COUNTERPRODUCTIVE
WORK BEHAVIOR

COUNTERPRODUCTIVE WORK BEHAVIOR

INVESTIGATIONS OF ACTORS AND TARGETS

EDITED BY SUZY FOX AND PAUL E. SPECTOR

AMERICAN PSYCHOLOGICAL ASSOCIATION • WASHINGTON, DC

Published by
American Psychological Association
750 First Street, NE
Washington, DC 20002
www.apa.org

To order
APA Order Department
P.O. Box 92984
Washington, DC 20090-2984
Tel: (800) 374-2721
Direct: (202) 336-5510
Fax: (202) 336-5502
TDD/TTY: (202) 336-6123
Online: www.apa.org/books/
E-mail: order@apa.org

In the U.K., Europe, Africa, and the Middle East, copies may be ordered from
American Psychological Association
3 Henrietta Street
Covent Garden, London
WC2E 8LU England

Typeset in Goudy by World Composition Services, Inc., Sterling, VA

Printer: Sheridan Books, Ann Arbor, MI
Cover Designer: Mercury Publishing Services, Rockville, MD
Project Manager: Debbie Hardin, Carlsbad, CA

The opinions and statements published are the responsibility of the authors, and such opinions and statements do not necessarily represent the policies of the American Psychological Association.

Library of Congress Cataloging-in-Publication Data

Counterproductive work behavior : investigations of actors and targets / edited by Suzy Fox and Paul E. Spector.—1st ed.
    p. cm.
Includes bibliographical references and index.
ISBN 1-59147-165-6
1. Anger in the workplace. 2. Work environment—Psychological aspects. I. Fox, Suzy. II. Spector, Paul E. III. Title.

HF5548.5.E43C68 2005
158.7—dc22   2004010918

British Library Cataloguing-in-Publication Data
A CIP record is available from the British Library.

Printed in the United States of America
First Edition

CONTENTS

CONTRIBUTORS

Lynne M. Andersson, Temple University, Philadelphia, PA
Karl Aquino, University of Delaware, Newark
Julian Barling, Queen's University, Kingston, Ontario, Canada
Robert A. Baron, Rensselaer Polytechnic Institute, Troy, NY
Rebecca J. Bennett, University of Toledo, Toledo, OH
Robert J. Bies, Georgetown University, Washington, DC
Susan M. Burroughs, Washington State University, Vancouver
Ståle Einarsen, University of Bergen, Bergen, Norway
Robert Folger, University of Central Florida, Orlando
Suzy Fox, Loyola University Chicago
Steve Harvey, Bishop's University, Lennoxville, Quebec, Canada
Lawrence R. James, Georgia Institute of Technology, Atlanta
Loraleigh Keashly, Wayne State University, Detroit, MI
Manon Mireille LeBlanc, Queen's University, Kingston, Ontario,
    Canada
Joel H. Neuman, State University of New York at New Paltz
Christine M. Pearson, Thunderbird, The Gavin School of International
    Management, Glendale, AZ
Christine L. Porath, University of Southern California, Los Angeles
Charlotte Rayner, Portsmouth Business School, Portsmouth, England
Americus Reed II, University of Pennsylvania, Philadelphia
Daniel P. Skarlicki, University of British Columbia, Vancouver, Canada
Paul E. Spector, University of South Florida, Tampa
Stefan Thau, University of Groningen, Groningen, The Netherlands
Thomas M. Tripp, Washington State University, Vancouver
Dieter Zapf, Johann Wolfgang Goethe University, Frankfurt, Germany

COUNTERPRODUCTIVE
WORK BEHAVIOR

INTRODUCTION

SUZY FOX AND PAUL E. SPECTOR

Since the mid-1990s, there has been an explosion of research interest in behaviors at work that harm employees and organizations. Much of this interest has been stimulated by media attention given to workplace violence, especially that perpetrated by coworkers—for example, shootings within the U.S. Postal Service. Although such violence is quite rare, harmful behavior of lesser severity is commonplace. Research on milder forms has been featured in the national media, where it is often called "desk rage." As editors of this volume, we will call the domain of research *counterproductive work behavior* (CWB), although not all contributors will agree with this umbrella label.

There recently has been interest among researchers, managers, consultants, and the general public in the widely reported experiences people have of being recipients of harmful behavior at the hands of supervisors, coworkers, and others. These experiences can range from systematic, openly abusive bullying to milder, ambiguous episodes of incivility.

Research concerning counterproductive behavior at work has considered two major classes of factors—individual employee characteristics and characteristics of the workplace. A variety of personality variables, such as conscientiousness, locus of control, narcissism, trait anger and anxiety, and Type A impatience–irritability are among a few of the variables linked to these behaviors. Some researchers have focused on characteristics of the perpetrator, others on the victims, and still others stress the dynamic interplay between the two. Research has shown that factors related to job stress, including lack of control, excessive workloads, poor relations with coworkers and supervisors, and both intrarole and extrarole (e.g., work–family) conflicts have been linked to harmful behaviors. In addition, fair treatment and workplace justice are important factors.

As the domain matures, more emphasis is being placed on the ramifications for individuals and organizations of these kinds of harmful behaviors, as well as approaches to solving the problems they create. This may prove to be the most controversial aspect of counterproductive work behavior research, because opinions vary widely regarding the locus of accountability (e.g., selection approaches versus organizational change) and the gamut of options available and hurdles facing victims of bullying. Our own work has suggested that a focus on employee perceptions of control and emotions can lead to job design and human resource practices that reduce harmful behavior.

The relative recency of most CWB research has undoubtedly contributed to a rather disjointed literature, with different camps developing different terminology and looking at somewhat different sides of an overlapping set of behaviors. These phenomena have been variously labeled as aggression, antisocial behavior, deviance, delinquency, revenge, retaliation, and our preference, counterproductive work behavior (from the actor perspective), and abuse, bullying, incivility, and mobbing (from the target perspective). The earliest empirical studies in the area of workplace aggression were published in the mid-1970s (Inkson & Simpson, 1975; Spector, 1975). Other early studies included Hollinger and Clark's (1982) paper on organizational deviance; Matthiesen, Raknes, and Rokkum's (1989) study of workplace bullying; Leymann's (1990) seminal work on mobbing; and Morrill and Thomas's (1992) paper on retaliation at work. Most papers in the area have been published since 2000.

The rapid and recent development in parallel of different perspectives has not left sufficient time for integrative work. This issue was noted as one of the most important for the field at an interactive paper session at the 2001 Academy of Management conference in Washington, DC. The session participants found that they were studying overlapping sets of behaviors from somewhat different theoretical perspectives, and tended to focus on distinctions and what is unique in each contribution rather than on connections. A need was felt for substantial integrative work to better tie the work together. Several of the contributors to this book participated in that discussion, which inspired this volume.

The chapters in this book have been written by scholars who have adopted different perspectives, perhaps different vocabularies or labels, and who have studied somewhat different sets of possible causes, consequences, or solutions. We have emphasized the desirability of relating, where feasible, each contributor's work to work done from other perspectives. The goal of this volume is to offer an integrative perspective that highlights connections and distinctions among different people's work, as well as a discussion of how conditions–events in modern organizations contribute to CWB and on things organizations might do to combat it.

As noted earlier, we have chosen the global term of CWB because it seems to encompass the critical features of the domain without excluding the distinct contributions of the various conceptualizations. It is not the intent of this book to force everyone into taking the same perspective or using the same terminology. Rather, its purpose is to build bridges among the different perspectives, showing where they overlap and where they are different. One of the strengths of CWB research is that there are so many different ideas that are contributing to an understanding of the underlying causes and consequences of the various behaviors that we study. Each perspective adds something important to our overall understanding.

This volume is divided into two sections, based on whether the central object of study is the actor or the target of the behavior in question. Section I looks at counterproductive work behavior from the actor perspective. Seven chapters discuss CWB from a variety of theoretical vantage points, focusing often on different precursors and consequences.

Joel Neuman and Robert Baron, two of the earliest researchers in the areas of aggression and emotion in the workplace, lead off with chapter 1. Their central argument is that efforts to harm organizations or the individuals who work in them fall under the rubric of workplace aggression. They specify the boundaries of aggression, which they define as "any form of behavior directed toward the goal of harming or injuring another living being who is motivated to avoid such treatment" (chap. 1, this volume), requiring intent to cause harm, actions directed at other living beings, and motivation of targets to avoid such treatment. The authors discuss areas of overlap with related concepts and conclude with a proposed theoretical framework, the General Affective Aggression Model (GAAM), to inform additional research.

Chapter 2 by Manon Mireille LeBlanc and Julian Barling examines a subset of counterproductive behaviors experienced by people at work involving actual physical violence, although not necessarily that which is committed by organization members. The authors categorize violence into four types based on the perpetrator's relationship to the organization. First, there is violence by individuals unrelated to the organization, as in robbery. Second, violence can be perpetrated by a nonemployee with a legitimate connection to the organization (such as by a client). Third, a current or former employee might engage in violence against members of the organization. Fourth, violence can spill over from outside of work by an individual with no legitimate relationship to the organization but who has a relationship with an organization member, such as a current or former partner. The authors argue that each of these classes of workplace violence poses unique requirements for the efforts of researchers and practitioners to understand and confront such behaviors.

Chapter 3 by Robert Bies and Thomas Tripp looks closely at ideological assumptions, particularly managerial bias, that the authors argue pervades much research in the field. They express their preference for the umbrella concept of workplace aggression rather than counterproductive work behavior, because it does not contain the promanagement value judgments inherent in the "counterproductive," "counternormative," "deviant," or "dysfunctional" labels. They call for a more value-neutral modeling of revenge, which also takes into account potentially valuable functions of such behaviors from an employee-centered as well as manager-centered point of view.

Chapters 4 and 5 expand the domain to include broader ethical and philosophical considerations. In chapter 4, Robert Folger and Daniel Skarlicki begin with their original construct of Organizational Retaliatory Behavior (ORB), a way in which organization members seek to punish their organizations and its representatives for perceived injustice. Rather than a static, one-time event, the authors seek to unravel a process that may include additional retaliation or reconciliation. They broaden their focus with the notion of moral emotions, third parties to the process, and prospects for reconciliation. As in the previous chapter on revenge, retaliation is not necessarily viewed as counterproductive or dysfunctional for the organization. The concept of legitimate retaliation is considered, including the functions of holding managers accountable to moral codes of behavior and providing employees who feel mistreated with psychological restoration of equity. Folger and Skarlicki contribute a broadly interdisciplinary investigation of the origins and consequences of retaliation, notably an exploration of possible evolutionary origins of deontic emotion and moral outrage. Finally, they consider the process by which the continuation of mutual retaliation can be replaced by the alternative response of reconciliation.

Rebecca Bennett, Karl Aquino, Americus Reed II, and Stefan Thau in chapter 5 expand the original concept of workplace deviance with an exploration of moral identity. Their starting point is the original Robinson and Bennett (1995) delineation of employee deviance as "voluntary behavior that violates significant organizational norms and threatens the well-being of the organization, its members, or both" (chap. 5, this volume). With norms as the starting point of determining what is and what is not deviance, the core question becomes determining what the source of organizational and societal norms is. Who defines notions of propriety, and how are these notions transmitted to individuals within a culture? The authors go on to examine what happens when an individual within a culture views the norms of that culture to be deviant. They examine the role of moral identity in the ways in which individuals chose to behave within deviant organizational cultures.

In chapter 6, Susan Burroughs and Larry James offer a new tool for assessing employees' proclivity to engage in CWB. This chapter offers an individual-differences perspective, proposing that some people are dispositionally more inclined than others to respond aggressively in response to perceived negative stimuli. This motive to aggress or dispositional aggressiveness is difficult to assess because of self-protective behaviors, social desirability, and instrumental factors. The authors offer conditional reasoning as a tool for examining individuals' latent motives to engage in aggressive or counterproductive behavior. The measure taps several underlying justification mechanisms, social cognitive biases, and implicit theories that are more likely to be salient in people who are inclined to respond aggressively. A program of research is described, with the goal of using conditional reasoning to more fully understand and address the issues of counterproductive work behavior.

We (Paul E. Spector and Suzy Fox) conclude the first section with our own perspective. Chapter 7 is an attempt to specify the boundaries of the CWB construct, to clarify definitional ambiguities, and to outline areas of overlap and divergence from related concepts presented in the foregoing chapters. Specifically, CWB is compared and contrasted to notions of violence, aggression, retaliation, revenge, and deviance. Definitional questions needing clarification include the necessity–sufficiency of intent, realization of harmful outcomes, and emotionality versus instrumentality as motivation. The resulting model of CWB integrates the domains of human aggression and occupational stress, putting the construct within the framework of job stress. It offers a broad description of a process that includes emotional, cognitive, and behavioral responses to perceived environmental (organizational) conditions. Perceived antecedent conditions may include constraints that interfere with goals, injustice, interpersonal conflict, or other sources of job stress, all of which have the potential to elicit a range of negative emotions, which in turn may play a role in the individual's engagement in behaviors that harm the organization or its members. Perceived control, attributions, and personality inform perceptions, reactions, and choices throughout the process.

The second section of the book looks at various approaches to understanding causes and consequences to people who are the targets of socially, occupationally, emotionally, and psychologically harmful behavior. The four chapters in this section vary in the severity and overtones of behaviors being considered, as well as in approaches to studying the dynamics involved and solutions offered. Interest in this area began in Scandinavia and Central

Europe and attracted widespread interest in the United Kingdom before becoming a significant subject of interest in the United States.

In chapter 8, Christine Pearson, Lynne Andersson, and Christine Porath investigate workplace incivility. Of the harmful workplace behaviors covered in this book, incivility appears to be the most low-key, chronic, and ubiquitous form. The actor's intentions, indeed awareness, are not necessarily a factor in the effects of incivility on the target. The authors imply that, on the contrary, the opposite of incivility, or civility, may require a level of respect for one's fellow human beings that is often lacking in today's workplace. They define the construct as "low-intensity deviant (rude, discourteous) behavior with ambiguous intent to harm the target in violation of workplace norms for mutual respect" (chap. 8, this volume). The boundaries of the construct are basically set by workplace norms of civility. Incivility is thus viewed not as a single, static event but rather as an interactive process among individuals within a situational context. The authors link the widely shared perception that workplace incivility is a growing phenomenon to widespread changes in the culture and climate of today's organizations.

The behaviors in question escalate in chapter 9, by Loraleigh Keashly and Steve Harvey. By definition, emotional abuse deals with severe, hostile actions that have short- and long-term effects on the victim's self-perceptions and well-being. The authors have refined the definition of emotional abuse to emphasize the persistent, repetitive patterns of verbal and nonverbal (but nonphysical) behaviors that harm or are intended to harm the target. Similar to counterproductive work behavior, emotional abuse is studied in a job-stress framework, from the perspective of the target. The authors develop a comprehensive analysis of emotional abuse as a complex interplay among situational forces, actor characteristics, and target-oriented factors. All three sets of factors are required to understand emotional abuse as a socially constructed experience within the social cauldron of organizational life.

Dieter Zapf and Ståle Einarsen offer a continental perspective in chapter 10, which begins with a historical overview of the Scandinavian, German, and Austrian origins of this domain of research, in which the authors played a pioneering role. The chapter continues with a clarification of the definitional boundaries of the construct, including the nature and severity of mistreatment, the frequency and the duration of the mobbing behaviors, the target's reactions, the perpetrator's intent, and the imbalance of power between the parties. As emphasized in the chapters on emotional abuse and counterproductive work behavior, mobbing is viewed in the job-stress framework. However, this is carried to an extreme, following the effects on mobbing victims through a process that may be considered a form of posttraumatic stress disorder (PTSD). The chapter explicates the similarities and distinctions between bullying and mobbing and goes on to review empirical research on categories of mobbing; personal, social, and organizational causes; and consequences for the victim as well as the organization.

In chapter 11, Charlotte Rayner and Loraleigh Keashly summarize bullying at work. The authors provide perhaps the broadest definition of the phenomenon from the target's perspective, namely "persistent negative interpersonal behavior experienced by people at work" (chap. 11, this volume). Interest in bullying is traced from earlier work on bullying among schoolchildren, a research stream that, enriched by their discovery of continental European work on mobbing, was developed by the authors into the growing research domain in the United Kingdom and North America of workplace bullying. The authors discuss issues of definition, labeling, relationships, power, intent, perspective, causes, and consequences. Some of the empirical work of the authors, who have been active in developing measurements of bullying, is outlined. The chapter points to early efforts by organizations in the United Kingdom and the United States to develop guidelines and practices to address the problem of workplace bullying.

In chapter 12, we conclude this book with an effort to locate the key terms and principles that the foregoing conceptualizations have in common, as well as those that differentiate the perspectives. This concluding chapter considers weaknesses in the generally shared methodological approaches and outlines future directions for the field.

*   *   *

As these chapters show, there is a great deal of overlap in the phenomena studied from these varying perspectives. Although the literatures of the actor and target sides have been unrelated, the underlying phenomena are linked. Acts of bullying and mobbing are acts of CWB directed at coworkers, and they can vary from fairly mild verbal behaviors to fairly serious physically aggressive acts. It is our hope that this book will help stimulate integrative research that links the various aspects of CWB both within and between actor and target perspectives.

REFERENCES

Hollinger, R. C., & Clark, J. P. (1982). Formal and informal social controls of employee deviance. *Sociological Quarterly, 23,* 333–343.

Inkson, K., & Simpson, D. (1975). The assembly-line and alienation: A participant–observer study in the meat-freezing industry. *New Zealand Psychologist, 4,* 44–55.

Leymann, H. (1990). Mobbing and psychological terror at workplaces. *Violence and Victims, 5,* 119–126.

Matthiesen, S. B., Raknes, B. I., & Rokkum, O. (1989). Bullying at the worksite. *Tidsskrift for Norsk Psykologforening, 26,* 761–774.

Morrill, C., & Thomas, C. K. (1992). Organizational conflict management as disputing process: The problem of social escalation. *Human Communication Research, 18,* 400–428.

Robinson, S. L., & Bennett, R. J. (1995). A typology of deviant workplace behaviors: A multidimensional scaling study. *Academy of Management Journal, 38,* 555–572.

Spector, P. E. (1975). Relationships of organizational frustration with reported behavioral reactions of employees. *Journal of Applied Psychology, 60,* 635–637.

I

ACTOR PERSPECTIVES

1

AGGRESSION IN THE WORKPLACE: A SOCIAL–PSYCHOLOGICAL PERSPECTIVE

JOEL H. NEUMAN AND ROBERT A. BARON

In reviewing the table of contents for this volume, it is apparent that a broad array of behaviors can be characterized, in whole or in part, as counterproductive to the accomplishment of work in organizational settings. It is our contention, and the central thesis of this chapter, that to the extent these behaviors involve efforts by individuals to harm others at work, or the organizations in which this work occurs, they represent instances of *workplace aggression* (Baron & Neuman, 1996, 1998; Baron, Neuman, & Geddes, 1999; Neuman & Baron, 1997, 1998b), and we believe there are substantial theoretical and practical benefits to be derived in studying them as such.

In this chapter, we argue the merits of this position and provide theoretical and empirical support for this line of reasoning. We begin by focusing on the need for concept clarity and an integrating framework for exploring the many behaviors subsumed in this text and follow this discussion with a definition of aggression in general and of workplace aggression in particular. Within this discussion, we describe the defining characteristics of aggression and violence and then compare and contrast these characteristics with other forms of counterproductive work behavior. After building what we hope is a compelling case for the use of workplace aggression as one possible integrating construct, we present a contemporary theoretical model of aggression that has proven useful in exploring (and explaining) the many causes and mediating processes associated with a wide variety of harm-doing behaviors. We conclude with some recommendations regarding future work in this area and, in particular, the need to consider the dynamics of the process in which these negative workplace behaviors are embedded—a process, we believe, that often reveals the underlying nature of, and motive for, such acts.

DEFINITIONAL AND CONCEPTUAL ISSUES

In this section, we address basic definitional and conceptual issues related to aggression in general and workplace aggression in particular. We begin this discussion with the most basic conceptual issue of all—the benefit of conceptualizing many of the behaviors described in this chapter as aggression.

The Need for Concept Clarity and an Integrating Construct

There are a number of terms used to describe "negative" behaviors in work settings, and this includes, but is not limited to, *counterproductive work behavior* (Fox, Spector, & Miles, 2001; Spector, 2001); *dysfunctional, deviant,* or *unreliable workplace behavior* (Hogan & Hogan, 1989; Robinson & Kraatz, 1998); *workplace bullying* (Adams & Crawford, 1992); *work harassment* (Björkqvist, Österman, & Hjelt-Back, 1994; Brodsky, 1976); *mobbing* and *psychological terror* (Leymann, 1990); *emotional abuse* (Keashly, 1998); *organizational retaliatory behavior* (Skarlicki & Folger, 1997); *petty tyranny* (Ashforth, 1994); *abusive supervision* (Moberg, Ritter, & Fischbein, 2002; Tepper, 2000); *workplace incivility* (Andersson & Pearson, 1999); *social undermining* (Duffy, Ganster, & Pagon, 2002); *organizational aggression* (Spector, 1975); *workplace aggression* (Baron & Neuman, 1996; Neuman & Baron, 1997); *organization-motivated aggression* (O'Leary-Kelly, Griffin, & Glew, 1996); and *workplace violence* (Kinney & Johnson, 1993; Mantell, 1994).

As organizational scholars pursue their work in each of these areas, we believe, as did Braithwaite (1985), that there is a real danger that this fragmentation will impede the advancement of theory and practice. Although organizational scholars are just beginning to investigate this issue as it relates to the relatively new area of research on negative workplace behaviors, Bandura (1973) identified a similar proliferation of labels and definitions in the general aggression literature, which he described as a "semantic jungle." Because the main focus of this chapter centers on applying aggression theory to studying harmful behaviors in work settings, we begin our discussion by drawing a lesson from that literature. In the introductory comments of his text on aggression, echoing Bandura's (1973) concerns, Russell Geen began by asking (and then answering) the following question:

> Does it make sense to use the [word aggression] to refer to such dissimilar events as a gangland murder, the bombing of a restaurant, a fight at a football game, and a cutting remark at a cocktail party? . . . Science depends on precision and clarity of definitions. From that standpoint, we might do well to forget about a unitary concept such as "aggression" and to search instead for functional relationships between specific acts and their equally specific causes. The various behaviors now subsumed by the word "aggression" could undoubtedly be studied as individual phenomena defined in terms of their own antecedent conditions, intervening processes, and outcomes. Nevertheless, such studies would obscure the possibility that the aggressive behaviors noted above, however different they may seem, possess some commonalities. If we are to make any sense of the whole idea of aggression, it is these commonalities that we must seek. (1991, pp. 1–2)

As additional evidence of why there is a need to integrate much of the work being done, consider the following experiments. Suppose we conduct four separate studies, each designed to assess the effect of one particular variable on creative problem solving. Participants in the experimental conditions (in studies 1 through 4) receive (a) a free gift, (b) $10 in cash, (c) a chocolate cookie, or (d) a compliment about the way they are dressed, respectively. In each of these studies, participants in the control condition receive nothing and move directly to the experimental task. Experimental and control participants, in each of the four studies, are given the same problem-solving tasks to complete (the dependent measure) and "creativity" is operationalized as the number of problem-solving tasks completed successfully. Suppose that in each of these four studies, the experimental participants do significantly better on the problem-solving tasks—in other words, they are more creative than the participants in the control conditions. What conclusions can we draw? Analogous to much of the research presently being done on negative workplace behaviors, we could conclude that gifts, money, cookies, and compliments all enhance creativity. This conclusion, of course, overlooks the fact that the independent variables in each of the four experiments possess some commonalities, and it is these commonalities that we should seek if we wish to truly understand what is happening. In the case of our hypothetical experiments, a substantial number of such studies—and related theory development—by Alice Isen and her colleagues (e.g., Isen, 1984; Isen & Geva, 1987) reveals that it is the ability of these variables (gifts, money, etc.) to elicit positive affect that, in turn, enhances creativity, as opposed to any unique qualities (attributes) associated with gifts, cookies, money, or compliments.

In short, we believe that the advancement of theory and practice is being hampered by the fragmented nature of the field, and it is our position that a good deal can be gained by integrating much of this work around the concept of aggression.

Interpersonal Aggression

As discussed in detail elsewhere (Baron, 2004; Baron & Richardson, 1994; Berkowitz, 1993; Zillmann, 1979), during the 1960s and 1970s researchers struggled to find an adequate and accurate definition of aggression. The consensus that emerged holds that *aggression is any form of behavior directed toward the goal of harming or injuring another living being who is motivated to avoid such treatment* (Baron, 1977). Four themes are explicit in (and central to) this definition. First, aggression involves effortful (goal-directed) behavior; or, to put it simply, behavior that is *intentional* in nature. Second, aggression involves the nature of this intent, which is to *cause harm* to one or more individuals. Third, aggression involves actions (direct or indirect) against other living beings, as opposed to inanimate objects. Fourth, the fact that targets of aggression are motivated to avoid such treatment suggests that the behavior is not invited nor welcomed by the target.

Intentions and the Infliction of Harm

Within workplace aggression and related literatures, there has been some confusion (and honest disagreement) over the use of intentionality as a defining feature. Within the context of the definition offered earlier, and consistent with widely held views in the field of aggression research, the issue of intentionality focuses on the *actual intent* of the actor—as opposed to the intent (or lack of intent) perceived by the target. It is often the case that innocent behaviors are misperceived as hostile (i.e., aggressive) whereas truly hostile behaviors may go unnoticed or be viewed as accidental, benign, or in some instances intended to be helpful—when people engage in harm-doing but proclaim this is being done for "your own good." As noted by Andersson and Pearson (1999), many acts are ambiguous as to their intent. As a consequence, using intentionality in the definition of aggression often is problematic. For this reason, some authors recommend excluding intent as a defining characteristic and, instead, suggest that we focus on the outcome of an act rather than its precipitating factors. Following this reasoning, any act that results in harm to a target would be considered aggressive. Although this suggestion might seem at first quite reasonable, it is problematic for several reasons, which become clear in the following examples.

If a dentist inflicts pain on a patient in the course of a tooth extraction, does this constitute aggression against the patient? Assuming that the pain was an unfortunate byproduct of the dental procedure and not the result of an intentional act by the dentist, this would not seem to be the case. Indeed, it seems reasonable to suggest that the dentist's primary motive is that of helping the patient, not inflicting harm. Similarly, if a manager directs a subordinate to undertake a difficult and stressful job in the hopes of furthering this subordinate's personal and professional development, would this constitute an act of aggression—even if the subordinate experienced great psychological anguish or stress-induced physical illness (i.e., strain) as a result of complying with the manager's directive? Assuming that both the dentist and the manager *intended* their actions to be beneficial and acted in good faith, their behaviors should be judged—at least in part—by their motives. If not, we are left to judge their actions entirely on the basis of the consequences, and there would be no distinctions drawn between thoughtless, insensitive, accidental, or malicious behavior. Beyond mere definitional (and legal) considerations, this has implications for the prevention and management of aggression, which requires that we address the *actual causes* of behavior and not merely treat the consequences.

Solely focusing on the outcome of an act is problematic for another reason. The mere failure to inflict harm on a target should *not* rule out the presence of aggression. For example, if I try to kill you with a handgun but the weapon misfires or the bullets miss their mark and you escape unharmed, is this not an act of aggression? If I spread untrue, vicious rumors about you throughout the organization in an attempt to get you fired (so that I can assume your position) but these efforts fail to achieve their intended purpose, is this not an act of aggression? In summary, although the *perceived* intent of an actor is important (as will be discussed in some detail later), it is the *actual intent of the actor* to inflict harm that is critical to a definition of aggression and not whether or not harm is successfully visited on the target. Furthermore, as suggested earlier, intention to inflict harm is an important criterion in discriminating between aggression and many related but nevertheless nonaggressive behaviors, as described in more detail later. Conversely, intention to inflict harm serves to integrate a wide variety of behaviors that may share similar antecedent conditions, intervening processes, and outcomes.

The Targets of Aggression

As relates to the targets of aggression, our definition focuses on interpersonal aggression—actions that are intended to harm another living being (i.e., another person). This would of course exclude actions against inanimate objects, assuming that the only *intent* is to damage those objects. As will be explained, if the ultimate aim is to harm another person through the use (or abuse) of an inanimate object, this would in fact constitute an act of aggression.

Finally, the fact that targets of aggression are motivated to avoid such treatment suggests that the behavior is not invited nor welcomed by those individuals. For instance, one who enjoys being hurt or humiliated is *not* considered a "victim" of aggression when such acts are directed at that person by others (e.g., a lover, a boss). Only when actions produce harm the victim wishes to avoid does it make sense to describe such action as aggression.

Workplace Aggression and Violence

To this point, our discussion has been drawn from the general literature on human aggression. Continuing to build on this substantial theoretical and empirical base, we now shift our focus more specifically to workplace aggression which, based on the preceding discussion, can be viewed as *any form of behavior directed by one or more persons in a workplace toward the goal of harming one or more others in that workplace (or the entire organization) in ways the intended targets are motivated to avoid*. The definition of *violence* is related to the form and intensity of behavior, to which we now turn our attention.

FORMS OF AGGRESSION

Because aggression involves all forms of behavior intended to harm others, it is clear that an infinite number of behaviors could be classified as aggressive. As a result, many scholars have attempted to construct typologies for the purpose of organizing these behaviors into a more manageable number of dimensions. Related to this, there may be an infinite number of motives underlying each of these behaviors.

The Buss Typology

Of all the taxonomies and typologies proposed for organizing and classifying different forms of aggression, the most widely recognized was proposed by Buss (1961), and this has served as the basis for several studies of workplace aggression (Baron & Neuman, 1996, 1998; Baron, Neuman, & Geddes, 1999; Geddes & Baron, 1997; Neuman & Keashly, 2004). According to Buss (1961), aggression can be captured using three dichotomies:

(a) physical–verbal, (b) active–passive, and (c) direct–indirect. Physical aggression, as the label implies, involves physical actions on the part of the actor and might include pushing, shoving, assault, unwanted touching, or the defacement of property. Verbal aggression inflicts harm through words as opposed to deeds (e.g., yelling, shouting, unfair criticism, damaging gossip, etc.). With respect to direct forms of aggression, the actor harms the target directly, whereas in the case of indirect aggression, the actor might inflict harm on something the target values or someone the target cares about, such as a protégé. Finally, active aggression requires the actor to do something to harm the target, whereas passive–aggression involves withholding something that the target needs or values (refer to Table 1.1 for examples of these behaviors).

Violence Versus Aggression

Aggression refers to *all* forms of intentional harm-doing behavior, whereas *violence* refers primarily to intense instances of harm-doing that would be characterized within the Buss (1961) typology as physical, active, and direct in nature (Baron & Richardson, 1994; Neuman & Baron, 1997). This, of course, would include workplace homicides as well as nonfatal physical assaults.

Overt Versus Covert Aggression

Another important distinction, and one that is probably closely associated with perceptions of intent, relates to the overt or covert nature of the act (Baron & Neuman, 1998; Baron et al., 1997; Kaukiainen et al., 2001). Some behaviors are easily recognized as aggressive in nature (i.e., homicide, abusive verbal exchanges, slamming doors, pounding fists, throwing objects, etc.), whereas others are invisible, less visible, or more ambiguous in form and therefore covert in operation (e.g., withholding needed resources or information, failing to return phone calls or e-mail messages, showing-up late for meetings run by the target, damning with faint praise, various forms of sabotage, etc.). Regardless of their form or process, to the extent that these actions involve efforts by individuals to harm others with whom they work—or the organizations in which they are employed—they constitute workplace aggression.

Proactive (Instrumental) Versus Reactive (Affective) Aggression

Up to this point, we have talked about the role of intent in a definition of aggression, but we have not really addressed the nature of that intent. As suggested earlier, there could be a large number of motives associated

TABLE 1.1
Examples of Eight Types of Workplace Aggression Categorized According to the Buss (1961) Typology

Physical–verbal dimension	Active–passive dimension	Direct–indirect dimension	
		Direct	Indirect
Physical	Active	Homicide and nonfatal assaults with weapon Rape/sexual assault Glared at in hostile manner Obscene/hostile gestures Interference with work activities	Theft Sabotage Defacing property Destruction of resources needed by target Hiding needed resources
	Passive	Excluded from work-related social gatherings Others "storm" out of room when target enters Intentional work slowdowns Refusing to provide needed resources Prevented from expressing self	Showing up late for meetings held by target Delaying work to make target look bad Failing to protect target's welfare Causing others to delay action on important matters Denied raise/promotion without a valid reason
Verbal	Active	Threats Yelling/shouting Sexual harassment Insults, sarcasm, rude/disrespectful comments Unfairly harsh criticism Negative comments about sexual orientation Unwanted terms of endearment Racist remarks	Blamed for others mistakes Talking behind target's back Spreading rumors Belittling opinions Attacking protégé Transmitting damaging info to higher levels Attempts made to turn others against target Others take credit for target's work
	Passive	Intentionally failing to return phone calls Giving the target the silent treatment Damning with faint praise Refusing the target's request Shown little sympathy during difficult time	Failing to transmit information Failing to deny false rumors about target Failing to defend target Failing to warn target of impending danger Failing to provide target with important feedback

with an equally large number of aggressive behaviors. Fortunately, aggression researchers have proposed two dimensions with which to capture many (if not all) of these motivations. Specifically, people either react to actions that they perceive as being provocative (reactive, hostile, affective, or "hot" aggression) or initiate acts of aggression against others as a means of obtaining some other desired end (instrumental, proactive, "cold" aggression). Although the majority of work in the aggression field has tended to focus on affective aggression, it is clear that "people often attack others with intent to harm without necessarily feeling any malice toward the victim. The primary goal of such aggression is not injury or harm to the victim; the aggression is simply a means to some other desired end" (Geen, 1991, p. 6). The world of work involves, by definition, the pursuit of an endless array of "desired ends" (e.g., raises, promotions, choice assignments, eye-catching offices, power, perks, etc.), and instrumental aggression often serves as a means to those ends. In fact, the dog-eat-dog business environment, characterizing many workplaces, glorifies the dispassionate use of power by management in achieving its ends. This is best captured in a remark made by Linda Wachner of the giant apparel maker Warnaco, who "advised an executive to fire people if he wanted to be taken seriously," or the behavior of Herbert Haft of the Dart Group, "who fired his wife and son because he thought they were usurping his power" (Dumaine, 1993, p. 39).

Having defined aggression and violence in general, and workplace aggression and violence in particular, we now compare and contrast this phenomenon with other counterproductive work behaviors.

COMPARING AND CONTRASTING WORKPLACE AGGRESSION WITH OTHER COUNTERPRODUCTIVE WORK BEHAVIORS

We began this chapter by asserting that any form of behavior directed by one or more individuals in a workplace toward the goal of harming one or more others in that workplace (or the entire organization) in ways the intended targets are motivated to avoid constitute instances of workplace aggression. In this section, we compare and contrast this phenomenon with other counterproductive work behaviors. We first wish to make two points. First, to facilitate and organize this discussion, we have grouped what we believe to be related constructs. However, it is important to note that this grouping was based on our reading and interpretation of the literature and not the result of statistical data-reduction procedures. Second, to be consistent with the overarching theme of this volume, we use the term counterproductive work behavior (CWB) to describe the full range of negative workplace behaviors that is the focus of this book. But, as we will explain later, no single term completely captures the array of behaviors explored in this volume.

Mobbing, Bullying, Psychological Terror, and Emotional Abuse

In reviewing the literature on mobbing, bullying, psychological terror, and emotional abuse, it seems clear that they all involve attempts by one or more individuals to harm others with whom they work who are motivated to avoid such treatment. The notion of intent is not necessarily explicit in the definitions associated with these phenomena. However, a careful reading of the literature in these areas suggests that excluding intent from these definitions has more to do with practical than theoretical considerations. For example, Rayner, Hoel, and Cooper noted that "if someone accused of bullying states that they did not intend it, then bullying would not have happened if intent were part of the definition" (2002, p. 12). In short, including intent would make implementing workplace behavior policies, or legal action, difficult (if not impossible). At the same time, Rayner et al. have written that "intent is an issue important to a target and essential when considering the interventions necessary, but cannot be included in a definition" (2002, p. 13). This position is echoed in the mobbing, psychological terror, and emotional abuse research in which the actual intent of the actors is seen as less important than the effects of these behaviors on the targets.

Although intent is not explicit in these definitions, the nature of the acts associated with these phenomena clearly suggests that they are largely goal-directed (i.e., intentional) and potentially harmful in nature. For example, according to Leymann, mobbing involves "harassing, ganging up on someone, or psychologically terrorizing others at work" (1996, p. 165). Similarly, Einarsen and Skogstad (1996) stated that bullying involves subjecting others to "negative acts" in the workplace, such as harassment, badgering, niggling, freezing out, or offending someone. According to Rayner et al., "workplace bullying constitutes unwanted, offensive, humiliating, undermining behavior towards an individual or groups of employees" (2002, p. xi), and Davenport, Schwartz, and Elliott (1999) view mobbing as an emotional assault that begins when an individual becomes the target of disrespectful and harmful actions that escalates into abusive and terrorizing behaviors.

In her work on bullying, emotional abuse, mobbing, harassment, and work trauma, Marais-Steinman (1998) stated that the most frequently reported incidents of these workplace hostilities involves instances of verbal aggression, including insults, shouting, name-calling, threats, damaging gossip, ridicule, cutting sarcasm, and false accusations. Keashly's (1998) work on emotional abuse identifies both hostile verbal and nonverbal behaviors, including yelling and screaming at someone, derogatory name-calling, giving someone the silent treatment, withholding necessary information, making aggressive eye contact, and explosive outbursts of anger.

In terms of conceptual overlap, it seems clear that mobbing, bullying, psychological terror, and emotional abuse are, to a large extent (if not completely), persistent acts of aggression most often directed against weaker targets who are unable to defend themselves readily.

Petty Tyranny and Abusive Supervision

In describing the attributes of a petty tyrant, Ashforth builds on the everyday usage of the term tyrant, as in the case of "a ruler who exercises absolute power oppressively or brutally" and then adds the qualifier "petty" to underscore the theme of "arbitrariness or small-mindedness" (1994, p. 755). Ashforth's (1994) factor analysis of behaviors associated with petty tyrants revealed six dimensions relating to arbitrariness and self-aggrandizement, including belittling subordinates, lack of consideration, a forcing style of conflict resolution, discouraging initiative, and the use of noncontingent punishment. Belittling others and the noncontingent use of punishment by definition would involve aggression. Arbitrariness involves the use of authority or position for personal gain, the "unfair" administration of organizational policies, and the tactic of "playing favorites" among subordinates. To the extent that these behaviors are used for self-aggrandizement at the expense of others, they would appear to involve instances of instrumental aggression. The consideration dimension involves not being friendly or approachable, failing to look out for the welfare of others, and doing little to make group membership a pleasant experience. To the extent that these are conscious actions, they might reflect instances of passive–aggression. Finally, in using a forcing style of conflict resolution, petty tyrants force acceptance of their point of view, demand to get their way, and do not take no for an answer. With respect to the discouragement of initiative, petty tyrants make it clear that the input of subordinates is not welcome, nor are the subordinates permitted to challenge the authority of the boss. Although it seems clear that supervisors may simply be poor managers, insensitive to the needs of their subordinates, it also seems clear that many of the tactics they use are aggressive in nature.

In the case of abusive supervision, the behaviors and underlying motivations are less ambiguous. Tepper described this phenomenon as "subordinates' perceptions of the extent to which supervisors engage in the *sustained display of hostile verbal and nonverbal behaviors, excluding physical contact*" (2000, p. 178), and Moberg, Ritter, and Fischbein (2002) suggested that it involves persistent, negative, aggressive interpersonal workplace behaviors. In particular, Tepper (2000) identified the following behaviors associated with supervisory abuse of subordinates: public and private ridicule, demeaning comments, ostracism, invasion of personal space, rude and discourteous behavior, lying, and taking credit for a subordinate's work. Similarly, Bies (2001) identified public criticism, loud and angry tantrums, rudeness, and coercion.

Social Undermining

According to Duffy, social undermining involves "behavior intended to hinder, over time, the ability to establish and maintain positive interpersonal relationships, work related success, and favorable reputation" (2002, p. 332). The definition of social undermining includes the notion of intent and, in fact, requires that the intent be obvious to the target. Also, the definition includes the concept of harm-doing and suggests that this harm-doing is "insidious" and occurs slowly over time (e.g., slowly weakening and, eventually, irreparably damaging social relationships). Finally, Duffy (2002) draws on the dimensions of the Buss (1961) typology to suggest that social undermining can take verbal, physical, active, and passive forms. Social undermining activities directed against targets would including talking behind their backs, hurting their feelings, putting them down in public, making them feel incompetent, belittling their ideas, giving them the silent treatment, or failing to defend them in front of others. As a point of information, all of these behaviors have been used in questionnaires designed to measure workplace aggression (e.g., Baron & Neuman, 1996, 1998; Baron et al., 1999; Neuman & Keashly, 2004) and have been discussed in detail in published theoretical papers (e.g., Neuman & Baron, 1997; Neuman & Baron, 1998b).

Revenge and Retaliation

Although the issue of intent is merely implicit in many of the definitions discussed earlier, it is quite explicit as relates to the concepts of revenge and retaliation. For example, in their vengeance scale, Stuckless and Goranson (1992) assessed attitudes toward revenge by asking respondents to indicate the extent to which they desired to get back at people who had wronged/ hurt them and the extent to which they believed in getting even—in other words, the extent to which they endorsed getting "an eye for an eye." This would clearly involve what we described earlier as reactive, hostile, or emotional aggression. However, in their thoughtful analysis of revenge, Bies and Tripp (1996) pointed out that revenge can motivate constructive change, promote cooperation, or serve as a constraint against the abuse of power (Axelrod, 1984; Bies, 1987; Donnerstein & Hatfield, 1982). In short, to the extent that the revenge has as its purpose the infliction of harm on the target, that would constitute aggression; however, the notion of "getting ahead" instead of "getting even" would constitute a nonaggressive reaction to an act of provocation. In terms of the prevalence of aggressive versus nonaggressive forms of revenge or the use of revenge fantasies, we defer to future empirical investigations and the musings of the reader.

Counterproductive, Unreliable, Deviant Workplace Behavior, Delinquency, Organizational Misbehavior, and Workplace Incivility

With some exceptions, in which phenomena are not explicitly defined in terms of the violation of any standards of conduct (e.g., Fox et al., 2001; Spector & Fox, 2002), it is our impression that the behaviors subsumed under the headings counterproductive, unreliable, deviant workplace behavior, organizational delinquency, organizational misbehavior, and workplace incivility (Andersson & Pearson, 1999; Hogan & Hogan, 1989; Hollinger & Clark, 1983; Murphy, 1993; Robinson & Bennett, 1995; Vardi & Weiner, 1996) share some conceptual overlap in that they involve, explicitly or implicitly, the violation of organizational or societal norms or standards of performance.

Employee/Organizational Deviance

In the case of employee deviance, Robinson and Bennett defined this as "voluntary behavior that violates significant organizational norms and in so doing threatens the well-being of an organization, its members, or both" (1995, p. 556). This would include violating formal and informal organizational policies, rules, procedures, or specific job-related performance standards. Robinson and Bennett (1995) identified two dimensions, pertaining to the seriousness–harmfulness of an act (minor vs. serious) and the targets (individuals or organizations). The resulting typology involves four categories of behavior subsumed within the two major dimensions. The two categories representing minor acts of deviance include production deviance (organizational) and political deviance (interpersonal), whereas serious acts involve property deviance (organizational) and personal aggression (interpersonal). With regard to the interpersonal–organizational dimension, we remind the reader that aggression, as we have defined it, involves actions against human beings. The question then becomes, is an organization an entity or a collection of people working together to accomplish work? It might be the case that when individuals set out to harm an organization they are, in fact, doing so with the intention of harming people—most often, people in leadership positions (often viewed collectively as "them"). Or there may be instances in which individuals view themselves as being victimized by the organization (its culture, norms, systems, etc.) or a given set of circumstances and engage in CWB without personalizing the situation. It would seem that in the latter situation, it probably makes more sense to view these actions as counterproductive or deviant in nature.

Within Robinson and Bennett's (1995) typology, the *personal aggression* category (involving sexual harassment, verbal abuse, coworker theft, and endangering coworkers) requires little discussion—because these behaviors are, by definition, aggressive. With respect to *property deviance* (characterized by sabotaging equipment, accepting kickbacks, lying about hours worked, stealing from the company), we believe that many of these behaviors may involve instrumental forms of aggression or reactive forms of aggression, to the extent that they are being perpetrated in response to some perceived injustice. In determining whether or not any or all of these acts are aggressive in nature, the issue again becomes intent and motive. This is true in many instances of *production deviance* (i.e., leaving early, taking excessive breaks, engaging in intentional work slow-downs, wasting resources) and *political deviance* (showing favoritism, gossiping about coworkers, blaming coworkers, competing nonbeneficially). These behaviors may (or may not) involve aggression, depending on the presence or absence of aggressive intentions and motives. However, we suggest that in thinking about these behaviors, instances involving reactive or instrumental forms of aggression are not difficult to imagine and may represent the prototypical image that comes to mind.

Hogan and Hogan (1989) view organizational deviancy as a syndrome (which they refer to as *organizational delinquency*) encompassing a wide array of counterproductive acts such as theft, drug and alcohol abuse, lying, insubordination, vandalism, sabotage, absenteeism, and, in their words, "assaultive actions." In viewing this as a syndrome, they make the case that employees who engage in some delinquent acts are more likely to engage in others (we revisit this assertion when we present a model of workplace aggression later in the chapter). This work builds on earlier work by Gough and colleagues (Gough, 1960; Gough & Peterson, 1952) that identified as a central element of this "delinquency syndrome" hostility toward rules and conventions of society as well as hostility toward authority. Although such delinquency is normally distributed, "past a certain point [on this continuum], their hostility will lead to conflicts with the law and eventually to incarceration" (Hogan & Hogan, 1989, p. 273). Although it is clear from the literature on delinquency that many of the behaviors subsumed by this syndrome are not aggressive in nature (e.g., actions related to thrill-seeking impulsiveness, social insensitivity, and alienation), the major emphasis on *hostility* presupposes that many of these destructive acts may involve reactive forms of aggression.

Counterproductive Work Behavior

As relates to CWB, the overarching theme of this volume, this has been defined as behavior that is *intended to have a detrimental effect* on organizations and their members (Fox et al., 2001; Spector & Fox, 2002). This reference to intentional harm-doing, especially as it relates to members of an organization, is aggression. Furthermore, as noted earlier, the detrimental effect on organizations constitutes aggression if the ultimate purpose of the act—either directly or indirectly—is to inflict harm on other individuals. With respect to indirect forms of aggression, in which individuals are harmed as a result of intentional injury to something (or someone) they value, this form of aggression is recognized within the Buss (1961) typology. Furthermore, the literature pertaining to displaced aggression addresses instances of "collateral damage," in which aggression toward one or more individuals is redirected toward other more convenient targets (Marcus-Newhall, Pedersen, & Miller, 2000). We believe that it also is important to note that, to a large extent, the CWB and workplace aggression literatures deal with many of the same antecedents, mediating processes, and outcome variables and rely on the same underlying causal theories (e.g., organizational stress and frustration, organizational justice, etc.). As noted, we believe that the CWB construct captures actions and situations not subsumed under the heading of aggression, but to the extent that behavior involves intentional harm-doing directed at others, there may be benefit to describing them as such.

Organizational Misbehavior

The definition of organizational misbehavior provided by Vardi and Wiener states that this involves "any *intentional action* by members of organizations that violates core organizational and/or societal norms" (1996, p. 151). As highlighted in the italicized portion of the definition, Vardi and Wiener believe that intentionality is a crucial element that serves to define three different types of organizational misbehavior: types S, O, and D. In type S, the misbehavior is intended to benefit the self (i.e., instrumental actions designed to benefit the actor), whereas in type O, the behavior is intended to benefit the organization (e.g., misrepresenting corporate earnings to inflate stock prices). Type D misbehavior is intended to inflict damage. With the exception of type D organizational misbehavior, it seems clear that behaviors designed to benefit the self or the organization may (or may not) involve aggression, and this brings us to what we believe is one dilemma in associating labels such as *counterproductive, deviant,* or *unreliable* with negative workplace behaviors. All of the behaviors described in this section rely to one degree or another on the violation of norms of behavior, and this allows for the possibility of norm-consistent instances of aggression or positive types of behavior that might be characterized as counterproductive. One clear example involves an organizational culture in which contentious dog-eat-dog behavior is not only permitted but encouraged. In this environment, the "deviant" might be the person who exhibits prosocial, nonaggressive behavior. A similar situation exists for those who blow the whistle on unethical or illegal business practices. Assuming that these behaviors are well-intentioned and not malicious, are they to be considered deviant? Conversely, not all acts of aggression are counterproductive. For example, revenge (or the threat of retaliation) often serves to discourage future acts of aggression and may serve as an informal behavioral control system leading to increased productivity (Bies & Tripp, 1996, 1998; Tripp & Bies, 1997). Finally, defining productivity is often quite complicated, because it may involve issues beyond simple efficiency and relate to issues of effectiveness and the time frame within which the determination is made (i.e., short- vs. long-term efficiency and effectiveness). Many actions may result in short-term gains (massive layoffs to inflate stock prices) and long-term consequences. Or things that seem counterproductive in the short-term (the time taken to carefully plan or acquire necessary resources) may pay large dividends over the long haul. We suggest parsing out, from these labels, those behaviors that are intended to harm others and identifying them for what they are—instances of aggression.

Workplace Incivility

To suggest that rude and disrespectful treatment is ubiquitous in the workplace, as well as other social contexts, is both true and unfortunate. As defined by Andersson and Pearson, "workplace incivility involves acting with disregard for others in the workplace, in violation of workplace norms for respect" as defined by "the norms of the community of which one is a part while at work, consisting of basic moral standards and others that have arisen out of the tradition of that community, including those prescribed by formal and informal organizational policies, rules, and procedures" (1999, p. 455).

In differentiating workplace incivility from workplace aggression and other forms of mistreatment at work, Andersson and Pearson stated that the "common aspect of all of these acts of aggression is the *obvious intent* to harm or injure someone physically or psychologically. A distinguishing characteristic of incivility, however, is that the intent to harm—as perceived through the eyes of the instigator, the target, and/or the observers—is ambiguous" (1999, p. 456, emphasis added). Although we certainly agree that the intent of an actor is often ambiguous, especially as relates to more covert (verbal, passive, and indirect) forms of aggression, as we stated earlier when defining aggression, the ambiguity (or clarity) of the intent is not the defining issue; rather, it is the real intent of the actor in a given circumstance. We recognize that there are many instances in social interaction in which intent to harm is completely lacking and yet rude or disrespectful treatment occurs or is simply perceived. It seems clear that these instances are best captured by the incivility construct and do not involve acts of aggression.

Andersson and Pearson (1999) described aggression as deviant behavior with intent to harm. As noted previously, we can point to instances in which aggression represents normative—as opposed to deviant—behavior. For this reason, we would characterize acts of intentional harm-doing as aggressive regardless of the conduct of others in that particular context— assuming that the target wishes to avoid such treatment. Next, contrary to the observation that researchers studying aggressive behavior in the workplace have given "rude comments, thoughtless acts, insinuating glances, and negative gestures that transpire within organizations little attention" (Andersson & Pearson, 1999, p. 466), with the exception of thoughtless acts, our research has focused on just those types of behaviors (Baron & Neuman, 1996, 1998; Baron et al., 1999; Neuman & Baron, 1997, 1998a, 1998b; Neuman & Baron, 2003) and, in defense of incivility as an important variable, our research continually shows that this is among the most frequently cited acts of CWB. Within the context of the general aggression literature, this comes as no surprise, because perceptions that one has been treated in a disrespectful or rude manner is continually cited by the targets of those behaviors as justification for their own aggression—in other words, retaliation (Harris, 1993; Torestad, 1990).

Finally, with respect to workplace incivility, in their seminal article on the subject, Andersson and Pearson (1999) adopted a social interactionist perspective and speak to the virtues of studying this phenomenon as a process of interactions playing out over time. This is an extremely important observation, and we say more about this in the next section of this chapter. For now, we point to the fact that if this is the case— and we believe that it is—ambiguity of intent becomes less of an issue as the parties in social exchange learn from, and react to, the behavior of the other. These reactions, of course, provide evidence of intent and motive (i.e., retaliation), and in describing this dynamic, Andersson and Pearson (1999) make extensive use of the general aggression literature, to which we now turn our attention.

THE BENEFITS OF USING AGGRESSION AS AN INTEGRATING FRAMEWORK

In all its many guises, "aggression, whether harmful to life and limb or merely painful to the ego, seems to be a real and important part of the human condition" (Geen, 1991, p. 1). In recognition of this fact, a significant amount of research has been devoted to factors that cause, facilitate, or exacerbate aggression, on the one hand, or that tend to prevent or reduce it on the other (e.g., Bandura, 1973; Baron & Richardson, 1994; Berkowitz, 1993; Geen, 1991; Zillmann, 1979). It has been (and continues to be) our belief that this considerable literature, empirical and theoretical—as well as the applications that have resulted from this scholarship—should be applied to aggression in work settings. To the extent that the behaviors discussed earlier constitute aggression, continuing research and applications should be theory-driven.

The General Affective Aggression Model

Although a thorough discussion of theory development in the area of interpersonal aggression is well beyond the scope of this chapter, the general affective aggression model (GAAM; Anderson, 1997; Anderson, Anderson, & Deuser, 1996; Anderson, Deuser, & DeNeve, 1995; Anderson, Anderson, Dill, & Deuser, 1998) serves as an excellent framework for understanding the current state of thinking in this area. Based on advances in many fields of behavioral science, this model suggests that aggression is triggered by a wide range of *input variables,* which in turn fall into two major categories: aspects of a current situation or tendencies individuals bring with them to that situation. Variables falling into the first category include frustration, provocation from another person (e.g., an insult, insensitivity), exposure to others behaving aggressively, the presence of stimuli associated with aggression (e.g., guns or other weapons), and virtually anything that causes individuals to experience discomfort or stress-reactions—everything from uncomfortably high temperatures to unpleasant noise or crowding in a workplace. Variables in the second category (*individual difference factors*) include traits that predispose individuals toward aggression (e.g., high irritability, trait anxiety, shame-proneness, Type A behavior, hostile–sinister attributional bias), attitudes and beliefs about violence (e.g., believing that it is acceptable or even appropriate), and specific skills related to aggressiveness (e.g., knowing how to fight or how to use various weapons; familiarity with various forms of organizational politics), or the ability to engage in aggression (e.g., power, status, hierarchical position).

According to the GAAM theory, these situational and individual difference variables then lead to aggression through their impact on several psychological processes—*arousal*, *affective states* (negative feelings and emotions), and *cognitions* (e.g., they can induce individuals to think hostile thoughts or bring hostile memories to mind). We refer to these physiological, emotional, and cognitive reactions as "critical internal states," and they play a central role in the dynamics of aggression, as we demonstrate.

Depending on how the people involved interpret various events in a given situation, the strength of restraining factors (e.g., fear of retaliation), and other variables, aggression then occurs or does not occur and takes a particular form and level of intensity. In short, modern theories such as the GAAM (refer to Figure 1.1), which is presented as an example of such views, note that aggression derives from a wealth of variables and conditions. Therefore, it can only be understood within the context of a complex interplay between cognitive, affective, and physiological processes, plus the impact of past experience and cultural influences. (For additional insights into this process, refer to the model of work frustration and aggression proposed by Fox & Spector, 1999.)

The Dynamics of Aggression

With the exception of the research on bullying, mobbing, and workplace incivility, much of the research on CWB tends to examine such actions as discrete events, as opposed to actions and reactions within a larger and often persistent dynamic (for exceptions see Glomb, 2002; Glomb & Liao, 2002; Glomb & Miner, in press). We often fail to consider the acts leading up to, and following, the behavior under examination. Failure to do this is important for several reasons. First, acts that are viewed in isolation are often ambiguous as to their cause, but this is less likely to be the case when the behaviors persist over time. For example, research related to attribution theory suggests that individuals infer the cause(s) of another person's actions on the basis of that individual's behavior in the same situation at other times, his or her behavior in other situations, and the behavior of others in that particular context (Kelley, 1971, 1972). Additional research demonstrates that this process is most likely to be used when individuals (a) are confronted with unexpected situations or (b) encounter unpleasant outcomes or events. Negative workplace behaviors represent unpleasant (or potentially unpleasant) events and (we hope) they often are unexpected, especially as relates to the initial encounter. Furthermore, as we have argued elsewhere (Baron & Neuman, 1996), individuals in work settings are often in repeated and prolonged contact with each other and are more likely to pay closer attention to the behavior of others than might

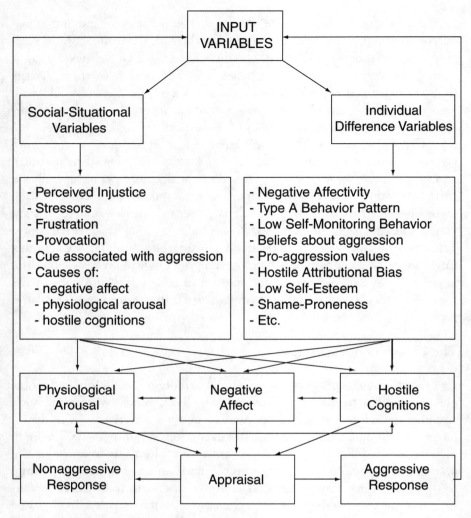

Figure 1.1. General affective aggression model.

be the case in other, less consequential, social encounters. In short, people in work settings are often in a good position to test their assumptions over time and uncover even the most covert and hidden intentions and motives on the part of others.

Second is the issue as it relates to the response of the target to a negative workplace behavior—or the response of an individual to the *perceived causes* of behavior. As suggested by Andersson and Pearson (1999), and strongly suggested in the social (Thibaut & Walker, 1975) and organizational justice literatures (Greenberg, 1987), the causes of others' behavior often are ambiguous, and issues of justice or intentionality are typically in the eye of the beholder (Cropanzano & Greenberg, 1997). If the behavior is judged to be aggressive (potentially harmful and intentional), the target may choose to respond in kind (i.e., engage in retaliation). At the same time, if the negative behavior of an actor is persistent over time, whether or not it is intentional, it is likely that the target of these repeated acts will perceive them as intentional and may try to retaliate to restore justice. The reasoning might be such that even if the actor did not "intend" harm to the target, he or she should have known better, with or without being told. Taking this even one step further, we suggest that even when the persistent acts are judged unintentional in nature, the negative affect that they elicit (resulting from frustration, stress, or simply annoyance) may, through the mechanisms outlined in the GAAM, result in an increased likelihood of aggression—through their impact on the critical internal states and the resulting cognitive appraisal process. As the preceding discussion suggests, by considering these social interactions in their entirety and embedding them in a theoretical framework, we are better able to understand the dynamics involved and the central elements shared by a wide range of variables—something that we are less likely to do if we consider these variables in isolation or as representing different phenomena.

Third, as noted above, there are instrumental reasons for engaging in aggression—it often pays! Referring again to Figure 1.1, the learning process is captured in the feedback loop between the resulting behaviors and the input to the model. Central to both cognitive and behavioral perspectives, people are likely to engage in behaviors that have "worked" for them in the past or those that reduce their level of discomfort (physiological or psychological). Although we may dispute the long-term benefits of engaging in coercive–aggressive behavior, abuses of power often are successful in forcing one's opponent to yield. Sabotaging a colleague's project so that you can take over, being generally unpleasant to avoid being given work, or being the squeaky wheel that all too frequently gets oiled are just a few of the many tactics that succeed more often than we would like to admit.

CONCLUSION

After reviewing the counterproductive work behaviors discussed, it should be clear that many of these actions look, feel, and sound like aggression. As noted previously, even when using different labels and terminology, scholars frequently refer to the actions they describe as aggressive, hostile, or coercive. Furthermore, many of the labels being used are synonymous with aggression (e.g., bullying, abusiveness, harassment, and tyranny, to name a few). Although advocating the use of aggression as an integrating framework for many of these behaviors, we realize (and freely admit) that not all of the actions that we have discussed (even the negative behaviors) necessarily involve aggression. Nor do we believe that the vast majority of behaviors in work settings are counterproductive or antisocial in nature. Furthermore, it is not our *intention* to corner the market on research or practice related to counterproductive work behaviors; rather, our *motive* (and the motivation for this volume) is to advance both theory and practice in this important area.

There is considerable value in many of the concepts described in this chapter, and this value will vary in accordance with the purpose for which the construct is being used. For example, in talking about many counterproductive work behaviors, the labels presently in use may prove helpful in describing the nature of the acts in question and identifying particular issues or research questions. Thus, in dealing with abusive supervision, petty tyranny, bullying, emotional abuse, or incivility, to name a few, the terms themselves seem to describe specific kinds of behaviors and suggest specific lines of inquiry. Not only does this facilitate communication among scholars and practitioners (or possibly the lay public), it focuses analysis on a circumscribed range and type of behavior—a desirable outcome when conducting research, designing applications, or implementing particular behavioral interventions. Also, it seems clear that regardless of the level of inclusiveness for any given integrative framework, there will be variability between the concepts subsumed by that construct. For example, although it is clear that bullying is a form of aggression, this phenomenon possesses unique characteristics not shared by aggressive behaviors in general. Specifically, bullying often occurs openly, in front of many observers, and societal norms that regulate aggression generally—and in most instances condemn aggression (especially repeated aggression) against weak or helpless victims as inappropriate—fail to apply, or apply only weakly, where bullying is concerned. In this case, merely identifying bullying as a particular form of aggression and failing to explore its unique characteristics will result in a loss of important information. Having said this, and being consistent with the argument we offered at the beginning of this chapter, working from a strong theoretical base (provided in this instance by the literature on human aggression) serves to highlight this important distinction for future research.

It strikes us that some of this discussion is reminiscent of the debate pertaining to the use of multiple versus composite criteria. Using a summative criterion such as grade point average (GPA) provides useful information about a student but tells us little about that student's performance in specific courses or specific academic areas. If we were to serve as an academic advisor, we would probably prefer to review the discrete elements that have contributed to a student's overall GPA to provide sound advice. However, if our purpose is to identify more general factors leading to academic success or failure in school, GPA may serve an important and useful function. An analogous situation occurs in organizational settings relating to the use of global versus facet measures of job satisfaction. Each type of measure is valuable in different ways at different times. In short, we believe that some of the variables described may prove useful at the *application* end of the continuum, whereas more integrative constructs and models make their contribution at the theoretical end of the spectrum.

In conclusion, over the years each of the scholars represented in this volume, and referenced throughout this chapter, have informed our thinking and helped guide our research. We believe that the discussion begun in this volume represents an important step in achieving concept clarity and working toward more integrative and paradigmatic research in this exciting and challenging area. We look forward to participating in this on-going process.

REFERENCES

Adams, A., & Crawford, N. (1992). *Bullying at work*. London: Virago.

Anderson, C. A. (1997). Effects of violent movies and trait hostility on hostile feelings and aggressive thoughts. *Aggressive Behavior, 23*, 161–178.

Anderson, C. A., Anderson, K. B., & Deuser, W. E. (1996). Examining an affective aggression framework: Weapon and temperature effects on aggressive thoughts, affect, and attitudes. *Personality and Social Psychology Bulletin, 22*, 366–376.

Anderson, C. A., Deuser, W. E., & DeNeve, K. M. (1995). Hot temperatures, hostile affect, hostile cognition, and arousal: Tests of a general model of affective aggression. *Personality and Social Psychology Bulletin, 21*, 434–448.

Anderson, K. B., Anderson, C. A., Dill, K. E., & Deuser, W. E. (1998). The interactive relations between trait hostility, pain, and aggressive thoughts. *Aggressive Behavior, 24*, 161–171.

Andersson, L. M., & Pearson, C. M. (1999). Tit-for-tat? The spiraling effect of incivility in the workplace. *Academy of Management Review, 24*, 452–471.

Ashforth, B. (1994). Petty tyranny in organizations. *Human Relations, 47*, 755–777.

Axelrod, R. (1984). *The evolution of cooperation*. New York: Basic Books.

Bandura, A. (1973). *Aggression: A social learning analysis*. Englewood Cliffs, NJ: Prentice-Hall.

Baron, R. A. (1977). *Human aggression*. New York: Plenum Press.

Baron, R. A. (2004). Workplace aggression and violence: Insights from basic research. In R. W. Griffin & A. M. O'Leary-Kelly (Eds.), *The dark side of organizational behavior* (pp. 23–61). San Francisco: Jossey-Bass.

Baron, R. A., & Neuman, J. H. (1996). Workplace violence and workplace aggression: Evidence on their relative frequency and potential causes. *Aggressive Behavior, 22*, 161–173.

Baron, R. A., & Neuman, J. H. (1998). Workplace aggression—The iceberg beneath the tip of workplace violence: Evidence on its forms, frequency, and targets. *Public Administration Quarterly, 21*, 446–464.

Baron, R. A., Neuman, J. H., & Geddes, D. (1999). Social and personal determinants of workplace aggression: Evidence for the impact of perceived injustice and the type A behavior pattern. *Aggressive Behavior, 25,* 281–296.

Baron, R. A., & Richardson, D. R. (1994). *Human aggression* (2nd ed.). New York: Plenum Press.

Berkowitz, L. (1993). *Aggression: Its causes, consequences, and control.* Philadelphia: Temple University Press.

Bies, R. J. (1987). The predicament of injustice: The management of moral outrage. In L. L. Cummings & B. M. Staw (Eds.), *Research in organizational behavior* (Vol. 9, pp. 289–319). Greenwich, CT: JAI Press.

Bies, R. J. (2001). Interactional (in)justice: The sacred and the profane. In J. Greenberg & R. Cropanzano (Eds.), *Advances in organizational justice* (pp. 89–118). Stanford, CA: Stanford University Press.

Bies, R. J., & Tripp, T. M. (1996). Beyond distrust: "Getting even" and the need for revenge. In R. M. Kramer & T. Tyler (Eds.), *Trust in organizations* (pp. 246–260). Thousand Oaks, CA: Sage.

Bies, R. J., & Tripp, T. M. (1998, August). Doing justice: The motivational dynamics of revenge. In A. M. O'Leary-Kelly & D. P. Skarlicki (Chairs), *Advances in organizational justice theories: The motivation to engage in dysfunctional behavior.* Symposium conducted at the meeting of the Academy of Management, San Diego, CA.

Björkqvist, K., Österman, K., & Hjelt-Back, M. (1994). Aggression among university employees. *Aggressive Behavior, 20,* 173–184.

Braithwaite, J. (1985). White collar crime. *Annual Review of Sociology, 11,* 1–25.

Brodsky, C. M. (1976). *The harassed worker.* Lexington, MA: Lexington Books.

Buss, A. H. (1961). *The psychology of aggression.* New York: Wiley.

Cropanzano, R., & Greenberg, J. (1997). Progress in organizational justice: Tunneling through the maze. In C. L. Cooper & I. T. Robertson (Eds.), *International review of industrial and organizational psychology* (Vol. 12, pp. 317–372). New York: Wiley.

Davenport, N., Schwartz, R. D., & Elliott, G. P. (1999). *Mobbing: Emotional abuse in the American workplace.* Ames, IA: Civil Society.

Donnerstein, E., & Hatfield, E. (1982). Aggression and inequity. In J. Greenberg & R. L. Cohen (Eds.), *Equity and justice in social behavior* (pp. 309–336). New York: Academic Press.

Duffy, M. K., Ganster, D. C., & Pagon, M. (2002). Social undermining in the workplace. *Academy of Management Journal, 45*(2), 331–351.

Dumaine, B. (1993, October 18). America's toughest bosses. *Fortune, 128,* 39–42, 44, 48, 58.

Einarsen, S., & Skogstad, A. (1996). Bullying at work: Epidemiological findings in public and private organizations. *European Journal of Work and Organizational Psychology, 5*(2), 185–201.

Fox, S., & Spector, P. E. (1999). A model of work frustration and aggression. *Journal of Organizational Behavior, 20,* 915–931.

Fox, S., Spector, P. E., & Miles, D. (2001). Counterproductive work behavior (CWB) in response to job stressors and organizational justice: Some mediator and moderator tests for autonomy and emotions. *Journal of Vocational Behavior, 59,* 1–19.

Geddes, D., & Baron, R. A. (1997). Workplace aggression as a consequence of negative performance feedback. *Management Communications Quarterly, 10,* 433–454.

Geen, R. G. (1991). *Human aggression.* Pacific Grove, CA: Brooks/Cole.

Glomb, T. M. (2002). Workplace anger and aggression: Informing conceptual models with data from specific encounters. *Journal of Occupational Health Psychology, 7,* 20–36.

Glomb, T. M., & Liao, H. (2002, August 12). Interpersonal aggression in work groups: Social influence, reciprocal, and individual effects. In P. J. Moberg (Chair), *Workplace abuse, aggression, bullying, and incivility: Conceptual and empirical insights.* Symposium conducted at the meeting of the Academy of Management, Denver, CO.

Glomb, T. M., & Miner, A. G. (2002). Exploring patterns of aggressive behaviors in organizations: Assessing model-data fit. In J. M. Brett & F. Drasgow (Eds.), *The psychology of work: Theoretically based empirical research* (pp. 235–252). Mahwah, NJ: Erlbaum.

Gough, H. G. (1960). Theory and measurement of socialization. *Journal of Consulting Psychology, 24,* 23–30.

Gough, H. G., & Peterson, D. R. (1952). The identification and measurement of predispositional factors in crime and delinquency. *Journal of Consulting Psychology, 16,* 207–212.

Greenberg, J. (1987). A taxonomy of organizational justice theories. *Academy of Management Review, 12,* 9–22.

Harris, M. B. (1993). How provoking! What makes men and women angry? *Aggressive Behavior, 19,* 199–211.

Hogan, J., & Hogan, R. (1989). How to measure employee reliability. *Journal of Applied Psychology, 74,* 273–279.

Hollinger, R. D., & Clark, J. P. (1983). *Theft by employees.* Lexington, MA: Lexington.

Isen, A. M. (1984). Toward understanding the role of affect in cognition. In J. R. S. Wyer & T. K. Srull (Eds.), *Handbook of social cognition* (pp. 179–236). Hillsdale, NJ: Erlbaum.

Isen, A. M., & Geva, N. (1987). The influence of positive affect on acceptable level of risk: The person with a large canoe has a large worry. *Organizational Behavior and Human Decision Processes, 39,* 145–154.

Kaukiainen, A., Salmivalli, C., Bjorkqvist, K., Osterman, K., Lahtinen, A., Kostamo, A., et al. (2001). Overt and covert aggression in work settings in relation to the subjective well-being of employees. *Aggressive Behavior,* *27*(5), 360–371.

Keashly, L. (1998). Emotional abuse in the workplace: Conceptual and empirical issues. *Journal of Emotional Abuse, 1,* 85–117.

Kelley, H. H. (1971). *Attribution in social interaction.* Morristown, NJ: General Learning Press.

Kelley, H. H. (1972). Causal schemata and the attribution process. In E. E. Jones, D. E. Kanous, H. H. Kelley, R. E. Nisbett, S. Valines, & B. Weiner (Eds.), *Attribution: Perceiving the causes of behavior* (pp. 1–26). Morristown, NJ: General Learning Press.

Kinney, J. A., & Johnson, D. L. (1993). *Breaking point: The workplace violence epidemic and what to do about it.* Chicago: National Safe Workplace Institute.

Leymann, H. (1990). Mobbing and psychological terror at workplaces. *Violence and Victims, 5,* 119–126.

Leymann, H. (1996). The content and development of mobbing at work. *European Journal of Work and Organizational Psychology, 5,* 165–184.

Mantell, M. R. (1994). *Ticking bombs: Defusing violence in the workplace.* Burr Ridge, IL: Irwin Professional.

Marais-Steinman, S. (1998). *The changing workplace.* Retrieved November 19, 2000, from http://www.worktrauma.org

Marcus-Newhall, A., Pedersen, W. C., & Miller, N. (2000). Displaced aggression is alive and well: A meta-analytic review. *Journal of Personality and Social Psychology, 78*(4), 670–689.

Moberg, P. J., Ritter, B., & Fischbein, R. (2002, August 12). Predicting abusive managerial behavior: Antecedents of supervisory job performance. In P. J. Moberg (Chair), *Workplace abuse, aggression, bullying, and incivility: Conceptual and empirical insights.* Symposium conducted at the meeting of the Academy of Management, Denver, CO.

Murphy, K. R. (1993). *Honesty in the workplace.* Belmont, CA: Brooks/Cole.

Neuman, J. H., & Baron, R. A. (1997). Aggression in the workplace. In R. Giacalone & J. Greenberg (Eds.), *Antisocial behavior in organizations* (pp. 37–67). Thousand Oaks, CA: Sage.

Neuman, J. H., & Baron, R. A. (1998a, August). Perceived injustice as a cause of—and justification for—workplace aggression and violence. In A. M. O'Leary-Kelly & D. P. Skarlicki (Chairs), *Advances in organizational justice theories: The motivation to engage in dysfunctional behavior.* Symposium conducted at the meeting of the Academy of Management, San Diego, CA.

Neuman, J. H., & Baron, R. A. (1998b). Workplace violence and workplace aggression: Evidence concerning specific forms, potential causes, and preferred targets. *Journal of Management, 24,* 391–419.

Neuman, J. H., & Baron, R. A. (2003). Social antecedents of bullying: A social interactionist perspective. In S. Einarsen, H. Hoel, D. Zapf, & C. L. Cooper

(Eds.), *Bullying and emotional abuse in the workplace: International perspectives in research and practice* (pp. 185–202). London: Taylor & Francis.

Neuman, J. H., & Keashly, L. (2004, April 4). Development of the Workplace Aggression Research Questionnaire (WAR–Q): Preliminary data from the Workplace Stress and Aggression Project. In R. J. Bennett & C. D. Crossley (Chairs), *Theoretical advancements in the study of anti-social behavior at work.* Paper presented at the meeting of the Society for Industrial and Organizational Psychology, Chicago, IL.

O'Leary-Kelly, A. M., Griffin, R. W., & Glew, D. J. (1996). Organization-motivated aggression: A research framework. *Academy of Management Review, 21,* 225–253.

Rayner, C., Hoel, H., & Cooper, C. L. (2002). *Workplace bullying: What we know, who is to blame, and what can we do?* London: Taylor & Francis.

Robinson, S. L., & Bennett, R. J. (1995). A typology of deviant workplace behaviors: A multi-dimensional scaling study. *Academy of Management Journal, 38,* 555–572.

Robinson, S. L., & Kraatz, M. S. (1998). Constructing the reality of normative behavior: The use of neutralization strategies by organizational deviants. In R. W. Griffin, A. M. O'Leary-Kelly, & J. M. Collins (Eds.), *Dysfunctional behavior in organizations: Violent and deviant behavior* (Vol. 23, pt. A, pp. 203–239). Stanford, CT: JAI Press.

Skarlicki, D. P., & Folger, R. (1997). Retaliation in the workplace: The roles of distributive, procedural, and interactional justice. *Journal of Applied Psychology, 82,* 434–443.

Spector, P. E. (1975). Relationship of organizational frustration with reported behavioral reactions of employees. *Journal of Applied Psychology, 60,* 635–637.

Spector, P. E. (2001, May/June). Counterproductive work behavior: The secret side of organizational life. *Psychological Science Agenda, 14*(3), 8–9.

Spector, P. E., & Fox, S. (2002). An emotion-centered model of voluntary work behavior: Some parallels between counterproductive work behavior (CWB) and organizational citizenship behavior (OCB). *Human Resources Management Review, 12*(2), 269–292.

Stuckless, N., & Goranson, R. (1992). The vengeance scale: Development of a measure of attitudes toward revenge. *Journal of Social Behavior and Personality, 7,* 25–42.

Tepper, B. J. (2000). Consequences of abusive supervision. *Academy of Management Journal, 43,* 178–190.

Thibaut, J., & Walker, L. (1975). *Procedural justice: A psychological analysis.* Hillsdale, NJ: Erlbaum.

Torestad, B. (1990). What is anger provoking: A psychophysical study of perceived causes of anger. *Aggressive Behavior, 16,* 9–26.

Tripp, T. M., & Bies, R. J. (1997). What's good about revenge? The avenger's perspective. In R. J. Lewicki, R. J. Bies, & B. H. Sheppard (Eds.), *Research on negotiation in organizations* (Vol. 6, pp. 145–160). Greenwich, CT: JAI Press.

Vardi, Y., & Weiner, Y. (1996). Misbehavior in organizations: A motivational framework. *Organization Science, 7,* 151–165.

Zillmann, D. (1979). *Hostility and aggression.* Hillsdale, NJ: Erlbaum.

2

UNDERSTANDING THE MANY FACES OF WORKPLACE VIOLENCE

MANON MIREILLE LeBLANC AND JULIAN BARLING

Thomas McIlvane, a former letter carrier for the United States Postal Service (USPS) in Royal Oak, Michigan, had a long history of verbally abusing and threatening his supervisors, coworkers, and customers. After being suspended several times for threats and poor performance, he was eventually fired for profane threats and insubordination. While awaiting the arbitration decision on his firing, McIlvane repeatedly threatened to kill people at the post office if he lost his arbitration. On November 14, 1991, the day after an arbitrator upheld his firing, McIlvane followed through on his threats. He shot and killed four USPS employees and wounded four others before killing himself (Report of the United States Postal Service Commission on a Safe and Secure Workplace, 2000).

Although violence committed by current or former employees, such as this tragic incident, is the stereotypical workplace violence scenario that comes to mind for many people, this is *not* the modal workplace violence

Preparation of this chapter was supported by funding from the Social Sciences and Humanities Research Council of Canada to Manon LeBlanc and Julian Barling. Comments from Kate Dupré, Michelle Inness, Aaron Schat, Niro Sivanathan, and Nick Turner on earlier versions of this chapter are gratefully acknowledged.

event. Consider this: Employee-initiated homicide accounted for 15% of workplace killings in the United States in 1998 (see Sygnatur & Toscano, 2000). In addition, worker-on-worker violence accounted for fewer than 10% of nonfatal violent injuries in a study examining eight southern California cities (see Peek-Asa, Schaffer, Kraus, & Howard, 1998). Instead, the vast majority of occupational violence is committed by nonemployees or outsiders (e.g., Peek-Asa, Runyan, & Zwerling, 2001; Sygnatur & Toscano, 2000).

Workplace violence has been categorized into four major types based on the perpetrator's relationship to the workplace (see Merchant & Lundell, 2001; Peek-Asa et al., 2001; University of Iowa Injury Prevention Research Center, 2001). In type I, the assailant has no legitimate relationship with the targeted workplace or its employees and enters the work environment to commit a criminal act (e.g., robbery). Individuals at particular risk for this type of violence include taxicab drivers, convenience store employees, and gas station attendants. In type II, the perpetrator has a legitimate relationship with the organization and commits an act of violence during a work-related interaction. Health care providers (e.g., nurses) and social service employees (e.g., social workers) are particularly vulnerable to this type of violence; ironically, the perpetrators are often the very people to whom care or services are being provided. In type III, the offender is an employee or former employee of the workplace. Typically, an employee targets a coworker or supervisor for perceived wrongdoing. Because McIlvane killed individuals at his former place of employment, his actions are categorized as type III violence. In type IV, the perpetrator does not have a legitimate relationship with the workplace but has a personal relationship with an employee (i.e., the intended victim). This category includes victims of intimate partner violence who are assaulted or killed while on the job.

The literature suggests that predictors of workplace violence depend on the type. For example, the risk for type I violence has been linked to characteristics of employee job tasks, such as exchanging money with the public and working alone at night (Castillo & Jenkins, 1994), while insider-initiated violence (type III) has been linked to both employee (e.g., trait anger; Douglas & Martinko, 2001) and organizational (e.g., perceptions of injustice; Barling, 1996; Folger & Skarlicki, 1998; Martinko & Zellars, 1998; O'Leary-Kelly, Griffin, & Glew, 1996) factors. Preliminary evidence suggests that there may be differential outcomes for victims, depending on the source of the violence (i.e., coworker vs. member of the public; LeBlanc & Kelloway, 2002), pointing to the importance of distinguishing between the different types of workplace violence. However, none of the types should be considered mutually exclusive (Meadows, 1998). For example, employees in certain industries (e.g., retail) are potentially at risk of type I violence such as robbery, and they may also experience type III events from coworkers.

Although the United States has seen a 35% decline in workplace homicides from 1992 to 2000 (Bureau of Labor Statistics, 2002), job-related violence remains an important issue. Homicide, the most severe form of workplace violence, is the third leading cause of death for all workers, accounting for 677 fatalities in 2000 alone (Bureau of Labor Statistics, 2002). Less severe forms of occupational violence (e.g., assault) are even more widespread. Between 1993 and 1999, American workers suffered an annual average of 1.7 million nonfatal violent victimizations (Bureau of Justice Statistics, 2001). Although Canadian workplaces experience lower levels of job-related violence, they are not immune from this phenomenon, as workplace killings at Concordia University, Montreal, Quebec, in 1992 (Montreal University staff gunned down, 1992) and Ottawa-Carleton Transpo, Ottawa, Ontario, in 1999 (Smith, 1999) show.

In the past decade, there has been an increase in studies published on workplace violence (cf. Baron, Neuman, & Geddes, 1999; Dupré & Barling, 2003). However, most of the focus has been on insider-initiated violence (type III)—the other three types have received far less attention. Hence, the purpose of this chapter is two-fold. First, we review the existing literature on all four types of workplace violence (including predictors and outcomes of violence). Second, we identify existing gaps in the workplace violence literature and potential opportunities for future research.

TYPE I: STRANGER-INITIATED WORKPLACE VIOLENCE

May 15, 2001, Antigonish, Nova Scotia, Canada: Yancy Meyer, a 19-year-old university student, was working alone at Need's Convenience Store when he was stabbed to death during a late night robbery. (Brooks, 2001)

August 2, 2002, Detroit, Michigan, United States: An employee of Happy's Pizza delivery was shot dead during an apparent robbery. Two weeks earlier, another employee of the organization was also killed on the job. (Another pizza delivery man killed, 2002)

More employees are killed each year as a result of type I violence than from all other types combined. Approximately 67% of workplace homicides recorded by the U.S. Bureau of Labor Statistics in 1998 were robbery-related (see Sygnatur & Toscano, 2000). A significant number of nonfatal injuries also fall within this category. For example, in a study of eight California cities, criminal acts accounted for 46% to 67% of violent assaults (Peek-Asa et al., 1998).

Epidemiological studies of work-related homicides (e.g., Castillo & Jenkins, 1994; Davis, 1987; Kraus, 1987; Loomis, Wolf, Runyan, Marshall,

& Butts, 2001) have identified several job tasks that may increase employee risk for type I violence. For example, Castillo and Jenkins (1994) examined the death certificates of individuals killed at work in 1980 to 1989. Their results suggest that interacting with the public, working alone or in small numbers, working in the late evening or early morning, guarding something of value, and exchanging money with the public are associated with increased risk for homicide. Earlier studies conducted by both Davis (1987) and Kraus (1987) reported similar findings. Based on the results of these studies, it should not be surprising that taxicab drivers have the highest risk for workplace homicide of any American occupation (see Davis, 1987; International Labour Organization [ILO], 1998; National Institute for Occupational Safety and Health [NIOSH], 1997)—they work alone, exchange money with the public, work outside of normal hours, and they may be asked to drive passengers to secluded locations.

In 1998, more restaurant workers were killed on the job in the United States than police officers (see Schlosser, 2002) or postal workers (see *Report of the United States Postal Service Commission on a Safe and Secure Workplace*, 2000), confounding stereotypes about workplace violence. Approximately four fast food employees are killed each month during the course of a robbery, which usually occurs early in the morning or late at night when few employees are present (see Schlosser, 2002).

About two thirds of the robberies at fast food restaurants involve current or former employees (see Schlosser, 2002), and although perhaps more common in fast food restaurants, the phenomenon is not limited to this industry. The following incident is not uncommon: In the early morning hours of Monday, July 8, 2002, Margaret McCarty, 32, and William Harrison, 36, two managers at Logan's Roadhouse restaurant in Livonia, Michigan, were killed during an early morning robbery when they were the only ones in the restaurant working (Garrett, Hall, & Shepardson, 2002). Three days later, the police arrested Ellis Robinson, a 31-year-old former meat manager for Logan's Roadhouse restaurant: He had been fired from the restaurant in early June (Garrett & Shepardson, 2002). Robberies and homicides perpetrated by current or former employees, such as the tragic incident just described, underscore the difficulty with categorizing workplace violent events into one of the four types. Should the events be categorized as type I violence because the primary motive appears to be robbery, or should they be categorized as type III events because the perpetrator is a current or former employee of the organization? We classify this as type I, thereby emphasizing that the intent of the action is more important in defining its nature than the background of the perpetrator.

We are unaware of any studies in the organizational psychology literature that have examined the outcomes for individuals exposed, either directly or vicariously, to type I violence. However, there is evidence in the criminology literature to suggest that being a victim of robbery can have negative consequences for employees and their organizations, even in the absence of physical injury. For example, Gabor and Normandeau (1989) reported on the findings of a five-year study of armed robbery. Using police files, they examined 1,266 cases of armed robbery in Quebec, Canada. Not surprisingly, the authors found that the targets of robbery were usually convenience stores and other small businesses. Two thirds of the victims interviewed experienced one or more of the following symptoms after the robbery: chronic nervousness, insomnia, nightmares, headaches, and changes in appetite. The most frequent complaints were fear of future hold-ups, moodiness, depression, a general distrust of others, and feelings of aggressiveness. Almost a quarter of the victims mentioned that the experience prompted them to modify their lifestyle, including changing jobs.

Leymann (1985) interviewed 221 employees involved in 73 bank robberies that took place in the greater Stockholm area during a four-year period. Respondents either witnessed the robbery or were in an adjacent room at the time of the incident. (Nineteen percent of their sample had experienced more than one robbery.) The most frequently experienced symptoms during the robbery were heart palpitations (41%), shaky hands (25%), and weak legs (26%); 17% also said they feared for their lives during the event. Four percent of respondents took sick leave following the robbery and 14% asked for and received treatment, including prescriptions for tranquillizers. Finally, 15 of the 221 respondents reported that exposure to robbery was the immediate cause of, or contributed to, their decisions to change employment.

Miller-Burke, Attridge, and Fass (1999) used a retrospective self-report methodology to examine employee perceptions of the consequences of being involved in a bank robbery. One third of employees reported psychological symptoms, including difficulty in falling or staying asleep, difficulty concentrating, headaches, exaggerated startle response, nightmares, and reexperiencing the event. More threatening incidents, such as being in close proximity to the perpetrator(s) during the robbery, feeling a greater threat to personal safety, and the use of a weapon by the perpetrator(s), were associated with workers experiencing more symptoms of posttraumatic stress, higher perceived stress, and worse physical health. Like Leymann (1985), they also showed that organizational functioning was impaired. Six percent of employees reported missing work because of the robbery, and more than 40% expressed less desire to continue working for their employer. In addition, more than half of the respondents reported declines in productivity following the experience, and 13% perceived that the robbery had a negative impact on their work relationships. Harrison and Kinner (1998) also found that severity of trauma was related to distress level in victims of armed robbery. As well, the researchers reported that victim vulnerability attributions (i.e., the belief that one is particularly vulnerable to victimization) and avoidant coping strategies were associated with higher levels of distress.

Anecdotal evidence suggests that the negative publicity that follows incidents of violence may also be costly for organizations. For example, Frank Portillo, Jr., president of Brown's Chicken and Pasta Restaurant chain, claims his organization lost $1 million in the three months following the 1993 robbery and murders in his Palatine, Illinois, restaurant, which left seven employees dead (see Lyndon & Zalud, 1997). It is not only the reactions of employees following robbery and violence that negatively influence organizational functioning.

Thus, being exposed to robbery has negative consequences for victims and their organizations. Victims experience a range of both physical and psychological symptoms varying in intensity and length of duration, and victim coping strategies and attributions affect employee recovery. For a percentage of employees, exposure to robbery results in declines in productivity and turnover. Nonetheless, it is clear that much more research is needed on the psychological and physical outcomes of type I workplace violence.

TYPE II: CLIENT–CUSTOMER–PATIENT-INITIATED WORKPLACE VIOLENCE

October, 3, 2001, Manchester, Tennessee, United States: Igic Damir, a 29-year-old passenger on a Greyhound bus, slit the throat of its driver, Garfield Sands, causing the bus to flip on Interstate 24. (McClure, 2001)

May 30, 2002, Montreal, Quebec, Canada: A psychiatric outpatient repeatedly stabbed a nurse during their scheduled appointment at the Sir Mortimer B. Davis Jewish General Hospital. The two had been regularly meeting for three years. (Davenport, 2002a, 2002b)

Compared to type I violence, type II violence is less likely to result in employee death. In 1997, 3% of workplace homicides in the United States were related to type II events (see Peek-Asa et al., 2001). However, more than 50% of nonfatal incidents fall within this category (see Peek-Asa & Howard, 1999). The perpetrators are typically customers, clients, or patients. Individuals employed in the service industries, such as health care, social services, retail, and food service, are the most likely targets of these incidents.

Recent data indicate that hospital workers are among those at highest risk for type II events (see, e.g., NIOSH, 2002). Although violent incidents can occur anywhere in hospitals, they are more likely to occur in geriatric and psychiatric wards, emergency departments, and waiting rooms (NIOSH, 2002; see also Health Services Advisory Committee, 1987). Most threats and assaults to health care workers are perpetrated by patients and, to a lesser extent, visitors (e.g., NIOSH, 2002). May and Grubbs (2002) conducted a survey of emergency department, intensive care unit, and general floor nurses in a Florida hospital. Seventy-four percent of nurses in their sample reported being physically assaulted in the past year by patients, family members, and visitors. Emergency department nurses reported the highest rate of assault (82%). Assaults were most commonly committed by patients with cognitive impairments (79%) and substance abuse problems (61%). The most common causes of assault by family members and visitors were anger at (a) enforcement of hospital policies (58%); (b) the patient's condition or situation (57%); (c) long wait times (48%); and (d) the health care system in general (47%). High rates of violence and aggression have been linked to low recruitment and retention rates of nurses (Jackson, Clare, & Mannix, 2002).

As stated earlier, individuals employed in the social services are also at risk. In fact, approximately 13% of nonfatal assaults that cause lost time from work occur in social service settings (see NIOSH, 2002). Guterman, Jayaratne, and Bargal (1996) surveyed 535 American and 591 Israeli social workers and found that approximately 49% of the former and 47% of the latter experienced at least one victimization experience over the past year, including physical assaults and threats of assault, threats of lawsuits, being sued, verbal abuse, and sexual harassment. There were no significant differences between social workers in the two countries in frequency of physical assaults, lawsuits, threats of lawsuits, and verbal abuse, suggesting that victimization from clients might cross national boundaries in similar ways.

Several job tasks are considered risk factors for type II violence. Providing service, care, advice, or education can put employees at increased risk for violence (Canadian Centre for Occupational Health & Safety [CCOHS], 1999), especially if clients, customers, or patients are experiencing frustration, insecurity, or stress (NIOSH, 2002; Painter, 1987; see also Lamberg, 1996). Workers may also be at risk if their jobs allow them to deny the public a service or request (Hearnden, 1988; NIOSH, 2002). Under these circumstances, client, customer, or patient anger and frustration may culminate in employee assault. Interacting with unstable or volatile populations (e.g., psychiatric patients, criminals), as well as individuals who are under the influence of drugs or alcohol, may also pose a risk to employees (CCOHS, 1999; NIOSH, 2002). Barling, Rogers, and Kelloway (2001) showed that working in clients' homes, away from the normal support and protection offered by the organization, was also a risk factor for experiencing workplace aggression and violence. Finally, working alone is also likely to increase risk (CCOHS, 1999; NIOSH, 2002).

Although occupational groups at risk for type I violence and type II violence share some (but not all) high risk job characteristics such as interacting with the public and working alone, they are believed to differ in perpetrator intent. Type I violence results from criminal behavior such as robbery and, as a result, is best described as instrumental aggression (see Anderson & Bushman, 2002). Type II violence, on the other hand, usually results from customer, client, or patient anger or frustration and may be best classified as reactive emotional aggression (see Anderson & Bushman, 2002).

Many of the studies examining employee and organizational outcomes of type II episodes have focused on the health care industry. A review of the literature suggests that exposure to violence results in employee fear, as well as declines in worker emotional, physical, and cognitive functioning (e.g., Barling et al., 2001; Rogers & Kelloway, 1997; Schat & Kelloway, 2000). Type II violence also has detrimental consequences for organizations (e.g., Barling et al., 2001; Levin, Hewitt, & Misner, 1998; Schat & Kelloway, 2000). Barling et al. (2001) conducted a study of health care providers who work inside their clients' homes and found that exposure to workplace violence (including physical aggression, sexual harassment, and psychological aggression) predicted employee fear of future violence. Fear of violence predicted worker negative mood (anxiety and anger), which in turn predicted cognitive difficulties. Health care providers who feared continued violence also reported a decline in affective commitment to their organization, turnover intentions, perceptions of injustice, and neglect of job duties. Negative mood also predicted a decline in affective commitment and an increase in perceptions of injustice. Hence, in this study evidence was found that the effects of workplace violence on personal and organizational outcomes were indirect, mediated by fear and negative mood.

Levin et al. (1998) used focus groups of emergency room nurses to investigate outcomes of assaults from patients for employees. Nurses reported experiencing short- and long-term emotional, physical, and personal difficulties, as well as changes in their professional lives following an experience of violence. Physical effects ranged from the immediate pain of the violent incident to long-term chronic pain. Other effects included anger, muscle tension, loss of sleep, feelings of isolation, nightmares, and flashbacks. Nurses who experienced assault also perceived a change in their experience of work, such as withdrawing from their patients and pulling away from their profession. It is interesting to note that nurses perceived nonintentional assaults by patients who were confused or under the influence of drugs or alcohol as more acceptable than intentional assaults.

Schat and Kelloway (2000) found that witnessing workplace violence may also result in negative outcomes for health care personnel and their organizations. Similar to Barling et al. (2001), these authors found that both direct and vicarious exposure to workplace violence predicted employee fear of future violence. Fear predicted employee emotional well-being, which in turn predicted somatic well-being and neglect of job duties. Employee training that targeted workplace violence was found to relate to enhanced perceptions of control. Worker perceptions of control were associated with a decrease in fear, as well as enhanced emotional well-being.

Investigators have recently begun to examine whether support buffers the negative consequences of workplace violence and aggression. For example, Leather, Lawrence, Beale, Cox, and Dickson (1998) examined the effects of intraorganizational (e.g., from the personnel department) and extraorganizational (e.g., from family) support on well-being, organizational commitment, and job satisfaction. They asked British pub licensees to indicate how often a variety of violent events occurred in their pubs; only vicarious violence was examined in this study. The authors found evidence for the moderating effects of intraorganizational support. More recently, Schat and Kelloway (2003) examined whether instrumental and informational organizational support moderate the relationship between workplace violence (including physical, psychological, and vicarious violence) and personal (fear of violence, emotional well-being, and somatic health) and organizational (job-related affect and job neglect) outcomes. In their study, instrumental support was operationalized as support received from coworkers, supervisors, and management following the experience of violence, whereas informational support was operationalized as whether employees received training on how to deal with aggressive or threatening behavior at work. Their sample consisted of employees in a health care setting. The authors found that instrumental support moderated the relationship between workplace violence and emotional well-being, somatic health, and job-related affect. Informational support interacted with workplace violence to predict emotional well-being. Neither type of support mitigated the effects of workplace violence on fear of future violence or job neglect.

Therefore, there is sufficient evidence to suggest that exposure to type II violence, whether direct or indirect, has detrimental consequences for employees and their organizations. Although prevention of workplace violence should be the primary goal of any organization, it is not always possible to prevent all violence. Thus, more research on organizational support and other possible psychosocial buffers is required.

TYPE III: INSIDER-INITIATED WORKPLACE VIOLENCE

April 7, 1999, Ottawa, Ontario, Canada: Pierre Lebrun, a transit worker of Ottawa-Carleton Transpo, shot and killed four of his coworkers and seriously wounded two others before killing himself. Reports suggest that Pierre Lebrun felt constantly taunted at work because of his stutter. (Smith, 1999)

December 26, 2000, Wakefield, Massachusetts, United States: Michael McDermott, an employee of Edgewater Technology, a software consulting firm, shot dead seven of his coworkers. The shootings were apparently not random—five of his victims worked in the accounting department, and McDermott had an outburst in that department the week before. (Valdmanis & Morrison, 2000)

Insider-initiated violence receives more media coverage than public-initiated violence, even though employees commit far fewer homicides and assaults than do members of the public (see, e.g., LeBlanc & Kelloway, 2002; Peek-Asa et al., 1998, 2001; Sygnatur & Toscano, 2000). However, it is not only the media that appear to be disproportionately focused on type III violence. It is apparent from even a cursory review of the academic literature that research is focused on insider-initiated violence. We are not suggesting that investigators abandon their interest in type III violence—its consequences can be devastating for victims and their organizations. Rather, we are calling for an increase in research attention dedicated to the other types of violence.

Research on type III workplace violence can be complex, because this phenomenon has multiple sources, targets, and causes (cf. Dupré & Barling, 2003). For example, perpetrators can be either employees or managers, and violence can be directed toward one or more of three different targets: current or former superiors, peers, and subordinates. Researchers have begun to distinguish between specific sources and targets of aggression; initial evidence suggests that factors that predict work-related violence vary depending on the target of aggression (Greenberg & Barling, 1999). In this section, we conduct a brief review of the predictors and consequences of type III violence. For a more thorough review of the literature, see Dupré and Barling (2003).

Unlike the first two types of violence discussed, employee task characteristics are not associated with risk for insider-initiated violence (also referred to as employee-initiated violence). In fact, there is no evidence to suggest that certain occupations or industries are more or less prone to this type of violence. Rather, investigators have suggested that type III workplace violence is likely the result of a complex interaction between perpetrator and organizational factors (e.g., Barling, 1996; Douglas & Martinko, 2001; Martinko & Zellars, 1998; O'Leary-Kelly et al., 1996).

Perpetrator factors have been hypothesized to contribute to insider-initiated violence (e.g., Barling, 1996; Martinko & Zellers, 1998), and some empirical work has examined the role of individual differences. One example is the study conducted by Douglas and Martinko (2001). Their sample consisted of managerial and nonmanagerial personnel. The authors reported that individual difference variables (e.g., trait anger, hostile attributional style, attitudes toward revenge, and previous exposure to aggressive cultures) accounted for 62% of the variance in their measure of workplace aggression.

Type A behavior pattern has also been linked to aggressive behavior on the job. For example, Baron et al. (1999) had employees in managerial and nonmanagerial positions rate the frequency with which they engaged in aggression against various targets, including their immediate supervisor, a coworker, a subordinate, a superior other than their immediate supervisor, and their organization. Higher scores on a measure of type A behavior pattern were associated with increased frequency of aggression toward immediate supervisors.

Alcohol consumption and history of aggression have also been linked to aggression in organizational settings (e.g., Greenberg & Barling, 1999; Jockin, Arvey, & McGue, 2001). For example, Greenberg and Barling found that binge drinking and history of aggression are related to psychological aggression toward coworkers and subordinates but not toward supervisors. Both Stuart (1992) and Graham (1991) have suggested that alcohol abuse is common in employees who kill at the workplace.

Although individual factors clearly play a role in workplace violence, some researchers argue that organizational factors are more important predictors of violence (e.g., Dupré & Barling, 2003; Inness, Barling, & Turner, in press). Inness et al. (in press) examined predictors (both situational and individual factors) of supervisor-targeted aggression among moonlighters (i.e., individuals who work two jobs, each with a different supervisor). In addition to confirming that supervisor-targeted aggression is a situationally specific phenomenon, their results showed that workplace factors account for more of the variance in aggression than do individual factors.

The majority of empirical work on insider-instigated aggression has focused on situational factors that might predict aggression on the job. Perceptions of interactional injustice, feeling overcontrolled, and electronic monitoring have all been hypothesized to predict type III violence (e.g., Barling, 1996; Folger & Skarlicki, 1998; Martinko & Zellers, 1998; O'Leary-Kelly et al., 1996).

Research indicates that feeling overcontrolled is associated with aggression toward the overcontrolling individual (Dupré & Barling, 2004; Ehrensaft, Langhinrichsen-Rohling, Heyman, O'Leary, & Lawrence, 1999). Dupré and Barling (2004) found that feeling overcontrolled and perceived injustice predicted employee aggression toward supervisors. These relationships were minimized, however, when employees perceived organizational sanctions against workplace aggression.

Perceptions of interactional injustice were also found to predict supervisor-targeted aggression in employees' primary place of employment, and it explained substantially more of the variance in workplace violence than did individual difference factors (Inness et al., in press). Folger, Baron, and McLean-Parks (1996) also found evidence of perceived interactional injustice as a predictor of physical assaults among employees (cf. Folger & Skarlicki, 1998). Finally, Greenberg and Barling (1999) found surveillance methods used to monitor employees were positively associated with psychological aggression against a supervisor.

Workplace aggression has negative consequences for both individuals and their organizations (e.g., Budd, Arvey, & Lawless, 1996). However, most of the literature on outcomes of violence comes from research focused on public-initiated aggression or from studies that inquire about employee experience of violence but do not ask participants whether the perpetrator was a coworker or a member of the public. It is possible that victims of violence experience different consequences depending on the source of the violence. In fact, two recent studies found evidence of differential effects of violence from coworkers and the public (i.e., LeBlanc & Kelloway, 2002; Santos & Leather, 2001).

LeBlanc and Kelloway (2002) examined employee and organizational outcomes of coworker-initiated psychological aggression (physical aggression from coworkers was negligible in this study) and public-initiated physical and psychological aggression. Exposure to psychological aggression from coworkers predicted emotional well-being, physical well-being, and affective commitment to the organization, which in turn predicted intent to turnover. Public-initiated aggression, including physical and psychological aggression, predicted employee perceptions of likelihood of future violence, which in turn predicted fear of future violence; it also predicted employee intent to turnover. Given the results of this study, researchers examining workplace violence might be advised to ask respondents to indicate who the source of the violence is.

In a study examining the effects of violence and aggression on police officers and civilian support staff in an English police force, Santos and Leather (2001) showed that both violence and aggression from the public and from coworkers have an impact on employee well-being and posttraumatic stress symptomology. However, the effects of violence and aggression from individuals within the organization were more detrimental to employee health and well-being than violence and aggression from the public.

Although employee-initiated violence is less common than public-initiated aggression, preliminary evidence suggests that the former may have more detrimental consequences for employee well-being (Santos & Leather, 2001). Although the reasons for the differences are unknown, O'Leary-Kelly et al. (1996) suggested that when harm is caused by a member of an organization, trust in coworkers and the organization may be damaged to a greater extent than when the violence is perpetrated by a member of the public.

TYPE IV: PARTNER-INITIATED WORKPLACE VIOLENCE

August 22, 1997, Santa Clara, California, United States. Kenneth McMurray shot and killed his estranged girlfriend, 33-year-old Maria Lualhati, at her place of employment, NEC Electronics, Inc., and then killed himself. (Man kills ex-girlfriend, 1997)

May 31, 2001, Kingston, Ontario, Canada. Michael Shawn Martin, 28, shot and killed his former girlfriend, 20-year-old Jeanine Perry, in the parking lot at her place of work and then killed himself. (Armstrong & Larsen, 2001)

Domestic abuse is rarely acknowledged in discussions of workplace violence. Yet, conjugal violence and its consequences do sometimes spill into the workplace. In 1997, 5% of homicides on the job were the result of domestic violence (see Peek-Asa et al., 2001); and, in a recent study, approximately 2% of nonfatal violent injuries on the job were the result of domestic disputes entering into the workplace (see Peek-Asa et al., 1998). Intimate partner violence may also pose a danger to the safety of other employees in the organization (Braverman, 1999) who "get in the way" of the perpetrator or who witness the violence. On October, 7, 1997, Charles Ruben White, 42, murdered his former girlfriend, Pamela Henry, 38, at her place of employment, Protocall, Inc. He also fatally shot one of her coworkers, Juanita Morin, 41, who tried to stop him (Hendricks & Tedesco, 1997). Given the high rate of domestic abuse and the real possibility that it can enter into the workplace, investigations need to be conducted examining domestic abuse in the context of the workplace. Currently, there is little empirical research on type IV workplace violence.

The physical and emotional effects of abusive relationships on victims are well documented. For example, a recent study conducted by Mertin and Mohr (2000) of Australian victims of domestic abuse found that 45% of their sample met all diagnostic criteria for posttraumatic stress disorder (PTSD). Morrell and Rubin (2001) reported that 62% of their sample met the criteria for PTSD. In addition to experiencing physical and emotional pain, domestic abuse victims may also lose their livelihood. For example, Kathy Evsich, vice president of Women Against Domestic Violence, an activist group based in the United States, recently went to Capitol Hill to tell her own story. She recounted how she was fired from two jobs because her employers would not tolerate her husband's frequent phone calls and threats (see Munn, 2002). A recent qualitative study (Swanberg & Logan, 2004) of intimate partner violence found that 20% of batterers made harassing phone calls to their victims, 10% made harassing phone calls to their victims' supervisors, 56% stalked their victims (i.e., watched them from afar) while they were at work, and 72% showed up at their victims' work site.

Recent data is shedding light on the frequency with which domestic abuse affects women's employment. Statistics Canada's 1999 General Social Survey on Victimization suggests that 32.9% of women in the sample had to take time off from everyday activities, including paid or unpaid work, as a direct consequence of being victimized (Johnson & Bunge, 2001). A recent study conducted by Riger, Ahrens, and Blickenstaff (2000) reported that 85% of female domestic abuse victims residing in a Chicago shelter who were employed missed work because of the abuse, and 53% were fired or quit for the same reason. Swanberg and Logan (2004) conducted a qualitative study of 32 women who had experienced domestic abuse in the past two years and were employed at the time the abuse occurred. More than 50% of victims missed work "with some regularity" (absenteeism ranged from once every two weeks to three or four times a month). The most prevalent reasons for missing work included sleep deprivation, physical evidence of the abuse, psychological distress, depression, anxiety, incarceration, hospitilization for an injury, physical restraint from going to work by the batterer, damaged car or hidden car keys, and batterer refusing to drive victim to work. In addition, almost 50% of respondents had been terminated from at least one job in the last year. Reasons for termination included poor work attendance, receiving too many phone calls at work, poor job performance, and batterer showing up at work too many times.

Some organizations (e.g., Liz Claiborne Inc., Polaroid Corp., Blue Cross Blue Shield of Massachusetts) have implemented domestic violence awareness programs, including enhancing security for employees involved in abusive relationships (see Jossi, 1999; Kolettis, 2000). Methods considered effective in dealing with domestic violence at work include relocating the victim within the organization, changing work schedules, changing an employee's phone extension, and providing security escorts to and from parking lots (Anderson, 2001; Munn, 2002). The situation is further complicated when both the abuser and victim are employed by the same organization.

Despite the fact that domestic violence sometimes spills into the workplace, it is often neglected in discussions of workplace violence, and it is poorly understood. Given that domestic abuse has devastating consequences for victims and their organizations, we strongly encourage researchers to investigate this phenomenon.

CHALLENGES FOR THE FUTURE

In this section, we first discuss some general challenges for future research; thereafter we discuss challenges specific to each of the different types of workplace violence. Throughout, the issues are presented as questions that need to be confronted.

Research on workplace violence has been impeded by lack of standard conceptual and operational definitions of violence. For example, Jenkins (1996) and LeBlanc and Kelloway (2002) defined violence as physical assaults and threats of assault directed toward employees, and Schat and Kelloway (2000) included psychological aggression (e.g., yelling) and vicarious violence in their definition. As a result of this inconsistency in defining violence, it is difficult to make comparisons across studies. Until researchers can agree on how narrowly or broadly to define workplace violence, current difficulties will continue.

Precise statistics on workplace homicide are difficult to acquire because no single agency is responsible for collecting data, and different agencies use different data collection techniques. For example, the Bureau of Labor Statistics (BLS), Department of Labor, collects Census of Fatal Occupational Injuries (CFOI) data. Sources of CFOI data include death certificates, workers' compensation reports and claims, reports to regulatory agencies such as the Occupational Safety and Health Administrations (OSHA), police reports, medical examiner reports, and media stories (see Peek-Asa et al., 2001). The National Institute for Occupational Safety and Health (NIOSH) also collects data on workplace homicide (i.e., National Traumatic Occupational Fatality Database [NTOF]), but it relies solely on death certificates (see Peek-Asa et al., 2001). It is even more difficult to attain precise statistics on nonfatal injuries because employees may underreport their experiences of violence (e.g., Lion, Snyder, & Merrill, 1981), and no coordinated surveillance system exists to collect this information (Merchant & Lundell, 2001). The lack of accurate data on nonfatal assaults makes it difficult for researchers to identify high-risk workers and to evaluate programs designed to reduce workplace violence (Peek-Asa et al., 2001). Information on the economic costs (e.g., impact on businesses affected; lost productivity) associated with both fatal and nonfatal events is also lacking (see Merchant & Lundell, 2001).

It is also critical that some uniformity be applied to the way in which the different types of workplace violence are categorized. As we noted with an example earlier, it is possible that the same situation might be categorized as more than one type. We would suggest the most appropriate way to resolve this is to classify the event in terms of the intent of the perpetrator, rather than the target of the event. Doing so emphasizes the importance of intent in understanding the meaning of the violent incident.

One last general question—whether all four types of workplace violence should fall under the counterproductive work behavior umbrella—has not yet been answered. Hence, we ask whether workplace violence should only reflect counterproductive work behaviors when the specific intent of the perpetrator is to cause harm to an employee or the organization, or perhaps when the target of the act is either the workplace or an employee? This issue certainly awaits conceptual clarification.

TYPE I VIOLENCE

There are many questions that remain unanswered about type I violence. Are programs aimed at training employees to cope with robbery successful? A recent study conducted by Schat and Kelloway (2000) found that employee training that targeted workplace violence (in a health care setting) related to enhanced perceptions of control. Worker perceptions of control were associated with a decrease in fear of future violence and enhanced emotional well-being. It is interesting to note that the trained group reported greater exposure to direct violence compared to employees that did not undergo training. The authors suggested that it is likely that the organization offered training to those employees most likely to face violence on the job. Another possibility is that training targeting workplace violence might give employees a false sense of control, which may place them at greater risk for future violence. It would be important to determine whether training aimed at potential robbery victims would be beneficial for employees. A large number of individuals aged 19 and younger are employed in various retail occupations such as convenience stores and restaurants (Janicak, 1999); hence, it would be important to understand whether young employees benefit from the same type of training as more mature employees. For many young individuals, working in a fast food restaurant or a convenience store is their first job. How does being exposed to violence and aggression at a first job influence later perceptions of employment? Do young workers suffer more severe consequences when exposed to violence compared to more mature employees?

It is also important to gather additional information on organizational responses to robbery. What forms of organizational support would most benefit employee victims of robbery? Would young employees benefit from the same type of support as more mature workers? What types of coping strategies are most effective for victims of robbery? Would young workers benefit from different coping strategies? There is evidence to suggest that employee vulnerability attributions and avoidance coping strategies following robbery may be counterproductive for victims (Harrison & Kinner, 1998). More research is also needed to better understand the impact of robbery on organizational functioning (e.g., productivity)?

TYPE II AND TYPE III VIOLENCE

Initial evidence suggests that there are differential effects of coworker- and public-initiated violence on personal and organizational outcomes (e.g., LeBlanc & Kelloway, 2002). More research would be needed to understand the extent of these differences. For example, are employees more likely to blame the organization (i.e., hold the organization responsible) when they are victimized by an insider rather than an outsider? What are the moderators (e.g., reprimand the perpetrator, discharge the perpetrator) of type III violence that would lessen the negative impact for the victim and organization? What are the repercussions for perpetrators of type III violence? In other words, do their supervisors and coworkers change their perceptions of and behavior toward them (e.g., do coworkers ostracize them, take sides)? Initial studies suggest that there are differential predictors of aggression toward coworkers, subordinates, and supervisors (Greenberg & Barling, 1999). Investigators should continue to explore this avenue of research.

How effective are organizational sanctions against violence in preventing employee-initiated aggression? A recent study conducted by Dupré and Barling (2002) found that organizational sanctions moderated the relationship between predictors of aggression and supervisor-targeted aggression. How effective are zero-tolerance policies against violence? What are the repercussions for perpetrators of public-initiated violence? How do organizations deal with the perpetrators and their victims? Does organizational response depend on the severity of the aggression? Do different industries respond differently? Do victims feel differently about the perpetrator if the violence was unintentional (e.g., the perpetrator was drunk, mentally ill)?

Is there a spill-over from public-initiated aggression to coworker-initiated aggression? A recent qualitative study suggested that exposure to robbery had a negative impact on work relationships (Miller-Burke et al., 1999).

TYPE IV VIOLENCE

To date, the topic of domestic violence in the workplace has received little attention in the empirical literature; hence, there are many potential avenues for future research. Practitioner-oriented journals suggest that trust in management is an important determinant of whether victims of domestic abuse confide in their supervisors, yet there is no empirical evidence to show that this is the case. Researchers could examine what the important organizational climate variables are that predict employee willingness to disclose domestic abuse. We know little about how organizations respond to disclosure. Do upper-level managers in organizations even recognize domestic violence as a problem for the organization, or do they consider it a personal problem? Are employees provided with support from their organizations following disclosure or are their problems ignored? A recent study conducted by Swanberg and Logan (2004) suggested that women who confided in their supervisors experienced short-term benefits, such as schedule flexibility and job relocation.

Are victims of domestic abuse more likely to confide in their supervisors or coworkers? What are effects of knowledge of domestic abuse on coworkers? What strategies are effective to prevent domestic violence from spilling over into the workplace? How should organizations handle the issue of domestic violence when both individuals in the relationship are employed in the organization? Anecdotal articles suggest that victims of abuse experience frequent harassment on the job (e.g., threatening phone calls; Zachary, 2000). How frequently victims are harassed on the job needs to examined in more detail.

CONCLUSION

Stereotypes about workplace violence abound. For example, it is believed that employee-initiated violence accounts for most violent situations in the workplace. Yet, as noted earlier, the data show that this is incorrect. This has critical implications for how workplace violence is seen in terms of counterproductive behaviors. Although we are not suggesting in any way that stranger-, customer-, employee-, or partner-initiated violence are any more acceptable or less detrimental, we must conclude this chapter by calling for conceptual clarification of the relationship between the four types of violence and counterproductive work behaviors. In addition, although a large body of research has developed relating to employee-based violence, research must now address the predictors and outcomes of all other types of workplace violence as well.

REFERENCES

Anderson, C. A., & Bushman, B. J. (2002). Human aggression. *Annual Review of Psychology, 53*, 27–51.

Anderson, T. (2001). The hostile customer and other grim tales. *Security Management, 45*, 64–75.

Another pizza delivery man killed. (2002, August 3). *Detroit News*. Retrieved August 25, 2002, from http://detnews.com/2002/metro/0208/03/metro-552778.htm

Armstrong, F., & Larsen, E. (2001, June 1). Two die in mall shooting. *Kingston Whig-Standard*, pp. 1, 8.

Barling, J. (1996). The prediction, experience, and consequences of workplace violence. In G. R. VandenBos & E. Q. Bulatao (Eds.), *Violence on the job: Identifying risks and developing solutions* (pp. 29–49). Washington, DC: American Psychological Association.

Barling, J., Rogers, A. G., & Kelloway, E. K. (2001). Behind closed doors: In-home workers' experience of sexual harassment and workplace violence. *Journal of Occupational Health Psychology, 6*, 255–269.

Baron, R. A., Neuman, J. H., & Geddes, D. (1999). Social and personal determinants of workplace aggression: Evidence for the impact of perceived injustice and the type A behavior pattern. *Aggressive Behavior, 25*, 281–296.

Braverman, M. (1999). *Preventing workplace violence: A guide for employers and practitioners*. Thousand Oaks, CA: Sage.

Brooks, P. (2001, June 5). Murder mask may ID killer: Skeleton hood found near store where clerk stabbed to death. *Halifax Chronicle-Herald*. Retrieved August 25, 2002, from http://www.canoe.ca/CNEWSLaw0106/05—halifax-par.html

Budd, J. W., Arvey, R. D., & Lawless, P. (1996). Correlates and consequences of workplace violence. *Journal of Occupational Health Psychology, 1*, 197–210.

Bureau of Justice Statistics. (2001). *Law enforcement officers most at risk for workplace violence*. Retrieved August 25, 2002, from http://www.ojp.usdoj.gov/bjs/pub/press/vw99pr.htm

Bureau of Labor Statistics. (2002). *National census of fatal occupational injuries, 2000*. Retrieved June 20, 2002, from http://data.bls.gov/servlet/SurveyOutputServlet?jrunsessionid=1026186073171104199

Canadian Centre for Occupational Health and Safety. (1999). *Violence in the workplace*. Retrieved August 31, 2000, from http://www.ccohs.ca/oshanswers/psychosocial/violence.html

Castillo, D. N., & Jenkins, E. L. (1994). Industries and occupations at high risk for work-related homicide. *Journal of Occupational Medicine, 36*, 125–132.

Davenport, J. (2002a, May 31). Patient stabs nurse: Her condition critical; police nab him at metro. *Gazette* (Montreal, Canada), p. A1.

Davenport, J. (2002b, June 1). Security boosted at psychiatric institute: Counseling provided to shaken staff after knife attack by patient leaves nurse in critical condition. *Gazette* (Montreal, Canada), p. A3.

Davis, H. (1987). Workplace homicides of Texas males. *American Journal of Public Health, 77*, 1290–1293.

Douglas, S. C., & Martinko, M. J. (2001). Exploring the role of individual differences in the prediction of workplace aggression. *Journal of Applied Psychology, 86*, 547–559.

Dupré, K. E., & Barling, J. (2003). Workplace aggression. In A. Sagie, S. Stashevsky, & M. Koslowsky (Eds.), *Misbehavior and dysfunctional attitudes in organizations* (pp. 13–32). New York: Palgrave.

Dupré, K. E., & Barling, J. (2004). *The roles of control, justice and organizational sanctions in the prediction and prevention of workplace aggression*. Manuscript submitted for publication.

Ehrensaft, M. K., Langhinrichsen-Rohling, J., Heyman, R. E., O'Leary, K. D., & Lawrence, E. (1999). Feeling controlled in marriage: A phenomenon specific to physically aggressive couples? *Journal of Family Psychology, 13*, 20–32.

Folger, R., Baron, R. A., & McLean-Parks, J. (1996, August). *Violence by disgruntled employees: Evidence on injustice and popcorn effects*. Symposium conducted at the Academy of Management Meetings, Cincinnati, OH.

Folger, R., & Skarlicki, D. P. (1998). A popcorn metaphor for employee aggression. In R. W. Griffin, A. O'Leary-Kelly, & J. M. Collins (Eds.), *Dysfunctional behaviour in organizations: Violent and deviant behavior* (pp. 43–81). Stamford, CT: JAI Press.

Gabor, T., & Normandeau, A. (1989). Armed robbery: Highlights of a Canadian study. *Canadian Police College Journal, 13*, 273–282.

Garrett, C., Hall, S., & Shepardson, D. (2002, July 9). Restaurant slayings shock quiet Livonia: Robbery at Logan's Roadhouse leaves 2 dead in city ranked among safest in U.S. *Detroit News*. Retrieved August 18, 2002, from http://detnews.com/2002/metro/0207/09/a01-532970.htm

Garrett, C., & Shepardson, D. (2002, July 24). Double murder suspect to stand trial: Police didn't need warrant to arrest him, judge rules. *Detroit News*. Retrieved August 30, 2002, from http://detnews.com/2002/wayne/0207/24/c03-544312.htm

Graham, J. P. (1991). Disgruntled employees—Ticking time bombs? *Security Management, 36*, 83–85.

Greenberg, L., & Barling, J. (1999). Predicting employee aggression against coworkers, subordinates and supervisors: The roles of person behaviors and perceived workplace factors. *Journal of Organizational Behavior, 20*, 897–913.

Guterman, N. B., Jayaratne, S., & Bargal, D. (1996). Workplace violence and victimization experienced by social workers: A cross-national study of Americans and Israelis. In G. R. VandenBos & E. Q. Bulatao (Eds.), *Violence on the job: Identifying risks and developing solutions* (pp. 175–188). Washington, DC: American Psychological Association.

Harrison, C. A., & Kinner, S. A. (1998). Correlates of psychological distress following armed robbery. *Journal of Traumatic Stress, 11*, 787–798.

Health Services Advisory Committee. (1987). *Violence to staff in the health services*. London: Her Majesty's Stationary Office.

Hearnden, K. (1988). *Violence at work (Industrial Safety Data File)*. London: United Trade Press.

Hendricks, B., & Tedesco, J. (1997, October, 8). 3 dead, 1 wounded in shooting at office. *San Antonio Express-News*, p. 1A.

Inness, M., Barling, J., & Turner, N. (in press). Understanding supervisor-targeted aggression: A within-person, between-jobs design. *Journal of Applied Psychology*.

International Labour Organization. (1998). *Violence on the job—A global problem*. Retrieved August 31, 2000, from http://www.ilo.org/public/english/235press/pr/1998/30.htm

Jackson, D., Clare, J., & Mannix, J. (2002). Who would want to be a nurse? Violence in the workplace—A factor in recruitment and retention. *Journal of Nursing Management, 10*, 13–20.

Janicak, C. A. (1999). An analysis of occupational homicides involving workers 19 years old and younger. *Journal of Occupational and Environmental Medicine, 41*, 1140–1145.

Jenkins, E. L. (1996). *Violence in the workplace: Risk factors and prevention strategies* (DHHS Publication No. 96-100). Washington, DC: U.S. Government Printing Office.

Jockin, V., Arvey, R. D., & McGue, M. (2001). Perceived victimization moderates self-reports of workplace aggression and conflict. *Journal of Applied Psychology, 86*, 1262–1269.

Johnson, H., & Bunge, V. P. (2001). Prevalence and consequences of spousal assault in Canada. *Canadian Journal of Criminology, 43*, 27–45.

Jossi, F. (1999). Defusing workplace violence. *Business and Health, 17*, 34–39.

Kolettis, H. (2000). Drawing the line. *Security, 37*, 18–24.

Kraus, J. F. (1987). Homicide while at work: Persons, industries, and occupations at high risk. *American Journal of Public Health, 77*, 1285–1289.

Lamberg, L. (1996). Don't ignore patients' threats, psychiatrists told. *Journal of the American Medical Association, 275*, 1715–1716.

Leather, P., Lawrence, C., Beale, D., Cox, T., & Dickson, R. (1998). Exposure to occupational violence and the buffering effects of intra-organizational support. *Work and Stress, 12*, 161–178.

LeBlanc, M. M., & Kelloway, E. K. (2002). Predictors and outcomes of workplace violence and aggression. *Journal of Applied Psychology, 87*, 444–453.

Levin, P. F., Hewitt, J. B., & Misner, T. S. (1998). Insights of nurses about assault in hospital-based emergency departments. *Image—The Journal of Nursing Scholarship, 30*, 249–254.

Leymann, H. (1985). Somatic and psychological symptoms after the experience of life threatening events: A profile analysis. *Victimology: An International Journal, 10*, 512–538.

Lion, J. R., Snyder, W., & Merrill, G. L. (1981). Underreporting of assaults on staff in a state hospital. *Hospital and Community Psychiatry, 32*, 497–498.

Loomis, D., Wolf, S. H., Runyan, C. W., Marshall, S. W., & Butts, J. D. (2001). Homicide on the job: Workplace and community determinants. *American Journal of Epidemiology, 154*, 410–417.

Lyndon, K., & Zalud, B. (1997). Fast-food mass murder triggers CEO involvement. *Security, 34*, 59–60.

Man kills ex-girlfriend, self at Santa Clara high-tech plant. (1997, August 23). *Los Angeles Times*, p. 21.

Martinko, M. J., & Zellars, K. L. (1998). Toward a theory of workplace violence: A cognitive appraisal perspective. In R. W. Griffin, A. O'Leary-Kelly, & J. M. Collins (Eds.), *Dysfunctional behavior in organizations: Violent and deviant behavior* (pp. 1–42). Stamford, CT: JAI Press.

May, D. D., & Grubbs, L. M. (2002). The extent, nature, and precipitating factors of nurse assault among three groups of registered nurses in a regional medical center. *Journal of Emergency Nursing, 28,* 11–17.

McClure, S. (2001, October 3). Six killed in Greyhound crash. *USA Today.* Retrieved August 30, 2002, from http://www.usatoday.com/news/nation/2001/10/03/buscrash.htm

Meadows, R. J. (1998). *Understanding violence and victimization.* Upper Saddle River, NJ: Prentice-Hall.

Merchant, J. A., & Lundell, J. A. (2001). Workplace violence intervention research workshop, April 5–7, 2000, Washington, DC: Background, rationale, and summary. *American Journal of Preventive Medicine, 20,* 135–140.

Mertin, P., & Mohr, P. B. (2000). Incidence and correlates of posttraumatic stress disorder in Australian victims of domestic abuse. *Journal of Family Violence, 15,* 411–422.

Miller-Burke, J., Attridge, M., & Fass, P. M. (1999). Impact of traumatic events and organizational response: A study of bank robberies. *Journal of Occupational and Environmental Medicine, 41,* 73–83.

Montreal University staff gunned down. (1992, August 25). *Calgary Herald,* p. A1.

Morrell, J. S., & Rubin, L. J. (2001). The Minnesota Multiphasic Personality Inventory—2, posttraumatic stress disorder, and women domestic violence survivors. *Professional Psychology: Research and Practice, 32,* 151–156.

Munn, M. (2002, July 26). The nation; domestic violence poses "double jeopardy"; workplace: The toll of abuse costs some victims their jobs. Senate panel considers protections. *Los Angeles Times,* p. A32.

National Institute for Occupational Safety and Health. (1997). *Violence in the workplace.* Retrieved August 30, 2000, from http://www.cdc.gov/niosh/violfs.html

National Institute for Occupational Safety and Health. (2002). *Violence: Occupational Hazards in Hospitals* (DHHS Publication No. 2002–101). Retrieved August 20, 2002, from http://www.cdc.gov/niosh/2002-101.html#intro

O'Leary-Kelly, A. M., Griffin, R. W., & Glew, D. J. (1996). Organization-motivated aggression: A research framework. *Academy of Management Review, 21,* 225–253.

Painter, K. (1987). "It's part of the job": Violence at work. *Employee Relations, 9,* 30–40.

Peek-Asa, C., & Howard, J. (1999). Workplace-violence investigations by the California Division of Occupational Safety and Health, 1993–1996. *Journal of Occupational and Environmental Medicine, 41,* 647–653.

Peek-Asa, C., Runyan, C. W., & Zwerling, C. (2001). The role of surveillance and evaluation research in the reduction of violence against workers. *American Journal of Preventive Medicine, 20,* 141–148.

Peek-Asa, C., Schaffer, K., Kraus, J., & Howard, J. (1998). Surveillance of nonfatal workplace assault injuries using police and employers' reports. *Journal of Occupational and Environmental Medicine, 40,* 707–713.

Report of the United States Postal Service Commission on a Safe and Secure Workplace. (2000). New York: National Center on Addiction and Substance Abuse at Columbia University.

Riger, S., Ahrens, C., & Blickenstaff, A. (2000). Measuring interference with employment and education reported by women with abusive partners: Preliminary data. *Violence and Victims, 15,* 161–172.

Rogers, K. A., & Kelloway, E. K. (1997). Violence at work: Personal and organizational outcomes. *Journal of Occupational Health Psychology, 2,* 63–71.

Santos, A., & Leather, P. (2001, November). *The comparative effects of "offender-initiated" and "colleague-initiated" violence upon employee well-being in the police force.* Paper presented at the annual meeting of the European Academy of Occupational Health Psychology, Barcelona, Spain.

Schat, A. C. H., & Kelloway, E. K. (2000). Effects of perceived control on the outcomes of workplace aggression and violence. *Journal of Occupational Health Psychology, 5,* 386–402.

Schat, A. C. H., & Kelloway, E. K. (2003). Reducing the adverse consequences of workplace violence and aggression: The buffering effects of organizational support. *Journal of Occupational Health Psychology, 8,* 110–122.

Schlosser, E. (2002). *Fast food nation: The dark side of the all-American meal* (2nd ed.). New York: HarperCollins.

Smith, G. (1999, June). Violence at work. *Benefits Canada, 23,* 22–27.

Stuart, P. (1992). Murder on the job (killing of coworkers). *Personnel Journal, 71,* 72–84.

Swanberg, J. E., & Logan, T. K. (2004). *Domestic violence and employment: A qualitative study of the effects of domestic violence on women's employment.* Manuscript submitted for publication.

Sygnatur, E. F., & Toscano, G. A. (2000, Spring). Work-related homicides: The facts. *Compensation and Working Conditions,* 3–8.

University of Iowa Injury Prevention Research Center. (2001). *Workplace violence: A report to the nation.* Retrieved May 31, 2002, from http://www.public-health.uiowa.edu/IPRC/NATION.PDF

Valdmanis, T., & Morrison, B. (2000, December 27). 7 colleagues killed in Mass.: Arrested software tester set to appear in court today. *USA Today,* pp. 1A, 3A.

Zachary, M. K. (2000). Labor law for supervisors. *Supervision, 61,* 23–26.

3

THE STUDY OF REVENGE
IN THE WORKPLACE:
CONCEPTUAL, IDEOLOGICAL,
AND EMPIRICAL ISSUES

ROBERT J. BIES AND THOMAS M. TRIPP

Over the past decade, there has been growing scholarly interest in revenge (Bies & Tripp, 1996, 2000; Bies, Tripp, & Kramer, 1997; McLean Parks, 1997; Tripp & Bies, 1997) and related topics such as retaliation (Allred, 1999; Skarlicki & Folger, 1997), deviant workplace behaviors (Robinson & Bennett, 1995), workplace aggression (Neuman & Baron, 1997; O'Leary-Kelly, Griffin, & Glew, 1996), and violence in the workplace (Folger & Skarlicki, 1998). Amid all this research, there has been considerable ambiguity about the validity and independence of these related constructs. If we are to advance our understanding of revenge and related behaviors and build a unified theory of these behaviors in the workplace, then we must bring some clarity to this conceptual confusion. We attempt such clarification in this chapter.

This chapter is divided into three sections. The first section analyzes the conceptual issues and ideological assumptions surrounding revenge and related topics and moves toward a unified conceptualization and definition of the construct. The second section reviews the empirical evidence on revenge—its etiology and the behavioral forms that it takes in the workplace. The third section concludes with a call for a more unified conceptual approach to guide research on revenge and related constructs, one that is "value-free" in its analysis.

CONCEPTUAL AND IDEOLOGICAL ISSUES: CLARIFICATION AND UNIFICATION OF RELATED CONSTRUCTS

What is missing in the theory and research on revenge and related topics is an assessment of the construct validity of each of the constructs. We argue that revenge is a value-added construct, one that is distinctive relative to others. But we also argue that revenge and related constructs fit more parsimoniously under the conceptual umbrella of workplace aggression.

The Construct Validity of Revenge: Definition and Distinctiveness

Aquino, Tripp, and Bies (2001) defined revenge as an action in response to some perceived harm or wrongdoing by another party that is intended to inflict damage, injury, discomfort, or punishment on the party judged responsible. As such, workplace revenge is uniquely different from the other workplace aggression constructs. Although revenge encapsulates the full range of aggressive behaviors, from verbal to physical, from covert to overt, from indirect to direct, and from interpersonally directed to organizationally directed, it attaches each of these aggressive behaviors to a singular motive.

Thus, *revenge* is not always, or even usually, the same thing as *incivility*, which can be motivated by competitiveness, sadistic impulses, or inattentiveness, none of which are revenge motives (Andersson & Pearson, 1999). Revenge is not the same thing as *bullying* (Randall, 2001), which is about individuals who instigate aggression, not about those who feel provoked to respond to aggression with more aggression. Revenge is not the same thing as *deviance*, either in terms of normative deviance or in terms of statistical deviance (Robinson & Bennett, 1995). In many contexts revenge is normative, such as in legal disputes, and sometimes in dealing with abusive customers, coworkers, or bosses. In many other contexts, revenge is not uncommon: In the numerous critical incident studies we have conducted, fewer than 10% of the respondents could not think of a time when they sought revenge (Bies & Tripp, 1995; Tripp & Bies, 1997). Revenge is not even the same thing as Skarlicki and Folger's (1997) organizational retaliatory behaviors (ORBs). ORB is revenge-motivated aggression that is targeted against the organization itself. Revenge, however, includes interpersonally directed as well as organizationally directed behaviors.

In summary, what makes revenge unique is that, unlike ORBs, revenge examines *interpersonal* aggression. Like ORBs, but unlike deviance, incivility, bullying, and abuse, revenge is concerned with reactions to perceived workplace *injustices*. Unlike all of the other mentioned constructs, our study of revenge-motivated aggression does not assume that such aggression is always dysfunctional and always needs to be weeded out. Our research has shown that revenge is often intended to help others more than hurt them, and that often this goal is reached.

Conceptual Proliferation and Unification

At the 2001 and 2002 Academy of Management national meetings, scholars in this area called for a resolution to the proliferation of overlapping and competing constructs on the "dark side" of micro-OB. We propose that workplace revenge should not be eliminated through subjugation to any other construct because workplace revenge is, if not a unique construct, at least a unique approach to workplace aggression. We also argue that the "workplace aggression" label should be promoted to the name of this field of study because (a) the workplace aggression construct encompasses all of the other related constructs (i.e., revenge, organizational retaliatory behavior, counterproductive work behavior, deviance, incivility, bullying, and abuse), and (b) it does not presuppose that all such behaviors are counternormative or dysfunctional.

In choosing a label for this field of study of aggressive, dark behaviors by individuals in the workplace, we should consider several criteria. First, the label should be specific enough to draw boundaries around a coherent set of phenomena; it should not be an amorphous label that means anything to anybody. Examples of labels that meet this criterion of specificity can be found in textbooks on organizational behavior under the chapter titles *motivation, power, teams, culture,* and so forth. One label that is often found in these textbooks that is too broad and amorphous for our purposes is *conflict.* Conflict does include workplace aggression, because it results from and produces conflict; however, conflict is not a good label in this instance because it also encompasses behaviors that are not necessarily aggressive, such as politics, mediation, and interest-based negotiation.

Second, the field label should not be so specific as to preclude avenues of inquiry that bear on the central phenomena. *Revenge, ORB, counterproductive work behaviors, deviance, incivility, bullying,* and *emotional abuse* all unduly limit the avenues of inquiry in the field because each construct label's uniqueness excludes other phenomena and values with which other constructs are concerned.

The one label that meets both of the criteria is *workplace aggression.* It is as defining as *motivation* or *power,* but does not restrict what kind of aggressive behaviors get studied nor prescribe any values or ideologies. In taking this position, it may seem, at first glance, that our analysis is at odds with the analyses of counterproductive work behavior (CWB; e.g., Fox, Spector, & Miles, 2001) and organizational deviance (Robinson & Bennett, 1995) in that withdrawal behaviors, such as tardiness and "pretending" to work hard, are included in those analyses but would not necessarily be considered aggression, which is central to our conceptualization of revenge. But a finer grained analysis suggests more similarity than difference. For example, in our previous research and analysis of revenge (e.g., Bies & Tripp, 1996, 1998b; Bies et al., 1997) as well as later in this chapter, we include withdrawal behaviors as part of revenge, as long as such withdrawal behavior was intended to inflict harm on the party judged responsible for the initial harm or wrongdoing. For us, withdrawal behavior is a passive–aggressive response and thus the enactment of revenge.

But in contrast to the CWB and deviance approaches, we do not promote the managerial-centered perspective over the employee-centered perspective. As an umbrella construct, of which all these other constructs are subsets, *workplace aggression* allows each scholar to study aggression from his or her own unique vantage point, and thus avoids constricting the variety of theoretical questions we can ask about the antecedents and consequents of aggressive behavior. For example, Andersson and Pearson (1999) can still ask, "How does aggression spiral out of control?" and Bies and Tripp (1996) can still ask, "What do employees do when they are treated unjustly?" Yet in answering these new questions, no new construct need be created and validated. Therefore, we must respectfully disagree with the editors of this book in their choice of a title. *Counterproductive work behavior* is not the best umbrella label because it violates the second criterion—in other words, it precludes the possibility, and thus the study of, aggression as sometimes prosocial, productive, and beneficial behavior.

This is more than just a semantic argument for us. In past research (e.g., Bies & Tripp 1998; Tripp & Bies, 1997) we have demonstrated that workplace revenge is not always perceived as *counterproductive* behavior. Sometimes, revenge-motivated aggression serves a purpose useful to not only the avengers but also to their victims, the bystanders, and even to the organization itself. Revenge, particularly as vigilante justice, can correct workplace injustices and thereby improve employee morale and productivity.

This view of revenge-motivated aggression as dysfunctional is not unique to the scholars who study counterproductive work behavior per se, but also to most scholars interested in the so-called dark side microbehaviors of organizations. For example, Robinson and Bennett (1995) studied deviant workplace behaviors. *Deviance* denotes that such behaviors are counternormative, and all of the examples in the Robinson and Bennett typology are behaviors that make the employees or the organization itself worse off.

Similarly, Andersson and Pearson (1999) described aggressive behaviors as "incivility," which also denotes such behaviors as counternormative. Also, the European study of aggressive behaviors is on bullying (see chap. 11, this volume), which focuses on aggression that is the result of sadistic tendencies. Finally, Keashly (1998, 2001; chap. 9, this volume) is interested in *emotional abuse*, a label that suggests that all such behavior is morally wrong because it is abusive.

We are not saying that these authors are wrong—that people in the workplace never engage in behaviors that are counterproductive, deviant, uncivil, bullying, or abusive. However, we are concerned that in framing so much aggressive behavior as counternormative, we pay insufficient attention to those aggressive behaviors that are normative or beneficial. Moreover, in the battle of competing constructs that have proliferated in the workplace aggression field, we do not want the "winning" construct to exclude by definition the possibility that aggression can be a good thing, which the justice approach on workplace aggression (namely, workplace revenge and organizational retaliatory behaviors) assumes.

We are saying that how scholars have labeled constructs, which reflects in part how scholars have elevated the manager-centered perspective over the employee-centered perspective, punctuates aggressive conflict such that we see only *part* of the story. Because we see the retaliatory aggression but not the aggression that provoked the retaliation, we often do not see that second act of aggression as an act of revenge. We are like the referees who officiate professional sports, where fisticuffs often break out. The referees rarely see who threw the first punch, but they do see who threw the second punch, and as a consequence penalize only that second person. To serve justice, the referees would see the whole conflict, from beginning to end, and thus penalize both players (or neither player). Much like those referees need to do, workplace aggression scholars more often need to recognize retaliatory aggression as retaliatory, because distinguishing between unprovoked aggression and provoked aggression is necessary to develop adequate models to decrease harmful aggression and promote workplace justice.

In a recent study with our colleague Karl Aquino (Tripp, Bies, & Aquino, 2002), we found that judgments of aggression depend on the perception of the provocation that precedes the aggression. Specifically, we found that third parties harshly judged acts of revenge-motivated aggression that were disproportionate to the size of the provocation; yet third parties (slightly) approved of acts of revenge-motivated aggression that were similarly severe to the provocation. What did not matter at all was the absolute severity of the revenge; only the relative severity of the revenge to the provocation affected third-party judgments of the acceptability of the revenge-motivated aggression. In particular, severe acts of revenge were acceptable, so long as they were provoked by severe provocations. Also, mild acts of revenge that followed severe provocations were judged harshly—just as harshly as were judged severe acts of revenge that followed mild provocations. In short, severe acts of aggression are justified, at least partially, if they are in response to severe provocations.

This finding is familiar to scholars who study war between nations. The concept of the "just war" (Walzer, 1977) is applicable. To all but pacifists, it is appropriate to fight a war if it meets certain criteria. Of concern is the criterion of provocation. That is, a necessary but not sufficient condition to justify fighting a war is to be the victim of an unprovoked attack by the enemy. Only then, if even then, may a nation be permitted to kill people of another nation. This is one reason why so many more Americans felt justified fighting the Japanese in World War II—Japan, of course, began the war (or at least began the lethal phase of conflict with the United States)—than felt justified fighting the war in Vietnam, which did not have such an unambiguous provocation.

RESEARCH ON REVENGE: WHAT WE LEARNED FROM THE EMPIRICAL STUDIES

Research on topics related to revenge (ORBs: Skarlicki & Folger, 1997; retaliation: Allred, 1999) have primarily focused on cognitive variables, such as attributions or justice judgments, as the triggers for such behaviors. Allred (1999) has also looked at anger as a key motivator for retaliation. Although their findings have been informative and yielded keen insights, our research has taken a different direction, conceptually and methodologically.

Our research program on revenge has focused more on the avenger's perspective and has included the inductive, grounded theory approach. As a result, our studies have yielded a more richly textured and broader mapping of the cognitive and emotional variables that shape the dynamics of revenge. From the empirical studies, we can draw five tentative conclusions about revenge: (a) revenge is provoked; (b) emotions are figural elements; (c) revenge has a rationality and morality; (d) the emotions of revenge are shaped by social cognitive dynamics; and (e) revenge can take many forms.

Revenge Is Provoked

Our research (e.g., Bies & Tripp, 1996) and that of others (e.g., Allred, 1999; Skarlicki & Folger, 1997) makes is quite clear that revenge is a provoked behavior. Sources of provocation include (a) goal obstruction; (b) violation of rules, norms, and promises; and (c) status and power derogation. The latter two sources of provocation are rooted in the sense of injustice, whereas goal obstruction is not necessarily a justice event.

Goal Obstruction

When one frustrates the attainment of goals in organizations, it can lead to acts of revenge in response (Morrill, 1992). Goal obstruction can lead to frustration (Buss, 1962), and that frustration can lead to an aggressive response such as revenge (Neuman & Baron, 1997).

Violation of Rules, Norms, or Promises

Employees are motivated to seek revenge when the formal rules of the organization are violated (Bies & Tripp, 1996). One such example is organizational decision makers who change the rules or criteria of decision making after the fact to justify a self-serving judgment (Bies & Tripp, 1996). Another example of rule violation involves a formal breach of a contract between an employee and employer, which can lead to litigation (Bies & Tyler, 1993).

Violations are not limited to formal rules but also include breaches of social norms and etiquette. For example, when bosses or coworkers make promises but then break them, or even lie outright, the victims may be motivated to avenge such wrongs (Bies & Tripp, 1996). More broadly, any perceived inequities on the job or violations of fairness norms can motivate revenge (cf. Skarlicki & Folger, 1997). Examples of such inequities and violations include bosses or coworkers who shirk their job responsibilities, or take undue credit for a team's performance, or outright steal ideas (Bies & Tripp, 1996). The revenge motive may also be salient when private confidences or secrets are disclosed to others inside or outside the organization—that is, when people feel betrayed by someone they trusted (Bies, 1993).

Status and Power Derogation

Several studies suggest that attempts to derogate a person's status or power can motivate revenge (Bies & Tripp, 1996). For example, bosses who are hypercritical, overdemanding, and overly harsh—even cruel—in their dealings with subordinates over time can spark revenge cognitions and emotions (Bies & Tripp, 1996, 2000). Other revenge-provoking incidents include destructive criticism (Baron, 1988), public ridicule intended to embarrass a subordinate or coworker (Morrill, 1992), or when the employee is accused wrongly by a boss or peer (Bies & Tripp, 1996).

Emotions Are Figural Elements of Revenge

Many of the studies of revenge behavior focus on one strong emotion—anger—as the figural element in revenge (e.g., Allred, 1999). Anger is an emotion that is triggered by an assignment of blame for perceived harm or wrongdoing (Bies et al., 1997). Drawing on findings from our own research (Bies & Tripp, 1996, 2002), along with findings from studies of other researchers (Hornstein, 1996; Mikula, 1986; Mikula, Petri, & Tanzer, 1990), the emotions of revenge can be characterized in much richer terms and in terms of a variety of facets (Bies & Tripp, 2002). These facets include a sense of violation, feelings of helplessness, intensity, and an enduring nature.

Sense of Violation

When describing the experience of harm, people's initial descriptions of the emotions often reflect a sense of violation that was more than mere "unmet expectations." Indeed, the violation was much deeper, reflecting a violated psyche or sense of sacred self (Bies, 2001). For example, in Bies and Tripp (1996), one individual described a betrayed confidence as causing her world to be "shattered," what she assumed to be "sacred and true—the trust of a friend"—was violated, if not destroyed forever.

Feelings of Helplessness

The sense of violation created by the harm is often accompanied by feelings of helplessness. For example, Bies and Tripp (2002) found that people described initially reflecting a feeling of being confused or stunned by the harm. A typical comment was, "I couldn't believe what had just happened. I trusted him. When he attacked me in front of my coworkers, I was paralyzed and speechless." In addition, several respondents reported a variety of physiological symptoms, including uncontrollable crying, "knots in the stomach," and physical exhaustion.

Intensity

In many cases, the feelings of violation and helplessness give way to intense, action-oriented emotions. Indeed, in almost existential terms, people often focus on the intensity of the emotions they experience, often belying a strong visceral response of physiological and psychological pain. For example, the initial emotions are often described as quite hot and volatile, characterized by expressions of pain, anger, and rage (Bies & Tripp, 1996). In describing these emotions, people use such words as *furious* and *bitter* and describe how they felt engulfed in *white-hot* emotions. One person described herself as *inflamed* and *enraged,* and *consumed* by thoughts of revenge, and another person needed to satisfy the *burning desire of revenge*.

Enduring Nature

In addition, the emotions of revenge can create a psychological and physiological stranglehold over the individual. The emotions of revenge can endure over time, sometimes for days, even weeks and months, if not longer. Indeed, the emotions of revenge can act like a "social toxin" (Hornstein, 1996), "poisoning" their professional and personal lives over time. For an extreme example, Matthews (1988) recounted an example of an individual who let a harm-doer "live inside his head rent free" for more than ten years after the initial harm.

Revenge Has a Rationality and Morality

Thus far, we have argued that, relative to cognitions, emotions should become more figural elements in an analysis of revenge dynamics (Bies & Tripp, 1996, 2002). But, with that said, what frequently triggers the emotions is a cognitive appraisal of the action or the consequences (Lazarus & Lazarus, 1994). Whether an action or outcome triggers the revenge motive depends on how one makes sense of, or cognitively processes, the harm or wrongdoing (Bies et al., 1997). In particular, to provide a moral basis for revenge (i.e., it is not just a harm but an injustice), the assignment of blame is critical (Folger & Cropanzano, 2001).

In taking a sense-making perspective (Weick, 1995), a provoking incident is one that violates social or normative expectations, and such a violation triggers a search for causal explanation about why the event occurred (Wong & Weiner, 1981). In this causal analysis, people will search for factors that might discount the perpetrator's responsibility for the action (Kelley, 1972). If there are any mitigating circumstances to create reasonable doubt in people's minds, then the emotions are less likely to intensify (Bies, 1987; Bies & Tripp, 1996). However, given the evidence of a negativity bias in evaluation (Kanouse & Hanson, 1972) and the actor–observer effect (Jones & Nisbett, 1972), people will likely focus on the perpetrator as the causal agent responsible for the harm and wrongdoing. Indeed, whether the provoking incident arouses intense emotional reactions will depend on the outcome of a causal analysis (Bies, 1987).

If an individual can place blame on the harm-doer, then that person will likely construe the action as a personal attack (Bies, 2001). Following Cahn (1949), the attack is viewed as an act of aggression that will trigger emotions that are often described vividly (e.g., furious, enraged, hate). In other words, revenge is viewed as a "legitimate" and rational response of self-defense in response to an aggressive action by another. From our perspective, then, revenge should be viewed as part of a bilateral aggression between the victim and the harm-doer.

There is also clear and consistent empirical evidence that revenge has its own moral imperative (Bies & Tripp, 1996; McLean Parks, 1997). First, revenge is in many cases a response to a perceived injustice (Skarlicki & Folger, 1997). Second, revenge is most often intended to restore justice.

For instance, while engaging in revenge, people reported their strong belief that they were "doing the right thing" and that they were "doing justice" (Tripp & Bies, 1997). Third, although the act of revenge may serve self-interest, it often serves other interests, and it is usually justified in moral terms (Bies & Tripp, 1998). The justice rationality can be a powerful motivation and justification for revenge.

Social Cognitive Dynamics

What aspects of the justice-centered sense-making process can amplify the emotions of revenge? Our research on revenge has identified several such cognitive processes that can bias the blame-assignment process (Bies et al., 1997). First, there is the overly personalistic attribution (Bies & Tripp, 1996). For example, when individuals overattribute sinister and malevolent motives to others' actions (e.g., "she wasn't just being careless or even just selfish; she was mean-spirited"; and "she was out to get *me*; it wasn't just business, it was *personal*"), they may perceive harmful intent or believe they are being belittled even in their otherwise seemingly benign social encounters. Kramer (1994) referred to this general process as the sinister attribution error.

Second is the biased punctuation of conflict (Bies et al., 1997). Biased punctuation of conflict refers to a tendency for individuals to construe the history of conflict with others in a self-serving and provocative fashion. For example, in a tit-for-tat feud, each party perceives itself as the avenging victim and perceives its opponent as the aggressor against whom one must defend.

Third, a cognitive process that often acts to amplify the emotions of revenge is rumination and obsession (Bies et al., 1997). Indeed, we find that rumination and obsession are often at the foundation of more extreme emotions that can motivate revenge (e.g., bitterness, hatred). Further, rumination and obsession can become even more intense and enduring when they are reinforced in social gatherings when people vent their emotions (Bies & Tripp, 1996), which Morrill (1992) referred to as "bitch sessions."

Fourth, a cognitive process that may intensify blame is an ego-defensiveness. That is, when an unfavorable outcome occurs, one may search for someone to blame for the outcome, rather than oneself, so that the person feels better about him- or herself. Indeed, there may be a bias toward believing procedures are not fair when one receives an unfavorable or an unfair outcome. For example, Shah and Schroth (2000) found that it is better for recipients of unfavorable outcomes to believe that they got "screwed" by an unfair procedure (see also Brockner, 2001). Otherwise, if they believe the procedure was fair, then they are more likely to conclude that they *deserved* the unfavorable outcome as a result of some negative behavior or trait such as incompetence or laziness. Thus, people are biased to believe that the procedures are unfair every time they get hurt, particularly if no procedural information exists that says otherwise (Daly & Tripp, 1996; Lind, 2001). As a consequence, they may be more likely to see an injustice where perhaps none exists and further blame the decision maker for the outcome.

Revenge Can Take Many Forms

The enactment of revenge can take many forms, depending on the situation and the objective (Bies & Tripp, 1996, 2000; Skarlicki & Folger, 1997; Tripp & Bies, 1997). For example, some forms of revenge resembled inequity reduction responses. For example, people might avoid the perpetrators for a short period of time, refusing to greet them or even acknowledge their presence. Or, in a passive–aggressive response, people might withhold effort or work (Bies & Tripp, 1996; Tripp & Bies, 1997), such as deliberately not supporting the perpetrator when support is needed or intentionally turning in poor work performance. Other people sometimes transfer out of the job or department as the ultimate act of withholding support and friendship. In all these acts, the benefit the perpetrator receives from the avenger is reduced or eliminated, thus restoring equity in the relationship.

In other cases, the act of revenge may not only focus on the source of the harm or injustice but also focuses on retributive justice (Hogan & Emler, 1981)—to harm the perpetrator. In Bies and Tripp (1996) and Tripp and Bies (1997), we found retributive elements in the following types of revenge: public complaints designed to humiliate another person, public demands for apologies that are intended to embarrass the perpetrator, bad-mouthing the perpetrator, whistle-blowing, and litigation. Although whistle-blowing or litigation may not always be intended to harm the perpetrator— that is, it may be intended to stop the wrongdoing, perhaps even in the hopes of reforming the perpetrator or organization (as with pollution or unsafe practices)—our research finds a retributive motivation to get even with the perpetrator (Bies & Tripp, 1996).

THE CALL FOR A UNIFIED AND VALUE-FREE CONCEPTUAL FRAMEWORK: INTEGRATING THE MANAGER-CENTERED AND EMPLOYEE-CENTERED APPROACHES

It is time to unify the two major perspectives of the study of workplace aggression. One approach is the manager-centered approach, which views all aggressive employees as bad eggs to be predicted, selected, and eliminated before they can cause damage. By implication, it assumes that although avengers may *believe* that revenge can be functional, we researchers *know* that it is dysfunctional. The manager-centered approach diminishes the scholar's ability to understand, or even empathize, with avengers. The ideology of this approach elevates the good of the organization, as often defined by the upper echelon, over the good of the individual employee–avenger. Therefore, to the extent that scholars wholeheartedly buy into the manager-centered approach, they will relegate the theory of revenge to individual differences and personality literatures.

If the research stopped at looking for personality defects, our understanding of the causes of revenge would be incomplete. This would then be the danger of a biased theoretical perspective. What if avengers really can make themselves or others better off by getting even? For instance, what if avengers can eliminate the environmental triggers that might otherwise produce more severe conflict and motivation problems? Furthermore, what if scholars believed that such benefits were possible to various stakeholders? If scholars believe this, then a different research frame develops. What we are arguing is that a strict focus on the manager-centered perspective—on blaming dysfunctional employees—would miss the environmental triggers that set off employees.

Scholars have begun to move in the direction we are endorsing. The Fox et al. (2001) study is a good example. In this study, the researchers take a job stress-centered approach in their study of CWB, one that specifically dissociates itself from the selection solution and directs attention to organizational interventions to reduce the stressors and environments that foster CWB.

The other approach is the employee-centered approach, one that views aggressive acts as reactions to unjust attributes of the workplace environment. In following the employee-centered approach, scholars must investigate the organizational world *through the avenger's eyes*. Avengers are people who do not necessarily see themselves as stupid or evil. They often intend the harm they cause and do so for moral reasons (Tripp & Bies, 1997). For scholars to judge them as stupid or evil leads scholars away from seeing the world through the avengers' eyes. Although we do not propose that scholars *agree with* avengers' choices or values, we do argue that successful scholars will have to *empathize with* avengers' values and predicaments, as well as their choices to enact revenge. In taking this perspective, we recognize that some may argue that we are supporting actions that one might find morally repugnant (e.g., empathy for avengers who engage in lynch-mob justice or who bomb abortion clinics). But such an interpretation misses the central point of our argument: Understanding the causes of revenge and the enactment of revenge is a *scientific* objective not a *political* statement of whether we approve or disapprove of the revenge act. Indeed, our perspective is aligned with practice, as in the case of an FBI profiler who attempts to get into the mind of a serial murderer yet does not support the crimes of murder.

In other words, understanding does not mean agreeing with or condoning such behavior.

Obviously, both manager-centered and employee-centered approaches yield insights into the dynamics of revenge. We call for a unification of these two approaches to study revenge as a form of workplace aggression, one that is a result of both provocative environments and aggressive traits. After all, not every employee responds to the same provocations in the same contexts in the same way. However, rather than get into a classic trait-versus-situation debate over how much variance of aggressive behavior is explained by individual differences, it is better to look at the interaction between traits and situations. For example, Fox et al. (2001) examined the interaction effects between job stressors (including injustices), affective traits, and CWB. They found that affective traits (trait anger and trait anxiety) weakly moderated the relationship between injustice and CWBs but that autonomy did not moderate. In short, they found that chronically angry and anxious victims are more likely to avenge an injustice than are calmer victims. This is an important finding, and also is an example of research that does take a managerial-centered perspective by not blaming the aggressive employees for their aggressions. In fact, Fox et al. (2001) concluded the following:

> Still, our findings suggest that organizations may be able to reduce the levels of work behaviors that undermine their effectiveness by developing human resource policies and practices that take into consideration their possible emotional effects on employees. . . . The implications of this study suggest an alternative to the predominant "selection" solution to CWB, in which individuals with certain personality tendencies that may predict CWBs are screened out of the organization during the selection process. (p. 306)

CONCLUSION

We argue for a broader, more value-free modeling of workplace aggression, because our goal is to improve our understanding of workplace aggression (e.g., O'Leary-Kelly et al., 1996). Our concern is not political; it is scientific. Only by getting into the heads of avengers can we develop good scientific theories about revenge-motivated aggression. And we can only get into their heads if we take a more value-neutral approach to studying aggression. We believe that by promoting workplace aggression as the name of the subfield of dark organization behaviors—and thus by taxonomically subordinating all the overlapping constructs of deviance, bullying, mobbing, ORB, incivility, and counterproductive work behaviors—the study of workplace aggression will proceed more fruitfully.

REFERENCES

Allred, K. G. (1999). Anger driven retaliation: Toward an understanding of impassioned conflict in organizations. In R. J. Bies, R. J. Lewicki, & B. H. Sheppard (Eds.), *Research on negotiations in organizations* (Vol. 7, pp. 27–58). Greenwich, CT: JAI Press.

Andersson, L. M., & Pearson, C. M. (1999). Tit for tat? The spiraling effect of incivility in the workplace. *Academy of Management Review, 24,* 452–471.

Aquino, K., Tripp, T. M., & Bies, R. J. (2001). How employees respond to personal offense: The effects of blame attribution, victim status, and offender status on revenge and reconciliation in the workplace. *Journal of Applied Psychology, 86,* 52–59.

Baron, R. A. (1988). Negative effects of destructive criticism: Impact on conflict, self-efficacy, and task performance. *Journal of Applied Psychology, 73,* 199–207.

Bies, R. J. (1987). The predicament of injustice: The management of moral outrage. In L. L. Cummings & B. M. Staw (Eds.), *Research in organizational behavior* (Vol. 9, pp. 289–319). Greenwich, CT: JAI Press.

Bies, R. J. (1993). Privacy and procedural justice in organizations. *Social Justice Research, 6,* 69–86.

Bies, R. J. (2001). Interactional (in)justice: The sacred and the profane. In J. Greenberg & R. Cropanzano (Eds.), *Advances in organizational behavior* (pp. 89–118) Palo Alto, CA: Stanford University Press.

Bies, R. J., & Tripp, T. M. (1995). The use and abuse of power: Justice as social control. In R. Cropanzano & M. Kacmar (Eds.), *Organizational politics, justice, and support: Managing social climate at work* (pp. 131–145). New York: Quorum Press.

Bies, R. J., & Tripp, T. M. (1996). Beyond distrust: "Getting even" and the need for revenge. In R. M. Kramer & T. Tyler (Eds.), *Trust in organizations* (pp. 246–260). Newbury Park, CA: Sage.

Bies, R. J., & Tripp, T. M. (1998). The many faces of revenge: The good, the bad, and the ugly. In R. W. Griffin, A. O'Leary-Kelly, & J. Collins (Eds.), *Dysfunctional behavior in organizations, Vol. 1: Violent behaviors in organizations* (Vol. 23, pp. 49–68). Greenwich, CT: JAI Press.

Bies, R. J., & Tripp, T. M. (2000). A passion for justice: The rationality and morality of revenge. In R. Cropanzano (Ed.), *Justice in the workplace* (Vol. II). Mahwah, NJ: Erlbaum.

Bies, R. J., & Tripp, T. M. (2002). Hot flashes, open wounds: Injustice and the tyranny of its emotions. In S. Gilliland, D. Steiner, & D. Skarlicki (Eds.), *Emerging perspectives on managing organizational justice* (pp. 203–223). Greenwich, CT: IAP Press.

Bies, R. J., Tripp, T. M., & Kramer, R. M. (1997). At the breaking point: Cognitive and social dynamics of revenge in organizations. In R. A. Giacalone & J. Greenberg (Eds.), *Antisocial behavior in organizations* (pp. 18–36). Thousand Oaks, CA: Sage.

Bies, R. J., & Tyler, T. (1993). The "litigation mentality" in organizations: A test of alternative psychological explanations. *Organization Science, 4,* 352–366.

Brockner, J. (2001, August). The pleasure and pain of high procedural justice. In J. Greenberg (Chair), *Controversial issues in organizational justice.* Paper presented as part of a symposium at the annual meeting of the Academy of Management, Washington, DC.

Buss, A. H. (1962). *The psychology of aggression.* New York: Wiley.

Cahn, E. (1949). *The sense of injustice.* New York: New York University Press.

Daly, J. P., & Tripp, T. M. (1996). Is outcome fairness used to make procedural fairness judgments when procedural information is inaccessible? *Social Justice Research, 9*(4), 327–349.

Folger, R., & Cropanzano, R. (2001). Fairness theory: Justice as accountability. In J. Greenberg & R. Cropanzano (Eds.), *Advances in organizational justice* (pp. 1–55). Stanford, CA: Stanford University Press.

Folger, R., & Skarlicki, D. P. (1998). A popcorn metaphor for workplace violence. In R. W. Griffin, A. O'Leary-Kelly, & J. Collins (Eds.), *Dysfunctional behavior in organizations, Vol. 1: Violent behaviors in organizations* (pp. 43–82). Greenwich, CT: JAI Press.

Fox, S., Spector, P. E., & Miles, D. (2001). Counterproductive work behavior in response to job stressors and organizational justice: Some mediator and moderator tests for autonomy and emotions. *Journal of Vocational Behavior, 59,* 291–309.

Hogan, R., & Emler, N. P. (1981). Retributive justice. In M. J. Lerner & S. C. Lerner (Eds.), *The justice motive in social behavior* (pp. 125–143). New York: Plenum Press.

Hornstein, H. A. (1996). *Brutal bosses and their prey.* New York: Riverhead Books.

Jones, E. E., & Nisbett, R. E. (1972). The actor and the observer: Divergent perceptions of the causes of behavior. In E. E. Jones, D. E. Kanouse, H. H. Kelley, R. E. Nisbett, S. Valins, & B. Weiner (Eds.), *Attribution: Perceiving the causes of behavior* (pp. 79–94). Morristown, NJ: General Learning Press.

Kanouse, D. E., & Hanson, L. R. (1972). Negativity in evaluations. In E. E. Jones, D. E. Kanouse, H. H. Kelley, R. E. Nisbett, S. Valins, & B. Weiner (Eds.), *Attribution: Perceiving the causes of behavior* (pp. 47–62). Morristown, NJ: General Learning Press.

Keashly, L. (1998). Emotional abuse at work: Conceptual and empirical issues. *Journal of Emotional Abuse, 1,* 85–95.

Keashly, L. (2001). Interpersonal and systemic aspects of emotional abuse at work: The target's perspective. *Violence and Victims, 16,* 211–245.

Kelley, H. H. (1972). Attribution in social interaction. In E. E. Jones, D. E. Kanouse, H. H. Kelley, R. E. Nisbett, S. Valins, & B. Weiner (Eds.), *Attribution: Perceiving the causes of behavior* (pp. 1–26). Morristown, NJ: General Learning Press.

Kramer, R. M. (1994). The sinister attribution error. *Motivation and Emotion, 18,* 199–231.

Lazarus, R. E., & Lazarus, B. N. (1994). *Passion and reason: Making sense of emotions*. Oxford, England: Oxford University Press.

Lind, E. A. (2001, August). When and how are heuristics used in making judgments? In J. Greenberg (Chair), *Controversial issues in organizational justice*. Paper presented as part of a symposium at the annual meeting of the Academy of Management, Washington, DC.

Matthews, C. (1988). *Hardball: How politics is played—Told by one who knows the game*. New York: Summit Books.

McLean Parks, J. M. (1997). The fourth arm of justice: The art and science of revenge. In R. J. Lewicki, R. J. Bies, & B. H. Sheppard (Eds.), *Research on negotiation in organizations* (Vol. 6, pp. 113–144). Greenwich, CT: JAI Press.

Mikula, G. (1986). The experience of injustice: Toward a better understanding of its phenomenology. In H. W. Bierhoff, R. L. Cohen, & J. Greenberg (Eds.), *Justice in interpersonal relations* (pp. 103–123). New York: Plenum Press.

Mikula, G., Petri, B., & Tanzer, N. (1990). What people regard as just and unjust: Types and structures of everyday experiences of injustice. *European Journal of Social Psychology, 20*, 133–149.

Morrill, C. (1992). Vengeance among executives. *Virginia Review of Sociology, 1*, 51–76.

Neuman, J. H., & Baron, R. A. (1997). Aggression in the workplace. In R. A. Giacalone & J. Greenberg (Eds.), *Antisocial behavior in organizations* (pp. 37–67). Thousand Oaks, CA: Sage.

O'Leary-Kelly, A. M., Griffin, R. W., & Glew, D. J. (1996). Organization-motivated aggression: A research framework. *Academy of Management Review, 21*, 225–253.

Randall, P. (2001). *Bullying in adulthood: Assessing the bullies and their victims*. New York: Brunner-Routledge.

Robinson, S. L., & Bennett, R. J. (1995). A typology of deviant workplace behaviors: A multidimensional scaling study. *Academy of Management Journal, 38*, 555–572.

Shah, P. P., & Schroth, H. A. (2000). Procedures, do we really want to know them? The effects of procedural justice on performance self-esteem. *Journal of Applied Psychology, 85*, 462–471.

Skarlicki, D. P., & Folger, R. (1997). Retaliation in the workplace: The roles of distributive, procedural, and interactional justice. *Journal of Applied Psychology, 82*, 434–443.

Tripp, T. M., & Bies, R. J. (1997). What's good about revenge? The avenger's perspective. In R. J. Lewicki, R. J. Bies, & B. H. Sheppard (Eds.), *Research on negotiation in organizations* (Vol. 6, pp. 145–160). Greenwich, CT: JAI Press.

Tripp, T. M., Bies, R. J., & Aquino, K. (2002). Poetic justice or petty jealousy? The aesthetics of revenge. *Organizational Behavior and Human Decision Processes, 89*, 966–984.

Walzer, M. (1977). *Just and unjust wars: A moral argument with historical illustrations.* New York: Basic Books.

Weick, K. E. (1995). *Sensemaking in organizations.* Thousand Oaks, CA: Sage.

Wong, P. T., & Weiner, B. (1981). When people ask "why" questions, and the heuristics of attributional search. *Journal of Personality and Social Psychology, 40,* 650–663.

4

BEYOND COUNTERPRODUCTIVE WORK BEHAVIOR: MORAL EMOTIONS AND DEONTIC RETALIATION VERSUS RECONCILIATION

ROBERT FOLGER AND DANIEL P. SKARLICKI

The editors of this volume invited our contribution so that we could address the place of organizational retaliatory behavior (ORB) in the conceptual domain covered by counterproductive work behavior. We trace the origins of ORB to earlier work by Folger and his colleagues (e.g., Cropanzano & Folger, 1989; Folger, 1986, 1987; Folger & Martin, 1986; Folger, Rosenfield, & Robinson, 1983) on referent cognitions theory, which in turn led to research on retaliation by Skarlicki and colleagues (Skarlicki & Folger, 1997; Skarlicki, Folger, & Tesluk, 1999). The interests that led us to study retaliation, however, have now grown to encompass a broader focus. In this chapter we address the reasons for an expanded orientation of retaliation that deals with moral emotions experienced by third parties as well as victims of offensive treatment. We introduce the term *deontic retaliation*, which refers to individuals' moral assumptions regarding how human beings *should* be treated (Folger, 2001). We also explore the prospects for reconciliation or continuing hostilities that are likely to include retaliation.

BACKGROUND ON ORGANIZATIONAL
RETALIATION BEHAVIOR

We grounded our initial work on ORB within the literature on organizational justice. Simply put, we predicted an increased likelihood of retaliatory tendencies as a function of perceived unfair treatment at work. We defined ORB as "a subset of . . . negative [workplace] behaviors . . . used to punish the organization and its representatives in response to perceived unfairness" (Skarlicki & Folger, 1997, p. 435). Although future research in ORB would benefit from identifying a generic set of items that generalize across a range of organizational settings, in this initial study we sought to focus on a set of items that were most relevant to the employees at this research site. We obtained our site-specific list of ORB by using two focus groups of seven employees each as subject-matter experts in an exercise based on the critical incident technique (Flanagan, 1954).

Before asking these two groups of employee subject-matter experts about critical incidents, we first instructed them as follows:

> Research suggests that when people perceive that they have been treated unfairly at work, they tend to find ways to "strike back" and somehow even the score. This retaliation may be direct or indirect and may be focused toward the organization or someone within the organization.

Additional instructions asked these employee groups to conduct a discussion focusing on examples of such actions they had observed during the previous 6 to 12 months, including (a) what the person did that was retaliatory and (b) why he or she considered it as an instance of retaliation.

When we followed this measurement development work by conducting the main study itself (at the same work site but among a different sample of employees), we obtained measures of our perceived-injustice predictors from one set of employees and responses to the ORB criterion measure from a yoked set of coworker peers. The peer assessment instrument asked respondents for ratings of a "coworker on his or her work behaviors" and told them that they had been assigned at random (from among those familiar with the coworker's behavior) to the person whose name they found listed on the questionnaire. This questionnaire included, along with positive items (e.g., "do more work than is required"), a set of 17 ORBs from the list generated by the focus-group employees (see Exhibit 4.1). The instructions called for frequency responses ("never," "once," "twice," "3–5 times," and "6 or more times") of "this person's activity on the job" over the preceding month (e.g., "calls in sick . . . when not ill"). In reference to more specifically targeted actions, relevant

EXHIBIT 4.1
List of Retaliation Behaviors Reported in Skarlicki and Folger (1997)

- On purpose, damaged equipment or work process.
- Took supplies home without permission.
- Wasted company materials.
- Called in sick when not ill.
- Spoke poorly about the company to others.
- Refused to work weekends or overtime when asked.
- Left a mess unnecessarily (did not clean up).
- Disobeyed a supervisor's instructions.
- "Talked back" to his or her boss.
- Gossiped about his or her boss.
- Spread rumors about coworkers.
- Gave a coworker the "silent treatment."
- Failed to give coworker required information.
- Tried to look busy while wasting time.
- Took an extended coffee or lunch break.
- Intentionally worked slower than necessary.
- Spent time on personal matters while at work.

portions of a generic stem referred either to "behaviors directed toward other coworkers or his/her supervisor" or to "behavior directed toward the company in general"; the questionnaire, however, did not contain the word *retaliation* or its like.

These details about our methodology add to our formal definition of ORB by showing how our research (Skarlicki & Folger, 1997; Skarlicki et al., 1999) linked the operationalization of measures quite closely to construct meaning. Additional support for the construct validity of this ORB measure comes from evidence that ORB responses differed as a function of unfairness antecedents as stipulated in the construct's definition. Recall that we defined ORB as elicited "in response to perceived unfairness" and that the pilot identification of ORB items came from asking for striking-back actions "when people perceive that they have been treated unfairly at work." Our research showed that at the individual level of analysis, coworkers rating employees with relatively higher unfairness scores reported having seen ORB exhibited by them on significantly more occasions than did coworkers rating employees who had less of a tendency to view themselves as victims of workplace unfairness. Note that these ORB raters did not know the unfairness questionnaire responses of the employee for whom they reported the frequency of observed ORB.

Unlike other counterproductive work behavior (CWB) such as deviance, incivility, or antisocial behavior, ORB can have both functional and dysfunctional implications for individuals and organizations. Retaliation can be dysfunctional for the organization because it can involve damage and loss to goods (e.g., sabotage) and resources (e.g., stealing time). It can also be detrimental to the retaliator in terms of feelings of guilt, anxiety, and stress associated with such things as the worry of getting caught for the retaliation. Moreover, a preoccupation with retaliation has the potential to detract from one's own personal performance.

On the other hand, and in contrast to CWB, acts of retaliation can also have potentially functional consequences. Whereas "deviant behavior" presumes wrongful and inherently negative conduct on the part of the employee, some mistreatment makes retaliation more legitimate than deviant. Just as conflict can sometimes be used constructively for change, legitimate retaliation under some circumstances might provoke needed organizational changes and, therefore, would qualify as more constructive than some instances of similar behavior exhibiting mere deviance or antisocial behavior. Examples of functional organizational consequences include keeping employee mistreatment in check and holding managers accountable to moral codes of behavior. Functional consequences for the individual include the psychological restoration of equity.

ORB also differs from other CWB constructs in an important way: Whereas other perspectives label the individual *actor as transgressor*, ORB activities represent an individual's *response to the transgressor*. By framing the behavior as a reaction to another person's provocation (or to an offense by the organization as an entity), ORB provides an interesting benefit for researchers—namely, we believe it increases participants' willingness to discuss their behavior. This is because participants are able to view their reactions as more legitimate than bad. For instance, in our research we were readily able to get job incumbents to talk about their ORB.

Reactions to unfairness are often known primarily by the person who engages in the behavior. This can be problematic from a measurement perspective because self-ratings of both the predictor (i.e., perceptions of unfairness) and the criterion (i.e., reactions to injustice) can contribute to common method variance in statistical analysis. In our research, ORB was developed to circumvent this problem by defining ORB in terms of behavior that is observable by one's peers or supervisors. Our procedure ensured that our ORB measure was content valid for our research site and was defined in terms of observable behavior rather than a person's traits (e.g., deviant or antisocial). Moreover, because we did not impose on our respondents a preconceived notion of what specific actions "getting even with the organization" might mean, we were able to uncover a variety of subtle responses to perceived injustice that constitute the behavioral repertoire of employees at this company.

ORGANIZATIONAL RETALIATORY BEHAVIOR: REFERENT COGNITIONS AND FAIRNESS THEORY AS PREDICTOR-CONSTRUCT FOCUS

To this point we have referred only to a generic antecedent of ORB: unfairness. Justice theorizing, however, has developed a more fine-grained approach in two respects. First, the types of injustice experienced have been differentiated as distributive, procedural, and interactional. Those terms refer respectively to the unfairness of outcomes received, the procedures used in making decisions that determine outcomes, and the aspects of an individual's interpersonal conduct (e.g., informative communications—such as thorough, forthright, reasonable explanations—and sensitive consideration) regarded as treating another individual with respect and dignity. The second kind of development within the organizational justice literature has been the treatment of different kinds of explanatory mechanisms.

Three theoretical perspectives have received attention. Thibaut and Walker (1975) first proposed what has become known as an instrumental or control-based perspective that linked procedural and distributive justice by treating the fairness of the former as a means for achieving fairness in the latter. Lind and Tyler's (1988) review of evidence inconsistent with that position, however, led them to propose a group-value model as an alternative, which was later updated and renamed a relational model (Tyler & Lind, 1992). The relational approach stressed the value of fair treatment for confirming one's acceptance into a group regarded as important from the standpoint of self-identity.

We pursued investigations on ORB guided by yet a third type of approach—one based on the perspective originally called referent cognitions theory (RCT) by Folger (e.g., 1986, 1987), then later modified and renamed fairness theory in work with Cropanzano (Folger & Cropanzano, 1998, 2001). RCT focuses on reactions to unfair treatment (e.g., resentment, moral outrage) that are characterized as counterfactual emotions, defined as those that arise when an actual state of affairs is compared with more favorable states of affairs that were possible—the more easily imagined, the greater the perceived unfairness (for a discussion of the counterfactual in moral emotions, also see Blair, 1995; Turiel, 1983).

Fairness theory (Folger & Cropanzano, 1998, 2001), which built on RCT, proposes that people evaluate, whether consciously or not, the fairness of their experience by assigning blame for injustice through judgments about what *would, could,* and *should* have happened. To determine the adversity of an experience, people assess what the event *would* potentially have felt like if it were different by comparing the event to a referent standard (i.e., an alternative event). People also assess whether the event *could* have been different. Finally, people make judgments about what *should* have happened based on normative standards of ethical conduct. Thus, unfairness judgments and subsequent reactions are a function of counterfactual processes in which actual states compare unfavorably to alternative states of affairs.

Fairness theory made more explicit that not only counterfactual emotions but also retaliatory behaviors increase in likelihood as a function of considerations about moral accountability. This notion of moral accountability has, in turn, become a bridge to the perspective on moral emotions we develop later in the chapter. It suffices for now to note that the nature of accountability identified by fairness theory relates to dual components of a perceiver's experience: (a) aversive implications of that experience (e.g., present conditions as a state of affairs inducing negative affect because of their implications—including the implications of comparison with counterfactual states made cognitively accessible and salient by moral norms); and (b) implications linking the aversive experience to a social agent deemed morally accountable for its existence (e.g., someone whose pursuit of his or her own self-interest did not show sufficient restraint and instead indicated a willingness to impose aversive states without regard for others' interests). This view of accountability cuts across earlier distinctions among forms of injustice and collapses their psychologically significant features into one or both of the two key categories, state and source. Interactional injustice, for example, often has the capacity to evoke especially strong reactions because it so often seems to meet both conditions in a transparent and compelling way: (a) It feels aversive to be treated without respect; (b) usually it is clear which person or persons treated you disrespectfully and whether or not they deserve to be held accountable for doing so. Moreover, given the nature of such processes as the fundamental attribution error (e.g., Ross, 1977), violations of interactional justice are often seen by victims and observers as purposeful rather than a function of situational factors.

INTRODUCTION TO DEONANCE: MORAL EMOTIONS, RETALIATION, AND RECONCILIATION

Having briefly touched on the nature of the developments that originally led to our work on ORB, we now introduce the broadly generic concept of *deonance* as an umbrellalike term used to include several kinds of moral emotions relevant for understanding retaliation. We base that term on the Greek *deon*, most commonly translated as referring to duty and obligation, often treated as virtually synonymous with morality. As Rawls (1971) noted, by reason of their humanity, individuals are entitled to the right to be treated in a way that fosters self-regard. Folger (2001) proposed that people are motivated toward fairness because it is the right thing to do. One's reaction to a moral violation arises out of holding someone accountable for his or her actions and to the motivation to help prevent the transgressor from making future violations of the rights of human dignity. Deontic justice seeks to continually validate the moral and ethical standards that regulate interpersonal conduct.

This orientation aims at broadening developments related to retaliation and, as we will explore in subsequent sections, other constructs related to CWB such as those addressed in this volume. Before discussing deontic anger, guilt, and shame, we first indicate why they matter.

BROADENING THE OUTLOOK ON RETALIATION

The focus of our new perspective began to develop in conjunction with research on possible functions of retribution—that is, the role of what might be called *retributive justice*. It struck us that studying the punishment of offenders might offer a unique venue for revealing actions less amenable to self-interest interpretations than seemed true of other approaches to explaining justice-related phenomena. Recall, for example, that the Thibaut–Walker approach linking procedural and distributive justice has been called an instrumental or control model because it treats the former as a means for obtaining the latter. If someone could control the process by which outcomes are distributed to serve his or her own self-interest, that person would have no need for a third-party decision maker (e.g., as mediator or arbitrator of a dispute)—because such direct control would allow the person simply to take what he or she wanted. Having a third-party decision maker follow a set of procedures for resolving conflicting interests about outcomes rather than having the competing parties battle it out between themselves, therefore, means surrendering direct control. Decision-making procedures then become means for exerting indirect control—that is, for attempting to influence the decision maker (e.g., when the procedures provide both opposing parties opportunities to present evidence and arguments).

Although addressing the topic of fairness, this instrumental or control model obviously speaks also to self-interest. Fair procedures represent the best available means by which to prevent something otherwise more detrimental to your interests—namely the prospect that each and every decision would unfairly allocate to you less than you deserve. The group-value or relational model (Lind & Tyler, 1988), for instance, proposes that procedural fairness has implications for individuals' sense of self. When the organization allows its members to have input into a decision, the organization has symbolically communicated its respect for its members; as a result the self-esteem and the self-identity of organization members is enhanced. Thus the reaction to unfair treatment stems from an interest in protecting and preserving self-identity. Lind (2001) explicitly referred to these two types of concerns—exploitation and exclusion—as reasons for caring about fairness. If you care about fairness because you do not want to be exploited or excluded, however, then you care about fairness for reasons of self-interest. The original RCT model was also based on self-interest, stating that resentment would be highest when people believe that their low outcome would have been more favorable if the procedures used to determine the outcome had been fair.

In construing fairness as involving moral accountability, which in turn refers to self-restraint obligations, fairness theory had begun going beyond the scope of RCT as a basis for thinking about the role of justice concerns in social relations. People held accountable to generally recognized moral norms are not supposed to pursue unbridled self-interest. This idea in turn not only suggests personal restraint as the basis for curbing self-interest but also implies a role for the public as moral watchdogs willing to act in ways consistent with constraining the actions of someone whose wanton disregard for the interests of others offends the public's moral conscience. In short, not only the victims of an offense but also third parties often feel the urge to condemn injustice and punish it as excessively self-interested, and such a moral stance demands that the condemners and punishers themselves not act out merely of their own self-interest.

Perhaps that all sounds too philosophically abstract, so a research illustration is in order. Before briefly summarizing one recent set of studies as an apropos example, however, first let us note the subtle shift from *retaliation*, as in ORB, or even *retribution*, as in retributive justice. Such language tends to connote (a) vengeful action-in-return by a victim oriented toward the offender and (b) evening the score, balancing things out, or restoring conditions to a rightful state. The line of research we are about to describe is specifically aimed at producing a situation in which the punishment of an offender would *not* fit those connotations. We explored punishment by third parties in which an action would seem offensive but, because actual harm had not occurred, no actual "victim" existed nor any need for restorative compensation. This also highlights compensatory restoration of conditions to a fair, even, and balanced state as a separable type of concern from punishment—much as courts sometimes separate compensatory damages from punitive damages (with the latter indicating the degree to which third-party jurors view as reprehensible the liability for which a defendant is held morally accountable).

The relevant research example pertains to studies conducted by Turillo, Folger, Lavelle, Umphress, and Gee (2002). The student participants in this research (a "dictator" decision game) acted as decision makers who had a choice of whether to award themselves $6 (choice A) or $5 (choice B), given information about consequences for other people that varied according to that choice. Either choice would have implications for two other people (labeled dictators). Both dictators were anonymous to the decision maker, who also remained anonymous.

Participants received information about what the two anonymous students from another class—person X and person Y—had decided under partially similar circumstances during a previous experimental session. Supposedly everyone in that session had the same two options: either (a) take $18 for yourself and leave another (anonymous, unknown) classmate with $2 or (b) take $10 for yourself and leave $10 for the classmate. The participants in that session had allegedly known that after indicating one or the other choice as a preference, payment in accordance with the indicated preference would occur only for a randomly drawn 10% of the students (putatively because of budgetary constraints).

X and Y were said to be drawn from among those not paid—but they were identified in terms of preference. X allegedly had indicated a preference for the $18/$2 split (i.e., keep $18 out of $20 and offer $2 to counterpart), whereas Y allegedly had indicated a preference for the $10/$10 split. The participants in the current study were asked to choose between two options: (a) Choice A would give the participant $6 and would also give $6 to X, the student in the former session who had tried (unsuccessfully) for the $18/$2 payoff. On the other hand, Y (who had tried unsuccessfully for a $10/$10 split) would receive nothing. (b) Choice B would give the participant $5 and would also give $5 to Y, who had tried for a $10/$10 split. On the other hand, X (who tried for $18/$2) would get nothing. The results replicated the original version of the dictator game findings (Kahneman, Knetsch, & Thaler, 1986) in that approximately three of every four participants punished the $18/$2 attempt by giving that person nothing even though it meant sacrificing $1 for themselves (i.e., taking $5 instead of $6).

In conjunction with design details we have omitted, the results affirm those data's relevance for ruling out each of the following possible sources of self-interest that failed to emerge as a significant determinant of behavior:

- *Public image:* Remaining anonymous, respondents could not get any credit from anyone else for "doing good for goodness' sake."
- *Public message:* Because no one other than the researchers would see the raw data, respondents were not able to use their punishment as a public message that "crime does not pay," thereby negating an explanation of general deterrence (sending a message to the general public) that might otherwise have been possible.
- *Perpetrator deterrence.* To have any hope that the punishment might deter the perpetrator from committing a similar transgression in the future, the respondent would have to believe that

the perpetrator was aware of being punished. But variations in such awareness (present versus absent) had no effect, indicating that self-interested deterrence was not influential.

In addition, the basic replication result itself (73% self-sacrificial punishment) also speaks against self-interest because participants chose to punish dictators who had not actually received payment but who had indicated an intention to be unfair in their allocation of the money. In this way, punishment served to deprive the $18/$2 dictator because of his or her presumed unfair intentions to collect $18 out of $20. Finally, the participants did not know the $18/$2 dictator's identity. They were merely third-party observers of his or her unfair intentions, not participants in a long-term exchange relationship. Therefore, anonymity made it implausible to foresee any long-term consequences from the participants' allocation decisions.

In summary, these respondents were willing to take loss to punish someone who behaved unfairly. The results cannot be easily explained by self-interest motives. Instead, these participants appear to have reacted to a moral affect, on which we now elaborate.

EVOLUTIONARY ROOTS OF DEONTIC EMOTION

Much of social science relies for explanation on narrowly defined self-interest and, therefore, has difficulty accommodating such data as those from the Turillo et al. (2002) studies we reported earlier. Even equity theory, a model concerned with fairness perceptions, can be interpreted as making self-interest the ultimate foundation of justice. For example, Berscheid and Walster (1978, pp. 125–126) believed that that groups develop equity norms to "maximize . . . collective reward." If the personal welfare of economic benefits were the only plausible source of human motivation, however, then results such as those found in Turillo et al. (2002) could not exist.

If not economic self-interest, then what could have motivated them? Our answer refers to a specific emotion, often simply called anger, which we label as *deontic anger* in this case. We argue that deontic anger has evolutionary roots linked with curtailing abuses of power otherwise free to run rampant (Boehm, 1999). The alternative to morality is a might-makes-right use of coercion by the powerful to maintain power. If absolute, unfettered power tends to corrupt absolutely, then a lack of any means for curtailing power would constitute a corrupting influence. We speculate that "corruption" in this sense would not enhance the survival of a species that required voluntary cooperation for sustaining effective access to resources—a feature, we believe, that characterizes humans. In other words, the existence of a checks-and-balances possibility (e.g., from third parties as moral specta-tors) relies on a human capacity for a type of moral affect related to disap-proval of wrongdoing (a condemnatory emotion).

The calculative self-interest seeking of rational-choice and standard neoclassical economic models entails only a forward-looking, instrumental aim at future goals. That is, such models assume that people respond strategi-cally based on what they assume will further their interests. A contrasting, backward-looking perspective (i.e., focused on antecedents, especially from an ancestral past history) comes from conceptualizing the function of affect in terms of adaptations favored by natural selection. This evolutionary viewpoint emphasizes emotions as adapted for emergencies: When environ-mental cues signal jeopardy, emotions save time by providing a built-in assessment of instrumental needs based on adaptively successful responses to such encounters in an ancestral past (Fiske, 2004). We turn, therefore, to natural selection as a source of such affects as deontic anger.

We suggest that self-sacrificial behavior exhibited by participants in the Turillo et al. studies was driven by deontic anger about injustice as the abuse of power. Furthermore, we suggest that claiming deontic anger has evolutionary roots in one sense simply accords with a truism—namely that natural selection has influenced the current biological architecture of the human species (e.g., neural circuitry relating to the experience of emotion). Bodies of literature across a diverse set of fields now provide both theory and research supporting that conclusion (e.g., Barkow, 1989; Katz, 2000; Tooby & Cosmides, 1990). Such assertions apply not only to emotions such as fear but also to those with moral connotations, such as guilt and moral outrage. To the extent that "people are motivated to behave morally not because they have rationally calculated that it is in their material interest to do that, but because they are emotionally predisposed to do so" (Frank, 1988, p. 288), it is important to consider evolutionary explanations about the possible origins of emotions.

It seems plausible that the earliest precursor to moral outrage remains physiologically and neurologically encoded, much as Damasio (2001) has postulated can occur via somatic markers within the lifetime of a single individual. Specifically, at least two types of data imply the existence of an unthinking, prepotent, and simplified core to what Panksepp (1998) called the RAGE system. First, humans exhibit ragelike behavioral tendencies when a neuroscience researcher electrically stimulates certain brain regions, whereas their own actions seem inexplicable to them both during and after the event. Common responses include verbalizations along the lines of "Get out of the way, I've got the urge to throw something at you." Second, infants as young as 14 months of age exhibit similarly expressive displays of rage when an experimenter pins their arms to their sides and holds tight (Stenberg & Campos, 1990).

Based on such indications combined with several supporting lines of theory and research (e.g., reviewed by Panksepp, 1998), we speculate that the anger of moral outrage (a base ingredient in the deontic anger syndrome) stems from adaptive responses to being attacked or having to fight against a resistant, opposing force—such as when a cornered prey cannot flee (e.g., perhaps partially and temporarily immobilized when grasped or pinned by a predator) and instead adopts the fight mode of the fight-or-flight response. In particular, we argue that from the standpoint of "hot" versus "cool" systems (see Ayduk, Mischel, & Downey, 2002; Metcalfe & Mischel, 1999), the hot emotional reactions to transgression and its aftermath have their roots in older aspects of visceral orientations associated with fight–flight arousal. In agonistic, competitive, or fighting situations against an opponent (conspecific or predator), the counterattacker gains an evolutionary advantage from using forcefully fierce displays in an intimidating fashion. Given the plasticity of behavioral adaptations garnered by humans, natural selection has operated so that it has also become possible to produce ritualistic displays of fierceness that can cause an opponent to cease and desist without an actual fight occurring. Resolving a dominance–submission confrontation by ritualistic displays of power and force allow conflict incidents to transpire at a reduced cost to reproductive resources—such as when the moral suasion of a sneer or raised eyebrow proves a sufficient deterrent. In general, then, humans have evolved beyond other species in the sophistication and subtlety by which they can apply negative sanctions against unwanted (e.g., transgressive, morally offensive) behavior.

We suspect that the emotions we feel as humans when experiencing aspects of the deontic anger syndrome build on the physiologically adaptive accompaniments of fighting back or fighting against. That is, we assume selection has favored bodily preparedness to attempt greater than ordinary exertions of force when circumstances appear to deem it necessary (e.g., often because of instigations that take the form of an obstructive or coercive, countervailing source of opposition or resistance)—hence the tendency to get angry at a stuck window you cannot lift at first. Relatedly, fearsome expressiveness and a foreboding posture such as the Darwinian (1872/1998) description of anger could motivate an opponent to quit rather than risk getting hurt. Put simply, an emotionally angry display and related forceful exertions can serve to help stop and possibly reverse an adverse trend from an opposing, resistant force. One could say, then, that outrage is the moral equivalent of "fighting fire with fire" because it betokens a counterattacking thrust against a force that broke through the bonds of moral restraint commonly taken for granted by members of society. Thus, the need to meet force with force calls for deontic anger oriented toward violators.

We believe that natural selection favored the development of moral emotions enabling ways to prevent (or reduce the frequency of) actions apt to jeopardize humans' survival chances as a species. For a perspective on the moral aspect of such emotions, consider moral goods as "social, personal, or spiritual obligations (e.g., justice, social harmony, self-actualization, piety, chastity) to which one appeals to justify or criticize the practices and behaviors of others, and which are felt to be binding on all people" (Haidt, Rosenberg, & Hom, 2003). This type of statement fits with our treating deontics as the study of moral experience. When people experience deontic emotions, feelings akin to the force of an obligation tend to be a concomitant ("I didn't really do it for any particular purpose—it just seemed like the right thing to do"). Moreover, the moral standards that contribute to such experiences also involve criteria for judging critically those who do not live up to such obligations.

We conceptualize deontic anger as being offended by transgressions and as one force that can drive individuals to oppose and curtail abuses of the moral system. Just as morality reflects the deontic characteristic of a constraint limiting an otherwise unfettered autonomy (on the related notion of *bounded autonomy*, see Folger, 1998), to impose a moral standard implies exerting one's will forcefully in opposition to the transgressor of that moral standard. Indeed, the language of power as an opposing force is part and parcel of the very concept of morality itself, once the moral domain is seen as being opposed to anyone's efforts to maximize his or her own self-interest exclusively (i.e., without considering potential harm to others as a result). The enforcement of restraint may come from self or others. For example, conscience means exercising self-restraint—opposing the power that pure self-interest would exert by forcing oneself to act in another fashion instead. Similarly, moral suasion is the effort by others to restrain excessive self-interest by appealing to a moral standard.

THE MORAL STATUS OF THIRD PARTIES: RISING ABOVE SELF-INTEREST

The reactions of third parties that we have highlighted also suggest that the experience of outrage in response to abuse of authority has a moral basis. Specifically, the lack of direct self-interest of third parties fits with how ethicists view morality: A canonical view suggests that morality "must bear on the interests or welfare either of society as a whole or at least of persons other than the judge or agent" (Gewirth, 1984, p. 978, quoted in Haidt, in press). Third parties, as we use the term, are those in the role of "moral spectator," as Adam Smith (1759/1971) called it, whose judgments reflect adopting a perspective outside the realm of personal interest (often exercised in line with the interests of the moral community as a whole).

Turillo et al. (2002) conducted their series of experiments in attempting to create third-party conditions without any form of direct self-interest as a payoff for the sacrificial-punishment response. As noted earlier, no harm had ever actually affected an individual, so empathizing with the victim was not a motivating factor. Also, punishing the greedy, first-party dictator could not make the world a better or safer place for the third-party: The respondents who chose punishment knew that neither the dictator nor anyone else would ever learn about the punishment. The conditions of anonymity also provided a punisher with no benefits in terms of a reputation enhanced by displaying virtuous, self-sacrificial behavior. Thus, it appears that the tendency for third parties to react to the abuse of power even though they are not directly harmed might stem from something like the evolved tendency to experience moral affect that we term deontic anger.

Deontic Anger and the Domain of Organizational Justice

The literature on organizational justice addresses factors influencing fairness perceptions in the workplace, as well as employee reactions when they perceive themselves to have been treated unfairly. We see justice as part of the larger domain of morality. Moral tenets and codes imply rules of conduct and the injunction not to break them. Descriptions of transgressive acts usually include the wrongdoing and a wrongdoer (the deed and the doer). Referring to the wrong itself, common usage will ordinarily have recourse to language about the state of the code or tenet at a prewrong and a postwrong time: Before the wrong, the code or tenet had not yet been broken (violated, etc.), whereas afterward the code or tenet has the status of brokenness (e.g., "she broke the rules"). Language describes the wrongdoer, therefore, as someone who *breaks, violates, transgresses,* and so on. Designating action as falling into the moral domain has the psychological connotation that others feel legitimately entitled to hold the actor accountable and answerable for wrongdoing. The person's freedom, rather than conceived as infinitely open to the person's own discretion, has a circumscribed area within which its exercise needs no justification. Once outside the bounds of morality, however, the person becomes answerable to others. "I answer to no one" will strike members of the moral community as intolerable (Rawls, 1971; Scanlon, 1998).

We argue that in light of such conceptions of moral conduct, the evolutionary bases of moral outrage is particularly applicable to understanding individuals' reactions to injustice in organizational settings. Organizations are characterized by power-laden dynamics, with clear hierarchical lines of authority and privilege. Those at the top of the organizational ladder can have power and privilege over those at the bottom. Those at the bottom of the organizational ladder accept hierarchy as a legitimate form of organization, but as we might expect (given our evolved predisposition), they react with moral indignation at particular forms of injustice—those involving abuses of power. This is especially the case when a superior (boss) abuses his or her power over a subordinate (worker). Stated differently in first-person terms, this sentiment can be summarized as, "No matter where I am in the hierarchy, I still expect to be treated as an equal human being."

Generally in organizations, individuals assume and tolerate the presence of legitimate hierarchy. They likely do so for the benefits that it confers to all members of the group (Boehm, 2000). Even those who are conferred dominance, however, can overstep their bounds of authority. Superiors who abuse the power invested in them by forcefully pursuing their own interests to the detriment of their subordinates are no longer using their power to legitimate ends. Social influence that is legitimate or endorsed instead becomes coercion or intimidation. Although this type of social influence or wielding of power might be submitted to out of fear of negative consequences, it is ultimately less stable than power that is granted or endorsed (Blau, 1964). Perhaps the reason that it is less stable is that intimidation and coercion as abuses of power invoke strong moral responses of injustice and outrage that often compel individuals to react despite their position of subordination. Responses to this abuse of power can range from individual feelings of indignation and retaliatory behaviors (Bies, 1987; Skarlicki & Folger, 1997) to coalition formation and attempts to sanction undue domination and victimization (Boehm, 2000, p. 85). This is the case because abuses of power threaten to undermine "the useful web of co-operation that everyone profits from" (Boehm, 2000, p. 90).

In essence, authority figures in organizations may act rulerlike (dominantly) so long as they are also "being ruled" by the moral code. Like all members of the organization, a superior's behavior is circumscribed by a moral boundary. Within the boundary, exercised power needs no justification. An abuse of power that has been legitimately conferred, however, symbolizes a step outside the bounds, an attempt to "break the bounds" of moral codes. And a moral boundary crossing is met with a moral response—which, in this case, starts with the emotion we call deontic anger (e.g., moral outrage, indignation, and the like).

We might think of the moral response as like the triggering of a node in an associative neural network, or we could conceptualize it as analogous to tacit knowledge (e.g., the "muscle memory" available after sufficient practice of a sport-relevant skill). We emphasize, however, that the deed done by wrongdoers actually has two victims rather than one: a person or persons harmed (in the sense that morality involves social relations and due regard for other individuals) and the structural integrity of the moral system itself.

On the one hand, of course, the moral structure itself does not actually suffer harm: It exists as an abstraction, in the world of pure thought, as an ideal. On the other hand, the breaking the rules connotations do imply a sense in which something once treated as if impenetrable (or supposed to receive that treatment) now shows itself as porous. Someone has escaped its boundaries, so *breaking* means *breaking through*. We might use the metaphor of cell bars in a jail: When a jail breakout occurs, nothing in the jail might exist now in a literally broken state (e.g., the bars remain intact but a prisoner slipped through them or used subterfuge that precluded their effectiveness). In using such metaphors and figures of speech within our argument, we obviously cannot claim the status of deductive proof for our conclusions. Conceding that point, we now play our psychological gambit with even greater transparency. The remaining discussion, in other words, relies even more heavily on taking for granted certain kinds of assumptions about human nature that others might question.

We hold that natural selection has favored an evolution of moral emotions. People experience strongly aroused feelings when they perceive events in moral terms. It may not involve too much exaggeration to suggest that humans treat morals anthropomorphically with respect to authoritative force: The moral injunction *is* the final authority on the matter. By this psychologic, then, "breaking" the "rules" gains the anthropomorphic status of regicide.

If the concerns about abusing one's relative rank connotations of morality have indeed affected human moral emotion as we speculate, then the reactions to an unfair abuse of power in the dictator-game data collected by Turillo et al. (2002) make even more sense than ever. Moreover, the greater the truth to the speculations, the richer the implications. Here we note just a few as related to organizational justice.

First, we acknowledge explicitly and quite readily that more than one type of characterization could faithfully capture the nature of the transgression in the Turillo et al. (in press) studies as it affected the responses of the research participants. That is, we posit no need for them to have consciously perceived that a norm has been violated. Frankly, we would be surprised if any participant ever referred to the abuse of authority as the essence of the transgression. Mentioning allocation norms of distributive justice (e.g., equity, equality) seems much more likely.

Because such a situation involves a decision maker's choice among alternative allocations, it makes sense to apply norms of distributive justice to assess the fairness of the amounts received by each party. Although the relevant norm may also depend on cultural socialization, we argue that even when a perceiver compares the actual distribution with a normative standard for the distribution, the moral norm functions as an authoritative (hierarchically dominant) injunction (for a related argument, see the discussion of authority ranking by Fiske, 1991). For example, ire toward the $18/$2 dictator in the Turillo et al. studies might have encouraged punishment not only because that person violated an equality norm by not making the evenly balanced choice of $10/$10 but also because that person acted as if corrupted by power (failed to show self-restraint when granted total autonomy over someone else's welfare).

That, simply put, is the gist of our claim—that violating *any* moral mandate has an inherent structure analyzable as a violation of rank privilege, thereby doing something that exceeds the authority of one's rank. Again, by definition, the moral mandate *is* the ultimate authority, so breaking a moral rule is analogous to killing a ruler. The language of regicide may sound overly anthropomorphic, but we use it because others (e.g., Fiske, 1991) emphasize regicide as among the quintessential or worst wrong when considering ranked domains.

Of course, retaliation is only one response to perceived wrongdoing. In the next section we move our discussion to consider the conditions under which other reactions, such as reconciliation, are possible.

From Wrath to Reconciliation

We propose that victims and third-party observers will increase their reconciliation-facilitating tendencies—that is, will feel appeased—to the extent that they perceive deontic guilt versus deontic shame on the part of the transgressor. Our thinking borrows from Tangney (1996), who proposed that shame and guilt are self-conscious and self-evaluative emotions. Shame is connected to a more global assessment of the self, whereas guilt refers more to specific behaviors than to the whole person. People who experience shame feel less control over their situation and tend to engage in withdrawal behaviors, whereas people experiencing guilt feel they have relatively more control over the situation and are more likely to engage in reparation behaviors.

Deontic guilt refers to the transgressor demonstrating any of the "four Rs" of reconciling apologies: accepting responsibility for the offense, expressing or manifesting remorse and a willingness to repair (or make restitution for at least some of the damage, and expressing or manifesting repentance, indicating a disinclination to offend similarly in the future. Unapologetic transgressors are viewed as committing intentional violations, which provoke greater deontic anger and more retaliation than unintentional acts of harm (Dyck & Rule, 1978). Expressions of remorse take the sting out of an offense because they affirm the status of the victim and acknowledge that the victim has been treated unjustly. Crucial to this construct is that an apology per se is not always so important to reconciliation between the parties as, say, the offender's apologetic manner or sincere intent to make amends, as *perceived* by the victim or observer.

Where complete reconciliation represents one pole of the continuum, continued antagonism and retaliation—fueled by the offender's deontic shame—is the other extreme. Borrowing loosely from Tangney (1996), we see the distinction between deontic guilt and deontic shame as a difference in *approach*. Although either process can be initiated from a single event or offense, deontic guilt describes the reconciliatory movement of the transgressor toward the victim or observer. Deontic shame, in contrast, refers to the transgressor's avoidance of the victim or observer and thus to any of a variety of factors inhibiting or causing movement "away from reconciliation." (Similarly, the literature on guilt-compliance effects focuses on offenders' tendencies to act prosocially to reconcile; the literature on victim derogation by offenders focuses on conflict-exacerbating themes that can be interpreted as Tangney's shame concept.)

Tangney (1996) described shame as concentrating negatively evaluative focus on the self, rather than attention on the victim and such things as the harm or suffering the victim has experienced. Shame turns any victim-related thoughts into "bad self" themes rather than "poor victim" themes. Deontic shame makes the offender want to "crawl under the table," to run and hide or cover up the shameful act. These consequences correspond to the distancing behaviors that have been observed in earlier research (Folger & Skarlicki, 1998), in which we interpreted the indication of reduced amounts of time set aside for meeting with a laid-off employee (to deliver the news, for example) as evidence of a desire to avoid contact with the victim. In fact, the role-playing students indicated distancing tendencies even if the vignette informed them that someone else—their boss, the CEO—might be considered the true offender because the boss was the one who had actually made the decision. Hence, it appears that transgressors are not the only individuals who can feel deontic shame. "Guilt by association" can have its counterpart in "shame by association."

Shame–rage syndrome or shame–rage cycles also fall into the category of deontic shame. In effect, when an offender cannot escape accusatory, condemning confrontations that arouse or exacerbate shame, the offender becomes more likely to behave defensively. Consider, for example, the spouse or lover who has wronged a partner. Even if the offender initially orients contritely, his or her tendencies to become defensive can be aroused if the other person "won't let go" or continues a diatribe on every aspect of the offender's shameful behavior. Again, these behaviors have power–force and dominance–submission themes at their core.

The perception of a dominance-like characteristic as central to moral violation, however, may not be salient at the level of full consciousness. Just as people are unlikely to consciously monitor increased levels of hormones in their bloodstream when they are angry, it might be even less likely that we register with full awareness our tacit–implicit coding of an offense along power–force–dominance lines. People might agree, if asked, that a moral violation strikes them as similar to an act of bullying, but such language might not occur to them without this suggestion. We believe, however, that some type of inner representation of power–force–dominance, when combined with the element of the aversive state, does help to distinguish actions as being offensive in the first place. The aversiveness element and the power–coercion elements go hand in hand.

CONCLUSION

The primary distinction between ORB and other forms of CWB is that whereas labels such as *deviance* can refer to the employee as instigator of negative actions, *retaliation* refers to an employees' response to a provocation. From the perspective of the retaliator, his or her actions are justifiable based on the perception that the transgressor has committed a misdeed, and not reacting violates a moral imperative—in essence creates a second wrong. The first wrong is the transgressor's misdeed; the second wrong is the individual's failure to take steps to redress the wrong. Moreover, although there can be negative and dysfunctional consequences for ORB, some consequences can also be functional in terms of initiating change and keeping potential violations at bay.

Although we first studied and defined ORB as an act of revenge by a disgruntled employee for a perceived wrongdoing (i.e., a largely self-interested motive on the part of the retaliator), we have come to understand that there may be more to the motivation than self-interest. By viewing retaliation in purely self-interest terms, researchers risk oversimplifying individuals' reactions to organizational misdeeds. Although we believe self-interest is indeed important, we instead prefer to think of the importance of self-interest retaliation as an individual's reaction to another person's unbridled self-interest. We label the emotional reactions to others' misdeeds as deontic emotion, defined as the moral experience of another person's wrongdoing. Guilt and shame are similarly deontic in reference to one's own putative wrongdoing. Often these reactions are highly compelling and preconscious, probably a derivation of human evolution. Viewing retaliation as deontic has an important advantage over self-interest motives in that it can help explain the reactions by third-party observers as well as victims. Deontic explanations of retaliation also help explain why people can engage in self-sacrifice in pursuit of retaliation.

Although organizational misdeeds can often result in retaliation by victims and observers, it is also important to consider the conditions under which reconciliation might occur. Building on Tangney's (1996) research, we propose that the degree to which the transgressor experiences deontic shame, the more likely that he or she will avoid the victim or observers, resulting in heightened anger and retaliation by the latter. To the degree that transgressors experience deontic guilt, in terms of extending an apology, enhanced tendencies for the victim to move toward reconciliation can occur. Contrition by transgressors, however, will depend on their willingness to exhibit submissiveness to moral authority rather than defensive protection of self-interested autonomy. We leave to readers' imaginations (and to the scope of future research investigations) the questions of when and why organizational authorities will refrain from defending their ranked positions as grounds for a "might makes right" stance toward subordinates.

REFERENCES

Ayduk, O., Mischel, W., & Downey, G. (2002). Attentional mechanisms linking rejection to hostile reactivity: The role of "hot" versus "cool" focus. *Psychological Science, 13*, 443–448.

Barkow, J. H. (1989). *Darwin, sex, and status: Biological approaches to mind and culture.* Toronto, Canada: University of Toronto Press.

Berscheid, E., & Walster, E. H. (1978). *Interpersonal attraction* (2nd ed.). Reading, MA: Addison-Wesley.

Bies, R. J. (1987). The predicament of injustice: The management of moral outrage. In L. L. Cummings & B. M. Staw (Eds.), *Research in organizational behavior* (Vol. 9, pp. 289–319). Greenwich, CT: JAI Press.

Blair, R. J. R. (1995). A cognitive developmental approach to morality: Investigating the psychopath. *Cognition, 57*, 1–29.

Blau, P. M. (1964). *Exchange and power in social life.* New York: Wiley.

Boehm, C. (1999). *Hierarchy in the forest: The evolution of egalitarian behavior.* Cambridge, MA: Harvard University Press.

Boehm, C. (2000). Conflict and the evolution of social control. *Journal of Consciousness Studies, 7*, 79–101.

Cropanzano, R., & Folger, R. (1989). Referent cognitions and task decision autonomy: Beyond equity theory. *Journal of Applied Psychology, 74*, 293–299.

Damasio, A. R. (2001). Emotion and the human brain. In A. R. Damasio, A. Harrington, J. Kagan, B. McEwen, H. Moss, & R. Shaikh (Eds.), *Unity of knowledge: The convergence of natural and human science. Annals of the New York Academy of Sciences* (Vol. 935, pp. 101–106). New York: New York Academy of Sciences.

Darwin, C. (1998). *The expression of the emotions in man and animals*. New York: Oxford University Press. (Original work published 1872)

Dyck, R. J., & Rule, B. G. (1978). Effect on retaliation of causal attributions concerning attack. *Journal of Personality and Social Psychology, 36*(5), 521–529.

Fiske, A. P. (1991). *Structures of social life: The four elementary forms of human relations*. New York: Free Press.

Fiske, A. P. (2004). *Emotions are proximate motives to sustain social relationships*. Unpublished manuscript.

Flanagan, J. C. (1954). The critical incident technique. *Psychological Bulletin, 51*, 327–358.

Folger, R. (1986). Rethinking equity theory: A referent cognitions model. In H. W. Bierhoff, R. L. Cohen, & J. Greenberg (Eds.), *Justice in social relations* (pp. 145–162). New York: Plenum Press.

Folger, R. (1987). Reformulating the preconditions of resentment: A referent cognitions model. In J. C. Masters & W. P. Smith (Eds.), *Social comparison, social justice, and relative deprivation: Theoretical, empirical, and policy perspectives* (pp. 183–215). Hillsdale, NJ: Erlbaum.

Folger, R. (1998). Fairness as a moral virtue. In M. Schminke (Ed.), *Managerial ethics: Moral management of people and processes* (pp. 13–34). Mahwah, NJ: Erlbaum.

Folger, R. (2001). Fairness as deonance. In S. W. Gilliland, D. D. Steiner, & D. P. Skarlicki (Eds.), *Research in social issues in management* (pp. 3–31). Greenwich, CT: Information Age.

Folger, R., & Cropanzano, R. (1998). *Organizational justice and human resource management*. Thousand Oaks, CA: Sage.

Folger, R., & Cropanzano, R. (2001). Fairness theory: Justice as accountability. In J. Greenberg & R. Cropanzano (Eds.), *Advances in organizational justice* (pp. 1–55). Stanford, CA: Stanford University Press.

Folger, R., & Martin, C. (1986). Relative deprivation and referent cognitions: Distributive and procedural justice effects. *Journal of Experimental Social Psychology, 22*, 531–546.

Folger, R., Rosenfield, D. D., & Robinson, T. (1983). Relative deprivation and procedural justifications. *Journal of Personality and Social Psychology, 45*, 268–273.

Folger, R., & Skarlicki, D. P. (1998). When tough times make tough bosses: Managerial distancing as a function of layoff blame. *Academy of Management Journal, 41*(1), 79–87.

Frank, R. H. (1988). *Passions within reason: The strategic role of the emotions*. New York: Norton.

Gewirth, A. (1984). Ethics. *Encyclopaedia Britannica*. Chicago: Encyclopaedia Britannica.

Haidt, J. (in press). The moral emotions. In R. J. Davidson (Ed.), *Handbook of affective sciences*. Oxford, England: Oxford University Press.

Haidt, J., Rosenberg, E., & Hom, H. (2003). Differentiating diversities: Moral diversity is not like other kinds. *Journal of Applied Social Psychology, 33,* 1–36.

Kahneman, D., Knetsch, J. L., & Thaler, R. H. (1986). Fairness and the assumptions of economics. *Journal of Business, 59,* s285–s300.

Katz, L. D. (Ed.). (2000). *Evolutionary origins of morality: Cross-disciplinary perspectives.* Bowling Green, OH: Imprint Academic.

Lind, E. A. (2001). Fairness heuristic theory: Justice as pivotal cognitions in organizational relations. In J. Greenberg & R. Cropanzano (Eds.), *Advances in organizational justice* (pp. 56–88). Stanford, CA: Stanford University Press.

Lind, E. A., & Tyler, T. R. (1988). *The social psychology of procedural justice.* New York: Plenum Press.

Metcalfe, J., & Mischel, W. (1999). A hot/cool-system analysis of delay of gratification: Dynamics of willpower. *Psychological Review, 106,* 3–19.

Panksepp, J. (1998). *Affective neuroscience: The foundations of human and animal emotions.* New York: Oxford University Press.

Rawls, J. (1971). *A theory of justice.* Cambridge, MA: Harvard University Press.

Ross, L. (1977). The intuitive psychologist and his shortcomings: Distortions in the attribution process. In L. Berkowitz (Ed.), *Advances in experimental psychology* (Vol. 19, pp. 173–220). New York: Academic Press.

Scanlon, T. M. (1998). *What we owe to each other.* Cambridge, MA: Harvard University Press.

Skarlicki, D. P., & Folger, R. (1997). Retaliation in the workplace: The roles of distributive, procedural, and interactional justice. *Journal of Applied Psychology, 82,* 434–443.

Skarlicki, D. P., Folger, R., & Tesluk, P. (1999). Personality as a moderator in the relationship between fairness and retaliation. *Academy of Management Journal, 42,* 100–108.

Smith, A. (1971). *The theory of moral sentiments.* New York: Garland. (Original work published 1759)

Stenberg, C. R., & Campos, J. (1990). The development of anger expression in infancy. In N. Stein, B. Leventhal, & T. Trabasso (Eds.), *Psychological and biological approaches to emotion* (pp. 247–282). Hillsdale, NJ: Erlbaum.

Tangney, J. P. (1996). Conceptual and methodological issues in the assessment of shame and guilt. *Behaviour Research and Therapy, 34,* 741–754.

Thibaut, J., & Walker, L. (1975). *Procedural justice: A psychological analysis.* Mahway, NJ: Erlbaum.

Tooby, J., & Cosmides, L. (1990). The past explains the present: Emotional adaptations and the structure of ancestral environments. *Ethology and Sociobiology, 11,* 375–424.

Turiel, E. (1983). *The development of social knowledge: Morality and convention.* Cambridge, England: Cambridge University Press.

Turillo, C. J., Folger, R., Lavelle, J., Umphress, E., & Gee, J. (2002). Is virtue its own reward? Self-sacrificial decisions for the sake of fairness. *Organizational Behavior and Human Decision Processes, 89,* 839–865.

Tyler, T. R., & Lind, E. A. (1992). A relational model of authority in groups. In M. P. Zanna (Ed.), *Advances in experimental social psychology* (Vol. 25, pp. 115–191). New York: Academic Press.

5

THE NORMATIVE NATURE OF EMPLOYEE DEVIANCE AND THE IMPACT OF MORAL IDENTITY

REBECCA J. BENNETT, KARL AQUINO,
AMERICUS REED II, AND STEFAN THAU

Robinson and Bennett, (1995, 1997, 2000) defined *employee deviance* as voluntary behavior that violates significant organizational norms and threatens the well-being of the organization, its members, or both. Understanding norms and their influence on behavior is central to this definition, but norms alone are insufficient to describe employee deviance. In this chapter we consider the interaction between societal, organizational, and individual-level factors. The first part of the chapter explores employee deviance as a violation of common performance norms and connects this notion with organizational norms endorsed by organizational culture. The second part explains how the impact of culture on deviant behavior might be influenced by one element of a person's mental self-representation: their moral identity. The third part speculates on what might happen when the self-importance of moral identity (self-conception organized around a set of moral trait associations) competes with deviant organizational norms.

BEHAVIORAL NORMS: DEFINITIONS AND ASSUMPTIONS

The determination of what is "good," "right," or "moral" is based on social norms (Rest, 1984). Social norms take the following form: "In a situation with X circumstances, a person ought to do Y." More specifically, norms are behavioral expectations directed toward possessors of social positions (e.g., job holders, church or government officials, parents). Doctors should help their patients, not harm them; priests ought to counsel parishioners, not have affairs with them; and parents should protect their children, not exploit them. Norms frequently become codified rules (legislation) enforced by the power of authorities.

Roles are positions connected to behavioral expectations. These expectations are usually less explicit than institutional rules. Social norms specify what behavior might be appropriate or inappropriate for that role. Because Katz and Kahn (1966) popularized the sociological concept of roles in organizational behavior research, norms and expectations have often been used to explain employee behavior (Van Dyne, Cummings, & McLean Parks, 1995). The central assumptions of role theory are simple: An organization fills jobs, which consist of sets of role expectations. These role expectations anticipate certain behaviors that presumably advance organizational goals—in other words, enhance performance. In reality, a job holder's behavior can either conform to or violate (i.e. "be deviant" in the classical role terminology) norm expectations. Deviance from norms can be either positive (e.g., organizational citizenship behaviors) or negative (e.g., employee deviance behaviors), but we are interested only in negative deviations from social expectations in this chapter.

The determination of whether nonconforming workplace behaviors are positive or negative has been approached in two ways. First, the organizational outcome (productive vs. counterproductive) evidences whether work behaviors are positive (desired) or negative (not desired). The problem with this definition is that it does not allow an empirical test of the link between these individual behaviors and the organizational outcome. That is, if the behaviors are defined by their outcome, contradictory findings (e.g., no relationship between sales level and altruism or employee theft) must lead to the conclusion that these behaviors were simply neither positive discretionary nor negative discretionary workplace behaviors. Conceptually, it makes more sense to disentangle the individual-level construct from its proposed outcome and to state falsifiable hypotheses about their macro outcomes later. (For another review of this aspect of the definition of employee deviance, see Bennett & Robinson, 2003.)

Second, work behaviors can be measured against a shared standard of behavioral expectations. Determining what behaviors are good or bad would thus depend on the chosen standard. Later on, we will show that an explanation of employee deviance is correlated to the standard that is chosen to determine the desirability of a given behavior.

THE ROLE OF NORMS IN DEVIANCE: ORGANIZATIONAL CULTURE

Robinson and Bennett, in their 1997 elaboration on their earlier (1995) definition of employee deviance, suggested that employee deviance is measured against the standard of the dominant administrative coalition of the organization rather than against societal norms. Workplace deviance was originally defined as "voluntary behavior of organizational members that violates significant organizational norms and, in so doing, threatens the well-being of the organization and/or its members" (Robinson & Bennett, 1995, p. 556). But how are significant norms defined within an organizational setting? Who sets the expectation of what's acceptable behavior within the organization? Where do these norms come from? Who determines that aggressive competition between peers is allowed or is not allowed? Who determines rules for resource allocation? Who determines how hard one should work and whether one is allowed extra breaks during the day? Robinson and Bennett (1997) have argued that it is the dominant coalition— the leaders of the organization—who define expected role behavior for the employees.

Social learning theory (Bandura, 1977) finds that children are most likely to model competent, powerful people, so it is no surprise that adult employees emulate the behavior of organizational leaders. In addition to social learning theory, both cultural anthropology and sociobiology suggest that the imitation of the successful (e.g., the leadership) is the best strategy to be successful oneself (Flinn & Alexander, 1982). Thus, the idea that successful people are the best ones to imitate is widely supported by social science research.

In organizations, the understanding of what behaviors are expected and appropriate within an organization are defined through organizational culture (Deal & Kennedy, 1982; Schein, 1983; Trice & Beyer, 1984). Organizational culture is the set of beliefs, values, and assumptions that guide behavior within the organization (Ott, 1989). Therefore, the sum of an organization's norms constitutes a large portion of an organization's culture. Employees are made aware of these written and unwritten norms through the socialization process (Allen & Meyer, 1990; Chatman, 1991). Many organizations have elaborate orientation and training procedures to help employees adopt the organization's standards of behavior. These strong expectations take on a sense of morality within the organization. For instance, in Disney's training program, employees are taught to consider "what would Walt have done?" in troubleshooting a problem, hence implying a "right" way of thinking about the problem. As a result of the socialization process, employees become aware of organizational norms. If the socialization process is successful, employees react with internal controls if they violate the norm. For example, the socialization process of a chronically tardy employee should result in guilt or shame because of the mismatch between her action and the norms against this behavior. That mismatch and its accompanying discomfort should lead the employee to a correction of that misfit by choosing the "correct" (organizationally sanctioned) action.

The initial organizational culture and hence organizational-specific norms are largely derived from the personality and management style of the founder of the organization (Schein, 1983). However, norms evolve and are transformed over time, intentionally and unintentionally, by virtue of what behaviors the dominant coalition of the organization chooses to espouse and to reward. Robinson and Bennett's (Bennett & Robinson, 2003; Robinson & Bennett, 1995, 1997) perspective that organizational norms are idiosyncratic allows for incorporating the concept of organizational culture. Because each dominant coalition is unique, each culture presumably has the potential to have unique components. For instance, Enron's corporate culture has widely been described as a "cowboy culture" in which it seemed the top managers engaged in reckless fraud without constraints (Eavis, 2001; Ledbetter, 2002; Sims & Brinkmann, 2003). Hence in that organization, fraud against stockholders, although harming the organization, would be considered nondeviant because it is not against the norms of the dominant coalition. In this chapter, we take the perspective that although organizational cultures may vary in the degree to which they implicitly or explicitly condone behaviors that may harm other individuals or the long-term health of the organization, there is a broader standard against which such behaviors can be judged as deviant. We use shared performance-enhancing norms[1] as the common standard against which employee deviance is judged from outside the organization.

We believe the theory of employee deviance can be meaningfully extended by incorporating contextual influences. Context variables operate outside of the individual but significantly affect individual decisions by shaping their possibilities and defining the situation the actor is in (Coleman, 1990b). Some context variables are specific to the organization but cannot

---

[1]Rational and behavioral perspectives on organizational behavior both assume that organizations desire to enhance their performance. Consequently, behaviors that are widely viewed as enhancing performance (e.g., working harder or more efficiently, going beyond job requirements to help the organization) are viewed as functional whereas those that are viewed as detracting from performance (e.g., calling in sick to work when not, stealing from the organization or coworkers, harassing coworkers or customers, etc.) are viewed as dysfunctional or deviant.

be traced back to behaviors of the members within (e.g., the organization's location), whereas others are the product of aggregated effects of corporate responses to individual behaviors (e.g., attendance norms; cf. Lazarsfeld & Menzel, 1969). Norms belong to the latter conceptual class. Our subject of interest turns to properties of organizational culture as a potential context effect for individual actions: What influence does the overall organizational culture have on an individual's likelihood of engaging in behaviors that violate performance-enhancing norms (i.e., deviant workplace behaviors)?

Berger and Luckmann (1966) claimed that the power of norms is defined by the overall acceptance of them within the culture. Therefore, organizational members may be subject to norms that are widely accepted within their organizational environment but are not necessarily acceptable in other organizations or by overall societal standards. Organizational culture is reflected in the reinforcement and punishment systems therein. Are deviant actions of employees sanctioned? Are there explicit orientation and training sessions to make employees aware of the organization's norms and standards and consequences for violating them? Do symbols, stories, language, and ceremonies of the organization seem to emphasize the shared values? Do the CEO and other organizational leaders speak publicly about corporate values and also seem to follow those norms in their own actions? A person in a position of power and authority sets a clear example by acting (or *not* acting) in accordance with his or her stated principles. Hence, the consistent modeling and reward behavior of its leadership strengthen a corporation's culture.

We assume corporate leaders to be the most salient models for employees because of their status and sanction power. They typically have the most effective communication strategies within the organization, and therefore their social influence might be *a priori* higher than the influence of other individuals or groups within the organization (see Latane, 1996, for the concept of social influence). If, however, the organization's guiding philosophy emphasizes profitability rather than moral values, if the reinforcement system directly or indirectly rewards deviant behaviors, and if the organization's leadership does not appear to exemplify moral values in their own behavior ("borrowing" from employees' pension funds, for instance, or verbally assaulting subordinates), then the organization can be said to have a culture that supports (or at least does not discourage) employee deviance.

To conclude, we extend the range of the construct of workplace deviance for this chapter to the following: *Employee deviance is the voluntary behavior of organizational members that has the potential to cause harm to the organization or to those within, and in so doing violates significant performance-enhancing norms.*

THE ROLE OF NORMS IN DEVIANCE: INTERNAL INFLUENCES

One central issue in this chapter is determining what happens when the organizational culture is deviant. What happens if the dominant coalition of the organization shares beliefs that are viewed by society as dysfunctional or harmful? We expect broad organizational norms endorsed and rewarded by the organizational leadership to affect deviant behavior by employees in that organization as well. In other words, if the organizational culture endorses deviant behaviors, employees within that organization will be more likely to behave in ways that harm the organization or its members. This proposition is intuitively obvious and grounded in both social learning (Bandura, 1977) and social information processing (Salancik & Pfeffer, 1978) theories. It has also received empirical support (e.g., Aquino & Douglas, in press; Robinson & O'Leary-Kelly, 1998).

But like other situational predictors of behavior, this relationship will not be perfect, and so it is in specifying the conditions under which the relationship will be stronger or weaker that theoretical advances can be made. Obvious sources of variability in employees' responsiveness to the influence of organizational norms are individual characteristics such as personality traits, personal beliefs, or values. Some factors that have been found to either directly affect or moderate the propensity to engage in employee deviance are trait anger (Deffenbacher, 1992; Fox & Spector, 1999), negative affectivity (Skarlicki, Folger, & Tesluk, 1999), aggressiveness (Aquino, Galperin, & Bennett, in press), and hostile attribution bias (Greenberg & Alge, 1999).

In this chapter, we introduce to the field of organizational behavior a new and unstudied construct as a possible moderator of the relationship between situational factors and deviant behavior. This construct is moral identity. Moral identity is one of the many possible identities that make up a person's overall self-schema. Any identity can be broadly defined as a mental representation of one aspect of the self that is held internally and projected to others. The specific content of a moral identity is what differentiates it from other identities such as those based on ethnicity, gender, occupation, or organizational affiliation. We propose that the mental representation of a moral self acts as a cognitive regulator of behaviors that are perceived as having moral implications; that is, they express some level of responsiveness to the needs and interests of others. The self has been a topic of empirical study in psychology for more than 100 years and of philosophical speculation for millennia, yet almost no research in organizational behavior has focused on the role that specific personal identities might play in guiding deviant workplace behavior. We propose that moral identity represents a clear theoretical link to deviant behavior because such behaviors, by definition, possess moral content in that they aversely affect the welfare of others.

In the following section, we explain how moral identity may influence the decision to either comply with or reject deviant organizational norms. We then consider some key outcomes of compliance and noncompliance in the context of a deviant organizational culture.

MORAL IDENTITY AND THE SELF-REGULATION
OF MORAL CONDUCT

The cognitive developmental approach historically has provided the dominant paradigm for examining moral behavior in organizations (e.g., Ferrell & Gresham, 1985; Jones, 1991; Kohlberg, 1969; Rest, 1979; Trevino, 1986). These rationalist models assume that moral behavior is largely the product of a conscious, deliberative, reasoning process. Contemporary developments in psychology, however, suggest that social–cognitive frameworks (e.g., Bandura, 1999; Cervone & Shoda, 1999; Lapsley, 1998) that incorporate a person's mental representation of the self may be an additional predictor of moral behavior in concert with the ability to engage in complex moral reasoning. The construct of *moral identity* as conceptualized by various writers (e.g., Aquino & Reed, 2002; Blasi, 1984, 1993; Damon & Hart, 1992; Hart, Atkins, & Ford, 1998; Reed & Aquino, in press) falls within this domain. A moral identity approach complements rationalist models by emphasizing that self-regulatory processes resulting from the formation of a personal identity can act as precursors of moral behavior in organizations perhaps even in the absence of sophisticated moral reasoning.

According to Erikson (1964), two key properties of a personal identity are that it is rooted in the very core of one's being and involves being true to oneself in action. In his later writings, Erikson (1968, p. 39) argued that morality and identity stand in mutually supportive relation and that an ethical capacity is the "true criterion of identity." Hart et al. (1998, p. 515) defined moral identity as "a commitment to one's sense of self to lines of action that promote or protect the welfare of others." Blasi (1984, p. 129) proffered a broader definition, suggesting that moral identity consists of "certain conceptual features of the moral self." In yet another definition, Lapsley and Lasky (2001, p. 347) described a person who has a moral identity as "one for whom moral schemas are chronically available, readily primed, and easily activated for information processing."

In an effort to develop a more precise definition that can be used to construct a measure of moral identity, Aquino and Reed (2002) adopted Erikson's (1964) conception of what constitutes an identity. Aquino and Reed (2002) defined moral identity as a self-conception organized around a set of moral trait associations. This definition is congruent with contemporary theorizing on social cognitive definitions of the self (e.g., Brewer &

Gardner, 1996; Kihlstrom & Klein, 1994) that consider traits to be the relevant elements of self-knowledge that define a personal identity. The self has long been seen as having multiple identities (Brewer & Gardner, 1996) that are hierarchically ordered (Stryker, 1980). As a consequence, the self-importance of moral identity may vary from person to person relative to other identities as a function of place and time (Hart et al., 1998). Nevertheless, there is evidence that moral identity predicts outcomes reflecting a person's level of concern for the needs and interests of others.

In a series of studies, Aquino and Reed (2002) presented empirical evidence supporting their trait-based conceptualization of moral identity, and they devised a measure of two of the dimensions of identity described by Erikson (1964)—identity as being rooted in the very core of one's being and identity as being true to oneself in action. Moreover, they showed that scores on this instrument predicted morally relevant cognitions and behaviors, including the emergence of a spontaneous self-concept organized around moral themes, self-reported volunteering, and the donation of food to the needy (Aquino & Reed, 2002).

Although moral identity is linked to specific traits, Aquino and Reed (2002) proposed that these traits may evoke a distinct mental image of what a moral person is likely to think, feel, and do. This means that moral identity can have a social referent such as a membership group (e.g., the Peace Corp.), an abstracted ideal (e.g., God), a known individual (e.g., Big Brother in a mentoring program), a public figure (e.g., Mother Teresa), or any social construction. As long as the person attempts to see the world in terms of the proscriptive implications of the moral traits linked to that social construction, the person has adopted moral identity as part of his or her social self-schema. Hence, moral identity constitutes one of many possible social identities that people use to define the self (Reed, 2002) and guide the selection of appropriate goals, values, and actions.

In line with this premise, moral identity can be viewed as a particular kind of self-representation that sometimes acts as a self-regulatory mechanism. For example, Verona and her colleagues (Verona, Reed, & Aquino, 2003) have posited the existence of a system of higher level self-representations that execute self-regulatory, control, and intentional processes that are akin to executive cognitive functioning. Presumably, when any environmental or social stimulus motivates a person to behave dysfunctionally (e.g., engage in organizationally deviant behavior), these processes may promote problem solving, examination of alternatives, and presumably inhibition of inappropriate responses (Verona et al., 2003). To empirically test this premise, Reed and Aquino (in press) showed that higher order self-representations predict the likelihood of not accepting postretaliatory harm that may come to incidental individuals loosely associated with a highly salient intergroup conflict. Hence, an internal self-regulatory mechanism may act as a buffer, and through the evaluative implications of these self-representations allow the person to more quickly and effectively dial down implicit reactions to salient organizationally deviant norms. If the person's moral identity is sufficiently self-important, that person may try to focus on positive aspects of the situation or to reconcile the conflict created by the incongruence between the implicit reaction to engage in deviant behavior and the evaluative self-proscriptions that may counteract this urge. Therefore, in some people, especially among those who have greater cognitive controls, the accessibility of higher level moral self-representations that are inconsistent with organizational deviance may override the more automatic or socialized cues that justify or even encourage such behavior.

In this regard, an individual-level variable that has not received either theoretical or empirical attention in the deviance literature is the concept of a moral self. A moral self-representation is important to consider in theoretical explanations for deviance because of its potential to act as a countervailing motivational force to deviant organizational employee norms. In psychology, and certainly in organizational research, almost no theoretical research has systematically examined the relationship between the self-importance of a moral self and its relationship to the motivation to comply with role expectations linked to deviant norms. We describe links between moral identity and deviant organizational culture in the next section.

THE SELF-REGULATION OF MORAL IDENTITY AND DEVIANT ORGANIZATIONAL CULTURE

When moral identity occupies a more important place within the person's overall self-schema relative to other identities, we propose that the person is more likely to express attitudes, cognitions, and behaviors that are consistent with the traits around which their moral self-definition is organized. It is in this way that moral identity corresponds to a conception of the self as being a relatively stable mental representation (Epstein, 1973; Pinker, 1997; Robins, Norem, & Cheek, 1999). This stable mental representation may be important for understanding why employees may react differently to a deviant organization's norms because a person's self-identity or one or more of its dominant facets can control, regulate, and organize the stimuli that enter the mind as well as the processes and operations of which the mind is ultimately composed (Robins et al., 1999). Like other individual-difference variables, we argue that a person's moral identity can moderate the relationship between deviant organizational norms and individual deviant behavior.

Brown (1998) outlined three aspects of the cognitive self-regulation process: goal selection, preparation for action, and a cybernetic cycle of comparing present with desired states and assessing progress. Both self-awareness and stable self-representations (e.g., moral identity) play a key role in ongoing self-regulatory efforts. As a consequence, high-level self-representations function as both goals to be pursued and standards against which outcomes are evaluated. In terms of goal-directed behavior and self-regulation, research shows that it is important for an individual to try to live up to and to meet his or her internal standards of right and wrong (Cialdini, Finch, & De Nicholas, 1990; Hales, 1985). The higher order self-representations that are indexed by a person's moral identity are likely to motivate a person to pursue goals that are consistent with the evaluative implications of his or her identity. For example, it may be important for a person to see him- or herself as fair and just, resulting in a higher likelihood that he or she would pursue the goals of cooperation and honesty in his or her dealings with others. In this way, the self is an antecedent to the choice of what set of goals to pursue in the first place. Second, the self then acts as a dynamic standard by which a person judges the extent to which his or her attitudes, emotions, and actions are congruent with his or her self-representation. In fact, if one's self-image and behavior are inconsistent, an individual will often use a variety of ego-defensive mechanisms such as motivated reasoning (Kunda, 1990), self-handicapping (Jones & Berglas, 1978), and verbal rationalizations (Scott & Lyman, 1968) to justify or neutralize the violation of self-standards. These goal-directed activities that underlie self-regulatory mechanisms maintain the experience of the self as being moral, competent, good, stable, and capable of choice and control (Bershoff, 1999; see also Steele, 1988). Hence, the self prioritizes and organizes goal-directed behavior in the face of complex and multiple structures of goals and subgoals. These well-established functions of the self lead us to propose that relative accessibility of certain types of identities that form a part of the person's overall self-schema can either compete against or support the influence of deviant organizational norms.

Figure 5.1 presents a model that depicts the relationship between deviant organizational norms and individual behavior. The model shows how a specific personal identity—the moral identity—acts as a high-level regulator of moral conduct by influencing whether or not the employee complies with deviant organizational norms. This identity is only one of many possible identities that make up the person's overall self-schema, so it is represented by a single circle inside a larger box. The box represents the totality of other possible identities that make up the self, some of which may be either more or less self-important than moral identity. The model goes on to show how the conformity to deviant norms at the individual level has implications for the maintenance of deviant cultures at the organizational level, a point we discuss more fully in the following section.

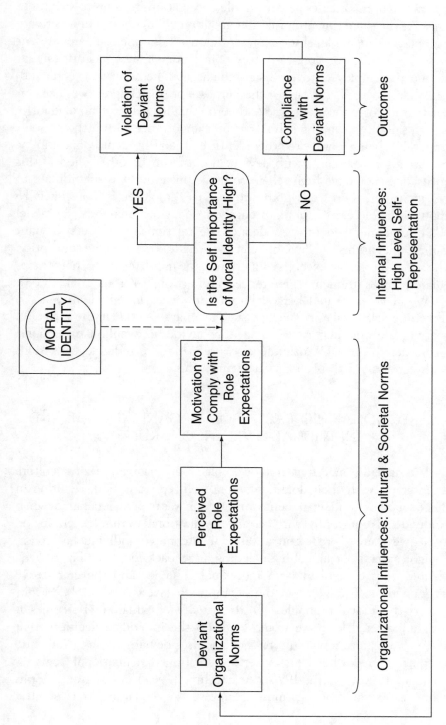

Figure 5.1. Relationships among deviant organizational norms, moral self-identity, and individual behavior.

The rationale for the model is as follows. First, the presence of deviant organization norms creates perceived role expectations to comply with those norms. At the same time, information about prevailing norms may activate the employee's higher level self-representation as he or she compares present with desired states or goals. At this point, one or more identities that make up the employee's overall self-schema may be activated (Forehand, Deshpande, & Reed, 2002). For the purposes of this chapter, we focus on the activation of moral identity. We theorize that if a person's moral identity has high salience, meaning it holds greater importance within the person's overall self-schema relative to other identities, then this identity may inhibit the motivation to comply with deviant norms. On the other hand, if this identity does not have high self-importance, meaning it is subordinate to other identities, then we hypothesize that the employee is more likely to comply with role expectations to engage in deviant behavior. The model predicts that moral identity moderates the relationship between deviant organizational norms and deviant behavior. This follows from the conception of the self as serving an executive function in the mind, meaning that it helps regulate peoples' thoughts, preferences, and actions (Verona et al., 2003).

We have presented a model that introduces moral identity as an intervening self-regulatory mechanism that may counteract the effects of deviant organizational norms on deviant behavior. In the following sections, we consider the possible macrolevel consequences of individual decisions to either comply with or violate deviant norms.

BIDIRECTIONAL FEEDBACK FROM ORGANIZATIONAL AND INDIVIDUAL-LEVEL INCONGRUITY

We have assumed that employees face a given organizational culture that interacts with their dominant moral self-representation, resulting in either deviant or nondeviant behavior. Our aim was to predict behavior when an individual is confronted with certain organizational norms. Depending on whether we desire to predict organizational outcomes or individual behavior, we might extend our model by including a feedback loop (see Figure 5.1). This allows us to explain both individual behavior and the cumulative effects on those behaviors on the organization (see Coleman, 1990b, for the meta-theoretical rationales). In the interest of explaining outcomes at the organizational level we would focus on the individual decisions that lead to an organizational culture that endorses deviant norms. Norms do not come from nowhere but rather are solutions to situational demands (Coleman, 1990a; North, 1990). As Hechter (1987) pointed out, norms are not an explanation but must themselves be explained. It is of little practical or theoretical use to answer the question, "Why is the organizational culture deviant?" with "Because of the organizational norms." Given that norms are based on collective interests, fraud against stakeholders might be the self-interested outcome of the behavior of individuals who benefit from this norm. They might experience their behavior as intrinsically (e.g., feelings of amusement or superiority) and extrinsically (e.g., peer group approval) rewarding. The collective phenomenon of deviant norms within organizations would be the result of the behavior of a powerful subgroup establishing general expectations for intraorganizational behavior. Outside of this powerful subgroup, however, will be those whose moral identities might prescribe actions that contradict the dominant norm. These persons may not exhibit deviance because doing so would act against the fulfillment of an internalized moral self-representation (Opp, 1989). On the other hand, employees whose moral identity has low self-importance might participate to maintain the culture or because they find doing so self-serving. These mechanisms constitute the linkage of individual behaviors to organizational culture. Individuals' compliance with these "deviant" norms, therefore, can solidify and reinforce the deviant culture. But cumulative individual violations of these norms can transform the norms and culture of the organization to one that upholds nondeviant norms.

To return to the postulated mechanism for deriving organizational culture from individual behavior, we hypothesized a moderating effect of a self-important moral identity on behavioral reactions to a deviant organizational culture. In turn, this results in a higher likelihood of noncompliance with overall deviant norms. This effect might be moderated by variables. One crucial factor we believe to be important on both transitions (individual level → organizational level, organizational level → individual level) is the saliency of norms through a strong organizational culture. Whereas saliency of internalized moral standards (e.g., by support from significant others, White, Hogg, & Terry, 2002) might contribute to the emergence of a self-important moral identity, the saliency of organizational norms may be best understood by its connected sanctioning mechanisms. That is, a deviant organizational culture with strong levels of informal control that sanctions those acting against the dominant culture might constrain employees with a high internal demand to act in accord with their moral principles. Organizational norms with stronger sanction mechanisms constrain behavioral patterns, because violators expect punishment (Koford & Miller, 1991). For example, coworkers might isolate whistle-blowers. If being isolated affects fulfillment of job duties, employees might weigh the pros and cons of staying with their job against acting in accordance with their moral identity. Thus, there are important and interesting situational preconditions that either restrict or enhance the likelihood of the described moderator effect.

CONCLUSION

This chapter had three aims: First, we discussed the normative nature of employee deviance, explaining the necessity of clarity in defining whether the organization or society is the reference point for employee behavior and also in separating the proposed outcome of harm from the behaviors proposed to be "deviant." Second, we demonstrated the importance of organizational context variables (such as organizational culture) and their potential differential effects on employees. Specifically, we proposed moral identity as a potential moderator of a hypothesized organizational culture—employee deviance relationship. Third, we speculated on what might happen when the self-importance of moral identity competes with behavioral predictions of deviant organizational norms.

We believe that advancement in employee deviance theory requires understanding and application of sociological and economical theories on deviance along with an explanatory core of the reciprocating effects of individual and organizational causal effects. We argued in this chapter that the particular normative frames of the organization (organizational culture) interact with the chronic accessibility of moral traits. We believe this illustrates a more generalized model of human behavior. People pursue goals, but they are restricted in their self-interested behavior by normative expectations of their immediate context (Fazio, 1990; Gollwitzer & Schaal, 2001; Lindenberg, 2001). Whether employees will engage in deviant behavior will be influenced by an interplay of personal incentives, organizational sanctions for these behaviors, and opportunities to engage in these behaviors.

However, before the research program of employee deviance begins to fish in "variable science" by correlating the usual suspects of organizational behavior (e.g., job satisfaction, turnover intention, and commitment), we want to underline the usefulness of understanding possible relationships among variables. That is, crucial to a theory is a law, which explains *why* variable x is correlated with variable y (Bacharach, 1989; Esser, 1996). We do not claim that moral identity is the key determinant of deviance. For sure, there might be other salient and highly accessible individual-level variables, such as hedonistic goals, which might oppose moral identity. As Stryker (1980) pointed out, self-identities are hierarchically ordered and so are personal goals. In this chapter, we argued that the saliency of these goals will be determined by internal factors (e.g., a priori strength of particular goals/identities; see Forehand et al., 2002) and external factors (e.g., the degree of situational ambiguity; see Fazio, 1990). Thus, we hope that future research will elaborate on this model.

REFERENCES

Allen, N. J., & Meyer, J. P. (1990). Organizational socialization tactics: A longitudinal analysis of links to newcomers' commitment and role orientation. *Academy of Management Journal*, 847–858.

Aquino, K., & Douglas, S. (2003). Identity threat and antisocial behavior: The moderating effects of individual differences, aggressive modeling, and hierarchical status. *Organizational Behavior and Human Decision Processes*, 90, 195–208.

Aquino, K., Galperin, B. L., & Bennett, R. J. (in press). Social status and aggressiveness as moderators of the relationship between interactional justice and workplace deviance. *Journal of Applied Social Psychology*.

Aquino, K., & Reed, A., II. (2002). The self-importance of moral identity. *Journal of Personality and Social Psychology*, 83, 1423–1440.

Bacharach, S. B. (1989). Organizational theories: Some criteria for evaluation. *Academy of Management Review*, 14, 496–515.

Bandura, A. (1977). *Social learning theory*. Englewood Cliffs, NJ: Prentice-Hall.

Bandura, A. (1999). Moral disengagement in the perpetration of inhumanities. *Personality and Social Psychology Review*, 3, 193–209.

Bennett, R. J., & Robinson, S. L. (2003). The past, present and future of deviance research. In J. Greenburg (Ed.), *Organizational behavior: The state of the science* (2nd ed., pp. 247–281). Mahwah, NJ: Erlbaum.

Berger, P. L., & Luckmann, T. (1966). *The social construction of reality*. Garden City, NY: Doubleday.

Bersoff, D. M. (1999). Why good people sometimes do bad things: Motivated reasoning and unethical behavior. *Personality and Social Psychology Bulletin*, 25(1), 28–39.

Blasi, A. (1984). Moral identity: Its role in moral functioning. In W. Kurtines & J. Gewirtz (Eds.), *Morality, moral behavior and moral development* (pp. 128–139). New York: Wiley.

Blasi, A. (1993). The development of identity: Some implications for moral functioning. In G. G. Naom & T. E. Wren (Eds.), *The moral self* (pp. 99–122). Cambridge, MA: MIT Press.

Brewer, M. B., & Gardner, W. (1996). Who is this "we"? Levels of collective identity and self representations. *Journal of Personality and Social Psychology*, 71, 83–93.

Brown, J. D. (1998). *The self*. New York: McGraw-Hill.

Cervone, D., & Shoda, Y. (1999). *The coherence of personality: Social–cognitive bases of consistency, variability, and organization*. New York: Guilford Press.

Chatman, J. A. (1991). Matching people and organizations: Selection and socialization in public accounting firms. *Administrative Science Quarterly*, 36, 459–484.

Cialdini, R. B., Finch, J. F., & De Nicholas, M. E. (1990). Strategic self representation: The indirect route. In M. J. Cody & M. L. McLaughlin (Eds.), *The psychology of tactical communication* (pp. 194–206). Clevedon, England: Multilingual Matters.

Coleman, J. S. (1990a). The emergence of norms. In M. Hechter, K. D. Opp, & R. Wippler (Eds.), *Social institutions: Their emergence, maintenance and effects* (pp. 35–59). New York: de Gruyter.

Coleman, J. S. (1990b). *Foundations of social theory*. Cambridge, MA: Belknap.

Damon, W., & Hart, D. (1992). Self-understanding and its role in social and moral development. In M. Bornstein & M. E. Lamb (Eds.), *Developmental psychology: An advanced textbook* (3rd ed., pp. 421–464). Hillsdale, NJ: Erlbaum.

Deal, T. E., & Kennedy, A. A. (1982). *Corporate cultures: The rites and rituals of corporate life*. Reading, MA: Addison-Wesley.

Deffenbacher, L. J. (1992). Trait anger: Theory, findings, and implications. In C. D. Spielberger & J. N. Butcher (Eds.), *Advances in personality assessment* (Vol. 9, pp. 177–201). Hillsdale, NJ: Erlbaum.

Eavis, P. (2001). *Enron reaps what its cowboy culture sowed*. Retrieved on January 3, 2004, from http://www.thestreet.com/markets/detox/10004675.html

Epstein, S. (1973). The self-concept revisited or a theory of a theory. *American Psychologist, 28*, 405–416.

Erikson, E. H. (1964). *Insight and responsibility*. New York: Norton.

Erikson, E. H. (1968). *Identity: Youth and crisis*. New York: Norton.

Esser, H. (1996). What is wrong with variable sociology? *European Sociological Review, 12*, 159–166.

Fazio, R. H. (1990). Multiple processes by which attitudes guide behavior: The MODE model as an integrative framework. In M. P. Zanna (Ed.), *Advances in experimental social psychology* (Vol. 23, pp. 75–109). New York: Academic Press.

Ferrell, O. C., & Gresham, L. C. (1985). A contingency framework for understanding ethical decision making in marketing. *Journal of Marketing 49*, 87–96.

Flinn, M. V., & Alexander, R. D. (1982). Culture theory: The developing synthesis from biology. *Human Ecology, 10*, 383–400.

Forehand, M., Deshpande, R., & Reed, A., II (2002). Identity salience and the influence of differential activation of the social self-schema on advertising response. *Journal of Applied Psychology, 87*, 1086–1099.

Fox, S., & Spector, P. E. (1999). A model of work frustration–aggression. *Journal of Organizational Behavior, 20*, 915–931.

Gollwitzer, P. M., & Schaal, B. (2001). How goals and plans affect actions. In J. M. Collins & S. Messick (Eds.), *Intelligence and personality: Bridging the gap in theory and measurement* (pp. 139–161). Mahwah, NJ: Erlbaum.

Greenberg, J., & Alge, B. J. (1999). Aggressive reactions to workplace injustice. In R. W. Griffin, A. O'Leary-Kelly, & J. M. Collins (Eds.), *Dysfunctional behavior in organizations: Violent and deviant behavior* (pp. 83–117). Stamford, CT: JAI Press.

Hales, S. (1985). The inadvertent rediscovery of the self in social psychology. *Journal for the Theory of Social Behavior, 15*(3), 237–282.

Hart, D., Atkins, R., & Ford, D. (1998). Urban America as a context for the development of moral identity in adolescence. *Journal of Social Issues, 54,* 513–530.

Hechter, M. (1987). *Principles of group solidarity.* Berkeley: University of California Press.

Jones, E. E., & Berglas, S. (1978). Control of attributions about the self through self-handicapping strategies: The appeal of alcohol and the role of underachievement. *Personality and Social Psychology Bulletin, 4*(2), 200–206.

Jones, T. M. (1991). Ethical decision making by individuals in organizations: An issue contingent model. *Academy of Management Review, 20,* 366–395.

Katz, D., & Kahn, R. L. (1966). *The social psychology of organizations.* New York: Wiley.

Kihlstrom, J. F., & Klein, S. B. (1994). The self as a knowledge structure. In R. S. Wyer, Jr., & K. Thomas (Eds.), *Handbook of social cognition: Vol. 1. Basic processes; Vol. 2. Applications* (2nd ed., pp. 153–208). Hillsdale, NJ: Erlbaum.

Koford, K. J., & Miller, J. B. (1991). Habit, custom, and norms in economics. In K. J. Koford & J. B. Miller (Eds.), *Social norms and economic institutions* (pp. 21–36). Ann Arbor: University of Michigan Press.

Kohlberg, L. (1969). Stage and sequence: The cognitive–developmental approach to socialization. In D. A. Goslin (Ed.), *Handbook of socialization theory and research* (pp. 348–480). Chicago: Rand-McNally.

Kunda, Z. (1990). The case for motivated reasoning. *Psychological Bulletin, 108*(3), 480–498.

Lapsley, D. K. (1998). An outline of a social–cognitive theory of moral character. *Journal of Research in Education, 8,* 25–32.

Lapsley, D. K., & Lasky, B. (2001). Prototypic moral character. *Identity, 1,* 345–363.

Latane, B. (1996). Dynamic social impact: The creation of culture by communication. *Journal of Communication, 46,* 13–25.

Lazarsfeld, P. F., & Menzel, H. (1969). On the relation between individual and collective properties. In A. Etzioni (Ed.), *A sociological reader on complex organizations* (pp. 499–516). London: Holt, Rinehart & Winston.

Ledbetter, J. (2002). Cowboy capitalism. *TIME Europe* [On-line]. Retrieved January 2, 2004, from http://www.time.com/time/europe/magazine/printout/0,131 55,901021028-66279,00.html

Lindenberg, S. (2001). Social rationality versus rational egoism. In J. H. Turner (Ed.), *Handbook of sociological theory* (pp. 635–668). New York: Kluwer.

North, D. C. (1990). *Institutions, institutional change and economic performance.* Cambridge, England: Cambridge University Press.

Opp, K. D. (1989). The economics of crime and the sociology of deviant behavior: A theoretical confrontation and basic propositions. *Kyklos, 42,* 405–431.

Ott, J. S. (1989). *The organizational culture perspective.* Pacific Grove, CA: Brooks/Cole.

Pinker, S. (1997). *How the mind works*. New York: Norton.

Reed, A., II. (2002). Social identity as a useful perspective for self-concept based consumer research. *Psychology and Marketing, 19*(3), 235–266.

Reed, A., II, & Aquino, K. F. (2003). Moral identity and the expanding circle of moral regard towards out-groups. *Journal of Personality and Social Psychology, 84*, 1270–1286.

Rest, J. R. (1979). *Development in judging moral issues*. Minneapolis: University of Minnesota Press.

Rest, J. R. (1984). The major components of morality. In W. M. Kurtines & J. L. Gewirtz (Eds.), *Morality, moral behavior, and moral development* (pp. 24–38). New York: Wiley.

Robins, R. W., Norem, J. K., & Cheek, J. M. (1999). Naturalizing the self. In L. A. Pervin & O. P. John (Eds.), *Handbook of personality* (2nd ed., pp. 443–477). New York: Guilford Press.

Robinson, S. L., & Bennett, R. J. (1995). A typology of deviant workplace behaviors: A multidimensional scaling study. *Academy of Management Journal, 38*(2), 555–572.

Robinson, S. L., & Bennett, R. J. (1997). Workplace deviance: Its definition, its manifestations, and its causes. *Research on Negotiation in Organizations, 6*, 3–27.

Robinson, S. L., & Bennett, R. J. (2000). Development of a measure of workplace deviance. *Journal of Applied Psychology, 85*(3), 349–360.

Robinson, S. L., & O'Leary-Kelly, A. M. (1998). Monkey see, monkey do: The influence of work groups on the antisocial behavior of employees. *Academy of Management Journal, 41*, 658–672.

Salancik, G., & Pfeffer, J. (1978). A social information processing approach to job attitudes and task design. *Administrative Science Quarterly, 23*, 224–253.

Schein, E. H. (1983, Summer). The role of the founder in creating corporate culture. *Organizational Dynamics*, 713–726.

Scott, M. B., & Lyman, S. M. (1968). Accounts. *American Sociological Review, 33*, 46–62.

Skarlicki, D. P., Folger, R., & Tesluk, P. (1999). Personality as a moderator in the relationship between fairness and retaliation. *Academy of Management Journal, 42*(1), 100–108.

Sims, R. R., & Brinkmann, J. (2003). Enron ethics (Or: Culture matters more than codes). *Journal of Business Ethics, 45*, 243–256.

Steele, C. M. (1988). The psychology of self-affirmation: Sustaining the integrity of the self. In L. Berkowitz (Ed.), *Advances in experimental social psychology* (Vol. 21, pp. 261–302). New York: Academic Press.

Stryker, S. (1980). *Symbolic interactionism: A social structural version*. Menlo Park, CA: Benjamin/Cummings.

Trevino, L. K. (1986). Ethical decision making in organizations: A person–situation interactionist model. *Academy of Management Review, 11*, 601–617.

Trice, H. M., & Beyer, J. M. (1984). Studying organizational culture through rites and ceremonies. *Academy of Management Review, 9,* 653–669.

Van Dyne, L., Cummings, L. L., & McLean Parks, J. M. (1995). Extra-role behaviors: In pursuit of construct and definitorial clarity (A bridge over muddied waters). In L. L. Cummings & B. M. Staw (Eds.), *Research in organizational behavior* (Vol. 17, pp. 215–285). Greenwich, CT: JAI Press.

Verona, E., Reed, A., II., & Aquino, K. F. (2003). *Automatic and controlled processes of aggression activation and regulation: The role of negative affect, ruminative content and identity driven self-control mechanisms* Unpublished manuscript, University of Pennsylvania.

White, K. M., Hogg, M. A., & Terry, D. J. (2002). Improving attitude–behavior correspondence through exposure to normative support from a salient ingroup. *Basic and Applied Social Psychology, 24,* 91–103.

6

ADVANCING THE ASSESSMENT OF DISPOSITIONAL AGGRESSIVENESS THROUGH CONDITIONAL REASONING

SUSAN M. BURROUGHS AND LAWRENCE R. JAMES

The study of counterproductive workplace acts has become an increasingly prominent issue among academicians and practitioners alike given the prevalence and costs of such damaging behavior in organizational settings. A sizable body of research has established that individual differences in personality (i.e., negative affectivity, disagreeableness, unreliability) play an influential role in performing counterproductive work behaviors (Aquino, Lewis, & Bradfield, 1999; Atkinson, 1978; Burroughs, 2001; Buss, 1961; Hogan & Hogan, 1989; McClelland, 1985; Skarlicki, Folger, & Tesluk, 1999; Watson & Clark, 1984). It appears that people with certain dispositions are more likely to engage in antisocial behaviors or to direct harmful actions against other people, groups, organizations, or entities (Geen, 1995). The personality trait of aggressiveness is the focus in this chapter because it continues to be a notable societal and workplace concern. We begin by discussing this attribute in some detail and then turn attention to describing a new tool to measure it.

Aggressiveness is an underlying trait that predisposes some individuals to aggress or attack more readily than others in response to perceived negative stimuli (Buss, 1961; Monahan, 1981). Research has found aggressive tendencies to be a consistently strong predictor of both unprovoked and provoked deviant behavior (Hammock & Richardson, 1992). Murray (1938) believed that certain people have a motive to aggress that consists of desires to overcome opposition forcefully, to fight, to revenge an injury, to attack another with intent to injure or kill, and to oppose forcefully or punish another. The motive to aggress has been described as "latent" because people with strong and dominant aggressive tendencies cannot explain why they experience an attraction toward acting in a counterproductive fashion. Rather, these individuals are aware of a strong desire to aggress toward others, compete and win, and anticipate and then experience the thrill of revenge. Contemporary work on aggression combines both the implicit and explicit components of this motive (Bing, Burroughs, Davison, Green, McIntyre, & James, 2004; Winter, John, Stewart, Klohnen, & Duncan, 1998) with trait-based behavior to describe the "aggressive individual." An aggressive individual (a) often uses some form of aggression to deal with frustrating situations and anger; (b) dislikes if not hates the target of aggression; (c) desires to inflict harm on this target; and (d) has diminished self-regulatory capacities, which suggests underdeveloped internal prohibitions or standards against aggressing (Bandura, 1973; Baron & Richardson, 1994; Baumeister, Smart, & Boden, 1996; Berkowitz, 1993; Crick & Dodge, 1994; Gay, 1993; Huesmann, 1988; Millon, 1990; O'Leary-Kelly, Griffin, & Glew, 1996).

Aggressive individuals tend to behave in ways that others might describe as *antagonistic, belligerent, bellicose, combative, contentious, hostile, malicious, malevolent, offensive, obstreperous, pugnacious, truculent, unfriendly,* or *passive–aggressive*. It is important to note that aggressive people want to believe that their behavior is justified. That is, they want such things as fighting with peers, being insubordinate, withholding effort, or engaging in intentionally harmful criticisms of others to appear as rational and sensible as opposed to irrational or foolish (Anderson, 1994; Gay, 1993; James, 1998; Tedeschi & Nesler, 1993; Toch, 1993). To enhance the rational appeal of their acts, aggressive individuals often cast their aggression as a form of self-defense intended to ward off physical or verbal attack, as retaliation for previous attacks, or as justified retribution for being exploited and victimized (Anderson, 1994; Averill, 1993; Baron & Richardson, 1994; Baumeister et al., 1996; Berkowitz, 1993; Crick & Dodge, 1994; Felson & Tedeschi, 1993; Gay, 1993; Huesmann, 1988; James, 1998; Millon, 1990; Tedeschi & Nesler, 1993; Toch, 1993). These attempts to justify aggression are typically grounded in implicit biases such as an unconscious predilection to judge that arguments for retaliation are more reasonable than arguments for reconciliation.

ISSUES SURROUNDING THE ASSESSMENT
OF DISPOSITIONAL AGGRESSIVENESS

Individuals with aggressive tendencies tend to mask their hostile intentions before acting aggressively, thereby making their identification difficult (James, 1998). Self-report instruments have traditionally been used to measure dispositional aggressiveness even though an array of problems with this methodology have been identified in the literature, including a number of ego-protective and ego-enhancing biases (Fiske & Taylor, 1991; James, 1998; Schmitt, 1994; Spector, 1994; Stone & Stone, 1990). As summarized by Heneman, Heneman, and Judge (1997), individuals may distort their responses on self-report personality measures to avoid describing themselves in negative terms. In addition, because some answers are nearly impossible to verify, faking or response distortion may occur (Dwight & Alliger, 1997; Kroger & Wood, 1993; Moore & Stewart, 1989; Rosse, Stecher, Miller, & Levin, 1998). Furthermore, an assumption made when using self-report instruments is that aggressive individuals can accurately perceive themselves as such, and subsequently endorse items that attempt to acquire this information. Self-report measures are designed to assess the reputational (i.e., self-attributed) component of personality and concentrate on individuals' conscious cognitions (Hogan, 1991). This domain includes but is not limited to self-ascribed motives, values, beliefs, goals, interests, and behavioral dispositions (Greenwald & Banaji, 1995; McClelland, Koestner, & Weinberger, 1989).

Mounting evidence suggests that implicit or unconscious social cognitions may provide an additional, important, and often unique (in relation to self-reports) source of information about personality (Bing et al., 2004; Greenwald & Banaji, 1995; McClelland et al., 1989; Wegner & Vallacher, 1977; Westen, 1991, 1998; Winter et al., 1998). A less transparent measurement tool—one that is focused on accessing implicit social cognitions—may prove to be a superior methodology for gathering information regarding negative personality dispositions. Implicit social cognitions are (a) components of cognitive structure and cognitive process that determine individuals' perceptual, emotional, and behavioral adjustments to environments (Allport, 1937; James & Mazerolle, 2002; Millon, 1990) and are (b) not accessible to introspection by the individual (Epstein, 1994; Erdelyi, 1992; Greenwald & Banaji, 1995; Kihlstrom, 1999; Nisbett & Wilson, 1977; Westen, 1990, 1991; Winter et al., 1998). Implicit social cognitions include implicit motives, implicit theories, unconscious biases in reasoning, illusionary correlations, unrecognized proclivities to stereotype, downward comparisons, and selective attention (Baumeister, 1982; Baumeister & Scher, 1988; Bing et al., 2004; Brewin, 1989; Fiske & Taylor, 1984, 1991; Greenwald & Banaji,

1995; Kihlstrom, 1999; Miller, 1987; Nisbett & Wilson, 1977; Pyszczynski & Greenberg, 1987; Ross, 1977; Schneider, 1991; Taylor, 1991; Westen, 1990, 1991; Winter et al., 1998).

By virtue of being hidden from introspection, implicit social cognitions cannot be assessed by self-report inventories (Greenwald & Banaji, 1995; Nisbett & Wilson, 1977). To study implicit social cognitions, Greenwald and Banaji indicated that "indirect measurements are theoretically essential" (1995, p. 5). These authors also suggested that "investigations of implicit cognitions require indirect measures, which neither inform the subject of what is being assessed nor request self-report concerning it" (p. 5). Similar views were presented by Winter et al., who stated that "motives (like other cognitions) may often be implicit, that is, not accessible to consciousness and therefore measurable only by indirect means" (1998, p. 232). Indirect measures "are identifiable chiefly by their lack of the defining feature of direct measures, that is, by their not alerting the subject to the identity of the [variable] being measured" (Greenwald & Banaji, 1995, p. 8). Greenwald and Banaji based the following conclusion on a review of the current state of indirect measurement:

> Research on latency decomposition, projective tests, and miscellaneous other procedures indicate indirect measurement of individual differences in implicit social cognition is possible. At the same time, such measurement has not yet been achieved in the efficient form needed to make research investigation of individual differences in implicit social cognition a routine undertaking. (1995, p. 20)

These authors went on to state that when efficient indirect methods are developed and made available, "there should follow the rapid development of a new industry of research in implicit cognitive aspects of personality and social behavior" (p. 20). Such a new and unique measurement system is needed that enhances the ability to predict whether a person will act in a hostile manner (Borum, 1996; Grisso & Tomkins, 1996; Monahan & Steadman, 1996; Schopp, 1996). A description of such a system is the focus of the remaining portion of this chapter.

CONDITIONAL REASONING

Conditional reasoning (James, 1998) provides a powerful new tool for researchers to use when examining how aggressive latent motives engender counterproductive work behaviors.[1] This theory purports that reasoning

---

[1]The disposition of aggressiveness is the focus of this chapter; however, other individual difference variables can be applied to and measured with the conditional reasoning methodology. Interested readers are encouraged to read James (1998) for a review of how to assess other personality variables (i.e., achievement motivation) via conditional reasoning.

is "conditional" because the probability that an individual judges certain behaviors to be acceptable is dependent on the strength of that person's motive to engage in the behavior. Aggressive individuals reason that the behaviors they find attractive and perform (e.g., counterproductivity) are justified, which is to say rational or sensible as opposed to irrational and foolish. To justify employing desired behaviors, aggressive individuals engage in slants or biases in reasoning called *justification mechanisms* that are designed to enhance the logical appeal of counterproductive behaviors.

Justification mechanisms are tied into (conditional) reasoning when people use their underlying assumptions (e.g., beliefs, ideologies) to make judgments about what is and is not rational or sensible behavior. These different assumptions can be referred to as "implicit theories" (Wegner & Vallacher, 1977) and involve long-term, unconscious, and valued beliefs, explanations, and cognitive causal models about the effects of behavior. Implicit theories with embedded justification mechanisms typically go unrecognized by reasoners yet define, shape, and otherwise influence reasoning to enhance the rational appeal of behaving aggressively. They involve identifiable biases that attempt to enhance the logical appeal of trait-based or characteristic behavioral preferences (James & Mazerolle, 2002). The unrecognized use of justification mechanisms in what are believed to be rational implicit theories is the primary reason that aggressive and nonaggressive individuals can decide to behave differently and yet each group believes that its reasoning is logical (James, 1998).

Some of the more salient justification mechanisms and the implicit theories in which they tend to be embedded for aggressive individuals are described in Table 6.1. This list of justification mechanisms was identified after a thorough search of the aggression literatures in psychology and other social sciences as well as in the popular press (e.g., Anderson's 1994 account of street gangs in the *Atlantic Monthly*). The objective was to identify a seminal set of implicit biases that define, shape, and guide the myriad of specific instances of framing and implicit hypothesizing that aggressive individuals use to rationalize aggressive behaviors (James, 1998; James et al., 2004). The searches uncovered what appeared to be six primary implicit biases, discussed next.

Hostile attribution bias is a bias that consists of an unrecognized tendency to see malevolent purpose or harmful intent as the most reasonable explanations for the behaviors of others (Crick & Dodge, 1994; Dodge & Coie, 1987). This bias may permeate the cognitive system such that perceptions of others tend to pass through a prism that evaluates their actions from the perspective of hostile or malevolent intent (Anderson, 1994; Tedeschi & Nelser, 1993; Toch, 1993). To illustrate, aggressive individuals may map a hostile attribution bias (e.g., boss is out to get me) into judgments about the controllability of a specific event (e.g., decision to deny a raise increase).

TABLE 6.1
Justification Mechanisms for Aggression

Justification mechanism	Definition
Hostile attribution bias	The tendency to see malevolent intent in actions of others. Even benign or friendly acts may be seen as having hidden, hostile agendas designed intentionally to inflict harm. An especially virulent form of this bias occurs when benign or positive acts are attributed to selfish concerns and negative incentives (e.g., a helpful suggestion by a supervisor is interpreted by an aggressive subordinate as an intentional attempt to demean his or her work).
Retribution bias	The tendency to confer logical priority to reparation or retaliation over reconciliation. Reflected in implicit beliefs that aggression is warranted to restore respect or exact restitution for a perceived wrong. Bias is also indicated by whether a person would rather retaliate than forgive, be vindicated as opposed to cooperate, and obtain revenge rather than maintain a relationship. This bias underlies classic rationalizations for aggression based on wounded pride, challenged self-esteem, and disrespect.
Derogation of target bias	An attempt to make the target more deserving of aggression. A number of negative characteristics may be ascribed to the target (e.g., corrupt, dishonest, evil, immoral, underhanded, unethical, untrustworthy). Or the positive traits of the target may be ignored, undervalued, or depreciated.
Victimization by powerful others bias	The tendency to frame self as a victim and to see self as being exploited and taken advantage of by the powerful (e.g., government agencies). Sets the stage for arguing that aggression is acting out against injustice, correcting an inequity, redressing wrongs, or striking out against oppression.
Potency bias	The tendency to frame and reason using the contrast of strength versus weakness. For example, people with a strong potency bias tend to frame others on a continuum ranging from (a) strong, assertive, powerful, daring, fearless, or brave to (b) weak, impotent, submissive, timid, sheepish, compliant, conforming, or cowardly. This bias is used to justify aggression via arguments such as (a) aggression (e.g., confrontations with teachers, fights with coworkers) results in being perceived as brave or as a leader by others, and (b) weakness/submissiveness invites aggression because it shows that one is willing to submit.
Social discounting bias	The tendency to call on socially unorthodox and frequently antisocial beliefs to interpret and to analyze social events and relationships. Disdainful of traditional ideals and conventional beliefs. Insensitive, unempathetic, unfettered by social customs. Directly cynical or critical, with few subliminal channels for routing antisocial framing and analyses.

In this case, the reasoning process (inference about the raise) is a mirror reflection of the structural basis (justification mechanism—implicit theory) for the reasoning. With this bias in place, even benign or friendly acts by others may be inferred to have hidden, hostile agendas. Another example includes an offer made by another to assist on a project, which may be framed by an aggressive person as an attempt to sabotage his or her work or to make him or her appear incompetent.

Retribution bias involves an unconscious tendency to confer logical priority to reparation or retaliation over reconciliation (Anderson, 1994; Baumeister et al., 1996; Bradbury & Fincham, 1990; Crick & Dodge, 1994; Dodge, 1986; Laursen & Collins, 1994; Nisbett, 1993). This bias promotes judgments that aggression is a justifiable response if the intent of the response is to restore respect or to exact restitution for a perceived wrong. Retaliation thus appears more reasonable than forgiveness, vindication appears more reasonable than cooperation, and obtaining revenge appears more reasonable than maintaining a relationship. This bias often underlies justifications for aggression engendered by wounded pride, challenged self-esteem, and perceived disrespect (Baumeister et al., 1996).

Derogation of target bias and *victimization by powerful others bias* are two more justifications for aggression. The derogation of target bias consists of an unconscious tendency to characterize targets of aggression as evil, immoral, or untrustworthy (Averill, 1993; Gay, 1993; Toch, 1993). Such characterizations make the targets more deserving of aggression. In other words, by derogating the target, aggressive individuals label a victim of violence or a target of aggression as someone who "asked for it" (Bing et al., 2004). This derogation bias may or may not be accompanied by an implicit tendency to infer that one is a victim of inequity, exploitation, injustice, or oppression by powerful others. Powerful others include entities such as supervisors, teachers, employing organizations, or institutions such as the Internal Revenue Service. Framing, hypothesizing, and confirmatory searches for evidence both engender and reinforce unconscious inclinations to infer that one is being victimized by powerful others. Reasoning is thus said to be shaped implicitly by a victimization by powerful others bias. This reasoning is used to justify acts of aggression toward others as warranted corrections of inequities or legitimate strikes against oppression (Bies, Shapiro, & Cummings, 1988; Bies & Tripp, 1998; Bies, Tripp, & Kramer, 1997).

Potency bias is based on the premise that many aggressive individuals filter interactions with others through a prism that frames these interactions as contests to establish dominance versus submissiveness (Anderson, 1994; Baron & Richardson, 1994; Crick & Dodge, 1994; Gay, 1993; Hogan & Hogan, 1989; Millon, 1990; Tedeschi & Nesler, 1993; Wright & Mischel, 1987). Such framing is the cornerstone for reasoning that acting aggressively is a demonstration of strength, bravery, and fearlessness. Not acting aggressively is logically attributed to weakness, fear, cowardice, or impotence. An aggressive person may thus justify aggression by reasoning that (a) aggression is an act of strength or bravery that gains respect from others, or (b) to show weakness is to invite powerful others to take advantage.

Social discounting bias comprises an implicit tendency to favor socially unorthodox and antisocial reasons as logically probable causes of social events and relationships (Finnegan, 1997; Gay, 1993; Huesmann, 1988; Loeber & Stouthhamer-Loeber, 1998; Millon, 1990; Toch, 1993). Reasoning affected by this bias will reflect disdain for traditional ideals and conventional beliefs. This reasoning will further evidence a lack of sensitivity, empathy, and concern for social customs, often accompanied by the absence of rational prohibitions against behaving aggressively. Analyses of social events lean toward the cynical and critical, with a proclivity to associate positive outcomes with aggression.

The aforementioned justification mechanisms do not exhaust all possible implicit reasoning biases for aggression. They are, however, the biases that appeared significant in the literature searches conducted. It would also be premature to think of these six justification mechanisms as representing established factors (as in factor analysis) that define six separate and distinct domains of bias in reasoning about aggression. In fact, empirical research suggests that several of the justification mechanisms may operate in unison, such as the hostile attribution bias and the victimization by powerful others bias (James et al., 2004). Studies have shown that several of the justification mechanisms might not be empirically distinguishable, and additional findings will be forthcoming. Hence, the six justification mechanisms are offered as potentially promising implicit reasoning biases whose relationships and latent structures have yet to be ascertained.

It should also be noted that individuals who do not have aggressive personalities tend to lack a proclivity to frame and to analyze a situation in ways to justify counterproductive behaviors (James, 1998). Nonaggressive individuals are likely to have no unrecognized bias to see malevolent intentions in other's actions; instead, they favor cooperation and harmony over vengeance and retribution. Their perceptions of situations do not pass through a prism of potency that evaluates people or entities as dominant or submissive in relation to oneself (James & Mazerolle, 2002). Rather, nonaggressive individuals see an aggressive person's conditional reasoning as improbable and unlikely (but not illogical). Moreover, their own reasoning is based on cognitive repertoires that are much broader and include the assumption that until proven otherwise, the motives of others are reputable and constructive. Nonaggressive individuals are thus prone to discount reasoning based on justification mechanisms for aggression and to offer reasoning engendered by impartial, constructive, and prosocial beliefs and values (James, 1998).

In summary, aggressive people rely on justification mechanisms, which are implicit biases designed to rationalize aggression. Nonaggressive people tend to judge that reasoning based on justification mechanisms lacks logical persuasiveness. They are also prone to conclude that reasoning based on conventional premises is more convincing than reasoning based on justification mechanisms. The framing of aggressive behavior and conclusions about its justifiability may thus be said to be "conditional" on whether the individual doing the reasoning is aggressive or nonaggressive. James (1998) suggested the term *conditional reasoning* to refer to this dependency of reasoning on the personality of the reasoner.

CONDITIONAL REASONING MEASUREMENT SYSTEM FOR AGGRESSION

James and colleagues set out to empirically assess the extent to which justification mechanisms for aggression are instrumental in reasoning (Burroughs, LeBreton, Bing, & James, 2000; James, 1998; James et al., 2004; McIntyre, 1995). These researchers understood that they could not make the assessment with conscious cognitions (via self-reports) because individuals cannot introspect and report on the activity of justification mechanisms. Instead, as noted by Greenwald and Banaji (1995), an indirect process must be used, and such an indirect method was developed that is grounded in conditional reasoning (James, 1998). Specifically, James and colleagues proposed that a penchant to use justification mechanisms in reasoning is indicated (indirectly) if an individual finds arguments based on justification mechanisms for aggression to be logically persuasive. Conversely, a penchant to use justification mechanisms in reasoning is contradicted if an individual (a) is skeptical or doubtful of arguments based on justification mechanisms and (b) finds arguments based on more conventional assumptions to be the most logically convincing. The indirect measurement system that was constructed based on conditional reasoning is described next.

The Conditional Reasoning Test for Aggression (CRT–A; James, 1998) was developed to measure individual differences in the extent to which people use implicit reasoning biases to justify aggressive behavior. It contains items that appear to be reasoning problems such as those found in standardized tests of critical thinking, thereby circumventing respondents' inclinations to intentionally or unintentionally distort and enhance their responses. Respondents are not alerted to the identity of the variable(s) being measured but are informed that the task is a measure of reasoning skills. After reading a paragraph of information and a problem stem, the respondent is presented with four response options and is required to choose the most logical answer (option) given that more than one conclusion may appear reasonable. Of the four options, one response is designed to appeal to individuals relying on one or more of the justification mechanisms for aggressive behavior, one response is designed to appeal to nonaggressive (prosocial) individuals, and two responses are illogical. The purpose of the CRT–A is to determine the degree to which the respondent views the aggressive responses to be the logical and reasonable answers to the problems. The more justification mechanisms an individual has in place, the greater the willingness and implicit cognitive preparedness to aggress.

Two illustrative problems are presented in Exhibit 6.1. The stem of each problem consists of premises (e.g., data, events, logical arguments, explanations, assumptions) built around themes known to trigger justification mechanisms for aggressive individuals (e.g., robberies, gun control debates, traffic jams, etc.). The particular premise of the first problem focuses on the theme of a powerful other (i.e., American automobile manufacturers) taking advantage of and exploiting less powerful victims (i.e., customers). Respondents are asked to identify which one of the four alternatives most reasonably follows from the premise.

One alternative is "American car makers built cars to wear out 15 years ago so they could make a lot of money selling parts" (alternative d). This alternative offers respondents the opportunity to bestow logical priority to reasoning that is tacitly based on the hostile attribution bias and the victimization by powerful others bias. It is designed to appeal to aggressive individuals' implicit proclivity to favor hostile intent and exploitation of victims (over nonmalevolent and nonmanipulative intent) when making attributions about the most reasonable causes of the behaviors of powerful others. Selection of this alternative as the most logically persuasive of the inferences offered furnishes a single piece of indirect evidence that the hostile attribution bias and victimization by powerful others bias are implicitly instrumental in shaping and guiding reasoning.

One should note that there is potential for some respondents to select this alternative for reasons that differ from those provided earlier. For example, a respondent may have had negative experiences with an American automobile manufacturer that influences his or her reasoning on this problem. Hence, it is recommended that one should not place undue weight on the responses to a single problem. Rather, what is important for measurement is whether a respondent consistently selects reasoning based on justification mechanisms across a set of problems that vary in terms of inductive argument and subject matter.

Nonaggressive individuals are expected to acknowledge that alternative d is plausible and that it cannot be rejected (or accepted) with logical certainty. It is also expected that nonaggressive individuals will not, on average, find this inference to be logically persuasive. This is because it

EXHIBIT 6.1

Conditional Reasoning Test for Employee Aggression Example Items

1. American cars have gotten better in the past 15 years. American car makers started to build better cars when they began to lose business to the Japanese. Many American buyers thought that foreign cars were better made.

   Which of the following is the most logical conclusion based on the above?

   A. America was the world's largest producer of airplanes 15 years ago.
      - *illogical (+0)*
   B. Swedish car makers lost business in America 15 years ago.
      - *illogical (+0)*
   C. The Japanese knew more than Americans about building good cars 15 years ago.
      - *nonaggressive (−1)*
   D. American car makers built cars to wear out 15 years ago so they could make a lot of money selling parts.
      - *aggressive (+1)*

2. The old saying, "an eye for an eye" means that if someone hurts you, then you should hurt that person back. If you are hit, then you should hit back. If someone burns your house, then you should burn that person's house.

   Which of the following is the biggest problem with the "eye for an eye" plan?

   A. It tells people to "turn the other cheek."
      - *illogical (+0)*
   B. It offers no way to settle a conflict in a friendly manner.
      - *nonaggressive (−1)*
   C. It can only be used at certain times of the year.
      - *illogical (+0)*
   D. People have to wait until they are attacked before they can strike.
      - *aggressive (+1)*

Note. Scored answers are written in italics under each response option. To obtain a copy of the complete measure, please contact Dr. Lawrence James at Georgia Institute of Technology, School of Psychology, Atlanta, GA 30332-0170.

suggests that American car makers hold a deeply cynical attitude toward customers, where profit by any means overrides other concerns such as pride in product and attracting repeat customers. Nonaggressive individuals are expected to consider such reasoning improbable, extreme, and unrealistic.

A different alternative was designed to appeal to nonaggressive individuals' need for an answer that, to them, is more probable and realistic. This inference is "the Japanese knew more than Americans about building good cars 15 years ago" (alternative c). This inference follows logically from the premises but lacks the cynicism of the first conclusion. It offers a rational, prosocial alternative to d. Selection of this alternative as the most logically persuasive of the inferences offered provides a single piece of indirect evidence that the hostile attribution bias/victimization by powerful others bias are not implicitly instrumental in shaping reasoning.

Aggressive respondents are, on average, expected to acknowledge the plausibility of this second alternative. However, they should, with a significantly greater probability than nonaggressive individuals, determine that alternative d shows greater insight into the true intentions of American automobile makers.

To enhance the face validity of the task, and to protect the indirect nature of measurement, the alternatives are embedded within a set of four inferences, as shown in Exhibit 6.1. Two of the conclusions (i.e., alternatives a and b) are meant to be clearly illogical and rejected by respondents (which is usually the case). Alternative d is referred to as the aggressive alternative because it is designed to appeal to aggressive individuals. Alternative c is targeted for nonaggressive individuals and is referred to as the nonaggressive alternative.

The second problem displayed in Exhibit 6.1 further illustrates the conditional reasoning procedure. Alternatives a and c are clearly illogical. Alternative d offers respondents the opportunity to determine that reasoning based on the retribution bias and the victimization by powerful others bias have logical priority. This inference is designed to appeal to aggressive individuals' implicit favoring of retribution over reconciliation and reasoning that striking first is a justifiable means to avoid being attacked and becoming a victim. Selection of this conclusion as the most logically persuasive of the conclusions offered provides indirect evidence that the retribution bias and victimization by powerful others bias are implicitly instrumental in shaping reasoning.

It is expected that nonaggressive respondents will reject alternative d as extreme and unnecessarily provocative even though it appears to follow logically from the premises. Alternative b is targeted to appeal to nonaggressive individuals' desire for a more prosocial alternative to counterbalance the antagonistic and provocative tenor of alternative d. Selection of alternative b provides indirect evidence that the retribution bias and victimization by powerful others bias are not implicitly instrumental in shaping reasoning.

DEVELOPMENTAL WORK ON THE CONDITIONAL REASONING TEST FOR AGGRESSION

The CRT–A has been in development for approximately 8 years and the current version of this conditional reasoning test is considered provisionally complete. The CRT–A is composed of 22 conditional reasoning problems, including the two problems in Exhibit 6.1, plus three actual inductive reasoning problems (to further protect the indirect nature of the system). The average Flesch–Kincaid Grade Level score for the 22 conditional reasoning problems, an indicator of reading level provided by Microsoft Word, is approximately 7.0 (i.e., seventh grade). This reading level makes the CRT–A accessible to large segments of the population, including adolescents and applicants for entry-level jobs.

For less adept readers, a test based on a visual–verbal version of a subset of the conditional reasoning problems was designed to have a threshold reading level of approximately the fifth to sixth grade (Green & James, 1999). Referred to as the VCRT, this test consists of bare-bones versions of the conditional reasoning problems. The problems are presented both verbally and in written form using a video player and television. The written component consists of simplified prose, which is overlaid on a photograph consistent with the basic theme of the conditional reasoning problem. The current VCRT contains 14 conditional reasoning problems, 12 of which are shared with the CRT–A. Work continues on converting CRT–A problems to the VCRT format. There are no inductive reasoning problems in the VCRT.

More than 50 conditional reasoning problems were written and empirically tested before arriving at the current pool of 22 problems in the CRT–A. The problems were rooted in research results presented in professional journals, case studies or historical accounts of aggressive individuals, theoretical treatises of aggression, news events and editorials, and televised interviews with aggressive individuals (James et al., 2004). Furthermore, a series of interviews were conducted with people whose demonstrated behavior identified them as either aggressive or nonaggressive. Included in these interviews were (a) probes for ideas for conditional reasoning problems, (b) requests for verbal framing and analyses of premises for already evolving conditional reasoning problems, and (c) requests for verbal protocol analyses of new conditional reasoning problems to determine if interviewees' reasoning was consistent with the problem's intention.

The 22 surviving conditional reasoning problems evolved over a series of developmental studies (see James et al., 2004, for a detailed review of these studies). To be considered for retention, a conditional reasoning problem had to significantly predict behavioral indicators of aggression, preferably in more than one sample. A conditional reasoning problem also had to have low correlations with potential confounds, namely intelligence, gender, and race. A significant part–whole correlation (i.e., correlation of a problem with the total score) was required. Each problem was reviewed by a psychometrician for acceptability as an inductive reasoning task. Problems were rewritten or deleted based on these reviews. No formal evaluation was made in these reviews. Rather, if needed, a conditional reasoning problem was revised until it was deemed "acceptable." If revisions failed to produce a satisfactory problem, then the problem was deleted.

An attempt was made initially to have each of the six justification mechanisms in Table 6.1 represented in the conditional reasoning problems. Five of the six justification mechanisms are represented by three or more of the problems that survived to become members of the 22-problem pool. The exception, the derogation of target bias, is represented by only one problem in this pool. This is largely a result of the difficulty in writing problems to capture this bias and findings that the problems that were written did not survive the empirical tests described earlier.

An analysis of verbal protocols of individuals completing the conditional reasoning problems indicated that interviewees believed they were completing reasoning problems. Experiences with thousands of administrations of [V]CRTs also suggest that respondents generally believe that they have completed a test of reasoning skills. A number of respondents have inquired about their scores, and several instances of cheating have occurred in which a respondent copied the answer sheet of another respondent.

Scoring of the retained 22 conditional reasoning problems follows a straightforward method described by James (1998). Respondents are given +1 for every aggressive alternative they select, 0 for every logically incorrect alternative they select (an infrequent event), and −1 for every nonaggressive alternative they select. These scores are summed to furnish a raw composite score. These scores are then transformed, via linear transformation (to preserve the distribution of scores) into a standard scale that has a mean of 6.0 and a standard deviation of 1.67. A high score on a linear composite of conditional reasoning problems indicates that a respondent accords logical priority to a greater number of aggressive alternatives than other respondents. These scores serve as indirect indicators that justification mechanisms are instrumental in guiding and shaping the respondent's reasoning. Moreover, a strong proclivity to reason in ways that justify aggression suggests that the respondent is implicitly prepared and willing to engage in some form of aggressive behavior in the future (James, 1998). This suggests that he or she has a strong implicit cognitive readiness to aggress.

A low score on a linear composite of conditional reasoning problems indicates that a respondent tends to accord logical priority to nonaggressive alternatives when solving conditional reasoning problems. These scores serve as indirect indicators that justification mechanisms are not instrumental in guiding and shaping the respondent's reasoning. In contrast to those with high scores, a weak or nonexistent proclivity to reason in ways that justify aggression suggests that the respondent is not implicitly prepared to engage in aggressive behavior (James, 1998). This suggests that he or she has a weak (or lacks a strong) implicit cognitive readiness to aggress.

Scores ranging between the weak and strong poles on a linear composite of conditional reasoning problems indicate selection of a few but not a large number of aggressive alternatives (compared to other respondents). Justification mechanisms appear to be only sporadically instrumental in shaping and guiding reasoning. Implicit cognitive readiness to aggress is therefore likely to be only modest or indeterminate.

In summary, scores on linear composites of conditional reasoning problems are interpreted in terms of individual differences on a psychological scale labeled "implicit cognitive readiness to aggress." Individuals with high scores on the implicit cognitive readiness to aggress scale are expected to have a significantly greater probability of engaging in aggressive acts than individuals with low and moderate scores.

The degree to which scores from this scale correlate significantly with indicators of aggressive behavior has been established through many tests of the scales' empirical and construct validity (Burroughs, 2001; Burroughs, Bing, & James, 1999; Burroughs et al., 2000; James et al., 2004; McIntyre, 1995). Results confirm predictions that implicit cognitive readiness to aggress would correlate significantly with behavioral indictors of aggression. For example, the absolute values of eight uncorrected validity coefficients were all statistically significant and ranged from .32 to .55, with a mean of .43 (see Table 6.2 for samples, criteria, and validity coefficients). These validities overcome the personality coefficient range of .20 to .30 typically found in studies using self-report measures (Mischel, 1968, p. 78) and exceed the .04 to .31 range depicted in many studies using self-report measures of aggression, unreliability, and lack of agreeableness, which includes hostility (Barrick & Mount, 1991; Buss & Perry, 1992; Gottfredson & Hirschi, 1993; Hogan & Hogan, 1989; Hurtz & Donovan, 2000; Tett, Jackson, & Rothstein, 1991). In addition, scores reflecting implicit cognitive readiness to aggress correlated only modestly and often nonsignificantly with self-report measures of aggression. These results were expected and are comparable with previous studies in which measures of implicit cognitions (typically based on projective techniques) have a history of low and often nonsignificant correlations with measures of conscious cognitions (Greenwald & Banaji, 1995; James, 1998; Kihlstrom, 1999; McClelland et al., 1989; Winter et al., 1998). Furthermore, multiple reliability analyses indicated that measures of implicit cognitive readiness to aggress were internally consistent and stable over time. Scores on implicit cognitive readiness to aggress were also shown to be uncorrelated with the potential confounds of critical intellectual skills and race. Correlations between gender and implicit cognitive readiness to aggress were mixed, with a preponderance of evidence indicating no relationship. Overall, the CRT–A has been validated and monitored in different contexts (in job selection process, in a classroom, during training) and results are promising. Additional research is needed to expand on a theory of the instrument for the CRT–A.

TABLE 6.2
Uncorrected Validities for the Conditional Reasoning Test

Sample and criterion	Composition	Instrument	Experimental design	Uncorrected validity[a]
1. Supervisory rating—overall performance	140 patrol officers	CRT	Concurrent	-.49
2. Absences—lack of class attendance	188 undergraduate students	CRT	Predictive	.37
3. Lack of truthfulness about extra credit	60 undergraduate students	VCRT	Experiment	.49
4. Absences—lack of work attendance	97 nuclear facility operators	CRT	Postdictive	.42
5. Student conduct violations	225 undergraduate students	VCRT	Postdictive	.55
6. Attrition	135 restaurant employees	CRT	Predictive	.32
7. Absences—lack of work attendance	105 package handlers	CRT–A	Predictive	.34
8. Work unreliability	111 temporary employees	CRT–A	Predictive	.43

Note. [a]All correlations are statistically significant ($p < .05$). *Uncorrected* means not corrected for either range restriction or attenuation as a result of unreliability in either the predictor or the criterion. *Concurrent* means predictor and criterion data were collected at approximately the same time. *Predictive* denotes that predictor data were collected before criterion data. *Postdictive* refers to the use of archival criterion data to validate a contemporaneous predictor. VCRT = visual–verbal version of the Conditional Reasoning Test for Aggression. CRT = current version of the Conditional Reasoning Test for Aggression. CRT–A = developmental version of the Conditional Reasoning Test for Aggression. From *Organization Research Methods* (p. 155), by Lawrence R. James, 1998, Thousand Oaks, CA: Sage. Copyright © 1998 by Sage Publications. Reprinted with permission of Sage Publications.

CONCLUSION

The conditional reasoning measurement system is a work in progress. The effort began with thinking about what an efficient, indirect approach to the measurement of implicit personality might look like (James, 1998; McIntyre, 1995). Next came the idea to base a measurement system on reasoning biases embedded in solutions to inductive reasoning problems. Searches of professional and lay literatures for implicit reasoning biases, later designated *justification mechanisms*, followed. The initial attempts to map justification mechanisms into inductive reasoning problems were then made. Informal protocol studies of these problems were conducted, followed by pilot tests on samples. As results for the fledgling measurement system showed promise, additional conditional reasoning problems were written and then tested in empirical validation studies. Psychometric analyses accompanied validation analyses, and eight years later the CRT–A exists. This chapter provides a progress report on a continuously evolving research program that has accomplished some key objectives and is moving on to additional objectives.

A strong effort was made to ground the conditional reasoning measurement system in a rational psychological theory. However, additional theorizing is desired on a number of fronts, followed by empirical tests. Models are needed that specify how justification mechanisms arise and where justification mechanisms fit in cognitive networks that include other types of implicit cognitions (e.g., implicit motives; cf. Greenwald & Banaji, 1995). Theorizing and research are also needed on the processes by which justification mechanisms affect the cognitive operations involved in framing and analyses. Theories are also desired regarding alternative, indirect ways to measure justification mechanisms so that tests of convergent validity may be conducted. The CRT–A also needs to be investigated in populations other than work and academic settings.

The idea that implicit cognitions may improve on the often modest empirical validities engendered by explicit cognitions is noteworthy (Hurtz & Donovan, 2000). However, considerable theoretical and empirical effort is needed to delve further into the relationship between implicit cognitions and explicit cognitions. A potentially fruitful direction for this undertaking is the "channeling hypothesis" proposed by Winter et al. (1998), wherein conscious cognitions (measured with self-reports) direct the manifestations of implicit cognitions (measured with the Thematic Apperception Test; Morgan & Murray, 1935). In that model, the two sets of cognitions interact to predict behavior. The focus is on integrating power and affiliation motives with the trait of extraversion. Similar research conducted by Bing, Burroughs, Davison, Green, McIntyre, and James (2004) replicated these results using an integrative model focusing on aggression that blends conscious cognitions (measured with self-reports such as Jackson's Personality Research Form [PRF; Jackson, 1984] and Hogan's Personality Inventory [HPI; Hogan & Hogan, 1995]) and implicit cognitions (measured with James's CRT–A). Empirical tests of the integrative model were conducted with data from laboratory, university, and organizational settings using criteria such as dishonesty and peer ratings of workplace deviance. Results demonstrate that the validity of self-reported aggression is often dependent on the nature of the latent motive as assessed via the conditional reasoning test and that an integration of these methodologies may be more advantageous than either one used alone. Such information may provide assistance in making more informed personnel selection decisions and better predictions of counterproductive work behaviors.

One final question to ask for all of the research conducted heretofore on conditional reasoning has been, "Does it work?" It appears that this question can be answered affirmatively, so now it is sensible to design research that addresses this issue. Establishing limits of generalizability is therefore a reasonable objective for future research.

In closing, Greenwald and Banaji (1995) encouraged investigators to develop efficient, indirect approaches to measure implicit social cognitions. James and colleagues have attempted to construct such an approach. It is hoped that this chapter stimulates others to consider research on implicit social cognitions and indirect measurement systems, particularly researchers attempting to identify and understand reasons for counterproductive workplace behaviors that waste a tremendous amount of both financial and human resources. One of the many ways to contribute to this mission is to use a new and unique measurement system that enhances our capability to predict whether a person will act in a counterproductive manner.

REFERENCES

Allport, G. W. (1937). *Personality: A psychological interpretation*. New York: Holt.

Anderson, E. (1994, May). The code of the streets. *Atlantic Monthly*, 81–94.

Aquino, K., Lewis, M. U., & Bradfield, M. (1999). Justice constructs, negative affectivity, and employee deviance: A proposed model and empirical test. *Journal of Organizational Behavior, 20*, 1073–1091.

Atkinson, J. W. (1978). The mainsprings of achievement-oriented activity. In J. W. Atkinson & J. O. Raynor (Eds.), *Personality, motivation, and achievement* (pp. 11–39). Washington, DC: Hemisphere.

Averill, J. R. (1993). Illusions of anger. In R. B. Felson & J. T. Tedeschi (Eds.), *Aggression and violence: Social interactionist perspectives* (pp. 171–192). Washington, DC: American Psychological Association.

Bandura, A. (1973). *Aggression: A social learning analysis*. New York: Prentice-Hall.

Baron, R. A., & Richardson, D. R. (1994). *Human aggression* (2nd ed.). New York: Plenum Press.

Barrick, M. R., & Mount, M. K. (1991). The big five personality dimensions and job performance: A meta-analysis. *Personnel Psychology, 44,* 1–26.

Baumeister, R. F. (1982). A self-presentational view of social phenomena. *Psychological Bulletin, 91,* 3–26.

Baumeister, R. F., & Scher, S. J. (1988). Self-defeating behavior patterns among normal individuals: Review and analysis of common self-destructive tendencies. *Psychological Bulletin, 104,* 3–22.

Baumeister, R. F., Smart, L., & Boden, J. M. (1996). Relation of threatened egotism to violence and aggression: The dark side of self-esteem. *Psychological Review, 103,* 5–33.

Berkowitz, L. (1993). *Aggression: Its causes, consequences, and control.* New York: McGraw-Hill.

Bies, R. J., Shapiro, D. L., & Cummings, L. L. (1988). Voice and justification: Their influence on procedural fairness judgments. *Academy of Management Journal, 31,* 676–685.

Bies, R. J., & Tripp, T. M. (1998). Revenge in organizations: The good, the bad, and the ugly. In R. W. Griffin, A. O'Leary-Kelly, & J. M. Collins (Eds.), *Dysfunctional behavior in organizations: Violent and deviant behavior* (pp. 221–239). Stamford, CT: JAI Press.

Bies, R. J., Tripp, T. M., & Kramer, R. M. (1997). At the breaking point: Cognitive and social dynamics of revenge in organizations. In R. A. Giacalone & J. Greenberg (Eds.), *Antisocial behavior in organizations* (pp. 18–36). Thousand Oaks, CA: Sage.

Bing, M. N., Burroughs, S. M., Davison, H. K., Green, P. D., McIntyre, M. D., & James, L. R. (2004). *The integrative model of personality assessment for aggression: Implications for personnel selection and predicting counterproductive workplace behavior.* Manuscript submitted for publication.

Borum, R. (1996). Improving the clinical practice of violence risk assessment: Technology, guidelines, and training. *American Psychologist, 51,* 945–956.

Bradbury, T. N., & Finchum, F. D. (1990). Attributions in marriage: Review and critique. *Psychological Bulletin, 107,* 3–33.

Brewin, C. R. (1989). Cognitive change processes in psychotherapy. *Psychological Review, 96,* 379–394.

Burroughs, S. M. (2001). *The role of dispositional aggressiveness and organizational injustice on deviant workplace behavior.* Unpublished doctoral dissertation, University of Tennessee, Knoxville.

Burroughs, S. M., Bing, M. N., & James, L. R. (1999, April). Reconsidering how to measure employee reliability: An empirical comparison of self-report and conditional reasoning methodologies. In S. Burroughs & L. Williams (Chairs), *New developments using conditional reasoning to measure human reliability.*

Symposium presented at the annual conference of the Society for Industrial and Organizational Psychology, Atlanta, GA.

Burroughs, S. M., LeBreton, J. M., Bing, M. N., & James, L. R. (2000, April). *Validity evidence for the conditional reasoning test of employee aggression.* Paper presented at the annual conference of the Society for Industrial and Organizational Psychology, New Orleans, LA.

Buss, A. H. (1961). *The psychology of aggression.* New York: Wiley.

Buss, A. H., & Perry, M. (1992). The aggression questionnaire. *Journal of Personality and Social Psychology, 63,* 452–459.

Crick, N. R., & Dodge, K. A. (1994). A review and reformation of social information-processing mechanisms in children's social adjustment. *Psychological Bulletin, 115,* 74–101.

Dodge, K. A. (1986). A social information processing model of social competence in children. In M. Perlmutter (Ed.), *The Minnesota Symposium on Child Psychology, 18,* 77–125. Hillsdale, NJ: Erlbaum.

Dodge, K. A., & Coie, J. D. (1987). Social information-processing factors in reactive and proactive aggression in children's play groups. *Journal of Personality and Social Psychology, 53,* 1146–1158.

Dwight, S. A., & Alliger, G. M. (1997). Reactions to overt integrity test items. *Educational and Psychological Measurement, 57*(6), 937–948.

Epstein, S. (1994). Integration of the cognitive and the psychodynamic unconscious. *American Psychologist, 49,* 709–724.

Erdelyi, M. H. (1992). Psychodynamics and the unconscious. *American Psychologist, 47,* 784–787.

Felson, R. B., & Tedeschi, J. T. (1993). *Aggression and violence: Social interactionist perspectives.* Washington, DC: American Psychological Association.

Finnegan, W. (1997, December 1). The unwanted. *New Yorker, 73,* 60–78.

Fiske, S. T., & Taylor, S. E. (1984). *Social cognition.* Reading, MA: Addison-Wesley.

Fiske, S. T., & Taylor, S. E. (1991). *Social cognition* (2nd ed.). New York: McGraw-Hill.

Gay, P. (1993). *The cultivation of hatred.* New York: W. W. Norton.

Geen, R. G. (1995). Human aggression. In A. Tesser (Ed.), *Advanced social psychology* (pp. 383–417). New York: McGraw-Hill.

Gottfredson, M. R., & Hirschi, T. (1993). A control theory interpretation of psychological research on aggression. In R. B. Felson & J. T. Tedeschi (Eds.), *Aggression and violence: Social interactionist perspectives* (pp. 47–68). Washington, DC: American Psychological Association.

Green, P. D., & James, L. R. (1999, April). The use of conditional reasoning to predict deceptive behavior. In S. Burroughs & L. Williams (Chairs), *New developments using conditional reasoning to measure human reliability.* Symposium presented at the annual conference of the Society for Industrial and Organizational Psychology, Atlanta, GA.

Greenwald, A. G., & Banaji, M. R. (1995). Implicit social cognition: Attitudes, self-esteem, and stereotypes. *Psychological Review, 102*, 4–27.

Grisso, T., & Tomkins, A. J. (1996). Communicating violence risk assessments. *American Psychologist, 51*, 928–930.

Hammock, G. S., & Richardson, D. R. (1992). Predictors of aggressive behavior. *Aggressive Behavior, 18*, 219–229.

Heneman, H. G., Heneman, R. L., & Judge, T. A. (1997). *Staffing organizations*. Madison, WI: Mendota House/Irwin.

Hogan, R. (1991). Personality and personality measurement. In M. D. Dunnette & L. M. Hough (Eds.), *Handbook of industrial and organizational psychology* (Vol. 2, pp. 327–396). Palo Alto, CA: Consulting Psychologists Press.

Hogan, J., & Hogan, R. (1989). How to measure employee reliability. *Journal of Applied Psychology, 74*, 273–279.

Hogan, R., & Hogan, J. (1995). *Hogan Personality Inventory manual*. Tulsa, OK: Hogan Assessment Systems.

Huesmann, L. R. (1988). An information processing model for the development of aggression. *Aggressive Behavior, 14*, 13–24.

Hurtz, G. M., & Donovan, J. J. (2000). Personality and job performance: The Big Five revisited. *Journal of Applied Psychology, 85*, 869–879.

Jackson, D. N. (1984). *Personality Research Form manual* (3rd ed.). Port Huron, MI: Research Psychologists Press.

James, L. R. (1998). Measurement of personality via conditional reasoning. *Organizational Research Methods, 1*(2), 131–163.

James, L. R., & Mazerolle, M. D. (2002). *Personality in work organizations*. New York: Sage.

James, L. R., McIntyre, M. D., Glisson, C. A., Green, P. D., Patton, T. W., LeBreton, J. M., et al. (2004). *Conditional reasoning: An efficient, indirect method for assessing implicit cognitive readiness to aggress*. Manuscript submitted for publication.

Kihlstrom, J. F. (1999). The psychological unconscious. In L. A. Pervin & O. P. John (Eds.), *Handbook of personality: Theory and research* (pp. 424–442). New York: Guilford Press.

Kroger, R. O., & Wood, L. A. (1993). Reification, "faking," and the big five. *American Psychologist, 48*, 1297–1298.

Laursen, B., & Collins, W. A. (1994). Interpersonal conflict during adolescence. *Psychological Bulletin, 115*, 197–209.

Loeber, R., & Stouthhamer-Loeber, M. (1998). Development of juvenile aggression and violence: Some misconceptions and controversies. *American Psychologist, 53*, 242–259.

McClelland, D. C. (1985). *Human motivation*. Glenview, IL: Scott, Foresman.

McClelland, D. C., Koestner, R., & Weinberger, J. (1989). How do self-attributed and implicit motives differ? *Psychological Review, 96*, 690–702.

McIntyre, M. D. (1995). *A feasibility study of a conditional reasoning measure of aggressiveness and prosociability*. Unpublished doctoral dissertation, University of Tennessee, Knoxville.

Miller, S. M. (1987). Monitoring and blunting: Validation of a questionnaire to assess styles of information seeking under threat. *Journal of Personality and Social Psychology, 52*, 345–353.

Millon, T. (1990). The disorders of personality. In L. A. Pervin (Ed.), *Handbook of personality: Theory and research* (pp. 339–370). New York: Guilford Press.

Mischel, W. (1968). *Personality and assessment*. New York: Wiley.

Monahan, J. (1981). *The clinical prediction of violent behavior*. Rockville, MD: National Institute of Mental Health.

Monahan, J., & Steadman, H. J. (1996). Violent storms and violent people: How meteorology can inform risk communication in mental health law. *American Psychologist, 51*, 931–938.

Moore, R. W., & Stewart, R. M. (1989). Evaluating employee integrity: Moral and methodological problems. *Employee Responsibilities and Rights Journal, 2*, 203–215.

Morgan, C. D., & Murray, H. A. (1935). A method for examining fantasies: The Thematic Apperception Test. *Archives of Neurology and Psychiatry, 34*, 289–306.

Murray, H. A. (1938). *Explorations in personality*. New York: Oxford University Press.

Nisbett, R. E. (1993). Violence and U.S. regional culture. *American Psychologist, 48*, 441–449.

Nisbett, R. E., & Wilson, T. D. (1977). Telling more than we can know: Verbal reports on mental processes. *Psychological Review, 84*, 231–259.

O'Leary-Kelly, A. M., Griffin, R. W., & Glew, D. J. (1996). Organization-motivated aggression: A research framework. *Academy of Management Review, 21*, 225–253.

Pyszczynski, T., & Greenberg, J. (1987). Toward an integration of cognitive and motivational perspectives on social influence: A biased hypothesis-testing model. *Advances in Experimental Social Psychology, 20*, 297–339.

Ross, L. (1977). The intuitive psychologist and his shortcomings: Distortions in the attribution process. In L. Berkowitz (Ed.)., *Advances in experimental and social psychology*. New York: Academic Press.

Rosse, J. G., Stecher, M. D., Miller, J. L., & Levin, R. A. (1998). The impact of response distortion on preemployment personality testing and hiring decisions. *Journal of Applied Psychology, 83*, 634–644.

Schmitt, N. (1994). Method bias: The importance of theory and measurement. *Journal of Organizational Behavior, 15*(5), 393–398.

Schneider, D. J. (1991). Social cognition. *Annual Review of Psychology, 42*, 527–561.

Schoop, R. F. (1996). Communicating risk assessments: Accuracy, efficacy, and responsibility. *American Psychologist, 51*, 939–944.

Schwarz, N. (1999). Self-reports: How the questions shape the answers. *American Psychologist, 54,* 93–105.

Skarlicki, D. P., Folger, R., & Tesluk, P. (1999). Personality as a moderator in the relationship between fairness and retaliation. *Academy of Management Journal, 42,* 100–108.

Spector, P. E. (1994). Using self-report questionnaires in OB research: A comment on the use of a controversial method. *Journal of Organizational Behavior, 15*(5), 385–392.

Stone, E. F., & Stone, D. L. (1990). Privacy in organizations: Theoretical issues, research findings, and protection mechanisms. *Research in Personnel and Human Resource Management, 8,* 349–411.

Sutherland, K. M., & Flin, R. H. (1989). Stress at sea: A review of working conditions in the offshore oil and fishing industries. *Work and Stress, 3,* 269–285.

Taylor, S. E. (1991). Asymmetrical effects of positive and negative events: The mobilization minimization hypothesis. *Psychological Bulletin, 110,* 67–85.

Tedeschi, J. T., & Nesler, M. S. (1993). Grievances: Development and reactions. In R. B. Felson & J. T. Tedeschi (Eds.), *Aggression and violence: Social interactionist perspectives* (pp. 13–46). Washington, DC: American Psychological Association.

Tett, R. P., Jackson, D. N., & Rothstein, M. (1991). Personality measures as predictors of job performance: A meta-analytic review. *Personnel Psychology, 44,* 703–742.

Toch, H. (1993). Good violence and bad violence: Self-presentations of aggressors through accounts and war stories. In R. B. Felson & J. T. Tedeschi (Eds.), *Aggression and violence: Social interactionist perspectives* (pp. 193–206). Washington, DC: American Psychological Association.

U.S. Department of Justice. (1994, June 19). *Concern about neighborhood crime doubles among Black households.* Washington, DC: Author.

Warr, M. (1987). Fear of victimization and sensitivity to risk. *Journal of Quantitative Criminology, 3,* 29–46.

Watson, D., & Clark, L. (1984). Negative affectivity: The disposition to experience aversive emotional states. *Psychological Bulletin, 96,* 465–490.

Wegner, D. M., & Vallacher, R. R. (1977). *Implicit psychology: An introduction to social cognition.* New York: Oxford University Press.

Westen, D. (1990). Psychoanalytic approaches to personality. In L. A. Pervin (Ed.), *Handbook of personality: Theory and research* (pp. 21–65). New York: Guilford Press.

Westen, D. (1991). Social cognition and object relations. *Psychological Bulletin, 109,* 429–455.

Westen, D. (1998). The scientific legacy of Sigmund Freud: Toward a psychodynamically informed psychological science. *Psychological Bulletin, 124,* 333–371.

Winter, D. G., John, O. P., Stewart, A. J., Klohnen, E. C., & Duncan, L. E. (1998). Traits and motives: Toward an integration of two traditions in personality research. *Psychological Review, 105*, 230–250.

Wright, J. C., & Mischel, W. (1987). A conditional approach to dispositional constructs: The local predictability of social behavior. *Journal of Personality and Social Psychology, 53*, 1159–1177.

7

THE STRESSOR–EMOTION MODEL OF COUNTERPRODUCTIVE WORK BEHAVIOR

PAUL E. SPECTOR AND SUZY FOX

Although most research on workplace behavior has focused on factors that lead to effective employee functioning, ineffective and even destructive actions are ubiquitous in the modern work organization. Counterproductive work behavior (CWB) consists of volitional acts that harm or are intended to harm organizations or people in organizations. Included are acts of aggression, hostility, sabotage, theft, and withdrawal. These behaviors can arise from a number of precipitating conditions in the perpetrator and situation. In this chapter we discuss a model of CWB as the joint result of personality and stressful job conditions. It complements the other chapters in this book that either focus on other underlying mechanisms or provide alternative theoretical explanations.

NATURE OF COUNTERPRODUCTIVE WORK BEHAVIOR AND RELATED CONCEPTS

CWB consists of volitional acts that harm or intend to harm organizations and their stakeholders (e.g., clients, coworkers, customers, and supervisors). Specific CWBs include abusive behavior against others, aggression (both physical and verbal), purposely doing work incorrectly, sabotage, theft, and withdrawal (e.g., absence, lateness, and turnover). The key characteristic of CWB is that the action itself must be purposeful and not accidental—that is, the employee makes a choice or decision to behave in such a way that is either intended specifically to harm or harms by purposeful action even if unintentionally. Poor performance that is unintended (e.g., an employee tries but has insufficient skill to successfully complete job tasks) is not CWB because the purpose of the employee was not to perform the job incorrectly. If there is not an attempt to perform poorly, and the harm to the organization is not a result of purposeful action on the part of the employee, then the action is not CWB. Likewise, workplace accidents that occur despite the employee's efforts to follow accepted safe procedures are not included, even though they may cause harm. To qualify as CWB, the employee must purposely avoid using safe equipment or procedures, thus behaving in a reckless manner that results in injury, even though the injury itself was not desired. Alternately, the individual might engage in the behavior for the specific purpose of causing harm—for example, to damage equipment.

These two distinct motive states for CWB (volition of behavior versus intentionality of harmful outcome) are important in understanding the underlying processes. Much of the CWB research derived from the human aggression literature has tended to focus on intentional harm, which is often associated with anger and other negative emotions. Unintentional harm CWB involves acts in which the behavior was intentional but the harm was incidental. Theft, for example, can often be motivated purely by the desire for the stolen object and not by desire to harm others. In fact the perpetrator may rationalize the action by assuming the organization is wealthy and will not miss the stolen item or that the stolen item is no longer needed. A potential limitation to the CWB literature is that in most studies participants are asked whether or not they committed certain acts without collecting additional information about their motives. A consideration of motives will help inform a more thorough understanding of underlying processes leading to CWB.

Our definition is not unlike Sackett's (2002), who defines CWB as behavior that runs counter to an organization's legitimate interests. Unlike Sackett, we do not define CWB purely from the perspective of the organization as the entity that is harmed. We also extend the harm to employees, customers, and other stakeholders. Of course, if a stakeholder is harmed it is likely the organization is harmed as well. However, there could be instances in which an employee does something hurtful to a coworker or customer that has no adverse effect on the organization.

CWB is a general term that overlaps a number of related but distinct constructs. It is perhaps most similar to the idea of workplace aggression (Neuman & Baron, 1997, 1998; O'Leary-Kelly, Griffin, & Glew, 1996; Spector, 1975, 1978), which is defined as behavior intended to harm organizations or people in organizations. The distinction is that CWB does not require specific intent to harm but only that behavior was intentional. However, aggression consists of behaviors that we classify as CWB; for example, Neuman and Baron (1998) included the same behaviors we list as CWB under the categories of hostility, obstructionism, and overt aggression.

Violence is a term used to refer to some forms of aggression, and depending on the definition it can be synonymous. A narrow definition includes only physical acts of violence that are classified as crimes—that is, homicide, rape, robbery, and assault (Bulatao & VandenBos, 1996; LeBlanc & Kelloway, 2002). Robbery may be violence but it is not necessarily aggression, because in most robberies the victim is not physically harmed, but merely threatened. Others have distinguished physical from psychological violence, such as verbally abusive actions (Barling, 1996). In either case, definitions of violence may or may not involve intentions to harm but merely define the act in terms of its nature and result. It is narrower than CWB in focusing specifically on harm to people. It should also be noted that it is possible to commit unsuccessful violence that is still violence. Shooting a gun at someone and missing would still be considered a violent act even if no physical harm were done.

Retaliation is behavior in response to perceived organizational injustice that is intended to punish the party or parties perceived as the cause (Skarlicki & Folger, 1997). Like aggression, it is volitional behavior intended to harm, but the construct assumes an underlying motive to restore equity and justice, making this a special case of aggression. Most acts of retaliation as described by Skarlicki and Folger (1997) are subsumed under CWB; however, the latter term does not assume that the behavior is necessarily in response to injustice, although in many cases it may be.

Revenge (Bies, Tripp, & Kramer, 1997) consists of actions against perceived agents of harm or violation of social order. This can occur not only in response to injustice (retaliation) but in response to other events that cause harm. Furthermore, these actions can consist of acts generally agreed to be aggressive or otherwise counterproductive, but they can also consist of constructive action. Bies et al. (1997) have written about revenge as sometimes serving a positive social function of helping to regulate interpersonal behavior. The threat of revenge can inhibit CWB and other negative behaviors directed toward individuals who are perceived capable of striking back. Revenge overlaps with CWB in the extent to which it involves counterproductive acts, but it can involve other acts that might not be harmful to individuals or organizations. Rather, it involves a demonstration of power that can have positive social regulatory functions.

Deviance is volitional behavior that violates organizational norms and causes harm to the organization or its employees (Hollinger, 1986; Robinson & Bennett, 1995). The norms are those defined by the dominant management of organizations and are prescribed by both formal and informal policies, rules, and standards. Although deviance includes many behaviors considered CWB, it excludes behaviors that may harm but are normative. For example, in organizations in which abusive supervisory behavior is normative, such acts would not be considered deviance, although they would be CWB if they are harmful. Conversely, resistance to abusive supervisory behavior or unfair incentive practices would be considered deviant relative to organizational norms but perhaps not relative to work group (or societal) norms, and to the extent that such actions result in positive change, they might arguably *not* be considered counterproductive. Deviance is distinct from aggression, retaliation, and revenge in that there is no specification of underlying motive for the behavior—for example, causing harm (aggression and retaliation) or restoring social order (revenge).

An important distinction made by Robinson and Bennett (1995) is deviance directed toward organizations versus people. Although not every act can be clearly distinguished (stealing a coworker's laptop that is company property), many are directed specifically at one or the other (breaking one's own company laptop vs. hitting a coworker). Revenge, retaliation, and violence might most often be directed toward people, but it is possible to direct such behavior indirectly toward objects. For example, an employee might retaliate against a supervisor by doing work incorrectly. Aggression can be considered narrowly as directed against people or more broadly as directed toward organizations (e.g., Spector, 1978). CWB includes acts directed at both organizations and people.

The foregoing conceptualizations of deviance and revenge also serve as a reminder that power and politics in organizational life may play a nontrivial role in what becomes defined as counterproductive, as in the cases of whistle-blowing, labor actions, resistance to unfair or oppressive treatment, or organizing for change. What might be counterproductive from the organization's point of view (filing a grievance over unfair treatment) may be productive for the individual, and likewise, what may be counterproductive for the individual (being treated unfairly and not complaining) can benefit the organization.

Similarly, we might be remiss in declaring certain behaviors to be counterproductive, deviant, or retaliatory when they actually represent choices a "reasonable person" might accept in navigating conflicting roles and responsibilities. For example, some scales measuring CWB (Bennett & Robinson, 2000; Skarlicki & Folger, 1997) include spending time on personal matters while at work. In many cases, not doing so would be counterproductive, deviant, or antisocial from the point of view of an employee's family responsibilities and societal expectations.

So far we have discussed various CWB-related concepts that focus on the actor, but there exist four parallel concepts in which research has focused mainly on the recipient of the behavior. All four involve interpersonal acts done to one or more recipients that are harmful in some way. These acts range from quite mild forms of rudeness to physical aggression. These lines of research have tended to explore the effects of these acts on recipients, as well as recipient characteristics that are associated with being targeted.

The mildest of these concepts is incivility, which involves relatively mild forms of interpersonal behavior with ambiguous intent to cause harm (Andersson & Pearson, 1999). This includes insensitive and rude behavior, largely but not entirely verbal, that can be hurtful but is not necessarily intended to be so. Recipients and even at times actors will often deny the intent, saying that the comment was misinterpreted or was unintentional. The actor might say he or she did not realize the comment would be hurtful. Andersson and Pearson (1999) clearly distinguish incivility from other related constructs. They noted that incivility can include mild forms of aggressive behavior. They do not link incivility to actor motives or to norms, although they state that some incivility might be considered mild forms of organizational deviance.

Emotional abuse (Keashley, 1998), bullying (Hoel, Rayner, & Cooper, 1999) and mobbing (Zapf, Knorz, & Kulla, 1996) are closely related concepts that all involve harmful, mainly nonphysical behaviors that occur between an actor and recipient over a period of time. They fit our definition of CWB in that they are volitional acts that harm. Although for the most part, these various concepts concern the same sorts of acts, there are some subtle distinctions at least in definitions. For example, emotional abuse assumes an intent to harm (Keashley, 1998), whereas bullying does not (Hoel et al., 1999). Mobbing has focused in part on groups of actors targeting a single recipient (Zapf et al., 1996), the other two forms are concerned with acts of single actors, although bullying can involve multiple targets.

We feel that most research on the various constructs discussed previously is linked by the study of an overlapping set of behaviors. The underlying conceptions and definitions are clearly different, and the same acts can be considered from a variety of perspectives. Thus insulting a coworker can be an instance of aggression (verbal), bullying, deviance, emotional abuse, incivility, mobbing, retaliation, or revenge, and can be classified as CWB as well. Keep in mind that depending on the definition, contextual factors can be important, such as actor intent or duration and frequency of the behaviors. An inspection of the specific behaviors listed by various researchers shows a great deal of overlap, with most including items dealing with abusive and aggressive acts toward others. Those concerned with the actor also include damaging or dirtying the workplace, doing work incorrectly, not working when one is supposed to, and stealing. Table 7.1 lists examples of similar items from Bennett and Robinson's (2000) scale of deviance, Fox and Spector's (1999) scale of aggression, and Skarlicki and Folger's (1997) scale of retaliation. Studies of these various concepts can inform one another, and they each have contributed to our understanding of this class of behaviors, although they may be based on different theoretical foundations.

THE STRESSOR–EMOTION MODEL
OF COUNTERPRODUCTIVE WORK BEHAVIOR

Our stressor–emotion model of CWB is based on integrating human aggression and occupational stress. Most theories and models of human aggression have linked it to anger or frustration (e.g., Anderson, Deuser, & DeNeve, 1995; Berkowitz, 1989; Dollard, Doob, Miller, Mowrer, & Sears, 1939; Neuman & Baron, 1997). The seminal work of Dollard et al.'s (1939) frustration–aggression hypothesis provided the foundation for much of modern aggression work. Their model suggested that frustration, the interference with a person's goals or ongoing activity, would lead to aggression. Later work in the organizational arena (Fox & Spector, 1999) has looked at the connection between frustration as an environmental condition (i.e., interference), emotional reactions to such conditions (usually anger), cognitive elements, and aggression. It suggests that many human aggressive acts are in response to provocation that induces anger. Often it occurs in retribution for actions taken by another person that are seen as harmful or unjustified.

An important cognitive element in responses to environmental frustration (interference with goals) is the attributions made by the person concerning the intent of the agent of their frustration. Pastore (1952) noted that acts perceived as arbitrary and purposefully frustrating result in more aggressive response than acts seen as accidental or unintentional. Whether one conceptualizes the instigation of aggression to require frustration or not, the intent of the provoking agent can be more important than the objective nature of the situation itself (Greenwell & Dengerink, 1973). Folger and Baron (1996) tied this idea to responses to injustice. They argued that aggression is a response to aversive or unpleasant emotional states and that intentional acts induce more negative emotions. Situations that are perceived of as intentionally unfair or unwarranted induce high levels of negative emotions and therefore are more likely to lead to aggressive responses.

TABLE 7.1
Examples of Similar Items From Scales That Assess Aggression, Deviance, and Retaliation

Aggression	Deviance	Retaliation
Been nasty to a coworker	Acted rudely toward someone at work	Gave a coworker the "silent treatment"
Stolen something from work	Taken property from work without permission	Took supplies home without permission
Purposely littered or dirtied your place of work or your employer's property	Littered your work environment	Left a mess unnecessarily
Started or continued a damaging or harmful rumor at work	Repeated a rumor or gossip about your boss or coworkers	Spread rumors about coworkers
Told people outside the job what a lousy place you work at	Told someone about the lousy place where you work	Spoke poorly about the company to others
Purposely did not work hard when there were things to be done	Intentionally worked slower than you could have worked	Intentionally worked slower
Stayed home from work and said you were sick when you were not	Called in sick when you were not	Called in sick when not ill
Purposely ignored your boss	Neglected to follow your boss's instructions	Disobeyed a supervisor's instructions
Purposely came to work or came back from lunch breaks late	Taken an additional or longer break than is acceptable at your workplace	Took an extended coffee or lunch break
	Came in late to work without permission	
Withheld work-related information from a coworker		Failed to give coworker required information
Tried to cheat your employer	Falsified a receipt to get reimbursed for more money than you spent on business expenses	
	Worked on a personal matter instead of work for your employer	Spent time on personal matters while at work

Note. Aggression data are from Fox and Spector (1999) Table 5; deviance data are from Bennett and Robinson (2000) Table 2; retaliation data are from Skarlicki and Folger (1997) Table 1.

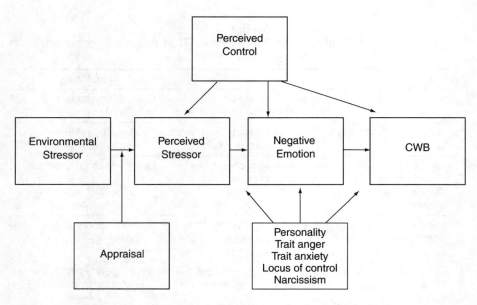

Figure 7.1. Stressor–emotion model of counterproductive work behavior.

Our model builds on these basic ideas. However, we include far more than interference with goals as precipitating conditions that induce negative emotion. First, stressful job conditions that do not necessarily involve interference with goals can induce negative emotions as well. Second, it is not only anger that is associated with CWB but many forms of negative emotions. Third, control is an important element of the model. Fourth, personality is a vitally important element in CWB. Given the same conditions, not all individuals will respond in the same manner.

Figure 7.1 illustrates the stressor–emotion model, showing a causal flow from the environment to perception–appraisal of the environment to emotion to behavior. Perceived control is an important moderator of both perceptions and behavioral reactions. Personality plays a role in perceptions, emotional responsiveness, and behavior. It should be kept in mind that we do not suggest that this model represents the only possible causal flows but merely it indicates some critical links in the CWB process. It should be recognized that causality likely runs in many directions. For example, CWB has effects on the environment and may well make it more stressful. Emotional state at a point in time will affect how a person perceives and appraises a situation. Thus an environmental event encountered while in a negative emotional state will be more likely to be perceived as a stressor than when in a positive emotional state. Even personality itself can be the effect as well as cause—for example after continued exposure to extreme emotion-arousing events (see Spector, Zapf, Chen, & Frese, 2000).

At the heart of the stressor–emotion model is the connection from the environment to perceptions, to emotions, and then to CWB. The CWB process begins at the left with job stressors. A stressor is an environmental condition that induces a negative emotional reaction (Spector, 1998). It is important to distinguish an environmental stressor from a perceived stressor. The environmental stressor is an objective feature of the workplace that tends to be perceived as a stressor by people. There are both intrapersonal temporal differences and interpersonal differences in how given situations are interpreted. Thus there is a less than perfect relationship between environmental and perceived stressors. In terms of the model, it is the perceived stressor that is most critical (Perrewé & Zellars, 1999) because it leads to emotional reactions and CWB. However, this is not to say that the environmental stressor is unimportant, and in fact the underlying processes linking objective reality to perceptions and emotional responses is a vital issue for research (Frese & Zapf, 1999; Schaubroeck, 1999).

It is presumed that people, whether at work or not, monitor their environments. Stimuli and information is continually perceived and interpreted. It is the appraisal process (Lazarus & Folkman, 1984) by which people interpret situations as stressors. Important elements include the extent to which the individual perceives a threat to well-being, the degree to which a situation might interfere with goals or ongoing activity, and the individual's attributions about the causes of events. Perrewé and Zellars (1999) discussed how specific attributions can lead to various negative emotions. For example, failure to perform a task properly can lead to guilt if the individual attributes the cause to his or her own lack of effort or anger if the failure is attributed to the supervisor's unreasonable demands. Martinko, Gundlach, and Douglas (2002) have discussed in detail the role of attributions in CWB, arguing that it is a fundamental element in most theories.

Although appraisal is a highly individual process, there are classes of events and situations that can be considered objective stressors because they tend to be perceived as stressors by a large proportion of people and because there is a level of consensus among people in reporting them. For example, Frese (1985) compared incumbents' reports of composite job stressors with both observers and peers, finding convergence ranging from .30 to .61. Kirmeyer (1988) reported a correlation of .59 between objective and incumbent measures of workload. Spector (1992) conducted a meta-analysis of convergence studies, comparing incumbents with other sources of data on stressors. Mean correlations ranged from .11 (role ambiguity) to .42 (workload).

Perceived stressors have been shown to relate to specific negative emotions. In a meta-analysis, Spector and Goh (2001) showed that anger and anxiety both related to a variety of perceived job stressors, with mean correlations ranging from .29 (anxiety and role conflict) to .49 (anger and organizational constraints). Fox, Spector, and Miles (2001) found that job stressors (conflicts with others and interpersonal constraints) were related to a composite measure of negative emotions. This emotion measure was also related to perceptions of injustice, which they also considered a type of job stressor.

STUDIES LINKING STRESSORS TO COUNTERPRODUCTIVE WORK BEHAVIOR

Some of our early work on CWB was based on the human aggression literature that tied behavior to frustration. Spector (1975) showed that frustration at work related to self-reported CWB. Storms and Spector (1987) showed that CWB was significantly related to a measure of organizational constraints that consisted of work conditions that interfered with job performance. A self-report measure of constraints correlated significantly with self-reports of several categories of CWB, including aggression (.36), hostility and complaining (.47), sabotage (.29), and withdrawal (.36), as well as with feelings of frustration (.55), which showed similar relations with CWB.

Later work expanded the range of theoretical precipitating conditions to stressful job conditions in general. Chen and Spector (1992) in a similar study included measures of role ambiguity, role conflict, interpersonal conflict, and workload along with organizational constraints. All five correlated significantly with hostility, and all but workload correlated significantly with aggression and sabotage. Subsequent studies have continued to find linkages between a variety of job stressors and CWB, although more recent studies have either used an overall measure of CWB (Miles, Borman, Spector, & Fox, 2002; Penney & Spector, 2002, 2003) or have classified the behaviors according to the Robinson and Bennett (1995) categories of organization versus person target (Fox & Spector, 1999; Fox et al., 2001; Goh, Bruursema, Fox, & Spector, 2003).

These six studies have investigated three stressors, two of which have been consistently associated with CWB. Organizational constraints have been assessed in all six and have been shown to consistently correlate with CWB when all variables were self-reported (ranging from $rs = .26$ for personal CWB to .48 for total CWB). Four of these studies included interpersonal conflict, finding significant correlations in all but one case (Goh et al., 2003, for organizational CWB) ranging from .19 (overall CWB) to .40 (personal CWB). In both Fox et al. (2001) and Goh et al. (2003), personal CWB correlated more strongly than organizational CWB with interpersonal conflict. This suggests that people's responses to conflict are more likely to target people than organizations. However, it is possible that the interpersonal conflict scale and CWB scale were picking up some of the same behaviors and incidents. For workload, Miles et al. (2002) found a significant correlation of .21 for overall CWB, but Goh et al. (2003) were unable to replicate it.

Using a different approach, Glomb (2002) interviewed employees about their experiences with personal CWB incidents at work. A content analysis showed that the most frequent antecedent of an aggressive encounter was a work stressor. Others included perceived injustice, perceived threats, and interpersonal conflicts both over job-related and personal matters. These results are consistent with our studies using quantitative scales.

A number of studies have linked CWB to injustice, although results have been somewhat inconsistent, especially for distributive justice. Looking at personal CWB, some studies have found a significant correlation (e.g., Aquino, Lewis, & Bradfield, 1999; Skarlicki & Folger, 1997), but others have not (e.g., Bennett & Robinson, 2000; Fox et al., 2001). Greenberg and Barling (1999) showed that the target of the CWB may be critical. They found that CWB directed toward supervisors related to distributive justice, but CWB targeting coworkers or subordinates did not. Results of distributive justice with organizational CWB have tended to be nonsignificant (Aquino et al. 1999; Bennett & Robinson, 2000; Fox et al., 2001). Results with procedural justice have been somewhat more consistent. Significant correlations were found with personal CWB in most (Aquino et al., 1999; Bennett & Robinson, 2000; Skarlicki & Folger, 1997) but not all (Fox et al., 2001) studies. With organizational CWB, Bennett and Robinson (2000) and Fox et al. (2001) found significant correlations, but Aquino et al. (1999) did not. Consistent significant findings have been published for interpersonal justice (Aquino et al., 1999; Bennett & Robinson, 2000; Skarlicki & Folger, 1997).

Taken as a whole, these studies support the idea that CWB can be a response to job stressors and other conditions that induce negative emotions. The number of such conditions studied has been rather limited, but they show that interpersonal conflict, organizational constraints, role ambiguity, role conflict, and perhaps workload are important. Injustice is also potentially important, although correlations with CWB tend to be more variable, suggesting that there might be additional moderating factors that may help determine when injustice leads to CWB and when it does not.

RELATIONS OF COUNTERPRODUCTIVE WORK BEHAVIOR WITH EMOTIONS AND JOB SATISFACTION

Our model suggests that CWB is a response to emotion-arousing situations in organizations, particularly feelings of anger and frustration. Such a connection has been found using different breakdowns of CWBs (Fox &

Spector, 1999; Storms & Spector, 1987). Chen and Spector (1992) found that a measure of workplace anger correlated more strongly with CWB than a measure of frustration. They found significant relations between frustration and both aggression and hostility but not for sabotage or theft. However, all four scales correlated significantly with a measure of anger.

In three studies (Fox et al. 2001; Goh et al., 2003; Miles et al., 2002), CWB was related to more general measures of both positive and negative emotions at work using the Job-Related Affective Well Being scale (Van Katwyk, Fox, Spector, & Kelloway, 2000), an instrument that assesses the experience of a variety of emotions at work. Correlations were significant for all cases for negative emotions with correlations as high as .45. Results were inconsistent with positive emotions, with only a third of correlations being significant. In all cases CWB was associated negatively with positive emotional experience.

Job satisfaction has been shown to relate to CWB (Chen & Spector, 1992; Duffy, Ganster, & Shaw, 1998; Fox & Spector, 1999; Goh et al., 2003; Kelloway, Loughlin, Barling, & Nault, 2002; Penney & Spector, 2003). Correlations tended to be larger for organization than personal CWB. For example, Fox and Spector (1999) found correlations of −.45 and −.14 for organization and personal, respectively, with the latter being nonsignificant. A similar pattern was found by Goh et al. (2003).

COUNTERPRODUCTIVE WORK BEHAVIOR AND CONTROL

We propose that control is an important element in CWB. There are two places in which one might expect control to have an effect. First, controllable situations are less likely to be perceived as stressors and therefore will be less likely to result in negative emotions (Spector, 1998).

Take the situation, for example, in which an individual is on tight deadline when an emergency request comes down from upper management for an additional report requiring extensive research. If the person believes he or she can juggle the "normal workload," it may be seen as a minor annoyance that might delay normal task completion for a short while. If, on the other hand, the person does not believe he or she can rearrange or restructure the timing and priority of tasks, likely the reaction will be anger or anxiety over not being able to complete the work. This will be especially extreme if the consequences for noncompletion are severe (being fired) and if the person has no access to additional resources.

As argued elsewhere (Spector, 1998), to affect perceptions of stressors, control must be over the environmental stressor itself. Having autonomy to set workloads, for example, may be effective in reducing the perception of workload as a stressor, but it will be unlikely to have much impact on social stressors. This is an important issue because there has been little attempt to assess control that is directly relevant to stressors. In most cases control instruments measure a limited range of control, focused mainly on autonomy in doing the job.

The second place control has effects is in the response to anger and how it leads to CWB. It has been suggested that human aggression, whether against others or inanimate objects (vandalism), can be a response to a sense of powerlessness. Allen and Greenberger (1980) argued that an individual can resort to violence as a means of restoring his or her sense of control.

All this suggests that control should relate to CWB and it should moderate the relationship between the emotional response and CWB. Unfortunately, there has been little attempt to explore the effects of control on CWB. Fox et al. (2001) included a measure of autonomy in their CWB study. It correlated significantly with organizational CWB (−.25) but not personal CWB ($r = -.05$). Goh et al. (2003), however, were unable to replicate these findings, in that autonomy was uncorrelated with either CWB measure. Fox et al. (2001) conducted moderator tests of autonomy on the relationship between stressors and CWB. They found a significant moderator effect in two of eight cases, personal CWB with interpersonal conflict and organizational constraints, but both were in a direction opposite to expectations. High autonomy participants were more likely to report CWB when they reported high levels of stressors. Apparently, having high autonomy increased the likelihood of responding to stressors with personal CWB, even though individuals with high autonomy were no more likely overall to engage in personal CWB. Perhaps this reflects that those with high autonomy are in higher power positions, making it easier for them to respond to stressors by engaging in CWB against others. In support of this proposition, Fox and Spector (1999) found that perceived ability "to hurt my company or mess things up at work" without being caught predicted both organizational and personal CWB ($r = .39$ and $r = .30$, respectively).

COUNTERPRODUCTIVE WORK BEHAVIOR AND PERSONALITY

It almost goes without saying that there are individual differences in CWB and that personality plays a critical role. A stream of CWB-related research can be found in the integrity testing area, where for years researchers have been attempting to refine measures that predict theft and other CWB behavior. Some of this research involves the use of personality tests, generally placed within the five factor (big five) model framework. Conclusions based on meta-analyses have generally been that such tests predict CWB, with conscientiousness being the best predictor (see Salgado, 2002, and reviews by Hough & Ones, 2001; Sackett & DeVore, 2001). Perhaps the biggest limitation to this work for our purposes is that most of it was not designed to offer insights into the CWB process but rather was conducted for more applied purposes of employee selection.

Several personality variables are specifically relevant to our model because of their connection to either emotions or control. Four are concerned with individual differences in emotional reactivity. Trait anger (Spielberger, Krasner, & Solomon, 1988) is the tendency to respond to situations with anger and can be thought of as a threshold for anger. Those high in trait anger report frequent experiences of anger and are hypersensitive to provocation. Trait anxiety is a similar variable, only concerned with the tendency to experience anxiety. More general affective tendencies are reflected in the variable of negative affectivity (NA; Watson & Clark, 1984), which is the tendency to experience negative emotions across situations and time. It is typically assessed with instruments such as the Positive and Negative Affect Scale (PANAS; Watson, Clark, & Tellegen, 1988) that cover a number of emotions, including anxiety. Emotional stability, one of the dimensions of the five factor model, is similar in covering a variety of emotions. Although there is overlap among NA and emotional stability with both trait anger and anxiety, they are all conceptually and operationally distinct.

All of these affective traits are concerned with an individual's tendency to experience emotions, either single emotions such as anger or anxiety or multiple emotions. Both NA and emotional stability are based on the assumption that there are general tendencies to experience a variety of negative emotions, so that an individual who might tend to experience anxiety might tend to experience anger or guilt. Trait anger and anxiety are quite distinct, with measures that assess them showing evidence for discriminant validity (e.g., .32 in Fox & Spector, 1999; and .43 in Fox et al., 2001).

According to our model, negative emotions are a precursor to CWB, so personality traits concerning emotional responsivity should be relevant to CWB. As might be expected based on the aggression literature, trait anger has been shown to correlate consistently with CWB (Douglas & Martinko, 2001; Fox & Spector, 1999; Fox et al., 2001; Miles et al., 2002; Penney & Spector, 2002). For example, Douglas and Martinko (2001) found a .68 correlation between a measure of trait anger and self-reports of CWB. Fox and Spector (1999) found somewhat lower correlations between trait anger and organization CWB ($r = .57$) and personal CWB ($r = .50$). Fox et al. (2001) conducted moderated regression to determine if trait anger would moderate the relationship between stressors and CWB. Only one of eight analyses was statistically significant, lending little support to this hypothesis. Part of the difficulty with this study was that it was entirely based on self-reports, so the moderator test was between stressor perception and CWB. It may well be that the effect of trait anger is in the perception of the environment, thus it may moderate the relationship between the environmental stressor and perceived stressor, which will then lead to anger and CWB. In other words by the time the perception is assessed, the moderating effect of trait anger has already occurred.

Another refinement of the dynamics of trait anxiety was demonstrated in Fox and Spector (1999). Spielberger and colleagues (Spielberger, Reheiser, & Sydeman, 1995; Spielberger & Sydeman, 1994) conceived of two correlated factors that make up trait anger: angry temperament (T–anger/T) and angry reaction (T–anger/R). T–anger/T describes individual differences in the general disposition to experience anger without specifying any provoking circumstances, resulting in displays of quick temper, outward expressions of unprovoked anger, and impulsiveness. T–anger/R describes angry reactions to specific situations involving frustration or criticism, and such reactions may be expressed or suppressed. Fox and Spector (1999) found angry temperament to be more strongly linked to CWB targeting individuals, whereas angry reaction was linked to CWB targeting the organization.

Trait anxiety has also been shown to relate to CWB. Both Fox and Spector (1999) and Fox et al. (2001) found significant correlations between trait anxiety and CWB that were somewhat smaller (rs = .20 to .40) than for trait anger. They also conducted moderated regression tests and found only two of eight significant for interpersonal conflict and organizational constraints with personal CWB. In both cases those high in trait anxiety showed a steeper slope in the relationship between the stressor and CWB. As with trait anger, part of the problem with finding support for the moderator effect is that it may occur preperception rather than postperception.

Similar correlations have been found with related but more general measures of affective traits. Jockin, Arvey, and McGue (2001) found a correlation of .22 between neuroticism and CWB. Douglas and Martinko (2001) found a correlation of .21, and Penney and Spector (2003) found a correlation of .31 with overall CWB using the NA subscale of the PANAS. Skarlicki, Folger, and Tesluk (1999) found a similar correlation between NA and coworker reports of incumbent CWB. Aquino et al. (1999) found correlations of .22 and .31 with organizational and personal CWB, respectively, using the NA scale of the PANAS. In his meta-analysis, however, Salgado (2002) failed to find a relationship between the five factor model dimension of emotional stability and CWB.

Penney and Spector (2002) investigated the possible role of narcissism in CWB. Based on the theory of threatened egotism and aggression (Baumeister, Smart, & Boden, 1996), Penney and Spector proposed that narcissistic individuals would be more likely to engage in CWB, especially in response to threat. The theory suggests that some individuals are hypersensitive to ego threat—that is, events or situations that challenge the favorable view of the self, leading to exaggerated anger responses and aggression. The narcissistic individual is one with an inflated and unrealistic view of his or her capabilities. A narcissist expects to be better than others and dominate in many situations and will be threatened by information that disconfirms this unfounded view, thus being easily provoked to anger and subsequent CWB. Penney and Spector found support for these ideas in that narcissism correlated significantly with CWB (r = .27). Furthermore, there was a significant moderator effect of narcissism on the relationship between organizational constraints and CWB. Those high on narcissism were more likely to respond to constraints with CWB. The relationship between narcissism and job constraints, however, was quite modest (r = .14), so it was not that narcissists were a great deal more likely to perceive constraints. In a follow-up study, Penney and Spector (2003) was able to replicate the correlation of narcissism with CWB but not the moderator effect.

Locus of control (Rotter, 1966) is a cognitive rather than affective trait concerning a person's generalized beliefs about control over events that have the potential to reward or punish. Internals are individuals who believe they have control, whereas externals believe control exists elsewhere, such as with fate, luck, or powerful others. As a personality variable, locus of control reflects an individual's tendencies and is distinct from perceptions of control in particular situations. As noted in the previous section, our model suggests that control will be a critical element in CWB, and so locus of control will be important as it reflects the tendency of an individual to believe in controllability.

Perlow and Latham (1993) provided the best evidence in support of the locus of control connection to CWB. They found that locus of control scores predicted subsequent employee termination for assaulting patients of a residential treatment facility. The relationship between locus of control and CWB has been replicated in two questionnaire studies (Fox & Spector, 1999; Goh et al., 2003), with both finding significance for organizational CWB (rs = .19 and .32) but only the former finding significance for personal CWB. These studies used the work-specific Work Locus of Control scale (Spector, 1988) rather than a general scale of locus of control.

Storms and Spector (1987) tested the work locus of control moderator effect on the relationship between frustration and CWB. Support was found in that those with an external work locus of control were more likely to respond to frustration with CWB, using both moderated regression and subgroup correlation comparisons. For example, the correlation between frustration and overall CWB was a nonsignificant .11 for the most internal third of the sample but was a significant .59 for the most external third. There was a small but significant correlation between work locus of control and overall CWB (r = .16). Fox and Spector (1999), however, were unable to replicate the moderator effect.

METHODOLOGICAL ISSUES IN THE STUDY OF COUNTERPRODUCTIVE WORK BEHAVIOR

Conducting research on CWB represents significant challenges because of the detrimental and even illegal nature of these acts. This has led in large part to an almost exclusive reliance on anonymous self-report questionnaires. Anonymity is required to allow participants to be honest in their responses, because being caught doing these behaviors could result in punishment and possibly even legal action. Questionnaires are necessary because the individual is in the best position to know what he or she has done. Many of these behaviors, especially organizational CWB, is done in secret. Considering that people are likely to be hesitant to admit to illegal and improper acts, it is a reasonable assumption that even with anonymous questionnaires, CWB is underreported. Most likely this would serve to attenuate correlations between CWB measures and other variables, because some individuals will be less honest in responses than others, thus introducing error into assessment. For example, perhaps those individuals who do the most CWB are paranoid about being caught, and so they tend to report no behaviors, whereas those who do the least tend to freely admit those they do.

The exclusive reliance on single source, cross-sectional designs limits the confidence with which conclusions can be reached. We cannot be certain that the correlations between CWB and other variables, all assessed via self-report of incumbents at one point in time, do not reflect unmeasured third variables. The relationship between CWB and other variables might be a result of some shared biases among scales, response sets, unmeasured environmental factors, or unrecognized personal characteristics. Clearly the self-report findings need replication using alternative methods.

There have been a small number of studies that have used alternative methods in an attempt to demonstrate that observed relations are not due solely to self-reports. For example, Perlow and Latham (1993), as noted earlier, administered a locus of control scale to a sample of employees at one point in time, and then conducted a follow-up of organizational records to see who had been dismissed for assaulting residential patients. The longitudinal nature of this study provided convincing evidence that locus of control played an important causal role in this form of CWB. Of course, it is possible that this relation is spurious and is due to the action of a variable that is related to locus of control. Future research will be required to rule out such possibilities.

Heacox (1996) administered a nonanonymous questionnaire to employees asking about their work frustration. She also asked supervisors to identify those employees who had been disciplined for doing CWB. She found that those who reported experiencing frustration on the job were more likely to be identified as having done CWB.

In their study of justice, Skarlicki and Folger (1997) had imcumbents report perceptions of distributive, interactive, and procedural justice. Coworkers were asked to complete a CWB measure on the participants. They found that all three measures of justice correlated significantly to CWB. What is interesting is that these correlations, ranging from −.44 to −.54, are larger than those found in studies in which justice and CWB were assessed via incumbent reports. In a subsequent paper with the same dataset, Skarlicki et al. (1999) found a correlation of .19 between NA and CWB. Penney and Spector (2003) found the same correlation between NA and coworker-assessed CWB.

Two studies used both incumbent and coworker reports of the incumbent's CWB. Goh et al. (2003) and Penney and Spector (2003) asked a sample of employees to complete an anonymous questionnaire containing measures of CWB, job stressors, and other variables. Included was a parallel questionnaire to be given to a coworker to be chosen by the employee. Instructions were to put a secret code on both questionnaires so the researchers could later pair them up without being able to identify either person. Both studies found convergence for overall CWB with correlations of .22 (Penney & Spector, 2003) and .29 (Goh et al., 2003). However, there was a considerable difference between organizational CWB (r = .13, nonsignificant) and personal CWB (r = .47) in Goh et al. (2003). They explain this as the more hidden nature of organizational CWB. Personal acts are done to people where someone, such as their coworkers, can see them. In fact unsolicited written comments made by a few coworkers noted that they were the targets of some CWB they were reporting. Organizational CWB is likely to be hidden, because these are behaviors that can get one fired or that cannot be readily detected as intentional behaviors. For example, not working as hard as one is able is a subjective judgment, depending on the individual's own assessment of ability and effort, whereas a coworker or supervisor may see only overt behaviors and outcomes.

Both studies also included other variables that were related to both incumbent and coworker reports of CWB, and in this instance results varied according to the specific variable in question. Both Goh et al. (2003) and Penney and Spector (2003) assessed interpersonal conflict and organizational constraints. In both studies, conflict was significant regardless of whether CWB was assessed from coworkers or imcumbents. However, with constraints both studies found significance with incumbents but not coworkers. With the Penney and Spector study, the incumbent correlations for conflict were significantly larger, but with the Goh et al. (2003) study the correlations were not significantly different. Likewise, both studies found similar results across sources of CWB for job satisfaction. Penney and Spector found no significant differences for corresponding correlations with CWB for NA or narcissism. Goh et al. (2003) found no significant differences for corresponding correlations for procedural and distributive justice, although none of the distributive justice correlations were themselves significantly different from zero.

Taken as a whole, these various studies that have relied on methods other than single-source methods have yielded results that are consistent with the single-source studies. In fact in some cases the correlations were larger in magnitude (although not significantly so) for the coworker than incumbent reports in Goh et al. (2003). The correlations with justice reported by Skarlicki and Folger (1997) using coworker reports were the largest of any reported in the studies we reviewed. This clearly suggests that monomethod bias (method variance) is not necessarily inflating the correlations within self-report questionnaires where CWB is concerned. This of course does not mean that there are not possible biases that might be affecting both coworkers and participants that have produced spurious correlations. Furthermore, even if these relations are not due to bias, causality cannot be assumed. It is possible that the conduct of CWB affects people's perceptions and their job satisfaction or that unmeasured third variables are the real cause of observed correlations.

One additional complication is that there may be other variables in which agreement is not found in correlations of incumbent versus coworker CWB with other variables. Goh et al. (2003) reported correlations with a general measure of negative emotions at work. They found significant correlations with both general and organizational incumbent-assessed CWB and significantly lower nonsignificant correlations with both general and organizational coworker-assessed CWB.

CONCLUSION

The work we have summarized has focused on understanding the underlying processes that lead to CWB. As suggested by our stressor–emotion model, job stressors, negative emotions, control, and personality are all important factors in at least some CWB. Individuals who have experienced stressful situations, are feeling negative emotions, and perceive little control over the situation are at risk for CWB. Most such acts are likely to be relatively minor and are often hidden from supervisors and even coworkers.

This is not to say that there is a single process underlying all CWB. As recognized in the human aggression literature, some CWB can be for instrumental purposes in which employees engage in CWB to achieve some goal or purpose other than causing harm. This is particularly true for theft, where in many cases the employee steals not in response to stress and emotion but because of antisocial tendencies. In other cases employees may resort to abusive behaviors in an attempt to exert power and influence over another.

However, it is our contention that a great deal of CWB is covered by our model. Certain acts are more likely to be stressor–emotion induced than others. For example, purposely doing work incorrectly is likely to be a response to a conflict with a supervisor or the perception of injustice. Many personal acts directed against coworkers can be a response to negative emotions.

Organizations would do well to consider how the treatment of employees can lead to CWB, and that CWB is often hidden. The new computer that is believed to be defective or the truck that always needs maintenance may be the result of purposeful acts by employees. Instituting fair procedures, reducing stress where possible, and empowering employees can go a long way toward reducing CWB and enhancing the well-being of both organizations and their stakeholders. The widespread practice of merely using integrity tests to weed out those with tendencies to engage in CWB without providing a healthy work environment may itself be counterproductive to the goal of reducing CWB.

REFERENCES

Allen, V. L., & Greenberger, D. B. (1980). Destruction and perceived control. In A. Baum & J. E. Singer (Eds.), *Applications of personal control* (pp. 85–109). Hillsdale, NJ: Erlbaum.

Anderson, C. A., Deuser, W. E., & DeNeve, K. M. (1995). Hot temperatures, hostile affect, hostile cognition, and arousal: Tests of a general model of affective aggression. *Personality and Social Psychology Bulletin, 21,* 434–448.

Andersson, L. M., & Pearson, C. M. (1999). Tit for tat? The spiraling effect of incivility in the workplace. *Academy of Management Review, 24,* 452–471.

Aquino, K., Lewis, M. U., & Bradfield, M. (1999). Justice constructs, negative affectivity, and employee deviance: A proposed model and empirical test. *Journal of Organizational Behavior, 20,* 1073–1091.

Barling, J. (1996). The prediction, experience, and consequences of workplace violence. In G. VandenBos & E. Q. Bulatao (Eds.), *Violence on the job: Identifying risks and developing solutions* (pp. 29–49). Washington, DC: American Psychological Association.

Baumeister, R. F., Smart, L., & Boden, J. M. (1996). Relation of threatened egotism to violence and aggression: The dark side of high self esteem. *Psychological Review, 3,* 5–33.

Bennett, R. J., & Robinson, S. L. (2000). Development of a measure of workplace deviance. *Journal of Applied Psychology, 85,* 349–360.

Berkowitz, L. (1989). Frustration–aggression hypothesis: Examination and reformulation. *Psychological Bulletin, 106*, 59–73.

Bies, R. J., Tripp, T. M., & Kramer, R. M. (1997). At the breaking point: Cognitive and social dynamics of revenge in organizations. In R. A. Giacalone & J. Greenberg (Eds.), *Antisocial behavior in organizations* (pp. 18–36). Thousand Oaks, CA: Sage.

Bulatao, E. Q., & VandenBos, G. R. (1996). Workplace violence: Its scope and the issues. In G. R. VandenBos & E. Q. Bulatao (Eds.), *Violence on the job: Identifying risks and developing solutions* (pp. 1–23). Washington, DC: American Psychological Association.

Chen, P. Y., & Spector, P. E. (1992). Relationships of work stressors with aggression, withdrawal, theft and substance use: An exploratory study. *Journal of Occupational and Organizational Psychology, 65*, 177–184.

Dollard, J., Doob, L. W., Miller, N. E., Mowrer, O. H., & Sears, R. R. (1939). *Frustration and aggression.* New Haven, CT: Yale University Press.

Douglas, S. C., & Martinko, M. J. (2001). Exploring the role of individual differences in the prediction of workplace aggression. *Journal of Applied Psychology, 86*, 547–559.

Duffy, M. K., Ganster, D. C., & Shaw, J. D. (1998). Positive affectivity and negative outcomes: The role of tenure and job satisfaction. *Journal of Applied Psychology, 83*, 950–959.

Folger, R., & Baron, R. A. (1996). Violence and hostility at work: A model of reactions to perceived injustice. In G. R. VandenBos & E. Q. Bulatao (Eds.), *Violence on the job: Identifying risks and developing solutions* (pp. 51–85). Washington, DC: American Psychological Association.

Fox, S., & Spector, P. E. (1999). A model of work frustration–aggression. *Journal of Organizational Behavior, 20*, 915–931.

Fox, S., Spector, P. E., & Miles, D. (2001). Counterproductive work behavior (CWB) in response to job stressors and organizational justice: Some mediator and moderator tests for autonomy and emotions. *Journal of Vocational Behavior, 59*, 291–309.

Frese, M. (1985). Stress at work and psychosomatic complaints: A causal interpretation. *Journal of Applied Psychology, 70*, 314–328.

Frese, M., & Zapf, D. (1999). On the importance of the objective environment in stress and attribution theory. Counterpoint to Perrewé and Zellars. *Journal of Organizational Behavior, 20*, 761–765.

Glomb, T. M. (2002). Workplace anger and aggression: Informing conceptual models with data from specific encounters. *Journal of Occupational Health Psychology, 7*, 20–36.

Goh, A. P. S., Bruursema, K., Fox, S., & Spector, P. E. (2003, April 11–13). *Comparisons of self and coworker reports of counterproductive work behavior.* Paper presented at the meeting of the Society for Industrial and Organizational Psychology, Orlando, FL.

Greenberg, L., & Barling, J. (1999). Predicting employee aggression against coworkers, subordinates and supervisors: The roles of person behaviors and perceived workplace factors. *Journal of Organizational Behavior, 20*, 897–913.

Greenwell, J., & Dengerink, H. A. (1973). The role of perceived versus actual attack in human physical aggression. *Journal of Personality and Social Psychology, 26*, 66–71.

Heacox, N. J. (1996). *The relationship between organizational frustration and aggressive behaviors in the workplace.* Unpublished doctoral dissertation, California School of Professional Psychology, San Diego.

Hoel, H., Rayner, C., & Cooper, C. L. (1999). Workplace bullying. In C. L. Cooper & I. T. Robertson (Eds.), *International review of industrial and organizational psychology: 1999* (pp. 195–230). Chichester, England: Wiley.

Hollinger, R. C. (1986). Acts against the workplace: Social bonding and employee deviance. *Deviant Behavior, 7*, 53–75.

Hough, L. M., & Ones, D. S. (2001). The structure, measurement, validity, and use of personality variables in industrial, work, and organizational psychology. In N. Anderson, D. S. Ones, H. K. Sinangil, & C. Viswesvaran (Eds.), *Handbook of industrial, work and organizational psychology* (Vol. 1, pp. 233–277). Thousand Oaks, CA: Sage.

Jockin, V., Arvey, R. D., & McGue, M. (2001). Perceived victimization moderates self-reports of workplace aggression and conflict. *Journal of Applied Psychology, 86*, 1262–1269.

Keashly, L. (1998). Emotional abuse in the workplace: Conceptual and empirical issues. *Journal of Emotional Abuse, 1*, 85–117.

Kelloway, E. K., Loughlin, C., Barling, J., & Nault, A. (2002). Self-reported counterproductive behaviors and organizational citizenship behaviors: Separate but related constructs. *International Journal of Selection and Assessment, 10*, 143–151.

Kirmeyer, S. L. (1988). Coping with competing demands: Interruption and the type A pattern. *Journal of Applied Psychology, 73*, 621–629.

Lazarus, R. S., & Folkman, S. (1984). *Stress, appraisal and coping.* New York: Springer.

LeBlanc, M. M., & Kelloway, E. K. (2002). Predictors and outcomes of workplace violence and aggression. *Journal of Applied Psychology, 87*, 444–453.

Martinko, M. J., Gundlach, M. J., & Douglas, S. C. (2002). Counterproductive workplace behavior: A causal reasoning perspective. *International Journal of Selection and Assessment, 10*, 36–50.

Miles, D. E., Borman, W. E., Spector, P. E., & Fox, S. (2002). Building an integrative model of extra role work behaviors: A comparison of counterproductive work behavior with organizational citizenship behavior. *International Journal of Selection and Assessment, 10*, 51–57.

Neuman, J. H., & Baron, R. A. (1997). Aggression in the workplace. In R. A. Giacalone & J. Greenberg (Eds.), *Antisocial behavior in organizations* (pp. 37–67). Thousand Oaks, CA: Sage.

Neuman, J. H., & Baron, R. A. (1998). Workplace violence and workplace aggression: Evidence concerning specific forms, potential causes, and preferred targets. *Journal of Management, 24*, 391–419.

O'Leary-Kelly, A. M., Griffin, R. W., & Glew, D. J. (1996). Organization-motivated aggression: A research framework. *Academy of Management Review, 21*, 225–253.

Pastore, N. (1952). The role of arbitrariness in the frustration–aggression hypothesis. *Journal of Abnormal and Social Psychology, 47*, 728–741.

Penney, L. M., & Spector, P. E. (2002). Narcissism and counterproductive work behavior: Do bigger egos mean bigger problems? *International Journal of Selection and Assessment, 10*, 126–134.

Penney, L. M., & Spector, P. E. (2003, April 11–13). *Workplace incivility and counterproductive workplace behavior*. Paper presented at the meeting of the Society for Industrial and Organizational Psychology, Orlando, FL.

Perlow, R., & Latham, L. L. (1993). Relationship of client abuse with locus of control and gender: A longitudinal study. *Journal of Applied Psychology, 78*, 831–834.

Perrewé, P. L., & Zellars, K. L. (1999). An examination of attributions and emotions in the transactional approach to the organizational stress process. *Journal of Organizational Behavior, 20*, 739–752.

Robinson, S. L., & Bennett, R. J. (1995). A typology of deviant workplace behaviors: A multidimensional scaling study. *Academy of Management Journal, 38*, 555–572.

Rotter, J. B. (1966). Generalized expectancies for internal versus external control of reinforcement. *Psychological Monographs, 80*(Whole no. 609).

Sackett, P. R. (2002). The structure of counterproductive work behaviors: Dimensionality and relationships with facets of job performance. *International Journal of Selection and Assessment, 10*, 5–11.

Sackett, P. R., & DeVore, C. J. (2001). Counterproductive behaviors at work. In N. Anderson, D. S. Ones, H. K. Sinangil, & C. Viswesvaran (Eds.), *Handbook of industrial, work and organizational psychology* (Vol. 1, pp. 145–164). Thousand Oaks, CA: Sage.

Salgado, J. F. (2002). The big five personality dimension and counterproductive behaviors. *International Journal of Selection and Assessment, 10*, 117–125.

Schaubroeck, J. (1999). Should the subjective be the objective? On studying mental processes, coping behavior, and actual exposures in organizational stress research. *Journal of Organizational Behavior, 20*, 753–760.

Skarlicki, D. P., & Folger, R. (1997). Retaliation in the workplace: The roles of distributive, procedural, and interactional justice. *Journal of Applied Psychology, 82*, 434–443.

Skarlicki, D. P., Folger, R., & Tesluk, P. (1999). Personality as a moderator in the relationship between fairness and retaliation. *Academy of Management Journal, 42*, 100–108.

Spector, P. E. (1975). Relationships of organizational frustration with reported behavioral reactions of employees. *Journal of Applied Psychology, 60,* 635–637.

Spector, P. E. (1978). Organizational frustration: A model and review of the literature. *Personnel Psychology, 31,* 815–829.

Spector, P. E. (1988). Development of the work locus of control scale. *Journal of Occupational Psychology, 61,* 335–340.

Spector, P. E. (1992). A consideration of the validity and meaning of self-report measures of job conditions. In C. L. Cooper & I. T. Robertson (Eds.), *International review of industrial and organizational psychology: 1992* (pp. 123–151). West Sussex, England: Wiley.

Spector, P. E. (1998). A control model of the job stress process. In C. L. Cooper (Ed.), *Theories of organizational stress* (pp. 153–169). London: Oxford University Press.

Spector, P. E., & Goh, A. (2001). The role of emotions in the occupational stress process. In P. L. Perrewé & D. C. Ganster (Eds.), *Research in occupational stress and well–being (Volume 1): Exploring theoretical mechanisms and perspectives* (pp. 195–232). Greenwich, CT: JAI Press.

Spector, P. E., Zapf, D., Chen, P. Y., & Frese, M. (2000). Why negative affectivity should not be controlled in job stress research: Don't throw out the baby with the bath water. *Journal of Organizational Behavior, 21,* 79–95.

Spielberger, C. D., Krasner, S. S., & Solomon, E. P. (1988). The experience, expression and control of anger. In M. P. Janisse (Eds.), *Health psychology: Individual differences and stress* (pp. 89–108). New York: Springer.

Spielberger, C. D., Reheiser, E. C., & Sydeman, S. J. (1995). Measuring the experience, expression, and control of anger. *Issues in Comprehensive Pediatric Nursing, 18,* 207–232.

Spielberger, C. D., & Sydeman, S. J. (1994). State–trait anxiety inventory and state–trait anger expression inventory. In M. E. Maruish (Ed.), *The use of psychological testing for treatment planning and outcome assessment* (pp. 292–321). Hillsdale, NJ: Erlbaum.

Storms, P. L., & Spector, P. E. (1987). Relationships of organizational frustration with reported behavioral reactions: The moderating effect of perceived control. *Journal of Occupational Psychology, 60,* 227–234.

Van Katwyk, P. T., Fox, S., Spector, P. E., & Kelloway, E. K. (2000). Using the Job-Related Affective Well-Being Scale (JAWS) to investigate affective responses to work stressors. *Journal of Occupational Health Psychology, 5,* 219–230.

Watson, D., & Clark, L. A. (1984). Negative affectivity: The disposition to experience aversive emotional states. *Psychological Bulletin, 96,* 465–490.

Watson, D., Clark, L. A., & Tellegen, A. (1988). Development and validation of brief measures of positive and negative affect: The PANAS scales. *Journal of Personality and Social Psychology, 54,* 1063–1070.

Zapf, D., Knorz, C., & Kulla, M. (1996). On the relationship between mobbing factors, and job content, social work environment, and health outcomes. *European Journal of Work and Organizational Psychology, 5,* 215–237.

II
TARGET PERSPECTIVES

8

WORKPLACE INCIVILITY

CHRISTINE M. PEARSON, LYNNE M. ANDERSSON,
AND CHRISTINE L. PORATH

A level of civility is fundamental to doing business. People tend to do business with those who grant them respect and make them feel good (Gonthier, 2002; Martin, 1996). Similarly, civility among employees fosters smooth relationships in the workplace, promoting harmony and goodwill. When civility is absent, work relations are strained. Rude treatment can make workers unhappy, and this can lead to cynicism, aggressive behavior, higher turnover, lower productivity, and lost customers (Connelly, 1994; Gonthier, 2002; Lewis, 2000; Walters, 1994). Uncivil behavior makes the work environment unpleasant, and it can negatively affect a company's bottom line (Pearson, Andersson, & Wegner, 2001).

Some contend that rudeness and insensitivity toward others have reached new heights in the United States. In a poll conducted by the research firm Public Agenda, 79% of 2,013 respondents said that a lack of respect and courtesy in American society is a serious problem. Sixty-one percent believe things have gotten worse in recent years (Remington & Darden, 2002). Organizational research reveals that a substantial percentage of employees see themselves as targets of rudeness (e.g., Cortina, Magley, Williams, & Langhout, 2001; Ehrlich & Larcom, 1994; Graydon, Kasta, &

Khan, 1994). Civility consultants, as well as guidelines for business "neti-quette" (i.e., civil behavior online) are proliferating.

Myriad examples of workplace incivility come to mind: taking credit for other's efforts, spreading rumors about colleagues, leaving office equipment jammed instead of taking the time to fix it, flaming coworkers through nasty email messages, neglecting to acknowledge subordinates, leaving snippy voice mail messages, and so on. As organizations have grown increasingly casual, there are fewer obvious cues about what constitutes "proper" business behavior (Gonthier, 2002; Martin, 1996). Given the speed, frequency, and complexity of work interactions in today's high-tech and global workplace, behavior has more nuances: There are more ways to show disregard for fellow workers (Carter, 1998; Gonthier, 2002).

DEFINING CIVILITY AND INCIVILITY

With more common use in the past decade, the terms *civility* and *incivility* have lost some of their original meaning. *Civility* has transcended its dictionary definition of "courtesy and politeness toward fellow human beings" to encompass everything from professional conduct to civic order and a moral imperative (Carter, 1998; Martin, 1996). Civil behavior involves treating others with dignity, acting in regard to others' feelings, and preserving the social norms for mutual respect (Carter, 1998; Elias, 1982; Morris, 1996). The basis for civility is a demonstration of respect for fellow human beings (Carter, 1998; Elias, 1982; Wilson, 1993).

Incivility implies rudeness and disregard for others, in violation of norms for respect in interpersonal relations (Brown & Levinson, 1987; Morris, 1996). Whereas civil behavior is expected and often goes unnoticed, uncivil behavior is conspicuous (Brown & Levinson, 1987; Carter, 1998).

Various conceptualizations of workplace incivility have emerged in management and social psychology. Described concisely by scholars as "impropriety" (Miller, 2000), "aversive behavior" (Winters & Duck, 2000), and "low-level workplace abuse" (Johnson & Indvik, 2001), incivility has been described in greater detail as "disrespectful behavior that undermines the dignity and self-esteem of employees and creates unnecessary suffering, indicating a lack of concern for the well-being of others and contrary to how individuals expect to be treated" (Zauderer, 2002). Recent scholarship in the federal courts has operationalized incivility as "interpersonal mistreatment" (Cortina et al., 2001; Cortina, Magley, & Lim, 2002). Qualitative research reveals the dimensions of disrespect–dishonesty, ignoring–exclusion, professional discrediting, silencing, gender disparagement, threats–intimidation, unprofessional address, and appearance comments (Cortina et al., 2002).

The precise definition of workplace incivility derived from our empirical (e.g., Pearson et al., 2001) and conceptual (e.g., Andersson & Pearson, 1999) work concurs with the work of these other scholars. We define incivility as *low-intensity deviant (rude, discourteous) behavior with ambiguous intent to harm the target in violation of workplace norms for mutual respect.*

We have established that workplace incivility involves acting with disregard for others in the workplace, in violation of workplace norms for respect. We recognize that particular norms differ across organizations, industries, and cultures, but we contend that in every workplace there are norms for respect for fellow workers and that incivility violates these norms. Whereas uncivil behavior in one setting may not be universally considered uncivil, we can hold a common understanding of workplace incivility as behavior that disrupts mutual respect at work.

Incivility is an interpersonal event—that is, an event in which two or more parties are involved (Brown & Levinson, 1987; Carter, 1998). We adopt a social interactionist perspective on the concept of incivility and its escalation in proposing that incivilities are exchanged between individuals. Unlike much of the recent research in which scholars model counterproductive work behavior as single acts in time, focusing on the motives of the instigator (e.g., Fox, Spector, & Miles, 2001; O'Leary-Kelly, Griffin, & Glew, 1996; Robinson & Bennett, 1997), our social interactionist perspective comprises the interpersonal and situational factors involved in the exchange. This perspective allows us to examine incivility as a process rather than an event.

In the remainder of this chapter we delve into the construct of workplace incivility. We provide a brief overview of the focus of the research that is amassing on this phenomenon. We provide a conceptual summary of the research, offering a comprehensive model that depicts the relationships among workplace incivility and other related constructs. In so doing, we attempt to untangle the construct of workplace incivility from other counterproductive work behaviors and delineate its uniqueness on several dimensions. Finally, we speculate about directions for future research, as well as practical implications for employees, organizations, and society.

RESEARCH ON WORKPLACE INCIVILITY: THE FOCUS

As scholarly interest in counterproductive work behavior has grown, a distinct stream of research focused specifically on lesser forms of interpersonal mistreatment in organizations is emerging (Keashly, 1998; Neuman & Baron, 1998; Rayner, Hoel, & Cooper, 2002). Research on workplace incivility, in particular, is gaining recognition as a unique form of interpersonal mistreatment characterized by ambiguity of intent and violation of workplace norms for mutual respect. Scholarship from multiple social science disciplines (e.g., criminal justice, health services, law, management, public administration, social psychology) is beginning to converge as scholars are recognizing, sharing, and incorporating the theory, measures, and techniques across disciplines. Nonetheless, substantial overlap of workplace incivility with constructs such as aggression, antisocial behavior, bullying, deviance, emotional abuse, petty tyranny, and social undermining at work (Andersson & Pearson, 1999; O'Leary-Kelly, Duffy, & Griffin, 2000) is ensuring that the stream remains open to novel, broader, and more intricate conceptualizations and explanatory frameworks.

Incivility has been defined as a conceptual construct and differentiated on multiple dimensions from other forms of counterproductive work behaviors (Andersson & Pearson, 1999). Empirical studies have examined the target–victim's perspectives on uncivil encounters (Cortina et al., 2001, 2002; Pearson et al., 2001), as well as the effects of instigator and target gender differences (Cortina et al., 2002; Cupach, Huggins, Long, & Metts, 2002; Porath & Pearson, 2000). Also, research on incivility has begun to address practical considerations, such as individual and organizational costs, as well as implications for managerial attention and action (Cortina et al., 2001; Pearson, Andersson, & Porath, 2000; Zauderer, 2002). The work of legal scholars has focused on incivility as it affects day-to-day professional conduct (e.g., Austin, 1988; Crain, 1997; Wegner, 1996), as well as the escalation from nasty words to violent behavior (MacKinnon, 1994). Finally, the relevance of incivility to those who are in the workforce has been documented in stories featuring this research that have been published in more than 500 newspapers and periodicals across the United States and in Canada, Australia, and Western Europe.

Emergent concepts and models of counterproductive work behaviors have been based on theories of attribution, frustration, social learning, social cognition, individual differences, social interactionism, and justice, among others (e.g., Andersson & Pearson, 1999; Douglas & Martinko, 2001; Fox & Spector, 1999; Martinko & Zellars, 1996; Neuman & Baron, 1998; Robinson & O'Leary-Kelly, 1998; Tedeschi & Felson, 1994). Thus far, the research across disciplines has been predominantly functionalist in seeking refinement of constructs through various means of causal analysis. Empirical investigation, even that seeking qualitative data, has been performed under a positivist set of assumptions viewing counterproductive work behavior as part of an objective organizational reality. In the investigation performed by Pearson and colleagues (2001), workplace incivility has been approached through an interpretive lens, and in that particular multiphase study the interpretive data were subsequently used to build testable hypotheses. But there is a dearth of interpretive, critical, and structural research on incivility and other counterproductive work behaviors; the stream would likely benefit from investigation from a nonmanagerial perspective. There is no denying the importance of deepening our understanding of incivility: The challenge for scholars is to continue to break new ground undaunted by academic epistemological battles.

RESEARCH ON WORKPLACE INCIVILITY: A CONCEPTUAL SUMMARY

That workplace incivility is ambiguous as to intent, low in intensity, and often a top-down phenomenon make it challenging to detect and understand. Also, because incivility exists in the eyes of the beholder, it presents its own research challenges. Scholars interested in the phenomenon face the difficulties inherent in examining individuals' reactions to their perceptual realities. Despite these hurdles, research is emerging regarding the potential causes, consequences, and moderators of incivility. In this section, we offer a conceptual summary of the research on workplace incivility in text and graphic forms (see Figure 8.1).

Potential Causes of Workplace Incivility

We suggest two conditions that can erode mutual respect at work and lead to incivility: social contextual shifts (as reflected in societal irreverence, altered psychological work contracts, and shifting demographics) and organizational pressures (as felt in corporate change initiatives, the surge of technology, inferior leadership, and compressed time and deadlines). These antecedents of workplace incivility seem to foster uncivil words and deeds between peers, from subordinate to superior or from superior to subordinate.

Social Contextual Shifts

The changing nature of work reflects social contextual shifts. Regarding the changes that some believe continue to blur the line between appropriate and inappropriate interaction, popular theory blames contingencies such as absentee parenting, poor schooling, media fascination with the dark side, and a relentless quest for individuality. In our everyday lives, in and out of the workplace, we seem to have become instigators of incivility when the phenomenon suits our self-interest (Carter, 1998).

In the workplace, psychological contracts are taking new forms: Whether from the perspective of employee or employer, long-term organizational investment seems to be declining. These changes can be seen as shifts in loyalty, retention, entitlement, short-term profitability, and informality. With minimal investment or trust in the long-term, some employees will focus sharply on taking care of themselves, neglecting the needs and desires

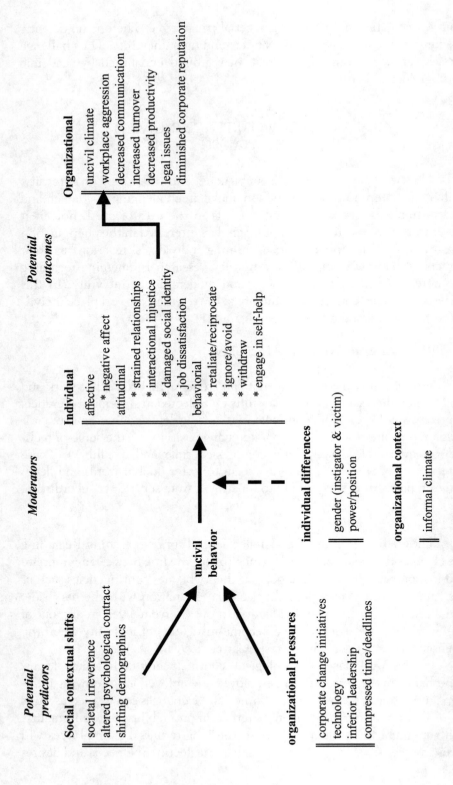

Figure 8.1. Conceptual summary of research on workplace incivility.

of colleagues. In some organizations, "me first" or "me only" attitudes have eroded former signals of respect (Pearson et al., 2000).

Shifting demographics may be potential predictors of uncivil behavior because smooth communications with those whose values differ from our own may require additional time and effort. Also, we may offend others inadvertently when value differences seep through our words and deeds.

Organizational Pressures

Corporate change initiatives can foster incivility. The uncertainty of downsizing, restructuring, and mergers can leave employees on edge about the future. They may be angry, tense, and fearful, and these negative emotions may result in less attention to acting respectfully toward colleagues. Also, contract labor, freelancing, outsourcing, and job-hopping can create a workforce segment that is unwilling to internalize organizational values or adhere to organizational norms.

Workplace technology can foster incivility. Technologies enable us to interact through impersonal and asynchronous contact, without the mediating filter inherent in personal interactions. Misunderstandings and misinterpretations in the use of electronic media can lead to perceived incivilities. And we can slam or "spam" electronic colleagues all too easily when technology takes away the human face (Pearson et al., 2000).

With the emergent organizational impact of technology, technical experts rise to leadership. In some cases, these promotions occur despite inferior competence, especially about the interpersonal requirements for managing people. Some of these new leaders may behave uncivilly themselves, therein modeling incivility. Others may attempt to avoid the messy and complex problems that underlie uncivil behavior rather than venture into areas in which they have little or no experience.

Incivility may also arise when people are required to do more with less, where initiatives to become lean and mean turn inward on the organization. Under conditions of work and information overload, feelings of time pressure intensify. Work hours tend to be longer, work responsibilities greater, and nonwork demands (e.g., single-parenting challenges, dual-career tensions, "sandwich generation" responsibilities) all the more taxing. People may simply have less energy, motivation, and time to attend to civility, to be ever mindful of the "niceties."

Potential Consequences of Workplace Incivility

Rudeness and disrespect among uncivil coworkers is expensive whether the incivility affects direct targets, their colleagues, their organizations, clients and customers, or even the instigators themselves. Whether direct or indirect, incivility can breed contempt, subvert legitimate authority, and anger bystanders (Andersson & Pearson, 1999). When someone withholds information (indirect incivility) or challenges another's reputation (direct incivility), participants and observers lose enthusiasm for work, loyalty to the organization, and respect for its leadership. In the worst case, incivility can spread throughout the organization and become the norm, whether interpersonally directed (e.g., as rounds of tit-for-tat rudeness or disrespect between instigator and target or others) or organizationally directed (e.g., as wasted work time, reduced productivity, or voluntary turnover resulting from experiencing or witnessing incivility; Andersson & Pearson, 1999; Pearson et al., 2000, 2001). Individuals and organizations, alike, experience the ill effects of incivility.

Individual Outcomes

Incivility feels bad. Targets experience negative affective responses when incivility occurs (Andersson & Pearson, 1999; Pearson & Porath, 2001), and their formerly positive attitudes about work may falter (Andersson & Pearson, 1999; Cortina, Magley, et al., 2002; Pearson et al., 2000). If the organization does not address the situation, the perceived unfairness of the situation may grow stronger as interactional injustice (Bies, 2000; Bies & Moag, 1986), or targets may believe that the interaction has tainted their reputation and identity within the organization. Often, targets find themselves less satisfied with their jobs and their work environments (Pearson et al., 2001). As a result, they may behave in ways that risk their reputation, efficiency, and sense of engagement or involvement as they purposefully reduce time, effort, and performance at work. Targets may waste time and other valuable resources by attempting to avoid the instigator. If they are successful at avoidance, they may miss opportunities that otherwise could have been facilitated by the instigator (Pearson & Porath, 2001; Porath & Pearson, 2000).

When the target chooses to retaliate against the instigator, their relationship may be strained and the target's reputation may be sullied in the eyes of the instigator, coworkers, or the organization at large (Pearson et al., 2001). When the target engages in nonwork activities to discharge the negative emotions evoked by incivility, additional time, energy, and attention must be spent to make up for this lost time. The effectiveness, productivity, and satisfaction of the target may be adversely affected immediately following the incivility or over time.

Perhaps the most interesting (and elusive) individual costs of incivility are those borne by the instigator. In addition to a direct compensatory toll exacted by the target (via actions or inaction that could be obvious to the instigator), what may be difficult for the instigator to reckon are the tolls imposed by the target indirectly. If the instigator's work performance is dependent even in part on the efforts or presence of the target, the costs of avoidance may be high for the instigator. If a target who had previously compensated for the instigator's inferior work disappears, his or her absence will hinder the instigator's work performance (Pearson & Porath, 2001). Furthermore, an instigator who has been avoided (rather than confronted) may continue to behave uncivilly: The target who avoids the instigator may reinforce future incidents inadvertently by seeming to take no offense from what has happened. In some cases, the instigator may even be unaware of causing ill feelings and, absent corrective feedback, may unknowingly repeat uncivil words or deeds.

Organizational Outcomes

Uncivil words and deeds may spiral or cascade, thus multiplying or intensifying deviant interactions (Andersson & Pearson, 1999; Baron & Neuman, 1996; Folger & Skarlicki, 1998). The phenomena of spiraling interpersonal conflict and escalating aggression have been well documented (e.g., Berkowitz, 1986, 1993; Bies & Tripp, 1995; Luckenbill, 1977; Tedeschi & Felson, 1994; Youngs, 1986). As Baron and Neuman (1996) have suggested, low-intensity aggression can constitute the initial steps in an upward spiral to more intense forms of aggression. We have theorized (Andersson & Pearson, 1999) that workplace incivility, specifically, may spiral into increasingly aggressive behaviors, including physical violence between target and instigator. Initial acts of incivility can yield an uncivil climate or they can serve as first steps in an upward spiral that surpasses incivility, leading to more intense forms of aggression (Andersson & Pearson, 1999; Porath & Pearson, 2000).

When incivility thrives, targets tend to limit their actions with instigators, as we have noted. This behavior curtails effective communication that may affect additional organizational stakeholders (Pearson et al., 2001). Some who experience incivility will leave their workplaces to avoid the instigator, thus increasing turnover. Others reduce their effort and time at work, thus decreasing productivity (Pearson et al., 2001). Organizations that condone incivility may find additional legal challenges (Cortina et al., 2002) as workers attempt to use the courts to right the perceived wrongs they have encountered at work. As employees experience or observe incivility and no organizational response is forthcoming, the reputation of the organization and its leaders may be spoiled internally. Customers or clients who witness uncivil encounters among employees may act in kind or absorb the incivility of the culture. Similarly, as employees describe these interactions to family and friends outside work, they may spoil the external reputation of the organization (Pearson & Porath, 2002).

Much of the empirical research on workplace deviance and related constructs suggests that organizational and group-level factors are important predictors of workplace deviance (e.g., Robinson & O'Leary-Kelly, 1998; Skarlicki & Folger, 1997). Those of different levels of power, as well as those of different genders, experience the workplace differently. We posit individual differences of status and gender, as well as organizational context as moderating factors related to incivility.

Individual Differences

Research investigating more serious forms of employee deviance at work suggests that organizational power differences among individuals may affect how likely they are to be targets of incivility. The ability to commit incivility may vary along power lines as well. Previous studies of the affects of gender differences at work suggest that men's and women's experiences of incivility differ in many ways, whether as instigator or as target. We consider these individual differences next.

Power and Position

It has been suggested that those of lesser power tend to retaliate in less aggressive ways (e.g., Epstein & Taylor, 1967; Ohbuchi & Saito, 1986). One reason offered is the ability of the powerful person to harm the less powerful person's career (Bies & Tripp, 1995; Neuman & Baron, 1998; Tedeschi & Felson, 1994). But what happens when the offense is subtle? In a recent study of more than 600 targets of incivility, we found that targets who are less powerful than their instigators tend to respond by avoiding the instigator and spoiling the instigator's reputation rather than outright, direct confrontation (Porath, Pearson, & Shapiro, 2002). Also, targets with less power than their instigators are more likely to respond with organization-ally directed deviance, rather than individually directed incivility. When there is a power differential that tips in favor of the instigator, targets will cut back their working hours and reduce their productivity, for example, rather than retaliate against their instigators. This strategy may be preferred because it allows greater safety through anonymity, as suggested by Aquino and colleagues (Aquino, Lewis, & Bradfield, 1999).

Gender: Instigator and Target

The occurrence of workplace incivility is gender blind. Male employees are just as likely to be targets of incivility as are their female colleagues (Pearson et al., 2000). But after an uncivil word or deed has happened, does gender make a difference in the target's reaction? Do men and women respond to incivility in the same ways? And if the responses differ, how do the differences affect the organization and beyond?

Meta-analyses of experimental studies reveal that in response to aggression, adult males are not only more physically aggressive than adult females but also more psychologically aggressive (Eagly & Steffen, 1986). Psychological forms of aggression more commonly expressed by males than females include vocal, nonverbal, and written aggressive responses (Eagly & Steffen, 1986). Moreover, in uncivil encounters, male targets tend to aggress more passively, as well as more overtly, against instigators of incivility than do women (Porath & Pearson, 2000). Men who have been targets of incivility respond with behaviors such as delaying action on the instigator's needs and withholding information needed by the instigator. Also, male targets of incivility are more likely than female targets to engage in aggression and to spoil the instigator's reputation (Porath & Pearson, 2000).

In general, women perceive active self-defense as antisocial, uncivilized, and irrational (Rothleder, 1992). Women may learn this conflict style early (e.g., Lindeman, Harakka, & Kettikangas-Jaervinen, 1997). Even as young girls, females are inclined to choose alternatives to direct conflict (Tannen, 1998). Studies of conflict resolution styles used in the workplace support these findings. Women defer more than their male counterparts and are more likely to rely on an accommodating style of conflict resolution (Sone, 1982; Zammuto, London, & Rowland, 1979). In regard to incivility specifically, we found that male targets are more likely than female targets to aggress against the instigator and to spoil the instigator's reputation, whereas female targets are more likely than male targets to avoid the instigator (Porath & Pearson, 2000).

When the target is male, the incivility spiral is more likely to be upward-bound in intensity, particularly when the instigator is also male (Porath & Pearson, 2000). A tit-for-tat behavior ensues in which each round has the potential to intensify. Interactions between males may quickly tip to additional aggressive behaviors, such as overt aggression, yelling, and direct threats. Men will try to get even. Also, by conveying that incivility will not go unanswered, uncivil behaviors toward the particular male are less likely to occur in the future (Axelrod, 1984). In contrast, women are more likely to "disappear" themselves (Fletcher, 1999) or intentionally distance themselves from the instigator. In so doing, they may attempt to rise above the situation, persevering despite the rudeness, or they may do something positive for themselves to offset the felt offense (Porath & Pearson, 2000).

Gender differences also affect the cascading and spillover of incivility within and beyond the organization. Male targets spread the word inside the organization as they attempt to build a workplace coalition of support.

Men tend to do this strategically. They spread the word from a power perspective, telling their own subordinates who are most likely to support them. After incivility has occurred, female targets are less likely than male targets to spread the word internally. Rather, they describe the incident to family members and friends outside the organization, thus damaging the reputations of the instigator and the organization in which the incivility occurred.

Organizational Context: The Informal Climate

It may be more difficult to discern appropriate behavior when the trappings of power and organizational membership vanish. As organizations have gone casual, cues about respect and politeness may have disappeared (Pearson et al., 2000). Formerly, artifacts of more formal attire, for example, may have signaled polite distance as the guideline to relating appropriately to coworkers within the work culture. For some who miss these cues, careless bantering may lead to thoughtless remarks, strained relationships, and an escalation of incivility (Pearson & Porath, 2002).

INTEGRATION WITH OTHER COUNTERPRODUCTIVE WORK BEHAVIOR CONSTRUCTS

Counterproductive work behavior (Fox et al., 2001; Martinko, Gundlach, & Douglas, 2002) has been described, modeled, and analyzed in various conceptual forms: as abusive (e.g., Keashly, 1998; Keashly, Trott, & MacLean, 1994; Tepper, 2000), aggressive (e.g., Baron & Neuman, 1996; Baron, Neuman, & Geddes, 1999; Neuman & Baron, 1998; O'Leary-Kelly et al., 1996), antisocial (e.g., Giacalone & Greenberg, 1997; Robinson & O'Leary-Kelly, 1998), bullying (e.g., Rayner et al., 2002); deviant (e.g., Aquino et al., 1999; Bennett & Robinson, 2002; Robinson & Bennett, 1995, 1997), mobbing (e.g., Leymann, 1990; Zapf, 1999), socially undermining (Duffy, Ganster, & Pagon, 2002), tyrannical (e.g., Ashforth, 1994), uncivil (e.g., Andersson & Pearson, 1999; Cortina, Magley, et al., 2001; Pearson et al., 2001), and violent (e.g., Dietz, Robinson, Folger, Baron, & Schultz, in press; Kinney, 1995; Pearson, 1998; VandenBos & Bulatao, 1996). Although there is great overlap among the various forms of counterproductive work behavior (O'Leary-Kelly et al., 2000), they tend to differ along a number of dimensions, including, but not limited to, intent to harm (e.g., absent, present, or ambiguous), target of the act (e.g., individuals, organizations, or both), type of norm violation (e.g., societal, organizational, work group, or none), persistence of the act (e.g., single act or act repeated over time), and the intensity and breadth of behaviors enacted (Martinko et al., 2002; O'Leary-Kelly et al., 2000). Nonetheless, all involve behavior that is intended to have a detrimental effect on organizations and their members (Fox et al., 2001; Martinko et al., 2002).

Aggressive behavior and violence have received the most attention in the U.S. academic and practitioner management literature (e.g., Baron & Neuman, 1996; Baron et al., 1999; Dietz et al., 2004; Kinney, 1995; Neuman & Baron, 1998; O'Leary-Kelly et al., 1996; VandenBos & Bulatao, 1996). Although there has been some disagreement among social scientists in the fields of criminology, psychology, and sociology about the definitions of and differences between aggression and violence (Tedeschi & Felson, 1994), researchers examining aggression and violence in organizations seem to concur that aggression is attempted injurious or destructive behavior and that violence is a high-intensity, physical form of aggression (Neuman & Baron, 1998).

A tremendous range and variety of acts constitute workplace aggression, from vandalism and sabotage to harassment, physical abuse, and homicide (Neuman & Baron, 1998). The common aspect of all of these acts of aggression is the obvious intent to harm or injure someone physically or psychologically (Neuman & Baron, 1998; Tedeschi & Felson, 1994). A distinguishing characteristic of incivility, however, is that the intent to harm—as perceived through the eyes of the instigator, the target, or the observers—is ambiguous. One may behave uncivilly as a reflection of intent to harm the target or one may behave uncivilly without intent (e.g., ignorance or oversight). Furthermore, the instigator may intend to harm the target, yet he or she may not even be conscious of such intent. Unlike instigators of aggression, instigators of incivility can easily deny or bury any intent, if present, in ignorance of the effect (e.g., "It wasn't meant as an attack"), in misinterpretation by the target (e.g., "I wasn't being rude; I was just in a hurry"), or in hypersensitivity of the target (e.g., "Don't take it so personally").

With incivility, the intent is not transparent and is subject to varying interpretation. Incivility is similar in intensity to several dimensions of petty tyranny (Ashforth, 1994), as well as several aspects of abusive supervision (Tepper, 2000). Both petty tyranny and abusive supervision include behaviors demonstrating a lack of consideration toward others, in which the intent to harm is ambiguous. Both petty tyranny and abusive supervision, however, are behavioral profiles attributed to leaders, referring also to a host of more intense negative behaviors associated with the instigator's abuse of position of authority.

The concepts of mobbing from research in Germany and Scandinavia and bullying from research in the United Kingdom are the conceptualizations of counterproductive work behavior most often grouped or confused with incivility in the human resource management media, policy, and practice. As opposed to incivility, however, conceptualizations of mobbing and bullying explicitly depict an obvious intent to harm the target and persistence of the behavior over time (Rayner et al., 2002; Zapf, 1999). Thus, both mobbing and bullying are acts of aggression, with bullying of low- to moderate intensity and more akin to incivility and mobbing of moderate- to high-intensity and more akin to violence.

Two other conceptualizations of counterproductive work behavior receiving recent attention in the United States are the overlapping constructs of deviant and antisocial employee behaviors. Robinson and Bennett have defined employee deviance as "voluntary behavior that violates significant organizational norms (including basic moral standards) and, in so doing, threatens the well being of an organization, its members, or both" (1995, p. 556). This definition implies a broad range of mistreatment—both of people and of property in organizations, with and without intent to harm—and is inclusive of workplace aggression and incivility. Even more broadly encompassing than employee deviance, and also inclusive of workplace aggression and incivility, is antisocial employee behavior, which Giacalone and Greenberg have defined as "any behavior that brings harm, or is intended to bring harm, to an organization, its employees, or stakeholders" (1997, p. vii). Antisocial behavior in the workplace, therefore, is essentially another term used to describe the broad spectrum of counterproductive behaviors at work.

To summarize, we illustrate how incivility differs from and overlaps with some of these other forms of counterproductive work behavior in Figure 8.2. This type of behavior, as action that has detrimental effects on the organization, its members, or both, is inclusive of all of the other conceptualizations. Deviant employee behavior is a type of counterproductive work behavior that violates workplace norms and includes employee aggression and incivility. Aggression includes violence, mobbing, emotional abuse, and bullying, as well as some forms of incivility (e.g., those with intent to harm, but in which the intent—as perceived by the instigator, the target, the observers, or any combination of these stakeholders—is ambiguous). Yet other forms of incivility (e.g., those without intent to harm but in which the intent is ambiguous, such as those that occur out of ignorance or oversight) lie outside the realm of aggression. Thus, like aggression, incivility is a deviant counterproductive work behavior, but one that is less intense and ambiguous as to intent to harm.

CONCLUSION

The research that is emerging regarding workplace incivility primarily regards targets' perceptions. Certainly, understanding the perspectives of

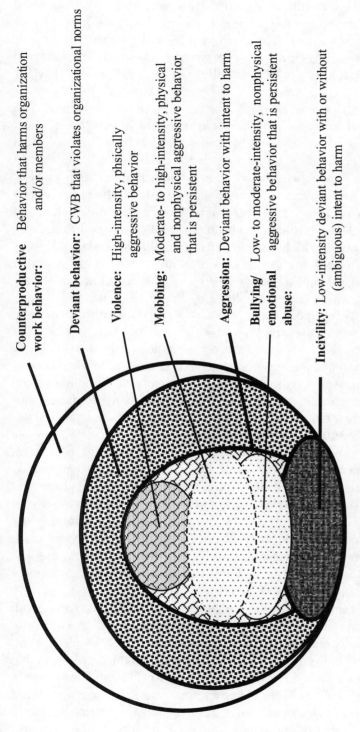

Counterproductive Behavior that harms organization
work behavior: and/or members

Deviant behavior: CWB that violates organizational norms

Violence: High-intensity, phsically
aggressive behavior

Mobbing: Moderate- to high-intensity, physical
and nonphysical aggressive behavior
that is persistent

Aggression: Deviant behavior with intent to harm

Bullying/ Low- to moderate-intensity, nonphysical
emotional aggressive behavior that is persistent
abuse:

Incivility: Low-intensity deviant behavior with or without
(ambiguous) intent to harm

Figure 8.2. Incivility and other forms of counterproductive work behavior in organizations.

other stakeholders, including instigators, witnesses, and additional third parties, would inform research and practice. Although scholars are clarifying the costs and consequences of incivility (as viewed through the targets' eyes), investigations of the instigator's perspective could help us understand why people behave uncivilly toward colleagues, as well as why they get away with it.

In general, the emergent studies of incivility have been limited in examining the nuclear dyad—that is, the target and the instigator. Although implications and attributions about other stakeholders have been collected from the target's perspective, to our knowledge, no research has examined the specific effects of workplace incivility as evaluated by third parties. How do varying reactions of supporters (internal or external to the organization) affect the targets' and instigators' behaviors? How does the experience of incivility affect colleagues or family within or outside the organization? Are there conditions under which unconstrained incivility at work is displaced in harmful ways outside the workplace on family or friends? In a similar vein, it would be valuable to study whether nonwork contingencies are displaced into the workplace as employee-to-employee incivility.

From a third-party perspective, it would also be useful to theory and practice to investigate how employee-to-employee incivility infests other work relationships. For example, how do customers respond when they encounter an uncivil work environment? Are there spillover effects of employee-to-employee incivility on vendors or suppliers? Although we are beginning to appreciate the impact of incivility on employee witnesses, thus far, we have no grasp of its effects on various other organizational stakeholders farther outside the nuclear dyad (Figure 8.3).

From an organizational perspective, it would be useful to understand how culture relates to incivility. Because culture is the enactment of organizational norms and values, it seems reasonable to assert that culture and incivility (in violation of those norms and values) will intermingle. Are there organizational or industrial practices that facilitate or inhibit the escalation or spread of incivility, and to what gain or loss? Do some workplace cultures intentionally encourage incivility? Does incivility prevail in some specific organizational functions or industrial sectors? How do differences among national cultures affect civility?

Similarly, examining incivility within the realm of electronic work would be intriguing. Increasingly, workplace interactions occur within the broad and constantly changing social context of cyberspace. Employees are, willingly or unwillingly, initiated into the esoteric and highly unstable world of online social conventions (Wallace, 1999). The different Internet venues—the World Wide Web, electronic mail, asynchronous discussion forums, synchronous chats, multiuser text domains, multimedia meta-worlds—vary in degree of anonymity, purpose, and moderating presence,

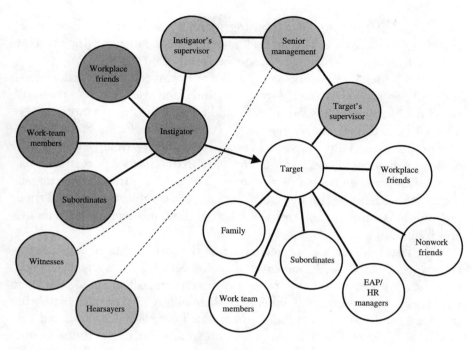

Figure 8.3. Stakeholder map of workplace incivility.

and thus require varying social rules, policies, and procedures. This begets the following questions, among others: Is the virtual workplace an inherently uncivil place because of factors such as perceived anonymity, lack of emotional reactivity, reproducibility, and uncontrollability (Kiesler, Siegel, & McGuire, 1984)? What behaviors are considered to be uncivil in the virtual workplace? How might incivility spiral in the virtual workplace?

Finally, explicitly linking incivility to financial impact would make an important contribution to practice. If managers and executives can calculate direct and indirect financial costs or benefits accrued in organizations that are uncivil, they could make deliberate and grounded decisions to squelch or ignore the phenomenon. From the data we have collected and the anecdotes we have heard, we tend to infer that organizations that insist on civil interactions will gain other benefits from their employees—but do they? Does an uncivil environment actually affect organizational costs, such as selection, retention, or productivity? As prospective employees evaluate their career options, for example, can a civil environment compensate for other perks or benefits that may be lacking? Learning more about the surface and hidden costs of incivility to organizations and their stakeholders could motivate executives to better manage incivility among their employees.

Incivility is expensive. Uncivil encounters at work can happen frequently. About 10% of respondents to a nationwide survey conducted across the United States reported witnessing incivility daily within their work-places. Roughly 20% said that they are the direct targets of incivility at work at least once per week (Pearson & Porath, 2002).

When incivility occurs, costs are borne by targets, coworkers, leaders, and instigators, as well as the target's family and friends, and others. A broad net of stakeholders, both inside and outside the organization, can be affected by and affect uncivil behavior (refer back to Figure 8.3). Targets of workplace incivility respond by wasting company time, reducing the quality of their work, and eliminating any extra efforts or organizational citizenship-type behaviors (Pearson et al., 2000, 2001). In addition, targets avoid and undermine the instigator, lose respect for their leaders and their organizations, and spread the word about their mistreatment to family and friends.

In research that we conducted across the United States and Canada (Pearson & Porath, 2002; Pearson et al., 2000, 2002), 80% of targets claimed that they lost respect for the instigator, more than half reported that they lost work time fretting and scheming about future interactions with the instigator, and roughly one half contemplated changing jobs to avoid the instigator. Add to this a reduction in organizational productivity as one fifth of targets reported decreasing their work effort intentionally and 12% actually left their jobs to escape the uncivil situation (Pearson et al., 2000). Given the low intensity of this phenomenon, the organizational costs can be staggering. By cutting back work effort, reducing the quality of their work, and putting in fewer hours, targets can undermine productivity. Furthermore, when targets leave their positions, they create gaps in organizational effectiveness and additional costs for resource replacement. Each of these organizational costs should capture the attention of management.

Even a target's indirect responses to incivility carry a toll. So those who are uncivil to colleagues at any level of the organization should beware. Although an immediate, more intense response may not be forthcoming, targets of incivility tend to retaliate. As we have noted, if you are uncivil, you may find your reputation spoiled, your requests ignored, and your ability to get things done stifled. You may find yourself trapped in an escalating battle with your targets as well as their colleagues. Or, if you work for savvy leaders, you may find your career stalled and, if your behavior is chronic, you may eventually be out of a job.

The most damaging threat to organizations is the occurrence of spirals and cascades. If leaders do not respond when incivility occurs, low-intensity breaches of conduct can ignite hostility, offend witnesses and others who hear about the interaction, and even escalate to physical aggression. Furthermore, new instigators (who witness or hear about the encounter) may initiate their own acts of incivility on additional coworkers if they have reason to believe that they can get away with it. As we have noted, incivility can spread in insidious ways to erode organizational values and fundamentally alter organizational norms. Unconstrained incivility can cause valued employees to leave, and those who stay may lose respect for the organization and its leaders.

Managers and executives can address these costs by setting norms for incivility (both by decree and by role modeling). Establishing an expectation about how employees treat one another provides a baseline against which infractions can be measured and corrected. Once set, it is critical that standards are reinforced. Those who take incivility seriously intervene to stop rudeness and disrespect among their workforce. In the case of chronic instigators, this may even require job termination.

The business world may have been one of the last bastions of civility. The relationship between coworkers was, for decades, characterized by formality yet friendliness, distance yet politeness (Elias, 1982). However, as we have argued, business has started to reflect social contextual shifts and organizational pressures that lead to negative outcomes for an array of stakeholders and their organizations. When someone neglects to acknowledge a colleague's contribution or does not respond to an e-mail request, although the target may feel offended, some coworkers may characterize the behavior as oversight or disregard rather than an outright intentional vengefulness. We assert that incivilities are negative behaviors and that insight is needed to manage the phenomenon in the workplace. We believe that such insight will come as researchers and managers consider not only the motives and actions of instigator, target, and others but also the context to better understand how incivility unfolds. As we continue to wrestle with this phenomenon, we believe that the subtleties of incivility, as well as the extensive net of stakeholders that it ensnares, compel additional investigation and informed practice.

REFERENCES

Andersson, L. M., & Pearson, C. M. (1999). Tit for tat? The spiraling effect of incivility in the workplace. *Academy of Management Review, 24,* 452–471.

Aquino, K., Lewis, M. U., & Bradfield, M. (1999). Justice constructs, negative affectivity, and employee deviance: A proposed model and empirical test. *Journal of Organizational Behavior, 20,* 1073–1091.

Ashforth, B. E. (1994). Petty tyranny in organizations. *Human Relations, 47,* 755–778.

Austin, R. (1988). Employer abuse, worker resistance, and the tort of intentional infliction of emotional distress. *Stanford Law Review, 41,* 1.

Axelrod, R. (1984). *The evolution of cooperation.* New York: Basic Books.

Baron, R. A., & Neuman, J. H. (1996). Workplace violence as a workplace aggression: Evidence on their relative frequency and causes. *Aggressive Behavior, 22,* 161–173.

Baron, R. A., Neuman, J. H., & Geddes, D. (1999). Social and personal determinants of workplace aggression: Evidence for the impact of perceived injustice and the type A behavior pattern. *Aggressive Behavior, 25,* 281–296.

Bennett, R., & Robinson, S. (2002). The past, present and future of deviance research. In J. Greenberg (Ed.), *Organizational behavior: The state of the science* (2nd ed., pp. 275–289). Mahwah, NJ: Erlbaum.

Berkowitz, L. (1986). Some varieties of human aggression: Criminal violence as coercion, rule-following, impression management, and impulsive behavior. In A. Campbell & J. J. Gibbs (Eds.), *Violent transactions* (pp. 87–103). Oxford, England: Basil Blackwell.

Berkowitz, L. (1993). *Aggression: Its causes, consequences, and control.* New York: McGraw-Hill.

Bies, R. J. (2000). Interactional (in)justice: The sacred and the profane. In J. Greenberg & R. Cropanzano (Eds.), *Advances in organizational justice* (pp. 89–118). Palo Alto, CA: Stanford University Press.

Bies, R. J., & Moag, J. S. (1986). Interactional justice: Communications criteria of fairness. In R. Lewicki & B. Sheppard (Eds.), *Research on negotiation in organizations* (Vol. 1, pp. 43–55). Greenwich, CT: JAI Press.

Bies, R. J., & Tripp, T. M. (1995). Beyond distrust: "Getting even" and the need for revenge. In R. M. Kramer & T. R. Tyler (Eds.), *Trust in organizations* (pp. 246–260). Thousand Oaks, CA: Sage.

Brown, P., & Levinson, S. C. (1987). *Politeness: Some universals in language usage.* New York: Cambridge University Press.

Carter, S. L. (1998). *Civility: Manners, morals, and the etiquette of democracy.* New York: Basic Books.

Connelly, J. (1994, November 28). Have we become mad dogs in the office? *Fortune,* 197–199.

Cortina, L. M., Lonsway, K. L., Magley, V. J., Freeman, L. V., Collinsworth, L. L., Hunter, M., et al. (2002). What's gender got to do with it? Incivility in the federal courts. *Law and Social Inquiry, 27,* 235–270.

Cortina, L. M., Magley, V. J., & Lim, S. G. P. (2002, August). *Individual differences in response to incivility in the workplace.* Paper presented at the annual meeting of the Academy of Management, Denver, CO.

Cortina, L. M., Magley, V. J., Williams, J. H., & Langhout, R. D. (2001). Incivility in the workplace: Incidence and impact. *Journal of Occupational Health Psychology, 6,* 64–80.

Crain, M. (1997, February). *Legal issues surrounding "violence" in the workplace: Update and conceptualization.* Paper presented at Festival of Legal Learning, University of North Carolina School of Law, Chapel Hill.

Cupach, W. R., Huggins, J., Long, L. W., & Metts, S. (2002, August). *Perceptions of impropriety: Role of embarrassability and perceiver sex.* Paper presented at the Western States Communication Association Annual Convention, Long Beach, CA.

Dietz, J., Robinson, S. L., Folger, R., Baron, R. A., & Schulz, M. (2004). The impact of community violence and an organization's procedural justice climate on workplace aggression. *Academy of Management Journal, 46,* 317–327.

Douglas, S. C., & Martinko, M. J. (2001). Exploring the role of individual differences in the prediction of workplace aggression. *Journal of Applied Psychology, 86*(4), 547–559.

Duffy, M. K., Ganster, D. C., & Pagon, M. (2002). Social undermining in the workplace. *Academy of Management Journal, 45,* 331–352.

Eagly, A. H., & Steffen, V. J. (1986). Gender and aggressive behavior: A meta-analytic review of the social psychological literature. *Psychological Bulletin, 100,* 303–330.

Ehrlich, H. J., & Larcom, B. E. K. (1994). *Ethnoviolence in the workplace.* Baltimore: Center for the Applied Study of Ethnoviolence.

Elias, N. (1982). *The history of manners.* New York: Pantheon.

Epstein, S., & Taylor, S. P. (1967). Instigation to aggression as a function of degree of defeat and perceived aggressive intent of the opponent. *Journal of Personality, 35,* 265–289.

Fletcher, J. K. (1999). *Disappearing acts.* Cambridge, MA: MIT Press.

Folger, R., & Skarlicki, D. P. (1998). A popcorn model of workplace violence. In R. W. Griffin, A. O'Leary-Kelly, & J. Collins (Eds.), *Dysfunctional behavior in organizations: Nonviolent dysfunctional behaviors* (pp. 43–82). Greenwich, CT: JAI Press.

Fox, S., & Spector, P. E. (1999). A model of work frustration–aggression. *Journal of Organizational Behavior, 20,* 915–931.

Fox, S., Spector, P. E., & Miles, D. (2001). Counterproductive work behavior (CWB) in response to job stressors and organizational justice: Some mediator and moderator tests for autonomy and emotions. *Journal of Vocational Behavior, 59,* 291–309.

Giacalone, R. A., & Greenberg, J. (Eds.). (1997). *Antisocial behavior in organizations.* Thousand Oaks, CA: Sage.

Gonthier, G. (2002). *Rude awakenings: Overcoming the civility crisis in the workplace.* Chicago: Dearborn Trade.

Graydon, J., Kasta, W., & Khan, P. (1994, November–December). Verbal and physical abuse of nurses. *Canadian Journal of Nursing Administration,* 70–89.

Johnson, P. R., & Indvik, J. (2001). Slings and arrows of rudeness: Incivility in the workplace. *Journal of Management Development, 20,* 705–713.

Keashly, L. (1998). Emotional abuse in the workplace: Conceptual and empirical issues. *Journal of Emotional Abuse, 1*(1), 85–115.

Keashly, L., Trott, V., & MacLean, L. M. (1994). Abusive behavior in the workplace: A preliminary investigation. *Violence and Victims, 9*, 341–357.

Kiesler, S., Siegel, J., & McGuire, T. W. (1984). Social psychological aspects of computer-mediated communication. *American Psychologist, 39*, 1123–1134.

Kinney, J. A. (1995). *Violence at work.* Englewood Cliffs, NJ: Prentice-Hall.

Lewis, D. E. (2000, October 8). From casual to rude. *Boston Globe*, p. J2.

Leymann, H. (1990). Mobbing and psychological terror at workplaces. *Violence and Victims, 5*, 119–126.

Lindeman, M., Harakka, T., & Keltikangas-Jaervinen, L. (1997). Age and gender differences in adolescents' reactions to conflict situations: Aggression, prosociality, and withdrawal. *Journal of Youth and Adolescence, 26*, 339–351.

Luckenbill, D. F. (1977). Criminal homicide as a situated transaction. *Social Problems, 25*, 176–186.

MacKinnon, C. (1994). *Only words.* New York: Basic Books.

Martin, J. (1996). *Miss Manners rescues civilization.* New York: Crown.

Martinko, M. J., Gundlach, M. J., & Douglas, S. C. (2002). Toward an integrative theory of counterproductive workplace behavior: A causal reasoning perspective. *International Journal of Selection and Assessment, 10*(1–2), 36–50.

Martinko, M. J., & Zellars, K. L. (1996, August). *Toward a theory of workplace violence: A social learning and attribution perspective.* Paper presented at the annual meeting of the Academy of Management, Cincinnati, OH.

Miller, R. S. (2000). Breaches of propriety. In R. M. Kowalski (Ed.), *Behaving badly: Aversive behaviors in interpersonal relationships* (pp. 25–42). Washington, DC: American Psychological Association.

Morris, J. (1996, Autumn). Democracy beguiled. *Wilson Quarterly*, 24–35.

Neuman, J. H., & Baron, R. A. (1998). Workplace violence and workplace aggression: Evidence concerning specific forms, potential causes, and preferred targets. *Journal of Management, 24*, 391–419.

Ohbuchi, K., & Saito, M. (1986). Power imbalance, its legitimacy, and aggression. *Aggressive Behavior, 12*, 33–40.

O'Leary-Kelly, A. M., Duffy, M. K., & Griffin, R. W. (2000). Construct confusion in the study of antisocial behavior. *Research in Personnel and Human Resources Management, 18*, 275–303.

O'Leary-Kelly, A. M., Griffin, R. W., Sr., & Glew, D. J. (1996). Organization-motivated aggression: A research framework. *Academy of Management Review, 21*, 225–254.

Pearson, C. M. (1998). Organizations as targets and triggers of aggression and violence: Framing rational explanations for dramatic organizational deviance. *Research in Sociology of Organizations, 15*, 197–223.

Pearson, C. M., Andersson, L. M., & Porath, C. L. (2000). Assessing and attacking workplace incivility. *Organizational Dynamics, 29*, 123–137.

Pearson, C. M., Andersson, L. M., & Wegner, J. A. (2001). When workers flout convention: A preliminary study of workplace incivility. *Human Relations, 54,* 1387–1420.

Pearson, C. M., & Porath, C. L. (2001, August). *Effects of incivility on the target: Fight, flee or take care of "me"?* Paper presented at the annual meeting of the Academy of Management, Washington, DC.

Pearson, C. M., & Porath, C. L. (2002). *Rude awakening: Detecting and curtailing workplace incivility.* London, Ontario, Canada: Richard Ivey School of Business, University of Western Ontario.

Porath, C. L., & Pearson, C. M. (2000, August). *Gender differences and the behavior of targets of workplace incivility: He "dukes" it out, she "disappears" herself.* Paper presented at the annual meeting of the Academy of Management, Toronto, Ontario, Canada.

Porath, C. L., Pearson, C. M., & Shapiro, D. (2002). *The consequences of incivility: Who reacts, how, and when?* Los Angeles: Marshall School of Business, University of Southern California.

Rayner, C., Hoel, H., & Cooper, C. L. (2002). *Workplace bullying: What we know, who is to blame and what can we do?* London: Taylor Francis.

Remington, R., & Darden, M. (2002). *Aggravating circumstances: A status report on rudeness in America.* New York: Public Agenda.

Robinson, S. L., & Bennett, R. J. (1995). A typology of deviant workplace behaviors: A multidimensional scaling study. *Academy of Management Journal, 38,* 555–572.

Robinson, S. L., & Bennett, R. J. (1997). Workplace deviance: Its definition, its manifestations, and its causes. *Research on Negotiations in Organizations, 6,* 3–27.

Robinson, S. L., & O'Leary-Kelly, A. M. (1998). Monkey see, monkey do: The influence of work groups on the antisocial behavior of employees. *Academy of Management Journal, 41,* 658–672.

Rothleder, D. (1992). Disappearing. *Philosophy Today, 36,* 173–180.

Skarlicki, D. P., & Folger, R. (1997). Retaliation in the workplace: The role of distributive, procedural and interactional justice. *Journal of Applied Psychology, 82,* 434–443.

Sone, P. G. (1982). The effects of gender on managers' resolution of superior–subordinate conflict. *Dissertation Abstracts International, 42*(11), 4914-A.

Tannen, D. (1998). *The argument culture: Moving from debate to dialogue.* New York: Random House.

Tedeschi, J. T., & Felson, R. B. (1994). *Violence, aggression and coercive actions.* Washington, DC: American Psychological Association.

Tepper, B. (2000). Consequences of abusive supervision. *Academy of Management Journal, 43,* 178–190.

VandenBos, G. R., & Bulatao, E. Q. (1996). *Violence on the job: Identifying risks and developing solutions.* Washington, DC: American Psychological Association.

Wallace, P. (1999). *The psychology of the Internet*. Cambridge, England: Cambridge University Press.

Walters, D. K. (1994, December 4). Read this story on rudeness: Now! *Los Angeles Times*, p. D1.

Wegner, J. W. (1996). Lawyers, learning and professionalism. *Cleveland State Law Review, 43*, 191–216.

Wilson, J. Q. (1993). *The moral sense*. New York: Free Press.

Winters, A. M., & Duck, S. W. (2000). You****!!! Swearing as an aversive and a relational activity. In R. M. Kowalski (Ed.), *Behaving badly: Aversive behaviors in interpersonal relationships* (pp. 59–77). Washington, DC: American Psychological Association.

Youngs, G. A., Jr. (1986). Patterns of threat and punishment reciprocity in a conflict setting. *Journal of Personality and Social Psychology, 51*(3), 541–546.

Zammuto, R., London, M., & Rowland, K. M. (1979). Effects of sex on commitment and conflict resolution. *Journal of Applied Psychology, 64*, 227–23.

Zapf, D. (1999). Organisational, work group related and personal causes of mobbing at work. *International Journal of Manpower, 20*(1–2), 70–85.

Zauderer, D. G. (2002). Workplace incivility and the management of human capital. *Public Manager, 31*(1), 36–43.

9

EMOTIONAL ABUSE IN THE WORKPLACE

LORALEIGH KEASHLY AND STEVE HARVEY

Judy receives a call from her old college roommate Cindy, now working as a caseworker at a child protection agency. Cindy, in tears, relates to Judy the mean things her boss has been doing to her (and others, she finds out later). He was nice enough when she first arrived at her job last year, but now he has become unbearable. Cindy listed some of the things he had done that week: "On Monday, he came in to work and told me that I was too slow and that I dragged down the whole department. The rest of the week he spent glaring at me each time he passed me in the hall. He threw a huge temper tantrum when I did not have a report ready prior to the deadline he had given me last week. I even heard a rumor suggesting that I was sleeping with a client, and I'm certain he started it. I just don't know what to do. What do you think, Judy?"

As Judy hung up, she began to ponder Cindy's problem. Several ideas ran through her mind. Could it be that Cindy is wrong about this? Is her performance a problem she is not sharing? Or maybe she is just blowing the situation up to be a bit worse than it is? No, Cindy always was a hard-working, determined individual. Maybe her boss was jealous of her competence and is punishing her by doing these things? Or maybe the boss is totally stressed out and is lashing out at those around him? Yeah, he does this to everyone at work, even the guys working with Cindy.

Many of us are all too familiar with these kinds of hostile work experiences, perhaps because they involve friends or family or even ourselves. It is this type of composite story that got our attention. We both knew of cases that had been shared with us independently of each other, so certainly this had to be a common enough experience, we thought. Based on informal discussions with self-reported victims, we soon realized that these experiences did not fit our traditional conceptions of harassment (e.g., sexual or racial), nor should it be classified as aggression (physical violence) in the workplace. The concept of emotional abuse in the intimate violence literature (e.g., Murphy & O'Leary, 1989; O'Leary, 1999), however, seemed to describe the same types and effects of the behaviors that we were hearing about. We thought the term *abuse* was particularly apt for two reasons. First, *abuse* captures the severity of and long-term effects on people that became apparent from written and oral accounts of people's experience. These behaviors are essentially hostile to the well-being of the target. Second, the emotional aspect helped to distinguish this phenomenon from physical, sexual, or racial hostility that are denoted by the form and content of the behaviors used. The emotional reference also seemed to capture the main focus of impact—in other words, the individual's feelings and thoughts about him- or herself as a competent person in the workplace. So, consistent with other developing literature at the time (Bassman, 1992; NiCarthy, Gottlieb, & Coffman, 1993), we decided to systematically examine whether emotional abuse was also a workplace phenomenon.

As the scenario that opens this chapter illustrates, emotional abuse in the workplace is a complex phenomenon that will take time to sort through given the various practical, social, theoretical, and research implications that typically envelop new areas of research. We by no means suggest that it is a new phenomenon, because clearly the evidence indicates that nonphysical hostility has existed as long as people have interacted with one another at work. What is new is our interest in studying this particular counterproductive work behavior from a scientific standpoint.

As excited as we are about sharing our thinking and work on emotional abuse, this was a difficult chapter to write, because the nature of the volume encourages each contributor to focus on our construct. This was tough because emotional abuse has been developed and refined in the larger cauldron of workplace aggression, hostility, harassment, bullying, and abuse as reflected in the diversity of this volume. Thus, our chapter makes reference to these constructs and the connection of emotional abuse to them.

We begin with a section that reviews the definition of emotional abuse as it has evolved over the past decade (Keashly, 1998; Keashly & Jagatic,

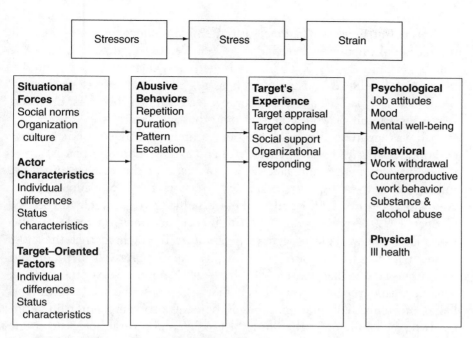

Figure 9.1. Emotional abuse process framework.

2003; Keashly, Trott, & MacLean, 1994). We tie this definition into other frameworks in which such connections are apparent (e.g., Barling, 1996; O'Leary-Kelly, Duffy, & Griffin, 2000). Much of what we cover in this chapter is summarized in Figure 9.1, which represents basic notions that capture some of the thinking and research that has driven and continues to influence research on emotional abuse. In general, the framework is predicated on the stress process, with each relevant concept cast within an antecedent–consequences framework. We return to this framework after establishing our definition of emotional abuse.

EMOTIONAL ABUSE: ALL-INCLUSIVE CONCEPT AND DEFINITION

An all-inclusive view of emotional abuse was apparent from the first definition constructed for our study of undergraduate work experiences (Keashly et al., 1994). By defining emotional abuse as "hostile verbal and nonverbal behaviors (excluding physical contact) directed by one or more persons towards another that are aimed at undermining the other to ensure compliance" (p. 342), we explicitly left open the possibility of any nonphysical behavior being construed as emotionally abusive. At the time, our belief was that many related concepts such as workplace bullying, harassment, and mistreatment were in fact measuring a similar—if not the same—general interpersonal phenomenon (Harvey, 1996; Keashly et al., 1994; Keashly, Harvey, & Hunter, 1997). There was nonetheless clear separation from the more well-developed constructs such as sexual harassment (Fitzgerald & Shullman, 1993). This first definition evolved through the years, however, in part as a result of work coming from other scholars.

It was apparent early on that other researchers' work corroborated that emotionally abusive behaviors were real and extensive in workplaces, albeit using different names and labels. Among some of the earliest and most influential work was that on workplace aggression (Baron & Neuman, 1996; Neuman & Baron, 1997) and workplace bullying (e.g., Hoel, Rayner, & Cooper, 1999). Applying Buss's (1961) theory on human aggression to the workplace, the workplace aggression literature highlighted that the most frequent forms of aggression were not physical as portrayed in the media but rather were verbal, passive, and indirect (Neuman & Baron, 1997). It was clear that the nonphysical behaviors they described fell within the behavioral domain of emotional abuse. There was also a burgeoning literature on workplace bullying in the United Kingdom and several European countries referring to essentially similar behaviors and actors (See Hoel et al., 1999, for a review). Other labels appeared during this time, including workplace mistreatment (Price Spratlen, 1995), generalized workplace abuse (Richman, Flaherty, & Rospenda, 1996), verbal abuse (Cox, 1991), psychological abuse (e.g., Sheehan, Sheehan, White, Leibowitz, & Baldwin, 1990), and psychological aggression (e.g., Barling, 1996). This profusion of terms prompted Keashly (1998) to review the literature and propose seven defining elements of emotional abuse that were either explicitly apparent or implied in the literature at the time. The seven defining features or dimensions included behaviors that are

1. verbal and nonverbal (excluding physical contact);
2. repetitive or patterned;
3. unwelcome and unsolicited by the target;
4. violations of a standard of appropriate conduct toward others;
5. harmful or cause psychological or physical injury to the target;
6. intended to harm or controllable by the actor; and
7. exploiting position power of the actor over target.

In her review, Keashly (1998) systematically reflected on the relevance of each dimension. For example, some of these features are sufficient reason to consider behavior emotionally abusive but are not in fact necessary for this determination. Exploiting power, for example, is not always an issue, but any time an actor behaves in a power *exploitative* fashion toward a target, one can typify such behavior as abusive. These dimensions are consistent with other proposed frameworks. In particular, O'Leary-Kelly et al. (2000)

invoke several similar dimensions to argue for and illustrate construct clarification in the area of antisocial behavior in general. In the end, their point is similar to ours in that various proposed constructs can be differentiated on several dimensions. The importance lies in researchers appreciating these differences and the impact they have on the study of the phenomenon of interest.

Since Keashly's 1998 review, a continued effort in the European bullying literature (e.g., Einarsen, Hoel, Zapf, & Cooper, 2003) has contributed to new insights on emotional abuse, as have several authors who have introduced additional distinct yet related constructs such as abusive supervision (Tepper, 2000), workplace incivility (Andersson & Pearson, 1999; see also chap. 8, this volume), and social undermining (Duffy, Granster, & Pagon, 2002). It is our view that, despite the initial confusion, these concepts have helped to develop the overall construct space of emotional abuse more precisely, particularly with regard to issues relating to the seven aforementioned features (Keashly, 1998; O'Leary-Kelly et al., 2000). The European bullying literature, for example, has solidified the importance of the notion of persistent hostility. Added to the growing longitudinal research on chronic workplace abuse (Rospenda, Richman, Wistar, & Flaherty, 2000; Tepper, 2000), this provides critical data on the effects of long-term exposure to nonphysical hostility for targets and their coworkers. Likewise, recent innovations in the workplace aggression literature (e.g., Glomb, 2002) introduce the notions of patterning and escalation to the area of hostile behavior. It is such additional contributions that prompted reconceptualization of emotional abuse to accommodate the findings other concepts seemingly developed in isolation.

Accordingly, Keashly and Jagatic (2003) visualized the concept of emotional abuse as a construct of hostile workplace relationships rather than as discrete and disconnected events. The element of time is now a central guiding feature in the definition of this construct (Keashly & Jagatic, 2003). In particular, the aspects of repetition (frequency), duration (over an extended period of time), and patterning (variety of behaviors involved) have become even more salient distinguishing features. That is, emotional abuse as a concept refers to repeated hostile verbal and nonverbal behaviors (excluding physical contact) directed at one or more individuals over a period of time such that the target's sense of self as a competent worker and person is negatively affected. It is clear that the definition now focuses on *persistent* nonphysical hostility that causes harm to the target. As such, any behavior referred to by several other concepts (e.g., generalized workplace abuse: Richman et al., 1996; workplace victimization: Aquino, Grover, Brackfield, & Allen, 1999; abusive supervision: Tepper, 2000; social undermining: Duffy et al., 2002) may feasibly fit into the definition of emotional abuse so long as they are seen to be *persistent*. Using Buss's (1961) framework,

Table 9.1 provides examples of the range and types of behaviors subsumed under emotional abuse.

A central underlying assumption of our research and theorizing on emotional abuse is that it is studied from the victim's perspective. Consistent with sexual and racial harassment literatures (e.g., Fitzgerald & Shullman, 1993; Schneider, Hitlan, & Radhakrishnan, 2000), we conceptualize emotional abuse to be a subjective experience. As highlighted in a review of the research and the assumptions underlying the framework in Figure 9.1, emotional abuse has always purposefully been understood and measured from the target's experiential perspective. This does not detract from valid concerns that research needs to also identify and study "objective" events—in other words, events corroborated by others as having occurred. As outlined in our model to be discussed shortly, subjective and corroborated forms of abuse are both part of a larger experiential process and should ultimately be studied in tandem to examine the points at which they are likely to differ and why. We have focused our attention largely on one part of this larger process, the subjective reports. Nonetheless in recognition of such concerns we have found it important to examine the impact that individual differences and situations (e.g., Harvey, 1996; Harvey & Keashly, in press; Keashly et al., 1997) have on victim's reports of emotionally abusive events at work.

Any discussion of definition would not be complete without an examination of measurement issues. Indeed, the challenge of succinctly defining emotional abuse over the years has been equaled only by concerns with its measurement.

MEASUREMENT OF EMOTIONAL ABUSE

Measurement of emotional abuse has not been as rigorous as one would hope. As noted by O'Leary-Kelly et al. (2000) in their consideration of the antisocial behavior literature, there has been a relative lack of construct research in contrast to a growing focus on substantive research about emotional abuse. By Schwab's (1980) standard of construct validity, this means that insufficient research has focused on the development of psychometrically sound measures of emotional abuse. The field has generally been hurried by a desire to discover the substantive issues at the expense of construct research. The danger is simply that unless we can be relatively confident of "what" we are measuring, we cannot be certain that the relationships we observe between measures are meaningful reflections of the presumed constructs (Schwab, 1980). It is fair to say that despite the attempt by many authors to clearly define the particular construct of interest, there has been

TABLE 9.1

Examples of Emotionally Abusive Behaviors

Behavioral source	Category	Behavioral examples
Verbal/active/direct	Name calling, use of derogatory terms	Baron and Neuman (1996); Bennett and Robinson (2000); Cortina et al. (2001); Glomb (2002); Keashly and Rogers (2001); Price Spratlen (1995); Tepper (2000)
	Subject to insulting jokes	Baron and Neuman (1996); Glomb (2002); Keashly and Jagatic (2000)
	Belittled; intellectually talked down to	Cortina et al. (2001); Duffy et al. (2002); Keashly and Jagatic (2000); Keashly and Rogers (2001); Price Spratlen (1995); Richman et al. (1997); Tepper (2000)
	Criticized harshly, attacked verbally in private or public; put down in front of others	Aquino et al. (1999); Cortina et al. (2001); Duffy et al. (2002); Keashly and Jagatic (2000); Keashly and Rogers (2001); Price Spratlen (1995); Richman et al. (1997); Robinson and Bennett (1995); Tepper (2000)
	Sworn at	Aquino et al. (1999); Glomb (2002); Keashly and Jagatic (2000); Keashly and Rogers (2001); Price Spratlen (1995); Richman et al. (1997);
	Lied to, deceived	Aquino et al. (1999); Duffy et al. (2002); Robinson and Bennett (1995); Tepper (2000)
	Yelled at, shouted at	Baron and Neuman (1996); Keashly and Jagatic (2000); Keashly and Rogers (2001); Price Spratlen (1995); Richman et al. (1997);
	Interrupted when speaking, working	Glomb (2001); Keashly and Jagatic (2000); Richman et al. (1997)
	Pressured to change personal life, beliefs, opinions	Cortina et al. (2001); Glomb (2002)
	Flaunting status	Baron and Neuman (1996); Duffy et al., (2002); Keashly and Jagatic (2000)
Verbal/active/indirect	Treated unfairly	Robinson and Bennett (1995)
	Subject to false accusations, rumors	Aquino et al. (1999); Baron and Neuman (1996); Duffy et al. (2002); Keashly and Jagatic (2000); Keashly and Rogers (2001); Richman et al. (1997); Robinson and Bennett (1995); Tepper (2000)
	Attempts made to turn others against you	Glomb (2002); Keashly and Rogers (2001); Tepper (2000)

(continues)

TABLE 9.1 *(Continued)*

Behavioral source	Category	Behavioral examples
Verbal/passive/direct	You or your contributions ignored; silent treatment	Aquino et al. (1999); Baron and Neuman (1996); Cortina et al. (2001); Duffy et al. (2002); Keashly and Jagatic (2000); Keashly and Rogers (2001); Price Spratlen (1995); Richman et al. (1997); Tepper (2000)
Verbal/passive/indirect	Had memos, phone calls ignored	Baron and Neuman (1996); Keashly and Jagatic (2000); Keashly and Rogers (2001)
	Been given little or no feedback, guidance	Keashly and Jagatic (2000)
	Deliberately excluded	Cortina et al. (2001); Keashly and Jagatic (2000); Keashly and Rogers (2001); Price Spratlen (1995); Richman et al. (1997); Schneider et al. (2000)
	Failing to pass on information needed by the target	Baron and Neuman (1996); Duffy et al. (2002)
Physical/active/direct	Glared at	Glomb (2002); Keashly and Jagatic (2000); Keashly and Rogers (2001); Robinson and Bennett (1995)
Physical/active/indirect	Theft or destruction of property	Aquino et al. (1999); Baron and Neuman (1996); Glomb (2002); Keashly and Jagatic (2000); Keashly and Rogers (2001); Robinson and Bennett (1995);
	Deliberately assigned with work overload	Robinson and Bennett (1995)
	Deliberately consuming resources needed by target	Baron and Neuman (1996)
Physical/passive/indirect	Expected to work with unreasonable deadlines, lack of resources	Robinson and Bennett (1995); Keashly and Rogers (2001)
	Causing others to delay action on matters of importance to target	Baron and Neuman (1996)

Note. From "By Any Other Name: American Perspectives on Workplace Bullying" (pp. 36–37), by L. Keashly and K. Jagatic, in *Bullying and Emotional Abuse in the Workplace: International Research and Practice Perspectives*, edited by S. Einarsen, H. Hoel, D. Zapf, and C. Cooper, 2003, London: Taylor & Francis. Copyright CRC Press, Boca Raton, Florida. Adapted with permission.

relatively little published research effort devoted to the validation of an emotional abuse measure or a portion of the theoretical space thereof.

Efforts at data collection and construct validation of workplace aggression measures that includes many emotional abuse behaviors are underway (e.g., Glomb, 2002; Neuman & Keashly, 2004), and such an exercise will require time. This measurement difficulty has been evidenced in many areas of organizational behavior, including the related domain of sexual harassment (Pryor & Fitzgerald, 2003). Indeed, it is clear from the focus of this volume that we are still looking for some certainty in defining the concepts, let alone how they should be measured. We identify what we believe to be some of the measurement challenges that have not been adequately addressed elsewhere in our writings (Keashly, 1998; Keashly & Jagatic, 2003; Keashly et al., 1994, 1997).

The structure of emotional abuse has generally been the most elusive of all development tasks. The work to date on the Workplace Aggression Research Questionnaire (Neuman & Keashly, 2004) has failed to identify stable, interpretable factors when a *full spectrum* of abusive behaviors have been analyzed via standard factor analytical techniques. This may be in part because conventional measurement wisdom has been applied to what is a fundamentally different type of measurement problem. For example, it may be that a Guttman scale is a more appropriate way of viewing these behaviors (Barling, 2002). The idea is that all behaviors are indeed part of one underlying dimension, patterned in this case according to their relative rank order on some criterion that has yet to be specified in theory (Schuessler, 1971). If, for illustrative purposes, the criterion was perceived severity of the abusive event, the behaviors could be ordered in terms of severity categories wherein each subsequent higher category presupposes the active presence of lower category behaviors. Continuing the example, this would entail that behavior such as "being glared at" is a lower level precursor to, but coexists with, other more serious categories of behavior, such as being the object of a verbal temper tantrum. In support of this approach, Glomb's (2002) analysis of specific aggressive encounters provides evidence of the cooccurrence of less severe behaviors with more severe ones. Taken a step further, the current definitional space of related concepts such as incivility at the less serious end of the spectrum and nonphysical verbal aggression at the other serious end of the dimension might be reconciled under such analyses. A scale analysis of this nature would require that the *full* range of events be measured and submitted to an appropriate scalogram analysis (Schuessler, 1971).

Including the full range of emotional abuse behaviors in a particular measure brings with it some disadvantages. In particular, the popular measure of emotional abuse (Keashly et al., 1994) and the extended versions since the Workplace Aggression Research Questionnaire (WAR–Q; Neuman & Keashly, 2004) can be criticized for being too long. Although not a psychometric problem per se, it is an important practical consideration when up to 60 items are included in a questionnaire measure along with any number of other relevant items. In fact, most research in recent years has adopted limited measures; some examples are Cortina, Magley, Williams, and Langhout's (2001) 7-item measure of incivility, Duffy et al.'s (2002) 13-item measure of social undermining, and Tepper's (2000) 15-item abusive supervision measure. From the perspective of the constructs considered in these studies, the measures seem adequate. Nonetheless, from a more inclusive view of emotional abuse, including the possibility of interrelatedness of these constructs, there remains the real problem of construct deficiency with a shorter version. This seems particularly likely given that the frequency of any one behavior has been noted to be low for certain abuser populations (Harvey, 1996; LeBlanc & Kelloway, 2002). It is clear that both concerns are important and that any shorter version would need to demonstrate that it correlates highly with a well-developed fuller version.

A critical point that we visit again in greater depth extends from the concern addressed by Keashly and Jagatic (2003) regarding the potential multiple sources of measurement for the behaviors of interest. They argued that measurement is often taken from a target perspective, but that various views are identifiable in theory, including the study of abuse from the actor and third-party perspectives. The basic issue is one of whether the measurement method fits the theoretical perspective proposed. With respect to emotional abuse, for instance, we propose that a target perspective has been the focus and that "perceptions" of abuse are of central concern. Although the accuracy of those perceptions of actual abuse is a valid research issue with practical implications for organizations, it is a distinctively different question than that addressed by research focusing on how the "experience" of abuse affects people. The real integrative value of volumes such as this will be to expose such issues and encourage research that closes the gaps. Many of these issues emerge in greater depth as we move on to consider the framework outlined in Figure 9.1.

A GENERAL FRAMEWORK

Consistent with the work of other researchers on aggressive workplace behaviors (e.g., Barling, 1996; Cortina, Magley, & Lim, 2002; Neuman & Baron, 1997; Richman et al., 1996), we chose to frame emotional abuse events as a workplace stressor, allowing us to draw on the rich thinking and research in organizational stress. In particular, we view emotional abuse behaviors as a chronic stressor as suggested by their frequency and endurance. Pratt and Barling's (1988) depiction of the stress process as one of stressor–stress–strain has been helpful in organizing our thinking about the diverse literatures on emotionally abusive behaviors. What is particularly appealing about this framework is the critical role of the individual's subjective experience in understanding their psychological and emotional responses to abusive behavior (Aquino & Bradfield, 2000; Barling, 1996). Indeed, we have defined emotional abuse from the perspective of the target and examined what factors relate to their experiences of these behaviors (Keashly, 2001).

The initial set of variables is classified as stressors and includes both distal and proximal factors. These are the objective, identifiable characteristics of the environment that impinge on individuals (Pratt & Barling, 1988). They may act as predictive or causal variables in the traditional sense, but they might also serve more complex mediating and moderating functions. Next is the stress experience, or the sense-making part of emotional abuse. This stage involves all factors related to the perception and psychological experience of the stressor. Whereas the stressor stage involves objective representations of events and any supporting factors, the stress process is purely perceptual by nature. Finally, strain includes all psychological, behavioral, and organizational outcomes that are typically thought to result from exposure to stressors in general (Jex & Beehr, 1991) and emotional abuse in particular (Keashly, 1998; Keashly & Jagatic, 2003). These outcomes themselves may become stressors and thus hold a more complex relationship to the framework variables than is depicted. Moreover, we acknowledge that some variables classified into one category could arguably occupy other categories or be part of a multidirectional effect framework—for example, target characteristics could be both social environment features setting the stage for mistreatment as well as influential in the subjective experience of the abuse. At this stage in the research process, we felt it was premature to specify a more complex framework with all subprocesses delineated.

In reviewing research from the perspective of this framework, we focus primarily on issues and studies since Keashly's (1998) treatment of the topic. The studies and sources we draw on are selective but representative. In some cases, we identify concepts that have received little to no attention in research on emotional abuse but that we think have much to offer in understanding this phenomenon. Hence, this framework provides a more complete picture of what we feel has been talked about or studied with respect to emotional abuse and what has yet to be examined but seems promising.

STRESSORS

As can be seen in Figure 9.1, we identify a diverse range of factors as stressors. Drawing on the extensive victimology literature, Aquino and his colleagues (Aquino & Bradfield, 2000; Aquino et al., 1999) discuss three groupings of factors related to people being victimized in the workplace:

situational forces, actor characteristics, and target-oriented factors. With the exception of the actual abusive events, these three groupings effectively capture the various factors we have identified from the extant literature on emotional abuse. Situational forces include those environmental and structural features of a work situation that enable the occurrence of abusive events—for example, regulatory failures such as nonexistent or unenforceable policies and structural inequities as reflected in perceived injustice and hostile organizational cultures (Elias, 1986). Actor characteristics include personality, beliefs, behaviors, and status-related features of the abusive actor that are associated with the propensity to behave aggressively—for example, type A personality, past aggressive behavior. Target-oriented factors include characteristics and behaviors of the target that may put them at risk for abusive treatment—for example, lower power position, being highly anxious or aggressive.

Situational Forces

These are the most distal factors in the framework and essentially set the stage for abusive behaviors to proliferate (or not). Our discussion of these forces will be at two levels: (a) the broader societal context and (b) the more specific organizational context.

At the risk of oversimplifying, the heart of the social situational argument is that people's behaviors are guided by and evaluated based on social norms of what is appropriate or inappropriate behavior. The assumption of the influence of societal norms is reflected in several authors' characterization of hostile and aggressive workplace behaviors as socially and organizationally deviant (e.g., Andersson & Pearson, 1999; Hornstein, 1996; Neuman & Baron, 1997; O'Leary-Kelly, Griffin, & Glew, 1996). And yet, according to research, these behaviors are frequent and persistent (see Keashly & Jagatic, 2003, for review). The existence of such deviant behaviors suggests therefore either a weakening or failure of societal norms (Neuman & Baron, 2003; Richman et al., 1996) or the existence of unspoken norms that effectively tolerate such treatment (Keashly, 2001). Either way, it appears that emotionally abusive behaviors are more likely to occur in a societal context that is either tolerant of such behavior or does not define it as problematic. Unfortunately, research on societal-level influences is somewhat limited. However, extrapolations from related research suggest to us there is a need to glean more knowledge about influences at this level of analysis. For example, Douglas and Martinko (2001) demonstrated that exposure to aggressive cultures (neighborhoods characterized by confrontation and argument) was linked to self-report of workplace aggression. Likewise, in an effort to get at some of the broader socially determined rules that may be related to abusive behavior, we are currently examining managers' accounts of respectful and disrespectful treatment of employees. What has struck us in the early stages of this research is that a set of common themes or rules runs through these different accounts (Williams & Keashly, 2001). For example, the notion of place (private or public) arises as central in the discernment of whether behavior is respectful or disrespectful. For example, criticism is to be delivered in private and not in public.

To get a complete picture of emotional abuse it seems necessary that these societal views of what is "abusive" be ferreted out. We need to better understand the societal context in which these behaviors occur and are experienced as well as explicitly examine the connections between such societal norms and the organizational norms that have received far more attention.

Systematic examination of social norms at the organizational level of analysis is more common. The notion that organizational (in)tolerance of various abusive behaviors plays an enabling role has been well supported in the sexual harassment literature (see Pryor & Fitzgerald, 2003, for review). Employees' perception of organizational (in)tolerance for certain behaviors is premised on the existence of effective regulatory mechanisms such as antiharassment policies (Pryor & Fitzgerald, 2003) and on direct or indirect experience with how the organization has responded to abusive behavior on the part of fellow employees (Keashly, 2001). This was clearly demonstrated in a study by Robinson and O'Leary-Kelly (1998), wherein the antisocial behavior of group members was shown to affect subsequent antisocial behavior by individuals. Consistent with propositions of social learning theory, individuals were less likely to conform to group antisocial behavior when there was a strong likelihood they would be punished—in other words, the organization would not tolerate such behavior.

Several studies are now consolidating the notion that organizations can influence emotionally abusive behaviors. This has been demonstrated through studies looking at facets of organizational culture (Jagatic, 2001; Keashly & Jagatic, 2000) and at the perception of unjust treatment by the organization (Tepper, Duffy, & Henle, 2002). Regarding organizational culture, we found that the more negatively employees (Keashly & Jagatic, 2000) and professionals-in-training (Jagatic, 2001) perceived their organization in terms of morale, quality of supervision and teamwork, and employee involvement, the greater the frequency of emotionally abusive behavior they experienced at the hands of their fellow employees. What is unclear from these studies is the nature of this causal link. Does a negative work environment result in more hostile employee behavior as suggested in the European literature on bullying (e.g., Hoel et al., 1999) and the American literature on toxic work environments (e.g., Neuman & Baron, 1997; Wright & Smye, 1996)? Or does hostile behavior left unchecked result in a more toxic environment as suggested by Andersson and Pearson's (1999) discussion of the development of "uncivil" workplaces? We suspect that this relationship is bidirectional. These are empirical questions that await additional research.

One characteristic of a toxic or hostile work environment would be a sense of unfair treatment by the organization. Perceived unfair treatment has been linked to subsequent aggressive behavior (Greenberg & Barling, 1999; Neuman & Baron, 1997; Tepper et al., 2002). Tepper et al.'s (2002) study on abusive supervision is particularly worthy of comment because supervisor-perceived injustice and abusive supervision were assessed within existing supervisor–subordinate pairs. Supervisors' perception of being treated unfairly by the organization was found to predict subordinates' assessment of the supervisor engaging in abusive behavior. Our confidence in this demonstrated link of organizational condition to subsequent abusive behavior is increased because the variables were not based on only the subordinate's perspective.

Actor Characteristics

The literature on workplace violence and aggression has tended to focus more on identifying and understanding the actors while the literature on workplace abuse and harassment has focused more on the target and the effects of the abuse. Thus, for this section, we will draw from the broader workplace aggression literature.

The popular literature on abusive bosses and coworkers describes them as psychopathological, often with roots as an abused child or as a schoolyard bully (e.g., Namie & Namie, 2000; Wyatt & Hare, 1997). The empirical literature has examined more specific personality characteristics and provides some support that an individual's personality does play an important role in their subsequent behavior. Not surprisingly, personality characteristics associated with anxiety or anger and hostility such as trait anger and self-control (Douglas & Martinko, 2001), depression (Tepper et al., 2002), type A personality (Neuman & Baron, 1998), negative affectivity (Neuman & Baron, 1998), neuroticism (Jockin, Arvey, & McGue, 2001), and attributional style (Douglas & Martinko, 2001) have all been linked to increased aggressive behavior. Characteristics associated with thoughtfulness, planning, tolerance, and collaboration such as tolerance for ambiguity (Ashforth, 1997), agreeableness and conscientiousness (Jockin et al., 2001), and high self-monitoring (Neuman & Baron, 1998) have been linked to lessened aggressive behavior. In a related vein, Ashforth (1997) found that managers who hold theory X beliefs (workers need to be forced to work) were more likely to behave aggressively toward subordinates. Thus, the personality and cognitive biases of actors do have an influence on engaging in aggressive behaviors.

Another set of actor characteristics relates to their organizational position and gender. These characteristics are important variables to consider because, unlike the actor's personality characteristics, these are features that targets can readily determine and let influence their perceptions. They would be expected to be important to targets because they are proxies for the actor's access to key resources and the resultant ability to influence others in the organization. Higher status actors have more control over resources that targets may need. Thus, actions by higher status actors would be expected to be viewed as more meaningful because the actor has the ability to deny access (Keashly & Rogers, 2001). Unfortunately, much of the research on emotionally abusive behaviors has either not assessed the status of the actor (usually the focus is on the target) or has focused explicitly on a particular type of organizational actor (e.g., supervisor: Tepper, 2000; supervisor and coworker: Duffy et al., 2002; faculty: Jagatic, 2001). Thus, the empirical evidence of the link to target experience is limited.

In terms of gender, the results are as yet unclear. Drawing on the social psychological literature on gender and aggression, Bowes-Sperry, Tata, and Luthar (2003) have argued that the nature of workplace aggression (primarily psychological and often provoked) suggests that there would be no gender differences. We have consistently found no gender differences in the reported actors of emotionally abusive behaviors (see Keashly & Jagatic, 2003, for review). It should be noted that only one nonscientific web-based survey of self-reported victims of bullies (Namie, 2000) found that women were more frequently identified as actors. Because gender has been an elusive variable in various areas of research, we believe that future research needs to continue examining potential effects.

The actor's role in the organization has been noted as an important variable in the emotional abuse literature, yet most studies tend to focus attention on one type of actor. Indeed, recent research suggests that explicitly examining more than one type of actor simultaneously may reveal different dynamics. For example, LeBlanc and Kelloway (2002) found that factors that predicted violence from a member of the public were different than those that predicted violence from an organizational insider. We have also found that different actors engage in different types of behaviors. In a study of health care workers, Keashly and Rogers (2001) found that patients were more likely to engage in sexually harassing and physically abusive behavior while coworkers and superiors were found to engage in emotionally abusive behaviors. Similarly, in an ongoing study of workplace stress and aggression in the U.S. Department of Veterans Affairs (VA; Keashly & Neuman, 2002), superiors were found to be more likely to engage in passive behaviors such as withholding praise while clients were more likely to engage in physical and active behaviors such as finger pointing and offensive gestures. These latter two studies also provide evidence of a moderating link between type of actor and target experience. Keashly and Neuman (2002) reported that targets were more bothered by persistent behavior from superiors than they were from coworkers or customers. Likewise, Keashly and Rogers (2001) found that client behavior was appraised as less threatening and easier to control than behavior coming from coworkers and supervisors. Overall, these results are consistent with the argument that the actions of more powerful actors (such as coworkers and superiors who control access to valued resources) will be experienced more negatively.

Moving a step away from inherent and positional characteristics to more person behaviors, two factors have received some empirical support: abuse history and alcohol use. Past aggressive or antisocial behavior and indicators of alcohol use and abuse both predicted self-reports of engaging in primarily psychologically aggressive behavior at work (Greenberg & Barling, 1999; Jockin et al., 2001). Abuse history has also been found to be important in a target's appraisal of the behavior. In both a scenario study (Keashly, Welstead, & Delaney, 1996) and an interview study of targets (Keashly, 2001), we found that previous hostile history with the actor was linked to judgments of the behaviors as abusive. Taken together, these studies provide strong support for the relationship of actor characteristics to subsequent emotionally abusive behavior. The evidence is much more limited but promising as to how relevant these factors are to the target's experience of these behaviors.

TARGET-ORIENTED FACTORS

The concept of provocative and submissive victims from the schoolyard bullying literature (Olweus, 1978) has made its way into the workplace aggression and abuse literatures (Aquino & Bradfield, 2000; Aquino et al., 1999). The premise of this perspective is that targets may behave in ways that contribute to them becoming the victim of another's hostility either by provoking another's anger—for example, by criticizing someone publicly—or placing themselves at risk—for example, being in the wrong place at the wrong time or confronting an aroused actor. Olweus described submissive victims as more anxious, insecure, and quiet than other students. The provocative victim exhibits both anxious and aggressive reactions. Thus, some people become targets because they are weak and some become targets because they provoke retaliation from others. Building on this work, Aquino and his colleagues (Aquino & Bradfield, 2000; Aquino et al., 1999) examined how target negative affectivity and dispositional aggressiveness (indicators of provocativeness) and self-determination (as an indicator of submissiveness) related to target perceptions of being victimized. They found support for the idea of provocative and submissive victims with targets high in aggressiveness and negative affectivity and low in self-determination perceiving higher levels of victimization.

Tepper et al.'s (2002) work on a person × situation interactional model of abusive supervision examined more specifically how target characteristics link to their victimization. Using intact supervisor–subordinate dyads, they demonstrated that target negative affectivity moderated the relationship between supervisor's depression and perceptions of organizational injustice and target's assessment of supervisor's abusive behavior. The relationship between supervisor characteristics and abusive supervision was strongest when subordinates were high in negative affectivity. These findings suggest that actors may express their dissatisfaction behaviorally when the opportunity is presented in the form of a ready (i.e., high negative affectivity) target (Tepper et al., 2002). Although these studies can be interpreted as placing responsibility for the actor's behavior on the target, an alternative interpretation is that they highlight ways in which people can reduce their chances of being chosen as the target. More fundamentally, these findings and those of Greenberg and Barling (1999) highlight the importance of pursuing an interactional approach to understanding when someone will behave abusively. Such an approach has implications for developing strategies designed to reduce if not prevent the occurrence of abusive behaviors.

As with actor characteristics, the social and organizational status of the target is a relevant consideration regarding who gets victimized. The basic premise is that low-status actors are more vulnerable. In terms of gender, the results are mixed. We have not found any gender differences in the frequency or number of emotionally abusive events reported (Keashly et al., 1994, 1997). Data from our ongoing study of workplace stress and aggression in the VA did not find differences between men and women in frequencies nor persistence of hostile behaviors (Keashly & Neuman, 2002). However, we did find gender differences for those behaviors that would be characterized as sexual harassment, such as inappropriate touching and obscene gestures. Cortina et al. (2001) found that women reported greater frequencies of incivility than did men. These contradictory findings may be the result of using different measures of emotionally abusive behaviors that tap the domain to varying degrees. What it clearly suggests is that research needs to look closely at the types of behaviors examined and, as with actor characteristics, determine whether different types of targets are differentially vulnerable to abusive treatment.

Support for the idea that organizational status affects vulnerability to abuse comes from two studies. In Cortina et al.'s (2001) study of employees in a federal circuit court district, employees in certain job positions experienced lower rates of incivility in contrast to other employees. Those "protected" (secretaries and attorneys) appear to be ones who occupied privileged status in the organization because they worked directly with federal judges. Unlike

Cortina et al. (2001), Aquino and his colleagues (Aquino & Bradfield, 2000; Aquino et al., 1999) did not find a relationship between organizational position or job status and perceived victimization. However, organizational status did appear to buffer the influence of target negative affectivity on perceived victimization such that the relationship only existed for lower status people (Aquino et al., 1999). Although seemingly contradictory, these two sets of studies highlight that targets can be differentially vulnerable for abusive treatment as a result of either their own position or the positions of those with whom they most closely work. Again, it appears that an interactional approach to understanding emotionally abusive behavior is necessary.

We have one final observation about the target research. The literature on victims–targets of emotional abuse and workplace aggression in general has tended to focus only on the direct target or victim. Research on other hostile workplace behaviors such as sexual harassment (Fitzgerald & Shullman, 1993; Schneider, 2000), racial harassment (e.g., Schneider et al., 2000), workplace incivility (Andersson & Pearson, 1999), and workplace violence (e.g., Rogers & Kelloway, 1997) indicates there are other victims. These other victims include those who witness the behaviors (e.g., coworkers) and those who hear about them from the target (e.g., family, friends, and others who support the person who is a target). When they have been the focus of research, these vicarious victims (Rogers & Kelloway, 1997) show similar kinds of negative effects as do the direct target. In addition, they alert us to the need to assess additional indicators of target strain such as work–family conflict and marital dissatisfaction (e.g., Barling, 1996; Barling & MacEwen, 1992; MacEwen, Barling, & Kelloway, 1992). Examining these other victims is also important in terms of understanding how toxic or hostile work cultures develop (Andersson & Pearson, 1999). A particularly interesting research issue concerns understanding those coworkers who observe the abuse and choose not to help the victim despite having the opportunity to intervene. Recent European work on mobbing (e.g., Zapf, 1999) has highlighted the devastating effects of coworkers who join in with an abusive supervisor to further traumatize the victim.

Abusive Behaviors

The actual behaviors are the most proximal factor to the stress experience (see Figure 9.1). In our discussion of the construct definition, we argued that persistence is a distinguishing feature of emotionally abusive behaviors. Persistence can be conceived as having four facets (Keashly & Jagatic, 2003): repetition (frequency of behaviors), duration (over some extended period of time), pattern (variety of behaviors cooccurring), and escalation (moving from less to more severe behaviors). Unfortunately, most of the studies on emotional abuse have only assessed frequency, and this assessment has been hampered by the use of vague scale anchors (e.g., "never" to "very often"). Duration has been difficult to assess because of the varying lengths of time provided to respondents (from one month to five years; usually one year). For example, in the European literature, bullying is defined by behavior that has endured at least six months (Hoel et al., 1999). However, recent research suggests that the use of the standard one-year time frame may not be sufficient to capture the typically longer duration of some forms of hostility. For example, Namie (2000) reports an average duration of 16.5 months for workplace bullying. Rospenda et al. (2000) found unique outcomes for those who have been exposed to generalized workplace abuse for a period of two years. Clearly, a discussion of what would be an appropriate time frame is needed.

Pattern or variety of behaviors has rarely been a consideration in most research. One simple indicator is to count the number of different events that have occurred. We have found the number of events to be uniquely linked to negative outcomes for targets (Keashly et al., 1997; Keashly & Neuman, 2002). A more detailed examination of patterning would involve looking at what behaviors tend to cooccur (e.g., Glomb, 2002; Keashly & Rogers, 2001) and to see how they connect over time (Glomb & Miner, 2002). Although escalation is a key aspect of the conflict literature (e.g., Rubin, Pruitt, & Kim, 1994), it has only recently become a topic for consideration in the workplace aggression literature (e.g., Andersson & Pearson, 1999; Barling, 1996; Glomb, 2002; Glomb & Miner, 2002). Thus, much remains to be done in fully fleshing out the critical dimensions of abusive behaviors.

As with the stressor characteristics research, the measurement of emotionally abusive events has been perceptual in nature. Although this is consistent with our framing of emotional abuse as a subjective phenomenon, we recognize that to understand it also as a social phenomenon it would be useful to compare the various potential sources (e.g., target, bystander, actor) of reported incidents for consistencies and discrepancies. Somewhat like research on influence tactics (e.g., Yukl & Falbe, 1990), we think a lot could be learned from getting reported behaviors from all players in the social context, wherever and whenever possible.

A Final Comment on Stressor Research

This discussion of the stressor characteristics has been challenging because there are two broad sets of relationships that extant research examines, creating two distinct research streams. The first set of relationships concerns the role of these factors as predictors of the emotionally abusive events—in other words, relationships among the stressor conditions. The second set of relationships concerns the links between these conditions and the target's subjective experience of the abuse—in other words, between stressor and stress. We cannot assume that what predicts emotional abuse will also be similarly influential in the target's experience of those behaviors. However, such research does provide us with important directions to pursue in understanding the target's experience (Keashly, 2001).

THE STRESS EXPERIENCE: EXPLORING THE BLACK BOX OF THE TARGET'S EXPERIENCE

We now move from the features of the abusive situation or stressor to how that situation is experienced and interpreted by the target. Consistent with the general stress literature (e.g., Lazarus & Folkman, 1984), what happens in this aspect has profound implications for the nature and degree of strain the target will experience. Relevant research for this topic includes target definition of experience, appraisal of threat, and coping responses.

Target Definition

We have discussed at some length earlier and in other venues (Keashly, 1998) what researchers as observers think are critical definition elements. Given that we have defined emotional abuse from the perspective of the target, we need to examine the elements that targets found important in labeling their experience with another as abusive. We were also curious to see how these elements linked to researcher-defined elements. In the mid-1990s, we conducted in-depth interviews with 29 people who self-identified as targets (Keashly, 2001). From this study we can highlight those elements that were influential for targets and see how those map on to researcher-defined elements of emotional abuse. Most of the researcher-defined elements (Keashly, 1998) were also spontaneously identified by the respondents. Specifically, respondents identified behaviors as abusive when there was a past history with the actor behaving in this way, when harm was experienced by the target, and when the boundaries or integrity of the target had been perceived to be violated by the actions. Relative power differential was also relevant in respondents' experiences. However, unlike researchers' conceptualization, an attribution of an actor's hostile intent was not a central element in respondents' labeling. This may be because of the link between past history (consistency) with attributions of intent. These findings stimulated our thinking and work on appraisal and coping, to which we now turn.

Target Appraisal

The appraisal process is a complex one, with the individual making a variety of judgments that involve addressing two broad questions: (a) What has happened and why? (event appraisal) and (b) what can be done about it? (action appraisal) If the target interprets the experience as a threat to future well-being and determines that he or she has little control over the actor or the incidents, they are more likely to experience negative outcomes (Keashly & Rogers, 2001; Neuman & Baron, 1997; Richman, Rospenda, Nawyn, & Flaherty, 1997).

Given the multifaceted nature of target appraisal, a number of different variables have been considered for their role in mediating the effects of exposure to aggressive or abusive behavior. In terms of event appraisal elements, Barling (1996) suggested that in the study of physical violence, fear of recurrence was an important mediator of the effects of exposure to violence and aggression. Although studies provide consistent support for fear of physical violence, the results are mixed in terms of nonphysical aggression (e.g., LeBlanc & Kelloway, 2002; Schat & Kelloway, 2000; Sinclair, Martin, & Croll, 2002). For example, LeBlanc and Kelloway (2002) found that the likelihood of future violence and fear of future violence were mediators for public-initiated violence but not for aggression from coworkers (which was exclusively nonphysical). However, Sinclair et al. (2002) in their study of the antecedents and consequences of antisocial behavior (including student aggression) for urban public school teachers found that fear of recurrence partially mediated the relationship with some outcomes. These mixed results may reflect different measures of fear of recurrence (physical violence only versus sense of safety) and a mismatch between type of behavior exhibited (nonphysical) and the behavior focused on in the measure (physical). So the question remains whether fear of future aggression is a relevant factor in the experience of emotional abuse. We believe more attention is needed on better defining, measuring, and anticipating under what conditions fear might apply. Harvey (1996), for instance, found that a different interpretation of fear, the fear of speaking up about work-related issues, was an important mediating variable between emotional abuse by supervisors and employees' work-related tension and job dissatisfaction.

Although we are not aware of research that has focused directly on either likelihood or fear of recurrence of nonphysical hostility, there has been work on factors that would be expected to relate to this assessment. As part of a larger study on target appraisal of aggressive and harassing events, Keashly and Rogers (2001) found that health care workers perceived events as more threatening when the actor was perceived as intending his or her behavior to harm them. As noted elsewhere, actor intent has been hotly debated as to its centrality in defining various aggression-related constructs (e.g., Andersson & Pearson, 1999; Keashly & Jagatic, 2003; Neuman & Baron, 1997). Because we view emotional abuse from the target's perspective, we suggest that actor intent be examined as a target attribution and for its role in appraisal and coping.

In terms of secondary appraisal, Richman et al. (1997) proposed that the target's sense of his or her ability to control either the abusive situation or the actor was a critical mediator of the impact of the abusive experience. Although this proposition is well-grounded in work-stress research, there has been limited empirical examination of the appraisal of control (or powerlessness) in emotional abuse in specific and workplace aggression in general. In the study mentioned earlier on health care workers, Keashly and Rogers (2001) found that emotionally abusive incidents were appraised as more difficult to control and hence more stressful than either physical or sexual incidents. Although this is a limited finding, it suggests the need to explicitly examine a target's appraisal of control and what factors contribute to this assessment. Drawing from the sexual harassment literature, Thacker (1992) has argued that perceived control is influenced by the target's resources to respond, both personal (e.g., self-esteem or conflict-management style) and organizational (e.g., policies on harassment and grievance procedures). Keashly and Rogers (2001) supported this argument with their finding that health care workers assessed aggressive incidents as more difficult to control when they perceived the existence of organizational barriers to their responding.

Although the research on target appraisal of emotionally abusive incidents is indeed in its infancy, the nature of emotionally abusive behaviors will require a careful understanding of the appraisal process. Behaviors classified as abusive are in isolation viewed at times as ambiguous, passive, and often indirect—maybe even harmless facts of life. How they become labeled and experienced as emotionally abusive clearly requires a better understanding of the judgment process involved. It requires that we have much better insight into the process. It also requires that we understand what follows an appraisal—in other words, attempts at coping.

Coping

According to Latack (1986), how well a person copes with a stressful situation such as abusive treatment can determine the extent to which the individual will experience negative effects from the stressor. Coping is interpreted as an ongoing psychological, sense-making, and reactive (behavioral) experience that the target is having in the presence of the stressor(s) (Hart & Cooper, 2001). Accordingly, we believe that the act of trying (or not) to cope with the stressor is linked to other variables identified in the "stress experience" category by others (e.g., mood, cognitive distractions, fear; Barling, 1996).

In an earlier study, Keashly et al. (1994) found that targets engaged in a variety of responses to abusive treatment, often choosing to do nothing or avoid the actor. In fact, some authors had linked this avoidance strategy to a sense of fear victims develop toward the abuser (Harvey, 1996; Ryan & Oestreich, 1991). Nonetheless, most of the strategies victims seemed to use created little perceived change on the part of the actor (Keashly et al., 1994). Recent research, however, has more systematically examined how coping may moderate the impact of exposure to abusive behaviors. Focusing on coping style, Jagatic (2001) found that those who used a confrontive or active style of coping with negative interpersonal events demonstrated a weaker relationship between exposure and negative effects (depression and intention to leave) than those who did not use an active style. The effectiveness of such direct coping appears to depend on the type of outcome examined. Fitzgerald, Hulin, and Drasgow (1992) found that assertive coping moderated the impact on physical and psychological outcomes but exacerbated the effect on job adjustment. Their interpretation was that job adjustment might reflect the problem of remaining on the job once one publicly grieves the harassment—in other words, others may retaliate or ostracize. In another study looking at abusive treatment over a two-year period, Richman, Rospenda, Flaherty, and Freels (2001) found active coping does little to end the abusive treatment itself and that when it is unsuccessful, failed coping leads to more severe long-term negative outcomes in terms of alcohol use and abuse. These data suggest that taking some action may be helpful but that the impact is limited, particularly for quality of life on the job. Also, if the action does not stop the abusive treatment, the outcomes for the target may become much worse. For example, confronting the actor or filing a grievance may result in retaliatory action, intensifying the hostility (Keashly, 2001). Richman, Rospenda, Flaherty, and Freels' (2001) study highlights the difference between persistent forms of hostility such as emotional abuse and bullying and the occasional or isolated forms of aggression that have been the subject of much workplace aggression research (Glomb, 2002).

Hostility that persists despite efforts to stop it may require organizational support, overt or systemic (Keashly, 2001; Richman et al., 2001). As such, these different forms may require different ways and levels of responding. Future research needs to examine the variety of responses that can be used by a target (e.g., subordinate resistance: Tepper, Duffy, & Shaw, 2001; coping style profiles: Cortina et al., 2002); the factors related to the selection of some coping responses over others (e.g., target disposition: Tepper et al., 2001; actor power: Cortina et al., 2002; Keashly, 2001; organizational policies and practices; Keashly, 2001), and the assessment of the impact of these coping behaviors on the abusive treatment itself (Keashly et al., 1994; Richman et al., 2001). We believe that how well these strategies work will be influenced to some degree by social support and organizational response strategies. Indeed, any social or organizational constraints the victims perceive as existing may serve to thwart their efforts at coping (Keashly & Rogers, 2001).

Social Support

The buffering effects of social support have been extensively examined for a variety of workplace stressors (Jex & Beehr, 1992; Kahn & Byosiere, 1992). One form of social support, talking to friends and family, has been referred to as a major form of coping in emotional abuse research (e.g., Jagatic, 2001; Jagatic & Keashly, 1998; Keashly et al., 1994; Richman et al., 1997), although its effectiveness in reducing the negative impact of emotional abuse has not been explored sufficiently until recently. One study by Richman et al. (1997) found that seeking support from others had limited buffering effects on exposure to workplace abuse. They noted that most of the support sought was from individuals who were not in a position to directly affect the hostile interactions—in other words, coworkers and family and friends. They argued that for social support to effectively buffer the target, it must come from people with the power and position to alter the situation, such as supervisors and other managers.

Recent findings from Duffy et al.'s (2002) study of social undermining suggest that even support from people internal to an organization, including supervisors, has limited buffering effect. In addition, if the supervisor who is engaging in social undermining is also the one who would be expected to be a major source of social support for the target, the effects of the undermining were magnified. As has been suggested in the social support literature (e.g., Eckenrode, 1991), the effectiveness of different types of support and supporters may likely depend on the social context and nature of the stressor. More than likely, to buffer someone from the effects of abuse the supporter would need to be an organizational member in an influential position and be capable of buffering the hostile interaction in some form.

Moral support alone seems to provide only small attenuation effects (Duffy et al., 2002). Hence, we now turn our attention to an extension of such social support in the way of organizational responding. Recent research has begun to identify ways in which organizational members—and by extension, the organization—responds to such behaviors (Keashly, 2001). Based on findings that perceptions of retaliation for blowing the whistle on sexual harassment lessens the likelihood that one reports incidents (Cortina &

Magley, 2003), we believe that organizational responding is equally a factor when more generalized forms of harassment are at issue.

Organizational Responding

It has been argued that how higher-ups respond to employee concerns tells employees something about how the organization values (or does not value) them (Folger, 1993). This is also true in terms of responses to grievances about emotionally abusive treatment. In her interview study with targets, Keashly (2001) found that the organization's response to the target's concerns had a powerful impact on the target's overall experience of feeling abused. To the extent the organization (as represented by its management) was viewed as having taken the target's concerns seriously and taken steps to alter the situation (such as moving the target, disciplining or firing the actor), targets felt valued and the effects of the mistreatment were viewed as easier to deal with. However, to the extent that the organization was viewed as leaving the responsibility for dealing with the abuse to the target (i.e., attributing problems to a personality conflict; minimizing the target's complaint; and in some cases, actively blaming the target for the behaviors), targets reported feeling that they were being abused again and the effects on them of their experience were intensified. In support of this argument, Keashly and Rogers (2001) found that perceived organizational barriers to responding were associated with appraisal of aggressive events as more threatening. Specifically, health care workers appraised events as more difficult to control when they perceived that the organization was preventing them from responding to the actor in the way they felt would be most effective.

The importance of organizational responses can be effectively studied from a justice perspective, as is demonstrated in one such study conducted by Tepper (2000). In this study, subordinates' perceptions of injustice were identified as the mechanism through which abusive supervision has its effects on outcome variables. He argued that the very existence of abusive supervision (which he defined as sustained and enduring hostile action) is suggestive to employees that the organization is not responding appropriately. Specifically, the continued behavior violated subordinates' sense of (a) being treated in a fair and respectful manner (interactional justice); (b) the organization as developing and enforcing procedures that discipline abusers (procedural justice); and (c) not receiving the same amount and type of positive input from supervisors that other coworkers do (distributive justice). In turn, these fairness perceptions were expected to have negative implications for subordinate attitudes and well-being. Indeed, Tepper found that organizational justice fully mediated the effects of abusive supervision on job and life satisfaction, organizational commitment, work–family conflict and depression, and partially mediated the effects on anxiety and emotional exhaustion.

What these initial studies indicate is that the organization's response can play a critical role in the target's overall appraisal of and response to abusive treatment. Research to date has only been suggestive of the nature of this role of the organization, and more systematic study of the dynamics needs to be undertaken. Indeed, more research is needed generally in this "black box" or stress section of the framework. There are many subprocesses (e.g., attribution theory), perceptual influences (e.g., selective perception), and individual differences (e.g., negative affectivity) that are also likely to affect the formation of an emotional abuse experience that we have not been able to cover in this chapter but that deserve equal consideration. We have highlighted the idea that coping, social support, and organizational responding all interact, among other factors, to contribute to the victim's appraisal process and ultimate experience of emotional abuse.

Strain

Our discussion of the elements of strain in our framework is briefer than the stressor and stress sections. It is our feeling that emotional abuse shares much with other stressors in terms of the personal and organizational outcomes that result from exposure (Keashly et al., 1997). Therefore, we refer readers to the more extensive reviews of stress and strain (see, e.g., Hart & Cooper, 2001; Jex & Beehr, 1991; Kahn & Byosiere, 1992) and focus on those elements that are of particular relevance to emotional abuse. Most of the strain variables identified in Figure 9.1 are based on a literature review by Keashly and Jagatic (2003). They are classified according to a psychological, behavioral, and physiological scheme common to stress parlance (e.g., Jex & Beehr, 1991; Kahn & Byosiere, 1992). See Table 9.2.

The most systematically studied outcomes of emotional abuse are those classified in the psychological domain. Research has typically supported the expected relationships in line with the stress literature. Emotional abuse correlates with a host of psychological outcome variables ranging from job dissatisfaction (e.g., Barling, 1996; Glomb, 2001; Harvey, 1996; Keashly et al., 1994, 1997) and lower organizational commitment (e.g., Pearson, Andersson, & Porath, 2000; Tepper, 2000) to intentions to leave the organization (e.g., Harvey, 1996; Rogers & Kelloway, 1997) and increased fears (e.g., Harvey, 1996; Schat & Kelloway, 2000). Most important is that emotional abuse appears to account for unique variance in predicting strain beyond the classic role stressors such as role overload, role conflict, and role ambiguity (Keashly et al., 1997; Rospenda, 2002). Hence, most studies in this area continue to demonstrate strong reason for including emotional

TABLE 9.2
Some Effects of Emotionally Abusive Behaviors on Targets

Category	Effect	Source
Direct		
Negative mood	Anger, resentment	Ashforth (1997); Richman et al. (1999); Richman et al. (2001)
	Anxiety	Keashly et al. (1994); Richman et al. (1999); Richman et al. (2001); Tepper (2000)
	Depressed mood	Richman et al. (1999): Richman et al. (2001)
Cognitive distraction	Concentration	Brodsky (1976)
Indirect		
Decreased psychological well-being	Lowered self-esteem	Ashforth (1997); Cortina et al. (2001); Price Spratlen (1995)
	Problem drinking	Richman et al. (1999); Richman et al. (2001); Rospenda et al. (2000)
	Depression	Tepper (2000)
	Overall emotional health	Keashly and Jagatic (2000), Rospenda (2002)
	Self-efficacy	Duffy et al. (2002)
	Life satisfaction	Tepper (2000)
Poor psycho-somatic function	Physical ill health (general)	Duffy et al. (2002); Price Spratlen (1995); Richman et al. (1999)
Reduced organizational functioning	Decreased job satisfaction	Cortina et al. (2001); Harvey (1996); Keashly and Jagatic (2000); Keashly et al. (1994); Keashly et al. (1997); Price Spratlen (1995); Sinclair et al. (2002); Tepper (2000)
	Job tension	Harvey (1996); Keashly et al. (1997)
	Greater turnover	Keashly et al., 1994; Sinclair et al. (2002); Tepper (2000)
	Work withdrawal behaviors	Cortina et al. (2001)
	Greater intention to leave	Ashforth (1997); Cortina et al. (2001); Harvey (1996); Keashly and Jagatic (2000); Keashly et al. (1994); Keashly et al. (1997); Tepper (2000)
	Increased absenteeism	Price Spratlen (1995)
	Decreased productivity	Ashforth (1997); Price Spratlen (1995)
	Organizational commitment	Duffy et al. (2002); Tepper (2000)
	Family–work conflict	Tepper (2000)
	Leadership endorsement	Ashforth (1997)
	Work unit cohesiveness	Ashforth (1997)
	Organizational citizenship behaviors	Zellars et al. (2002)
	Counterproductive behaviors	Duffy et al. (2002)

Note. From "By Any Other Name: American Perspectives on Workplace Bullying" (pp. 54–55), by L. Keashly and K. Jagatic, in *Bullying and Emotional Abuse in the Workplace: International Research and Practice Perspectives*, edited by S. Einarsen, H. Hoel, D. Zapf, and C. Cooper, 2003, London: Taylor & Francis. Copyright CRC Press, Boca Raton, Florida. Adapted with permission.

abuse in understanding stress and strain at work, particularly when psychological strain variables are of interest.

Although not as extensively studied as psychological outcomes, behavioral variables have been recently spotlighted with a growing body of research on emotional abuse and drinking behavior (e.g., Richman et al., 1999; Rospenda, 2002). Initially, these studies make it clear that emotional abuse can play a significant role in the prediction of problem drinking among men and women. These studies also suggest that future research in this area is likely to find similar relationships to other personal dysfunctional behaviors ranging from substance use (e.g., Chen & Spector, 1992) to family violence and aggression (e.g., Barling, 1996). A more direct examination of the full range of work-related withdrawal behaviors is an area in need of attention. As Fitzgerald and Shullman (1993) noted with respect to sexual harassment, and we believe this extends to emotional abuse, we need to examine the full range of withdrawal behaviors including "less than voluntary" early retirements, tardiness, avoiding tasks, as well as the traditional measures of absenteeism and turnover. We may find that effects are more noticeable for the less dramatic withdrawal behaviors that are under the victim's control. Most studies to date (with the exception of Tepper, 2000) have focused on intentions or self-reported behaviors of withdrawal (e.g., Chen & Spector, 1992; Cox, 1991). Future research must collect hard data wherever possible of the broad range of withdrawal constructs. Moreover, a broad array of destructive behaviors, such as retaliatory behaviors (Skarlicki & Folger, 1997) and various other forms of counterproductive behaviors more generally (Fox, Spector, & Miles, 2001) need to be examined in the context of exposure to emotional abuse.

The relationship of emotional abuse to outcome factors in the physiological domain has received little direct attention. This is a more difficult domain to research given the typically longer onset of effects. Because the interest in emotional abuse is relatively recent, it is understandable that research is just beginning in this area. Until more research is available, certain studies can provide interesting approximations to this type of research, with measures such as visits to the doctor and self-reported physical symptoms (e.g., Spector, Dwyer, & Jex, 1988). Nonetheless, in many cases we must extrapolate from anecdotal evidence or make educated guesses that measurement of reported causes such as "conflicts" at work approximate what is intended by emotional abuse. Although negative physiological effects appear probable, it is not until researchers carefully explore and document relevant emotional abuse items in future epidemiological and longitudinal research that some certainty can be cast on these ideas. For now, we must rely on behavioral research findings such as problem drinking, substance abuse, and the measurement of self-reported illness to substantiate the belief that physiological effects are likely to occur.

In closing this section it is worth noting that most of the assumptions we make with respect to emotional abuse and its predicted outcomes are from the literature on stress in general and sexual harassment in particular. Although many of the effects are likely to hold up, it is only through empirical means that this can be ascertained.

CONCLUSION

We started out in this area wondering if emotional abuse was also a workplace phenomenon. The answer was yes—and indeed it was a frequently experienced phenomenon. Knowing that it is real means we need to more rigorously and systematically study its nature and effects, the circumstances that enable or disable the actors, and the mechanisms that can mitigate the harm. It is clear that this area of research is in its early stages, although a recent surge of interest indicates that it is likely to develop quickly. As a result of emotional abuse's neophyte status in the counterproductive behavior literature, our review has raised more questions (and hence, future research directions) than provided definitive answers. Our review has also highlighted for us the need for an interactional approach. Although limited, studies that have investigated the person × situation interaction have offered additional insight into the mechanisms by which such behavior occurs and has an impact. In particular, this perspective highlights the critical role of the organization in the facilitation or mitigation of this phenomenon. Emotional abuse is a socially constructed and constituted experience, and the organization is the social cauldron within which the myriad of factors and influences we have identified come together. We hope that our review provides some ideas organizations can use to begin their own efforts in understanding and dealing with this costly problem.

REFERENCES

Andersson, L. M., & Pearson, C. M. (1999). Tit for tat? The spiraling effect of incivility in the workplace. *Academy of Management Review, 24,* 452–471.

Aquino, K., & Bradfield, M. (2000). Perceived victimization in the workplace: The role of situational factors and victim characteristics. *Organization Science, 11*(5), 525–537.

Aquino, K., Grover, S., Bradfield, M., & Allen, D. G. (1999). The effects of negative affectivity, hierarchical status, and self-determination on workplace victimization. *Academy of Management Journal, 42,* 260–272.

Ashforth, B. E. (1997). Petty tyranny in organizations: A preliminary examination of antecedents and consequences. *Canadian Journal of Administrative Sciences, 14,* 126–140.

Barling, J. (1996). The prediction, psychological experience, and consequences of workplace violence. In G. R. VandenBos & E. Q. Bulatao (Eds.), *Violence on the job: Identifying risks and developing solutions* (pp. 29–49). Washington, DC: American Psychological Association.

Barling, J. (2002, April). Comment from the discussant. In V. J. Magley & L. M. Cortina (Cochairs), *Intersections of workplace mistreatment, gender, and occupational health*. Symposium presented at the 17th annual conference of the Society for Industrial and Organizational Psychology, Toronto, Ontario, Canada.

Barling, J., & MacEwen, K. E. (1992). Linking work experiences to facets of marital functioning. *Journal of Organizational Behavior, 13*, 573–582.

Baron, R. A., & Neuman, J. H. (1998). Workplace aggression—The iceberg beneath the tip of workplace violence: Evidence on its forms, frequency, and targets. *Public Administration Quarterly, 21*, 446–464.

Bassman, E. S. (1992). *Abuse in the workplace*. Westport, CT: Quorum Books.

Bennett, R. J., & Robinson, S. L. (2000). Development of a measure of workplace deviance. *Journal of Applied Psychology, 85*, 349–360.

Bowes-Sperry, L., Tata, J., & Luthar, H. K. (2003). Comparing sexual harassment to other forms of workplace aggression. In M. Sagie, M. Koslowsky, & S. Stashevsky (Eds.), *Misbehavior and dysfunctional attitudes in organizations* (pp. 33–56). London: Palgrave MacMillan.

Brodsky, C. M. (1976). *The harassed worker*. Toronto, Canada: Lexington Books, D.C. Heath.

Buss, A. H. (1961). *The psychology of aggression*. New York: Wiley.

Chen, P. Y., & Spector, P. E. (1992). Relationships of work stressors with aggression, withdrawal, theft and substance use: An exploratory study. *Journal of Occupational and Organizational Psychology, 65*, 177–184.

Cortina, L. M., & Magley, V. J. (2003). Raising voice, risking retaliation: Events following interpersonal mistreatment at work. *Journal of Personality and Social Psychology, 8*, 247–265.

Cortina, L. M., Magley, V. J., & Lim, S. (2002, August). *Individual differences in coping with incivility*. Paper presented at the annual meeting of the Academy of Management, Denver, CO.

Cortina, L. M., Magley, V. J., Williams, J. H., & Langhout, R. D. (2001). Incivility in the workplace: Incidence and impact. *Journal of Occupational Health Psychology, 6*, 64–80.

Cox, H. (1991). Verbal abuse nationwide, part II: Impact and modifications. *Nursing Management, 22*, 66–69.

Douglas, S. C., & Martinko, M. J. (2001). Exploring the role of individual differences in the prediction of workplace aggression. *Journal of Applied Psychology, 86*, 547–559.

Duffy, M. K., Ganster, D. C., & Pagon, M. (2002). Social undermining in the workplace. *Academy of Management Journal, 45*, 331–351.

Eckenrode, J. (1991). *The social context of coping*. New York: Plenum Press.

Einarsen, S., Hoel, H., Zapf, D., & Cooper, C. (2003). *Bullying and emotional abuse in the workplace: International perspectives in research and practice.* London: Taylor Francis.

Elias, R. (1986). *The politics of victimization: Victims, victimology, and human rights.* New York: Oxford Press.

Fitzgerald, L. F., Hulin, C. L., & Drasgow, F. (1992, November). *Predicting outcomes of sexual harassment: An integrated process model.* Paper presented to the second APA/NIOSH Conference on Stress and the Workplace, Washington, DC.

Fitzgerald, L. F., & Shullman, S. L. (1993). Sexual harassment: A research analysis and agenda for the 90's. *Journal of Vocational Behavior, 42,* 5–27.

Folger, R. (1993). Reactions to mistreatment at work. In J. K. Murnighan (Ed.), *Social psychology of organizations* (pp. 161–183). Englewood Cliffs, NJ: Prentice-Hall.

Fox, S., Spector, P. E., & Miles, D. (2001). Counterproductive work behaviors (CWB) in response to job stressors and organizational justice: Some mediator and moderator tests for autonomy and emotions. *Journal of Vocational Behavior, 59,* 291–309.

Glomb, T. M. (2001). *Workplace aggression: Antecedents, behavioral components and consequences.* Unpublished manuscript, University of Minnesota, Minneapolis.

Glomb, T. M. (2002). Workplace aggression: Informing conceptual models with data from specific encounters. *Journal of Occupational Health Psychology, 7,* 20–36.

Glomb, T. M., & Miner, A. G. (2002). Exploring patterns of aggressive behaviors in organizations: Assessing model-data fit. In J. M. Brett & F. Drasgow (Eds.), *The psychology of work: Theoretically based empirical research* (pp. 236–252). Mahwah, NJ: Erlbaum.

Greenberg, L., & Barling, J. (1999). Predicting employee aggression against coworkers, subordinates, and supervisors: The roles of person behaviors and perceived workplace factors. *Journal of Organizational Behavior, 20,* 897–913.

Hart, P. M., & Cooper, C. L., (2001). Occupational stress: Toward a more integrative framework. In N. Anderson, D. S. Ones, H. K. Sinangil, & C. Viswesvaran (Eds.), *Handbook of industrial, work, and organizational psychology* (Vol. 2, pp. 93–114). Thousand Oaks, CA: Sage

Harvey, S. R. (1996). *Bosses' negative interpersonal behaviors: A latent variable test of personal and organizational outcomes.* Unpublished doctoral dissertation, University of Guelph, Ontario, Canada.

Harvey, S., & Keashly, L. (2003). Predicting risk for aggression in the workplace: Risk factors, self-esteem and time of exposure. *Social Behavior and Personality, 31,* 807–814.

Hoel, H., Rayner, C., & Cooper, C. L. (1999). Workplace bullying. In C. L. Cooper & I. T. Robertson (Eds.), *International review of industrial and organizational psychology* (pp. 195–229). Chichester, England: Wiley.

Hornstein, H. A. (1996). *Brutal bosses and their prey: How to identify and overcome abuse in the workplace.* New York: Riverhead Books.

Jagatic, K. (2001). *The influence of educational culture on experienced and witnessed hostility by faculty toward professionals-in-training.* Unpublished doctoral dissertation, Wayne State University, Detroit, MI.

Jagatic, K., & Keashly, L. (1998). *The nature and effects of negative incidents by faculty members toward graduate students.* Unpublished manuscript, Wayne State University, Detroit, MI.

Jex, S., & Beehr, M. (1991). Emerging theoretical and methodological issues in the study of work-related stress. *Research in Personnel and Human Resource Management, 9,* 311–365.

Jockin, V., Arvey, R. D., & McGue, M. (2001). Perceived victimization moderates self-reports of workplace aggression and conflict. *Journal of Applied Psychology, 86,* 1262–1269.

Kahn, R. L., & Byosiere, P. (1992). Stress in organizations. In M. D. Donnette & L. M. Hough (Eds.), *Handbook of industrial and organizational psychology* (2nd ed., Vol. 3, pp. 571–650). Palo Alto, CA: Consulting Psychologists Press.

Keashly, L. (1998). Emotional abuse in the workplace: Conceptual and empirical issues. *Journal of Emotional Abuse, 1,* 85–117.

Keashly, L. (2001). Interpersonal and systemic aspects of emotional abuse at work: The target's perspective. *Violence and Victims, 16*(3), 233–268.

Keashly, L., Harvey, S. R., & Hunter, S. (1997). Abusive interaction and role state stressors: Relative impact on student residence assistant stress and work attitudes. *Work and Stress, 11,* 175–185.

Keashly, L., & Jagatic, K. (2000, August). *The nature, extent, and impact of emotional abuse in the workplace: Results of a statewide survey.* Paper presented at the Academy of Management Conference, Toronto, Canada.

Keashly, L., & Jagatic, K. (2003). By any other name: American perspectives on workplace bullying. In S. Einarsen, H. Hoel, D. Zapf, & C. Cooper (Eds.), *Bullying and emotional abuse in the workplace: International perspectives in research and practice* (pp. 31–61). London: Taylor Francis.

Keashly, L., & Neuman, J. H. (2002, August). *Exploring persistent patterns of workplace aggression.* Paper presented at the annual meeting of the Academy of Management, Denver, CO.

Keashly, L., & Rogers, K. A. (2001). *Aggressive behaviors at work: The role of context in appraisals of threat.* Unpublished manuscript, Wayne State University, Detroit, MI.

Keashly, L., Trott, V., & MacLean, L. M. (1994). Abusive behavior in the workplace: A preliminary investigation. *Violence and Victims, 9,* 125–141.

Keashly, L., Welstead, S., & Delaney, C. (1996). *Perceptions of abusive behaviors in the workplace: Role of history, emotional impact and intent.* Unpublished manuscript, University of Guelph, Ontario, Canada.

Latack, J. C. (1986). Coping with job stress: Measures and future directions for scale development. *Journal of Applied Psychology, 71,* 377–385.

Lazarus, R. S., & Folkman, S. (1984). *Stress, appraisal, and coping.* New York: Springer.

LeBlanc, M. M., & Kelloway, E. K. (2002). Predictors and outcomes of workplace violence and aggression. *Journal of Applied Psychology, 87,* 444–453.

MacEwen, K. E., Barling, J., & Kelloway, E. K. (1992). Effects of short-term role overload on marital interactions. *Work and Stress, 6,* 117–126.

Murphy, C. M., & O'Leary, K. D. (1989). Psychological aggression predicts physical aggression in early marriage. *Journal of Consulting and Clinical Psychology, 57,* 579–582.

Namie, G. (2000, October). *U.S. hostile workplace survey 2000.* Paper presented at the New England Conference on Workplace Bullying, Suffolk University Law School, Boston, MA.

Namie, G., & Namie, R. (2000). *The bully at work: What you can do to stop the hurt and reclaim your dignity on the job.* Naperville, IL: Sourcebooks.

Neuman, J. H., & Baron, R. A. (1997). Aggression in the workplace. In R. A. Giacalone & J. Greenberg (Eds.), *Antisocial behavior in organizations* (pp. 37–67). Thousand Oaks, CA: Sage.

Neuman, J. H., & Baron, R. A. (1998). Workplace violence and workplace aggression: Evidence concerning specific forms, potential causes, and preferred targets. *Journal of Management, 24,* 391–411.

Neuman, J. H., & Baron, R. A. (2003). Social antecedents of bullying: A social interactionist perspective. In S. Einarsen, H. Hoel, D. Zapf, & C. Cooper (Eds.), *Bullying and emotional abuse in the workplace: International perspectives in research and practice* (pp. 185–202). London: Taylor Francis.

Neuman, J. N., & Keashly, L. (2002, April). *Development of the Workplace Aggression Research Questionnaire.* Paper presented at the annual meeting of the Society of Industrial/Organizational Psychology, Chicago, IL.

NiCarthy, G., Gottlieb, N., & Coffman, S. (1993). *You don't have to take it: A woman's guide to confronting emotional abuse at work.* Seattle, WA: Seal Press.

O'Leary, K. D. (1999). Psychological abuse: A variable deserving critical attention in domestic violence. *Violence and Victims, 14,* 3–23.

O'Leary-Kelly, A. M., Duffy, M. K., & Griffin, R. W. (2000). Construct confusion in the study of antisocial work behavior. *Research in Personnel and Human Resources Management, 18,* 275–303.

O'Leary-Kelly, A. M., Griffin, R. W., & Glew, D. J. (1996). Organization-motivated aggression: A research framework. *Academy of Management Review, 21,* 225–253.

Olweus, D. (1978). *Aggression in schools: Bullies and whipping boys.* Washington, DC: Hemisphere.

Pearson, C., Andersson, L., & Porath, C. (2000, Fall). Assessing and attacking workplace incivility. *Organizational Dynamics,* 129–137.

Pratt, L. I., & Barling, J. (1988). Differentiating between daily hassles, acute and chronic stressors: A framework and its implications. In J. R. Hurrell, L. R. Murphy, S. L. Sauter, & C. L. Cooper (Eds.), *Occupational stress: Issues and developments in research* (pp. 41–53). London: Taylor Francis.

Price Spratlen, L. (1995). Interpersonal conflict which includes mistreatment in a university workplace. *Violence and Victims, 10,* 285–297.

Pryor, J. B., & Fitzgerald, L. F. (2003). Sexual harassment research in the U.S. In S. Einarsen, H. Hoel, D. Zapf, & C. Cooper (Eds.), *Bullying and emotional abuse in the workplace: International perspectives in research and practice* (pp. 71–100). London: Taylor Francis.

Richman, J. A., Flaherty, J. A., & Rospenda, K. M. (1996). Perceived workplace harassment experiences and problem drinking among physicians: Broadening the stress/alienation paradigm. *Addiction, 91,* 391–403.

Richman, J. A., Rospenda, K. M., Flaherty, J. A., & Freels, S. (2001). Workplace harassment, active coping, and alcohol-related outcomes. *Journal of Substance Abuse, 13,* 347–366.

Richman, J. A., Rospenda, K. M., Nawyn, S. J., & Flaherty, J. A. (1997). Workplace harassment and the self-medication of distress: A conceptual model and case illustrations. *Contemporary Drug Problems, 24,* 179–199.

Richman, J. A., Rospenda, K. M., Nawyn, S. J., Flaherty, J. A., Fendrich, M., Drum, M. L., et al. (1999). Sexual harassment and generalized workplace abuse among university employees: Prevalence and mental health correlates. *American Journal of Public Health, 89,* 358–363.

Robinson, S. L., & O'Leary-Kelly, A. (1998). Monkey see, monkey do: The influence of work groups on the antisocial behavior of employees. *Academy of Management Journal, 41,* 658–672.

Rogers, K. A., & Kelloway, E. K. (1997). Violence at work: Personal and organizational outcomes. *Journal of Occupational Health Psychology, 12,* 63–71.

Rospenda, K. M. (2002). Workplace harassment, service utilization, and drinking outcomes. *Journal of Occupational Health Psychology, 2,* 141–155.

Rospenda, K. M., Richman, J. A., Wislar, J. S., & Flaherty, J. A. (2000). Chronicity of sexual harassment and generalized workplace abuse: Effects on drinking outcomes. *Addiction, 95,* 1805–1820.

Rubin, J. Z., Pruitt, D. G., & Kim, S. H. (1994). *Social conflict: Escalation, stalemate, and settlement* (2nd ed.). New York: McGraw-Hill.

Ryan, K. D., & Oestreich, D. K. (1991). *Driving fear out of the workplace.* San Francisco: Jossey-Bass.

Schat, A. C. H., & Kelloway, E. K. (2000). Effects of perceived control on the outcomes of workplace aggression and violence. *Journal of Occupational Health Psychology, 5,* 386–402.

Schneider, K. T., Hitlan, R. T., & Radhakrishnan, P. (2000). An examination of the nature and correlates of ethnic harassment experiences in multiple contexts. *Journal of Applied Psychology, 85*(1), 3–12.

Schuessler, K. (1971). *Analyzing social data.* New York: Houghton-Mifflin.

Schwab, D. P. (1980). Construct validity in organizational behavior. In B. M. Staw & L. Cummings (Eds.), *Research in organizational behavior* (Vol. 2, pp. 3–43). Greenwich, CT: JAI Press.

Sheehan, K. H., Sheehan, D. V., White, K., Leibowitz, A., & Baldwin, D. C. (1990). A pilot study of medical student "abuse": Student perceptions of mistreatment and misconduct in medical school. *Journal of the American Medical Association, 263,* 533–537.

Sinclair, R. R., Martin, J. E., & Croll, L. W. (2002). A threat-appraisal perspective on employees' fears about antisocial workplace behavior. *Journal of Occupational Health Psychology, 7,* 37–56.

Skarlicki, D., & Folger, R. (1997). Retaliation for perceived unfair treatment: Examining the roles of procedural and interactive justice. *Journal of Applied Psychology, 82,* 434–443.

Spector, P. W., Dwyer, D. J., & Jex, S. M. (1988). The relationship of job stressors to affective health and performance outcomes: A comparison of multiple data sources. *Journal of Applied Psychology, 73,* 11–19.

Tepper, B. J. (2000). Consequences of abusive supervision. *Academy of Management Journal, 43*(2), 178–190.

Tepper, B. J., Duffy, M. K., & Henle, C. A. (2002). *Development and test of an interactional model of abusive supervision.* Unpublished manuscript, University of Kentucky, Lexington.

Tepper, B. J., Duffy, M. K., & Shaw, J. D. (2001). Personality moderators of the relationship between abusive supervision and subordinates' resistance. *Journal of Applied Psychology, 86,* 974–983.

Thacker, R. A. (1992). A descriptive study of behavioral responses of sexual harassment targets: Implications for control theory. *Employee Responsibilities and Rights Journal, 5,* 155–170.

Williams, A., & Keashly, L. (2001, August). *Communication of respect in the workplace: The managers' perspective.* Poster presented at the fourth annual Wayne State University Minority Programs Research Day, Detroit, MI.

Wright, L., & Smye, M. (1996). *Corporate abuse: How lean and mean robs people and profits.* New York: Macmillan.

Wyatt, J., & Hare, C. (1997). *Work abuse: How to recognize and survive it.* Rochester, VT: Scheming Books.

Yukl, G., & Falbe, D. M. (1990). Influence tactics and objectives in upward, downward and lateral influence attempts. *Journal of Applied Psychology, 75,* 132–140.

Zapf, D. (1999). Organizational work group related and personal causes of mobbing/bullying at work. *International Journal of Manpower, 20,* 70–85.

Zellars, K. L., Tepper, B. J., & Duffy, M. K. (2002). Abusive supervision and subordinates' organizational citizenship behavior. *Journal of Applied Psychology, 87,* 1068–1076.

10

MOBBING AT WORK: ESCALATED CONFLICTS IN ORGANIZATIONS

DIETER ZAPF AND STÅLE EINARSEN

During the 1990s, a new research field emerged in Europe under the terms *mobbing* and *bullying* at work, which have in common that employees are systematically harassed by one or more colleagues or superiors on a regular basis and for a long time (Einarsen, Hoel, Zapf, & Cooper, 2003a). Such forms of persistent negative treatment had not been systematically described until Heinz Leymann, a Swedish family therapist, began investigating direct and indirect forms of conflicts in the workplace (Leymann, 1995). In 1982, Leymann began empirical work in various organizations, where he encountered the phenomenon of mobbing. He wrote the first report about the phenomenon (Leymann & Gustavsson, 1984) and published the first popular book (Leymann, 1986). A series of studies followed (see Leymann, 1996), and other research projects were begun in Finland (Björkqvist, Österman, & Hjelt-Bäck, 1994; Vartia, 1993) and Norway (Einarsen, Raknes, Matthiesen, & Hellesøy, 1994; Matthiesen, Raknes, & Røkkum, 1989). Because of German-born Leymann, the concept of mobbing became popular in the German-speaking countries, and some scientists started their own research, based on his work (Niedl, 1995; Zapf, Knorz, & Kulla, 1996).

The term *mobbing* was borrowed from the English word *mob* and originally was used in Swedish to describe animal aggression and herd behavior as well as bullying in the schoolyard (see Einarsen, Hoel, Zapf, & Cooper, 2003b; Leymann, 1993). Leymann (1986) then borrowed the term to describe nonsexual harassment in the workplace. Internationally, the term was later adopted in the German-speaking countries and, in part, in the Netherlands, as well as in some Mediterranean countries, whereas *bullying* became the preferred term in English-speaking countries (Roland & Munthe, 1989).

Interest among the lay public in the phenomenon of mobbing grew rapidly. Within a short period of time, the popular media in various European countries regularly reported almost unbelievable stories of how people were mistreated at work. Some people experienced coming back from vacation to find their office and tasks occupied by other employees and their desk moved to another floor. One victim got a room in the basement without daylight and without anything to do for months. Another one had no work tasks for more than four years and was invited to no meetings or social gatherings at all during these years. Others described how they were harassed, badgered, mistreated, and ostracized, how they fell ill and became physically and psychologically unable to work.

THE CONCEPT OF MOBBING

Mobbing is a description of a certain phenomenon rather than a psychological theory. It is a severe and highly stressful interpersonal conflict in which a power difference exists between the parties. Mobbing qualifies as a research topic because neither traditional conflict nor stress research adequately addresses this phenomenon. However, theories from these fields are important and useful to explain why mobbing occurs and why it has such extreme negative consequences for the target.

Various researchers (Einarsen, 2000; Einarsen et al., 2003b; Hoel, Rayner, & Cooper, 1999; Hoel, Zapf, & Cooper, 2002; Zapf, 1999b) identified the following characteristics when examining the concept of mobbing at work: the degree of mistreatment, the frequency and the duration of the mobbing behaviors, the nature of the behaviors involved, the reaction of the target, the imbalance of power between the parties, the intent of the perpetrator, and the question of subjective versus objective mobbing.

MOBBING AS A SEVERE SOCIAL STRESSOR

When starting his research with victims of mobbing, Leymann (1990b) discovered that victims were severely shaken by their experiences of being harassed, showing symptoms of psychological and physical illness. He also observed that these health problems were so severe that management and even health-care personnel did not believe them to be caused by experiences of mistreatment in the workplace. The victims reported typical stress symptoms, but of a degree beyond what was found elsewhere in organizational stress research (Zapf et al., 1996). Leymann diagnosed many of the victims to have psychiatric illnesses such as general anxiety disorder (GAD) or posttraumatic stress disorder (PTSD) resulting in permanent personality changes (Leymann & Gustafsson, 1996; cf., e.g., the case in Groeblinghoff & Becker, 1996). Assuming that organizational circumstances contribute to these disorders puts the problem of mobbing and its consequences into an organizational stress perspective. Many authors have claimed that mobbing must be seen as an extreme source of social stress at work. Using such a perspective, an extreme stress reaction is elicited by an organizational stressor comparable in severity to catastrophic occurrences such as a train operator driving over a suicide victim (Theorell, Leymann, Jodko, Konarski, & Norbeck, 1994) or a bank employee who is the victim of a bank robbery. Leymann (1993) argued that mobbing is caused by organizational factors such as a deficit in leadership, work design, and social climate. Moreover, Leymann understood mobbing as an extreme interpersonal conflict. The mobbing conflict had to be clearly different from the "normal" everyday conflicts in organizations, because the normal conflicts would never be thought to cause any traumalike psychiatric illnesses. Leymann (1993, 1995) had in mind that some kind of psychiatric disorder such as "PTSD due to mobbing" should become an official psychiatric diagnosis that could then be applied in practice and that should make it possible for the mobbing victims to receive a disability pension or other compensation for their suffering from their company. This background explains why much mobbing research has focused on the extreme conflict situations described in this chapter.

THE FREQUENCY AND DURATION OF THE EXPERIENCE

According to Leymann (1996), the frequency and the duration of the experience are key dimensions of mobbing. Many researchers have adopted this view (e.g., Björkqvist et al., 1994; Einarsen et al., 2003b; Einarsen, Raknes, Matthiesen, & Hellesøy, 1994; Niedl, 1995; Vartia, 1996; Zapf et al., 1996). Mobbing is not a single act or an occasional experience. Rather, to speak of mobbing, negative behavior directed against a target has to occur repeatedly and for a long time. Leymann (1993, 1996) suggested that the related behavior should occur at least once a week for at least 6 months.

Most mobbing behaviors are not necessarily extremely negative per se. For example, not greeting somebody may be a result of feeling sleepy in the morning or being distracted by something that just happened. However, never greeting a particular person has an entirely different quality and meaning. Shouting at somebody or making a person look foolish may sometimes be a result of a loss of self-control and may often be regretted afterward. Again, using every opportunity to show this behavior against a particular person and being convinced that the person "deserves" it is on a different plane.

According to Leymann (1996), it is this dimension of systematic and long-term aggression that effectively distinguishes what may be considered a normal interpersonal conflict from mobbing. However, several researchers have emphasized that there will be occasions in which mobbing may be established by a one-time negative act (Einarsen et al., 2003b; Hoel & Cooper, 2000; Zapf, 1999b). For example, in cases of severe aggression the effect may remain for a long time. There may be severe incidents in which the behavior induces sufficient fear that the behavior does not need to be repeated for the effect to remain. Some kinds of treatment, such as having work tasks taken away, may only happen once while the consequences of the act are experienced daily. In other words, flashbacks or the sheer sight or thought of a previous aggressor may recall memories of the act and may keep the victim in constant fear.

THE EFFECTS AND THE REACTIONS OF TARGETS

Although a stress reaction of the target is usually not part of the definition of mobbing, most mobbing researchers share the view that one can only speak of mobbing when the negative behavior manifests itself in a negative health outcome for the target (e.g., Einarsen & Mikkelsen, 2003; Einarsen et al., 2003b; Leymann, 1993). In this sense, mobbing stands in the tradition of reaction-oriented stress concepts (e.g., Lazarus & Folkman, 1984; Selye, 1971). Whereas perception and appraisal play a significant role in stress research, this is of secondary importance in mobbing research for a simple reason: Given the severity of the conflict situation it is highly unlikely that a mobbing victim will not appraise the stressors negatively and will not show stress reactions.

THE INTENT OF THE PERPETRATOR

Intent is not considered an essential element in mobbing research. The intent to cause harm on the part of the perpetrator as a key feature of mobbing has been suggested by some authors who consider aggression theory as an important explanatory concept (e.g., Björkqvist et al., 1994). From this perspective there is no mobbing when there is no intention to cause harm. However, it is normally impossible to verify the presence of intent (Hoel et al., 1999; cf. the research on sexual harassment, e.g., Pryor & Fitzgerald, 2003). Intent can be linked both to whether a single negative action was intended, whether mobbing as a process (i.e., frequent negative actions systematically aimed at the target) was intended, whether there were goals for which mobbing was used instrumentally, or whether the likely harmful outcomes of the mobbing behavior were intended (cf. Hoel et al., 1999).

Whereas single episodes of mobbing behavior may be conscious and intended, there may be no intent to cause severe harm on the part of the perpetrator. There are repeated anecdotal reports of perpetrators who were surprised when they were informed about the personal and health problems of the victims. They claimed their behavior only to be thoughtless (e.g., Leymann, 1993; Zapf, 1999b). On the other hand, people may be aware that somebody is a regular target of negative social behavior but they may not be fully aware of their own contribution to that situation.

Moreover, the mobbing behavior may be considered instrumental to achieve a certain goal—for example, to make a certain person leave the company or to receive a certain position at the cost of someone else. In empirical studies on the victims' perspective of mobbing, the intent to harass someone is usually taken for granted when victims say that "they want to push me out of the firm" or "a hostile person influenced others" (Zapf, 1999c, p. 76). The question is, "Was this a conscious goal right from the beginning or was it a result of the process?" Mobbing behavior is sometimes spontaneous (e.g., making an inappropriate joke), and employees may not really be aware of single negative behaviors (e.g., ignoring somebody, not greeting someone). In some cases, both victims and perpetrators may find themselves together in an uncontrollable and escalating conflict situation, and it may be difficult to say what exactly was intended and what was not.

In summary, although intent of the perpetrator is not a definitional criterion of mobbing, it seems highly unlikely that, given that mobbing is a long-lasting process, the perpetrators are entirely unaware of what they are doing. Even if there was no clear intent in the beginning, mobbing is typically justified and seen as no more than a fair treatment of a difficult person by most actors after the event.

THE IMBALANCE OF POWER

A central definitional feature of mobbing is the imbalance of power between the parties. Typically, targets of mobbing find it difficult to defend themselves against the behavior, because their opportunity for retaliation is more or less ruled out (Einarsen, 2000; Einarsen, Raknes, Matthiesen, & Hellesøy, 1994; Hoel et al., 1999; Leymann, 1993; Niedl, 1995; Vartia, 1996; Zapf et al., 1996). The imbalance of power is important both from the stress- and the conflict-theory perspective. Imbalance of power in the context of mobbing means that the person concerned has little control. Little control combined with high stressors has been described as particularly stressful (Kahn & Byosiere, 1992; Karasek & Theorell, 1990), thus explaining the severe health damage often observed in victims. Moreover, low or no control impedes almost all active conflict management strategies, and thus partly explains the long duration of mobbing conflicts. The imbalance of power often mirrors the formal power structure of the organizational context in which mobbing develops— for instance when someone is on the receiving end of negative acts from a person in a superior organizational position. Alternatively, the source of power may be informal, based on knowledge and experience as well as access to the support of powerful others (Einarsen, 1999; Hoel & Cooper, 2000). In the latter instances, conflicts between individuals of seemingly equal power may gradually escalate, leaving one of the parties increasingly defenseless. To emphasize the power difference we mainly use the terms *victim* and *perpetrator* instead of more neutral terms such as *actor* and *target* throughout the chapter. This does not imply that the victim necessarily is without any responsibility for the situation and hence the "good guy" in the conflict.

A DEFINITION OF MOBBING

The following definition of *mobbing* is suggested:

Mobbing at work means harassing, offending, socially excluding someone or negatively affecting someone's work tasks. In order for the label mobbing to be applied to a particular activity, interaction or process it has to occur repeatedly and regularly (e.g. weekly) and over a period of time (e.g. about six months). Mobbing is an escalating process in the course of which the person confronted ends up in an inferior position and becomes the target of systematic negative social acts. A conflict cannot be called mobbing if the incident is an isolated event or if two parties of approximately equal "strength" are in conflict. (Einarsen et al., 2003b, p. 15)

(For similar definitions, see Einarsen & Skogstad, 1996; Hoel et al., 1999; Leymann, 1996; Niedl, 1995; Zapf, 1999b, 1999c.)

MOBBING OR BULLYING? A QUESTION OF PERSPECTIVE

In Europe, two labels are used to signify severe nonsexual harassment at work: *mobbing* and *bullying*. Because research in this area was driven by the phenomenon and not by any specific theory, a variety of concepts and definitions of mobbing and bullying appeared, depending on the particular focus of the researchers. There have been attempts to bring these concepts and definitions together, especially in the books by Einarsen et al. (2003a) and Hoel et al. (1999). Although we were involved in this converging process, in this chapter we emphasize the differences between mobbing and bullying rather than their similarities.

Mobbing and bullying research has in common that they are both victim-oriented and that the negative outcomes for the victims are a vital issue. However, researchers who prefer the term *bullying* (e.g., in the UK: Randall, 1997; Rayner, 1997; in Australia: Sheehan, 1999) primarily focus on the bully. As an example, the influential book by Andrea Adams (1992) is full of stories about bullies, typically supervisors or managers, who mistreat and harass one or more—or even all—of their subordinates. Accordingly, a bully could be defined as someone who behaves aggressively toward others who have less power than him- or herself regularly and over a long period of time. Misuse of power, low social skills, and personality problems of the bully are frequently given as explanations for bullying. Moreover, bullying seems to be particularly concerned with aggression from someone in a managerial or supervisory position targeting his or her subordinates (e.g., Adams, 1992).

On the other hand, as described earlier, mobbing research has always had an exclusive focus on the victim. According to Leymann (1993, 1996), the choice of the term *mobbing* over *bullying* was a conscious decision. It reflected the fact that the phenomenon in question often refers to subtle, less direct forms of aggression as opposed to the more physical forms of aggression commonly identified with the term *bullying*. Mobbing is often concerned with aggression from a group of people but tends to be directed toward one single person. Leymann's interest was to demonstrate that work conflicts in which one person was singled out, harassed, and ostracized over a long period of time do lead to such severe health consequences that even health professionals such as physicians or psychologists may not believe that the health damages they observed could be due to conditions in the workplace.

The differing foci of these concepts are summarized in Figure 10.1. A bully is someone who bullies other employees and does this frequently and over a long period of time. However, if these bullying behaviors are distributed across several individuals, this does not necessarily imply that every

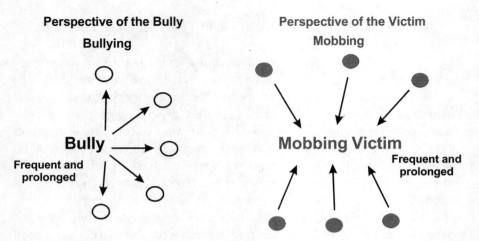

Perspective of the Bully
Bullying
Bully — Frequent and prolonged

Perspective of the Victim
Mobbing
Mobbing Victim — Frequent and prolonged

Figure 10.1. Bullying and mobbing: Victim and perpetrator perspectives.

individual becomes a victim harassed on a weekly basis and for at least 6 months. Rather, this can also mean that each individual is only occasionally exposed to the bully's negative behavior. Moreover, in this case the single individuals are not necessarily defenseless. Rather, several victims may support each other. Social support, as is known from stress research (e.g., Kahn & Byiosiere, 1992), is an important resource that can reduce the otherwise extreme effects of the bullying behavior.

In contrast, the concept of mobbing looks at the harassing behavior from the victim's perspective. One or more perpetrators exhibit negative behaviors that are systematically directed at a targeted person. This does not necessarily mean that each single perpetrator does a lot of mobbing. Rather, the personal contribution of one perpetrator may be small: a relatively insignificant event, such as gossiping, not greeting, not sharing information or an incidence of horseplay (Zapf & Einarsen, 2003). If in a group of five or six people everybody is teasing, ridiculing, or otherwise negatively treating a particular person, and if these individuals do so about once a month, the perpetrators may perceive their individual behaviors as occasional and unrelated events. For the person on the receiving end, however, this means that he or she experiences the negative behavior six times a month, which meets the criterion of weekly mobbing. Very likely, the person will perceive the negative behavior as intentional and systematically directed at him- or herself. This view is supported by Baumeister, Stillwell, and Wotman (1990), who analyzed narrative interviews and found that victims of aggression, anger, and harassment interpreted such experiences as a series of interrelated events.

The bullies, on the other hand, may not be aware of the effects of their behavior because of little communication between perpetrators and victims and because of the fact that perpetrators may not receive realistic feedback about their behavior (Zapf & Einarsen, 2003).

These different perspectives can also be found in empirical data. Comparing the percentages of supervisors, colleagues, and subordinates reported as bullies in various studies in Europe (see Zapf, Einarson, Hoel, & Vartia, 2003), the supervisors were involved in 50% to 70% of all cases. It is obvious that mobbing is a leadership problem in many respects. Yet, in most studies, mobbing among colleagues is equally frequent, showing that many victims are harassed by both superiors and colleagues. However, this is not so in some studies carried out in the United Kingdom, where the concept of bullying is used and where the percentage of colleagues involved in bullying is much lower compared to other European countries, whereas superiors are reported as the bullies in approximately 80% of cases (Rayner, 1997; UNISON, 1997). This can be taken as support of the somewhat differing views of bullying and mobbing. Thus, in spite of the efforts to achieve a widely accepted definition, as in the case of Einarsen et al. (2003b), one has also to be aware of the possibly differing connotations of the terms *mobbing* and *bullying* at work.

CATEGORIES OF MOBBING BEHAVIOR

Looking at the specific acts of mobbing, the question is whether mobbing is a homogeneous construct or whether there are different kinds or strategies of mobbing. Homogeneity of mobbing implies that the mobbing behaviors show similar frequencies, have similar causes and consequences, and occur under the same circumstances (Zapf et al., 1996). Correlational analyses based on general samples of employees (e.g., Niedl, 1995) show that different kinds of mobbing categories are highly correlated. Factor analyses also often lead to a single mobbing factor. If people are severely harassed, they tend to experience a large number of mobbing behaviors from different behavioral categories. However, if factor analyses are based on victim samples, a variety of mobbing strategies may be differentiated. Based on a revised version of the Negative Acts Questionnaire (NAQ; Einarsen & Hoel, 2001), applied to a random sample of 5,288 employees in the United Kingdom, Einarsen and Hoel empirically distinguished two basic factors: personal bullying (e.g., verbal aggression, rumors, ridiculing) and work-related bullying (affecting someone's work tasks and competencies). Using the Leymann Inventory of Psychological Terrorization (LIPT; Leymann, 1990a), which is a questionnaire of 45 items, Zapf et al. (1996) empirically differentiated seven factors in two samples: (a) organizational measures consisting of behaviors initiated by the supervisor or aspects directly related to the victim's tasks (corresponding to Einarsen and Hoel's work-related bullying); (b) social isolation, related to informal social relationships at work; (c) attacking the private sphere, related to individual attributes of the victim and the victim's private life usually aimed at derogating the victim's self-esteem; (d) verbal aggression; (e) spreading rumors; (f) physical violence, referring to sexual harassment as well as general physical violence or threat of violence; and (g) attacking the victim's attitudes about politics, nationalism, and religion (the mobbing strategies b–g corresponding to Einarsen and Hoel's personal bullying). Other studies in several countries using the LIPT found similar factor structures (e.g., Niedl, 1995; Vartia, 1993).

It appears that the first five categories can be considered typical for mobbing (Leymann, 1993; Niedl, 1995; Vartia, 1993; Zapf et al., 1996), whereas attacking attitudes and physical aggression are found in some studies but occur only occasionally in the context of mobbing, mostly in fewer than 10% of the cases (cf. Einarsen & Raknes, 1997; Zapf, 1999b). Moreover, with the exception of physical aggression, compared with nonvictims, the victims typically score higher on all mobbing strategies (e.g., Zapf, 1999b). There are also differences within the victim group. For example, victims harassed by their superiors tend to report more mobbing by organizational measures and less rumors and mobbing by social isolation compared to victims harassed by their colleagues (Zapf, 1999a). However, the differences among the victims are much smaller than the differences between victims and nonvictims.

EMPIRICAL RESEARCH ON MOBBING

In the following sections we will present empirical results on mobbing with regard to the frequency and duration of mobbing, the gender of victims and perpetrators, and the organizational status of the perpetrator.

The Frequency of Mobbing

It is difficult to provide a reliable estimate of the frequency of mobbing or bullying. The frequency of mobbing depends on the definition used and how frequency is measured (Hoel et al., 1999).

Most studies are based on self-report questionnaires. Some researchers provide a list of mobbing behaviors and estimate the frequency of mobbing based on a point score (Björkqvist et al., 1994). These studies estimate approximately 10% to 17% of people report mobbing (although the definition of mobbing in this instance does not necessarily correspond to the definition given earlier). Those studies using the LIPT maintain that to be considered a mobbing victim, the response to at least one item should be that it happens at least once a week, for at least 6 months. This method seems to result in 3% to 7% of respondents self-reporting mobbing (Zapf et al., 2003). Others have directly asked, "Have you been bullied during the last six months?" This question typically leads to a high percentage of bullying—usually with 10% to 25% replying affirmatively. This high number may be a result of the use of the terms *mobbing* or *bullying* in everyday language: Some may claim to have been bullied when only occasional minor actions have occurred. Another strategy is to give a precise definition of what mobbing is, for example, the definition given earlier. This method leads to 1% to 4% of respondents reporting mobbing (e.g., Einarsen & Skogstad, 1996).

The large and highly representative studies arrive at similar results for the prevalence rate of severe mobbing using the strict definition given earlier. Leymann (1996), based on a representative sample ($N = 2,438$) of the Swedish workforce, reported a prevalence rate of 3.5%. Einarsen and Skogstad (1996) in their total sample of $N = 7,787$ reported a prevalence rate of 1.2% weekly mobbing. Two large studies in Germany found 2.9% ($N = 1,989$; Mackensen von Astfeld, 2000) and 2.7% ($N = 2,765$; Meschkutat, Stackelbeck, & Langenhoff, 2002), and Hoel and Cooper (2000) found a prevalence rate of 1.4% in the United Kingdom ($N = 5288$). In all, most of the studies in Europe found a percentage of respondents reporting mobbing according to the definition given in this chapter of between 1.2% and 4% (Zapf et al., 2003).

Using a less strict definition of mobbing by giving up the six-months criterion and including mobbing "now and then" or "occasionally" leads to somewhat higher numbers. Hoel and Cooper (2000) found 10.6% reporting occasional mobbing; Einarsen and Skogstad (1996) found prevalence rates of 3.4% reporting mobbing "now and then" and 8.6% reporting "occasional" mobbing. From these and other studies, one may conclude that between 1% and 4% severe mobbing and up to 10% occasional mobbing is likely to exist (Zapf et al., 2003). However, between 20% and 25% of the employees are likely to be exposed to occasional negative social behavior, behavior that does not necessarily correspond to the strict definition of mobbing or bullying (Zapf & Holz, 2003; see also Keashly & Jagatic, 2003).

The Duration of Mobbing

Empirical studies support the view that mobbing typically is a long-lasting situation. In the large and representative samples in Sweden (Leymann, 1996), Norway (Einarsen & Skogstad, 1996), and Germany (Meschkutat et al., 2002), the average duration of mobbing was 15, 18, and 16 months, respectively. In studies of victim groups only, the average duration was much higher, with a mean of more than three years (e.g., Leymann & Gustafsson, 1996; Zapf, 1999b). This difference is attributable to the method: If one tries to find mobbing victims and contact them through counseling phone lines or self-help groups, one will receive a self-selected sample of more severe cases of mobbing. These numbers show that mobbing is not a short episode but a long-lasting, wearing-down process, often lasting much longer than one year.

Gender of the Victims

Although data exist on the gender of perpetrators and victims, there are not many studies focusing on this issue (an exception is Vartia & Hyyti, 2002). In most samples, there are about one third men and two thirds women among the victims, although a few studies are more balanced (see Zapf et al., 2003). Mobbing seems to occur more often in sectors such as the social services and health sector, where women are in the majority. Moreover, it is known from research on stress and health that women are more prepared to take part in studies on issues where personal problems or weaknesses play a role (Kasl & Cooper, 1987). Finally, mobbing is more often a top-down process than the other way around. Women are more often in subordinate positions (Davidson & Cooper, 1992), which may also contribute to their increased risk of becoming victims of mobbing. Although there is substantial evidence that women are at greater risk to become a victim of mobbing, there is, so far, little evidence that this is because of a specific female socialization.

Gender of the Perpetrators

In a study by Einarsen and Skogstad (1996), 49% of the victims reported all perpetrators to be males, whereas 30% reported their perpetrators to be females. The rest reported perpetrators of both genders. Similar results have been found in other studies (Zapf et al., 2003). Men seem to be overrepresented among the perpetrators in most studies. This result corresponds to similar findings in research on bullying at school (Olweus, 1994). Mobbing, at least in part, includes forms of direct aggression, such as shouting or humiliating somebody. There is substantial empirical evidence that this kind of aggression is much more typical for men than for women, who tend to prefer forms of indirect aggression such as social exclusion or spreading rumors (Björkqvist, 1994).

The Number of Perpetrators

Most studies on mobbing show that in 20% to 40% of all cases there was only one person harassing the victim, whereas in 15% to 25% there were more than four perpetrators involved (Zapf et al., 2003). Studies of Einarsen and Skogstad (1996) and Zapf and Gross (2001) showed that the mobbing behaviors occurred more frequently the longer mobbing lasted and that more people participated in the mobbing the longer it went on. Data on this issue suggest that it gets more and more difficult to remain a neutral bystander the longer mobbing lasts. Therefore, more and more people may become involved as time goes by. This may explain the higher mean number of perpetrators in the pure victims samples, which also show a higher mean duration of mobbing.

The Organizational Status of the Victim

Relatively little has been reported about the organizational status of the victim. Hoel, Cooper, and Faragher (2001) analyzed this issue and found similar rates of mobbing for workers, supervisors, and middle and senior management. A representative sample of Finnish employees showed that upper level white-collar employees experienced mobbing somewhat more often than lower level white-collar employees or workers (Piirainen et al., 2000). Salin (2001), however, found less mobbing at the higher levels of management. These findings show that it is not the weak and defenseless who become the primary victims of mobbing. Rather, there seem to be similar risks at all organizational status levels. Supervisors and senior managers may also experience a power imbalance relative to their colleagues and superiors.

The Status of the Perpetrator

By contrast, many studies have been interested in the organizational status of the perpetrators. Leymann (1993) introduced mobbing as a lasting conflict among colleagues. However, the Scandinavian studies identified people in superior positions as offenders in approximately equal numbers to peers, with only a small number harassed by a subordinate (Einarsen & Skogstad, 1996; Leymann, 1993). In contrast, British studies have consistently identified people in superior positions as bullies in an overwhelming majority of cases (Cowie et al., 2000; Hoel et al., 2001; Rayner, 1997). The results of studies in other European countries (e.g., Niedl, 1995; Zapf, 1999b) fall in between. In part, they topped the British numbers with regard to supervisor mobbing (e.g., Zapf, 1999b). However, the number of colleagues among the perpetrators was much higher in these studies compared to the British studies and equaled the number of superiors.

All in all, harassment of superiors by subordinates is rare. There are only a few cases in which superiors were exclusively harassed by their subordinates. Usually, subordinates harass a superior together with other supervisors or managers. The reason is, of course, that it is not easy to overcome the formal power of a superior by informal power. It may be possible if the superior is isolated (which points at tensions or conflicts within management) or new in the position, but it is almost impossible if the superior is backed up by superiors at the same level or by the senior management. One can certainly say that only isolated superiors who have lost or not yet gained the support of their colleagues and of the higher management carry a risk of becoming the victim of subordinates' mobbing. In summary, mobbing may be both a lasting conflict among colleagues and a case of harsh supervisory practice.

THE CAUSES OF MOBBING

There have been many controversial discussions about the causes of mobbing in Europe. One side in this controversy is represented by a part of the media and some employers. This side made the victims themselves responsible for being a target of mobbing. This side received support from many physicians and clinical psychologists who treated victims of mobbing and came up with diagnoses such as "querulous behavior" or "general anxiety disorder." They suggested that these disorders existed before the mobbing process began and that these disorders were the reason why a mobbing process developed.

The other side was represented by Leymann (1990b, 1996), the mobbing victims, and their organizational networks, claiming organizational factors, predominantly problems in the organization of work and leadership, were the primary causes of mobbing. There is not enough research by far to provide a definitive answer to the question of what may cause bullying and mobbing. The problem is partly of a methodological nature because the present studies are all cross-sectional (Zapf, 1999c). However, most researchers agree that there are four potential causes of bullying: the organization, the perpetrator, the social work group, and the victim (Einarsen, 1999, 2000; Hoel et al., 1999; Zapf, 1999c). The perpetrator as a cause usually overlaps with causes found in the social group and the organization if supervisors as perpetrators are involved.

Personal Causes of Mobbing: The Perpetrator

In some studies, the victims of mobbing were asked what causes they saw for being harassed. "They wanted to push me out of the company" was the most frequent reason in the studies of Zapf (1999c). Second came "there was a certain person responsible for bullying." At least from the victims' perspective the cause of mobbing is often seen in a certain perpetrator. Among many victims, envy is considered a core reason behind mobbing

(Björkqvist et al., 1994; Einarsen, Raknes, & Matthiesen, 1994; Vartia, 1996). A weak superior; competition for tasks, status, or advancement; or competition for the supervisor's favor are other perceived reasons for mobbing (Einarsen, 2000).

Einarsen (1999) suggested the concepts of dispute-related and predatory mobbing to explain the onset of two distinct kinds of mobbing. Whereas dispute-related mobbing is characterized by a highly escalated interpersonal conflict, *predatory mobbing* refers to cases in which the victim has personally done nothing provocative that may reasonably justify the behavior of the predator. In such cases the victim is accidentally in a situation in which a predator is demonstrating power or is exploiting the weakness of an accidental victim. The concept of petty tyranny proposed by Ashforth (1994) seems to apply to such kinds of mobbing. Petty tyranny refers to leaders who lord their power over others through arbitrariness and self-aggrandizement, the belittling of subordinates, a lack of consideration, and the use of an authoritarian style of conflict management. Zapf and Einarsen (2003) suggested that the concept of threatened self-esteem of Baumeister, Smart, and Boden (1996) may be applied to these mobbing cases. In summarizing their review of empirical research, Baumeister et al. (p. 26) concluded, "In all spheres we examined, we found that violence emerged from threatened egotism, whether this was labeled as wounded pride, disrespect, verbal abuse, insults, anger manipulations, status inconsistency, or something else. . . . Violence resulted most commonly from feeling that one's superiority was somehow being undermined, jeopardized, or contradicted by current circumstances." A study by Stucke (2002) supported the application of Baumeister et al.'s general findings to mobbing research. In her study, employees indicated first whether or not they actively used different kinds of mobbing behaviors. Second, measures of narcissism and stability of self-esteem were administered. Narcissism implies exaggerated self-esteem along with the disregard of others. Active mobbing behavior was highest for a group high in narcissism but low in self-esteem stability. These individuals had to stabilize their high but unstable self-esteem by treating other individuals negatively.

Another explanation stems from concepts of micropolitical behavior in organizations (e.g., Gandz & Murray, 1980; Neuberger, 1995, 1999), which assumes that members in organizations try to protect and improve their status and their interests in the organization. Part of the behavior is directed toward the striving for personal goals that may be opposed to the goals of other organizational members. Opponents in one situation may be coalition partners in another. Therefore, causing damage to somebody is usually not a primary goal in micropolitical behavior. However, in some cases, damage will be accepted and a person may actively use negative social behavior to reach her or his personal goals.

Organizational Causes of Mobbing

There are a number of indications that the causes of mobbing may also lie in the organization itself. One such indication can be found in the distribution of mobbing across industries. Although there are some differing results in the various European countries, mobbing seems to occur less often among factory workers and more often among office workers. There is evidence that there is more mobbing in the social and health care services and in the education, public administration, banking, and insurance sectors (Leymann, 1993; Meschkutat et al., 2002; Zapf et al., 2003).

There must be some differences in the organizations in these branches that lead to the different frequencies of mobbing, and one can speculate why this is so. First, this can possibly be explained in the more difficult career prospective within these branches. Opportunities for advancement either do not exist as in many parts of the social and health services or only to a small extent can they be influenced by achievement but instead depend heavily on seniority, time in the organization, and personal relationships. This situation may then increase micropolitical behavior and thus the likelihood of unresolved or unmanaged conflicts. Such conflicts may then escalate into mobbing. Second, the quality of the work and efforts of a teacher or a nurse may be more difficult to evaluate objectively compared to the work of an assembly line worker. This, again, may be a source of potential conflicts and it could make it easier to use organizational measures to harass someone (e.g., permanently criticizing one's work; giving someone humiliating or senseless tasks, etc.; Zapf et al., 1996). Third and most important, among the factory workers, many are relatively unskilled and can readily find equivalent alternative employment if the unemployment rate is not too high. They might simply leave the company if conflicts escalate. In the public sector, it is not as easy to leave the job and find new employment. People would not easily give up the privilege of high job security often found in public sector organizations in Europe. Hence, it may be difficult for a victim to leave the organization even if exposed to mobbing.

How does an organization produce conflicts that may escalate into mobbing? One possibility is a simple probability assumption. If the probability of conflicts is high in an organization, then the probability that a conflict might not be solved but will escalate is also high. Hassles in the work organization might make cooperation more difficult; unclear or contradictory goals might induce rivalry; and high time pressure might imply that there is little time for conflict management. An organization with such characteristics would be expected to have a higher risk for mobbing compared to an organization with no such characteristics. Several studies show that the victims of mobbing work under such conditions (high job stressors such as time pressure, high cooperational dependencies, high levels of role conflict and role ambiguity, and low control at work; see Einarsen et al., 1994; Vartia, 1996; Zapf, 1999c; Zapf et al., 1996).

Causes of Mobbing in the Victim and the Social Group

Contrary to the early statements of Leymann (1993), several studies have been carried out in recent years that point to potential causes of mobbing in the victim. These studies have found differences between victims and nonvictims of mobbing that seem more likely to be causes rather than consequences of mobbing.

Studies from various countries find increased levels of neuroticism among the mobbing victims (Coyne, Seigne, & Randall, 2000; Coyne, Smith-Lee Chong, Seigne, & Randall, 2003; Einarsen & Mikkelsen, 2003; Einarsen et al., 1994; Lindemeier, 1996; Matthiesen & Einarsen, 2001; Rammsayer & Schmiga, 2003; Vartia, 1996; Zapf, 1999c). Neurotic individuals tend to show high levels of emotional instability, anxiety, and depressive symptoms. Although it cannot be excluded that the victims' symptoms were a consequence of mobbing rather than a cause in these studies, it is unlikely that this was so in all cases.

It has been suggested that people high in negative affect (NA, including anxious, depressive, and neurotic symptoms) by their behavior create or enact adverse circumstances (Depue & Monroe, 1986) and thus may create or contribute to the development of conflicts at work (Spector, Zapf, Chen, & Frese, 2000). Moreover, there is evidence that other people may respond negatively to depressed individuals (e.g., Sacco, Dumont, & Dow, 1993). All this may increase the base rate of conflicts, may increase the likelihood of a conflict to escalate, and may eventually lead to mobbing (Zapf & Einarsen, 2003).

Psychological theories on group dynamics suggest that individuals who are seen as outsiders in some respect and who differ from the rest of the group on some salient factors carry a higher risk of getting in trouble with the others and may be forced into the role of a scapegoat (Schuster, 1996; Thylefors, 1987). A study on differences between characteristics of the group and the victims in a sample of victims and a control group (Zapf, 1999b; see also Zapf & Einarsen, 2003) showed that the victims saw themselves more often as being different from their colleagues compared with a control group. Most interestingly, the results showed that there were heterogeneous groups of victims. One victim group corresponded to what most people would expect: low in social competencies, bad conflict managers, unassertive, weak and neurotic personalities (see also Zapf, 1999c), a result corresponding to findings of both Coyne et al. (2000) and Matthiesen and Einarsen (2001). On the other hand, there was a group of victims who described themselves as more achievement-oriented and as more conscientious than their colleagues.

This group of victims was certainly not among the least efficient employees in the organization. Their problem was that they clashed with the norms of the work group to which they belonged. It is likely that in this case, the victims' conscientiousness went against a group culture characterized by rigidity and low tolerance for diversity. These victims were probably perceived as constant annoyances or even threats to the work group to which they belonged. As a consequence, the group may have started to harass these individuals, either to enforce conformity or to get rid of the person.

There is relatively little well-established knowledge about the causes of mobbing. However, taking all the existing empirical data together, there is sufficient evidence that there are many possible causes and probably often multiple causes of mobbing to be found in the organization, in the perpetrator, in the social system and in the victim.

THE CONSEQUENCES OF MOBBING

Both consequences for the organization, such as absenteeism, turnover, and costs for grievance procedures (e.g., Hoel, Einarsen, & Cooper, 2003) and consequences for the victim (e.g., Einarsen & Mikkelsen, 2003; Leymann & Gustaffson, 1996; Niedl, 1996; Zapf et al., 1996) have been discussed in mobbing research. In this chapter we focus on the effects on the victims using a stress perspective that is the dominant perspective in mobbing research. Most studies on mobbing conclude that it has severe and extreme negative effects on the health and well-being of the victims. See Figure 10.2 to understand the effects of mobbing on the victims.

Like most psychological stress theories, this model assumes that an external stressor, in this case mobbing, negatively affects an individual. An appraisal process, in which the individual evaluates how negatively he or she experiences the stressor and how well he or she can cope with the stressor, mediates the potential effect of the stressor. Coping behaviors exhibited by the victim may also mediate the actual stress outcomes. In addition, most stress concepts emphasize the importance of resources (Kahn & Byosiere, 1992; Lazarus & Folkman, 1984) and differentiate between internal resources (e.g., availability of coping strategies) and external resources such as control at work and social support. Most stress concepts assume that, in line with Karasek's job-demand-control model (Karasek & Theorell, 1990), the combination of high stressors and low resources—for example, low control—is most stressful for the individual.

In this sense, mobbing can be characterized as an extreme stress situation. By definition, the victims are exposed to frequent negative social behavior over a long period of time, making it a strong social stressor. For example, comparing social stressors (conflicts, verbal aggression; Frese &

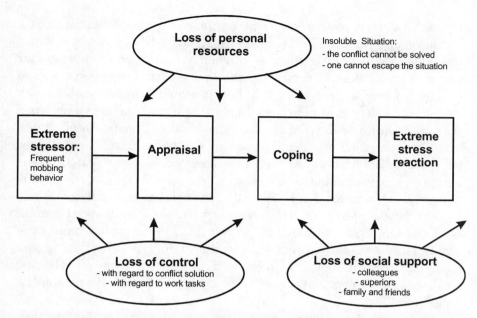

Figure 10.2. Mobbing and consequences of mobbing from the stress perspective.

Zapf, 1987) or mobbing behavior among victims and control groups usually shows tremendous differences. In Zapf et al.'s study (1996), mean social stressor scores of the mobbing victim sample were one standard deviation above various comparison samples.

Mobbing is also characterized by an almost complete lack of resources (e.g., energy, coping strategies, control, and social support). Most victims portray a range of problems and symptoms of ill health. Using Mohr's (1986) checklist of psychosomatic symptoms (e.g., headache, sleeping problems, feeling tense), mean scores in three mobbing samples (Zapf, 1999c; Zapf et al., 1996) were between one and two standard deviations above those in comparison samples (Frese, 1985; Zapf, 1993; Zapf, Vogt, Seifert, Mertini, & Isic, 1999). A substantial proportion of the victims investigated have received medical treatment (Einarsen & Mikkelsen, 2003; Zapf, 1999b). These may be indicators of the psychological exhaustion and depletion of energy many victims report. Moreover, analyzing the conflict strategies of the victims (see discussion later) shows that mobbing is a no-control situation for them. Studies of Meschkutat et al. (2002), Niedl (1996), and Zapf and Gross (2001) found that active coping strategies did not work to solve the mobbing conflict. More than 50% of the victims in these studies ultimately left their jobs.

Finally, responding to Frese's (1989) German translation of the social support scales used in Caplan, Cobb, French, van Harrison, and Pinneau (1975), mobbing victims' social support scores were two standard deviations below the scores of comparison samples without mobbing (Zapf et al., 1996). At the qualitative level, Leymann (1993) reported that victims of mobbing tended to talk about their situation with family, friends, and colleagues over and over again. Because these supportive people had few opportunities to help in a material sense, they may have resented being confronted with their own helplessness and hence started to withdraw from the victims. In a sense, the victims destroyed their own social network (Einarsen et al., 1994).

Without going into details, one can say that mobbing victims show the typical health effects we find in occupational stress research: These effects include psychosomatic complaints, depressive symptoms, and anxiety (Einarsen & Mikkelsen, 2003). Several researchers have found that mobbing victims show symptoms similar to posttraumatic stress syndrome (Leymann & Gustafsson, 1996; Mikkelsen & Einarsen, 2002). The predominant symptom is that the traumatic event occupies the victim's thoughts. The victims cannot help but think about what has been happening to them, often leading to sleeping problems and a variety of other psychological and somatic symptoms.

In summary, mobbing is a stress situation characterized by very high stressors and very low internal and external control, leading to symptoms of ill-health that are more severe than most other stress situations encountered in organizations.

COPING WITH MOBBING

In a study of targets of mobbing, Niedl (1996) investigated how individuals responded to the harassment. Far from responding with a simple fight or flight response, Niedl found that victims resorted to a number of constructive coping strategies when faced with mobbing. Using a model devised by Whithey and Cooper (1989), he reconstructed the responses of victims by mapping the acts of each individual according to four different behavioral strategies: voice, loyalty, neglect, and exit. *Voice* refers to individuals' attempts to raise the alarm within the organization or air their grievance, and *loyalty* relates to actively demonstrating one's commitment. *Neglect* as a strategy points to removal or withdrawal of commitment on the part of victims, and in *exit* the person decides to leave the organization altogether. The results show that there was no single common action pathway, and that most of the victims had tried a number of strategies before finally resorting to neglect or exit. These findings were replicated by Zapf and Gross (2001). Both studies showed that the victims mostly started with active and constructive strategies and mostly ended with passive strategies such as withdrawal behavior or leaving the organization, which is often a destructive strategy from the point of view of the organization.

Several studies using a quantitative approach showed that actions frequently taken in response to being harassed included discussing the problem with work colleagues or discussing the problem with the perpetrators. A substantial proportion of the victims went to the union–staff association, to the workers' representatives, or to the supervisor (Hoel & Cooper, 2000; Knorz & Zapf, 1996; Zapf & Gross, 2001). However, the studies showed that these actions did not prove successful. Rayner (1997) reported that "nothing" (positive) happened in a majority of cases, but a large number of negative outcomes resulted from the action. For example, after putting forward a group complaint, the majority (93%) of those currently bullied reported having been threatened with dismissal. In the study of Meschkutat et al. (2002), 83% of the participants reported that trials to clarify and solve the conflicts by talking to the bullies were unsuccessful, whereas only 7.7% were successful. In a recent diary study (Gross, 2003), fewer than 30% of the daily conflicts of mobbing victims could be solved, whereas more than 60% of the daily conflicts of nonvictims could be solved. The victims reported that in comparison to nonvictims, more conflict episodes were a continuation of former conflicts, that the overall conflict situation more often worsened, that they more often felt inferior and had less influence in the conflict situation.

Knorz and Zapf (1996) and Zapf and Gross (2001) investigated coping strategies of successful and unsuccessful victims. Only 9 out of a sample of 149 victims were identified as successful, whereas 67 out of 149 were identified as unsuccessful in the study of Zapf and Gross—in other words, their case worsened in spite of their coping efforts. The rest did not report substantial changes after their actions. In line with Rayner (1999), talking with the perpetrators was the most frequently used strategy. However, it was used significantly less often by successful compared to unsuccessful victims. This supports the view that mobbing victims are in an inferior position, with little opportunity to actively solve their problem. Most of the active strategies were more likely to worsen than to improve the overall situation. In addition, the successful victims were less likely to use absenteeism and sick-leaves as a coping mechanism. An interpretation of these results is that the most successful strategy to prevent the situation from escalating was to avoid giving the perpetrators additional grounds to harass.

Overall, most results on coping with mobbing at work support the view that mobbing is a no-control situation that can be characterized as a series of failing conflict management attempts (Niedl, 1995) in which active and constructive coping strategies do not prove useful but often make things even worse and in which conflict avoidance seems to be the only reasonable strategy (Gross, 2003; Hogh & Dofradottir, 2001; Knorz & Zapf, 1996; Niedl, 1995; Zapf & Gross, 2001). These results correspond to other findings in conflict research—for example, those of Aquino (2000), who found that the conflict management strategy of integrating was positively correlated with victimization when the individual held a lower power position.

Models of conflict escalation (Glasl, 1994) suggest that at a certain stage of escalation it seems to be impossible to find a solution in which victims and perpetrators work together and develop a positive personal relationship again. In the study of Meschkutat et al. (2002), 12.6% of the mobbing victims reported that defense strategies brought mobbing to an end, whereas 81% said that it was the separation of perpetrators and victims that brought mobbing to an end. Separation was also the most reasonable solution in the studies of Knorz and Zapf (1996) and Zapf and Gross (2001).

Even seeking help may make things worse, because the other party may perceive it as provocative. As a consequence, it is not surprising that most victims, when making recommendations for other victims, most often suggest leaving the company (Zapf & Gross, 2001). Therefore, any advice to the victims has to be given with utmost care. Suggesting they should leave is particularly problematic. First, employment is vital to most people and may not easily be found elsewhere. Second, leaving the organization may be perceived by the victim as self-betrayal in times of hardship and as a highly unfair solution.

MOBBING AND COUNTERPRODUCTIVE BEHAVIOR

In the final part of this chapter we discuss the relationship between mobbing and counterproductive behavior. This includes whether and in which respect mobbing is counterproductive behavior and what the relationship between mobbing and other concepts of counterproductive behavior is.

Determining If Mobbing Is Counterproductive Behavior

Mobbing is without doubt unethical behavior (Leymann, 1993). However, in which respect and for whom is it counterproductive? First, we may conclude that mobbing is counterproductive from the victim's perspective, which is the dominant perspective in mobbing research. As described in this chapter, mobbing has severe consequences for the psychological and physical health of the victim. These consequences may include the actual, perceived, or anticipated threat of being dismissed; the loss of career prospects; becoming unemployed; or taking a new job with worse conditions.

The situation is different for the perpetrators and the organization. As described earlier, with regard to the perpetrators, many mobbing cases fit the perspective of micropolitical behavior in organizations (Neuberger, 1999; Zapf, 1999b; Zapf & Einarsen, 2003). The fact that victims frequently report that there are people who want to kick them out of the firm suggests that some perpetrators may profit from mobbing. From the organizational perspective mobbing has repeatedly been called "human resource management with other means" (Leymann, 1993). Especially in countries with a strong social and legal system—as in Scandinavia and the German-speaking countries—it is almost impossible to dismiss somebody without the person's consent, even if performance is very low. If there are no legal means to get rid of somebody, one may be tempted to use other means. One may harass a person until he or she gives up and leaves the organization "voluntarily." Representatives of organizations of mobbing victims and trade unions often claim that this is indeed the case (Einarsen et al., 1994). However, if one looks at the description of mobbing cases in popular books on mobbing (e.g., Huber, 1993; Leymann, 1993; Walter, 1993) or if one looks at the qualitative material collected over the years (Einarsen et al., 1994; Knorz & Zapf, 1996; Zapf & Gross, 2001), it is difficult to support this view. The explanation we can offer is that both scientists and journalists who approach mobbing victims usually collect a sample of relatively severe cases. These cases can be characterized as lose–lose situations and as a collection of failed strategies to attaining goals. Organizations as well as individual members of organizations may use unethical or antisocial behavior to reach certain goals they cannot reach otherwise. However, overall, they calculate input and output (equity theories: Adams, 1965; and reciprocity theories: Buunk & Schaufeli, 1999). That means they would likely give up mobbing when the costs become too high. The more escalated a conflict is, the more likely it is that every party in the conflict will lose. As has been shown in research on conflict escalation (Fisher & Keashly, 1990; Glasl, 1994; Keashly & Nowell, 2003), the more a conflict escalates the more the original goal will recede into the background and the more motives such as "not losing face" and "win whatever it costs" will dominate. Such conflict strategies are likely counterproductive for the organization and for everybody involved. If this is true, then much depends on the concrete definition of *bullying, mobbing, harassment, emotional abuse*, and so forth. The more we look at the extreme cases, the more we will look at mixed-up conflicts where everybody loses and where hardly any reasonable win strategy can be identified. The less extreme the conflicts are, the more likely we will find cases of antisocial behavior, with reasonable albeit mostly ethically unacceptable strategies to reach personal or organizational goals (win–lose situations). For example, a sales manager of a supermarket might use verbal aggression and other kinds of negative social behavior to make certain employees work harder. However, he would not go beyond certain limits knowing that this would mean losing support of the good workers. A middle manager might threaten a young subordinate manager that she would do everything to undermine the young man's career perspectives in the firm, hoping that the young man would decide to look for another job. Again, the middle manager would not go beyond certain limits knowing that a public conflict would damage her own future career prospects.

In both examples, negative social behavior is used to reach certain goals at the expense of other people. In as far as the sales employees and the young manager have become targets and negative social behavior has repeatedly been shown, the criteria of a wider definition of mobbing may be met. If the sales employees work harder and if the young manager realizes that it is important for his career to look for another job elsewhere, this is a win–lose situation for the perpetrators because the mobbing strategies have been successful. However, because the perpetrators have limited their behavior to avoid doing damage to themselves, the frequency of mobbing behavior, the powerlessness and loss of support from colleagues that is important to make the victims defenseless, are limited. Therefore, a strict definition of mobbing may not be met. In the sales manager example the following scenario is possible: It may happen that one of the employees retaliates against the manager and attacks the manager's self-esteem. Anxious about losing face, the manager strikes back, thus escalating the conflict. She starts to use a variety of mobbing behaviors to get rid of the person who is now becoming a victim of mobbing. Because of the economic situation, the victim is unable to leave the organization without becoming unemployed. The other employees try to be neutral because mistakes have been made on both sides and because they fear losing their own jobs. The victim starts to develop the typical health symptoms related to mobbing, the sales manager is unable to reach her goal of getting rid of the victimized person, the social climate in the supermarket is getting worse, customer-oriented behavior suffers, and sales go down. Even if the victim finally leaves the organization, the conflict has turned into a lose–lose situation, with damage done on both sides. This is typical of cases that follow the strict criteria of mobbing.

Mobbing and Other Concepts of Counterproductive Behavior

As described, mobbing research is more about a phenomenon that has been largely ignored in the past than about a specific and coherent theory. Therefore, to describe and explain mobbing, the line of research has to borrow concepts and theories from other sources and fields. The main sources so far have been stress and conflict theories. Concepts of conflict escalation have become central in mobbing research (Einarsen et al., 2003b; Keashly & Nowell, 2003; Zapf & Gross, 2001). Although mobbing certainly has substantial overlaps with other concepts of counterproductive behavior, there are also differences. The recently developed concept of emotional abuse (Keashly, 1998) comes closest to mobbing. Because of the focus on the victim, mobbing is rather broad with regard to the possible behaviors included, although direct and indirect forms of psychological aggression prevail. Therefore, behaviors comprising concepts of social undermining (Duffy, Ganster, & Pagon, 2002), workplace aggression (Baron & Neuman, 1996, 1998), supervisor abuse (Tepper, 2000), or workplace incivility (Andersson & Pearson, 1999) also occur in the concept of mobbing (Keashly & Jagatic, 2003). Moreover, because of the victim perspective, mobbing seems to focus less or not at all on intentionality, whereas this plays a key role for the concepts of workplace aggression (Neuman & Baron, 1997) and social undermining. Single mobbing behaviors may be thoughtless, spontaneous, or a result of indifference or neglect. Although single acts of mobbing may be intentional, the perpetrator may not have foreseen or even wanted to follow the mobbing process. In this sense, workplace incivility may be closer to mobbing than workplace aggression or social undermining. Overall, however, the perpetrators cannot deny having some knowledge about their actions because of the time frame of the conflicts.

Also, justification is not an issue in mobbing research, although in the public view, the typical target of mobbing seems to be an innocent victim. A victim of mobbing can well be an annoying person, who actually has provoked the mobbing behavior, which, from a neutral standpoint, may be seen as a justifiable defense reaction.

Finally, power does not seem to be an issue in most other concepts (an exception is Ashforth, 1994). For mobbing, however, powerlessness, power differences, and loss of control are key elements. Summarizing the specific aspects of mobbing research, we believe that it has to offer the following:

1. Mobbing research has drawn public and scientific attention to an almost unknown phenomenon (until recently) that has been experienced by many employees. At least in many European countries there is now an increased awareness that negative social behavior in general and mobbing in particular is a reality in many organizations.

2. Mobbing research offers the victim's perspective. It focuses the attention on the effects on the victims, which have not really been addressed in conflict research. It is actually surprising that the effects of conflicts on ill health and well-being have attracted so little attention in this field (see, e.g., Thomas, 1992). Thus, mobbing research may help to bridge the gap between stress and conflict researchers.

3. Key definitional elements of mobbing are the repetition of aggressive behavior, the duration, and the focus on the target. In this respect mobbing or bullying do not belong to the "mild" forms of antisocial behavior, as suggested by Duffy, O'Leary-Kelly, and Ganster (in press), which can also be single acts.

Mobbing, by contrast, is constituted by its persistence and focus on the target. In this fashion, mobbing develops a destructive power that can equal the severe forms of physical violence or sexual harassment.

4. Although mobbing researchers focus on different degrees of escalation, they share the focus on (almost) insoluble situations in which the typically positively evaluated strategies to cope with stress and to manage conflicts obviously have failed to work. This is, of course, not a critique of these kinds of theories or the usefulness of these strategies. However, mobbing research makes the strong point that there are situations in organizations where these strategies have been reasonably applied but have all failed, as evidenced by the high numbers of victims who have finally left the company (Leymann, 1996; Meschkutat et al., 2002; Rayner, 1997; Zapf & Gross, 2001). To our knowledge, this is only found in mobbing and bullying research, where the center of interest lies in individuals with escalated conflicts and no control over the situation.

5. Related to the focus on severe conflicts, mobbing research can serve as a bridge to clinical psychology. In practical work the correct diagnoses of the victims' illnesses and complaints are important. Questions such as, "Do victims of mobbing develop symptoms of posttraumatic stress disorders, general anxiety disorders, or any kind of personality change?" usually go beyond the expertise of organizational psychologists and require collaboration with clinical psychologists and psychiatrists.

CONCLUSION

One cannot say that mobbing is a well-researched field. We therefore expect that it will profit from any collaboration with other approaches of counterproductive behavior. However, a strong momentum for research in this field does exist in Europe at present (see Einarsen et al., 2003a; Zapf & Einarsen, 2001), and one hopes this will further increase its contribution to the general knowledge base on counterproductive behaviors.

REFERENCES

Adams, A. (1992). *Bullying at work. How to confront and overcome it*. London: Virago Press.

Adams, J. S. (1965). Inequity in social exchange. In L. Berkowitz (Ed.), *Advances in experimental social psychology* (Vol. 2, pp. 276–299). New York: Academic Press.

Andersson, L. M., & Pearson, C. M. (1999). Tit for tat? The spiraling effect of incivility in the workplace. *Academy of Management Review, 24,* 452–471.

Aquino, K. (2000). Structural and individual determinants of workplace victimization: The effects of hierarchical status and conflict management style. *Journal of Management, 26,* 171–193.

Ashforth, B. E. (1994). Petty tyranny in organizations. *Human Relations, 47,* 755–778.

Baron, R. A., & Neuman, J. H. (1996). Workplace violence and workplace aggression: Evidence on their relative frequency and potential causes. *Aggressive Behavior, 22,* 161–173.

Baron, R. A., & Neuman, J. H. (1998). Workplace agression—The iceberg beneath the tip of workplace violence: Evidence of its forms, frequency and targets. *Public Administration Quarterly, 21,* 446–464.

Baumeister, R. F., Smart, L., & Boden, J. M. (1996). Relation of threatened egotism to violence and aggression: The dark side of high self-esteem. *Psychological Review, 103,* 5–33.

Baumeister, R. F., Stillwell, A., & Wotman, S. R. (1990). Victim and perpetrator accounts of interpersonal conflicts. Autobiographical narratives about anger. *Journal of Personality and Social Psychology, 59,* 994–1005.

Björkqvist, K. (1994). Sex differences in aggression. *Sex Roles, 30,* 177–188.

Björkqvist, K., Österman, K., & Hjelt-Bäck, M. (1994). Aggression among university employees. *Aggressive Behavior, 20,* 173–184.

Buunk, B. P., & Schaufeli, W. B. (1999). Reciprocity in interpersonal relationships: An evolutionary perspective on its importance for health and well-being. In W. Stroebe & M. Hewstone (Eds.), *The European review of social psychology* (Vol. 10, pp. 259–340). Chichester, England: Wiley.

Caplan, R. D., Cobb, S., French, J. R. P., van Harrison, R., & Pinneau, S. R. (1975). *Job demands and worker health.* Washington, DC: National Institute for Occupational Safety and Health.

Cowie, H., Jennifer, D., Neto, C., Angula, J. C., Pereira, B., del Barrio, C., et al. (2000). Comparing the nature of workplace bullying in two European countries: Portugal and the UK. In M. Sheehan, S. Ramsey, & J. Patrick (Eds.), *Transcending the boundaries: Integrating people, processes and systems. Proceedings of the 2000 conference* (pp. 128–133). Brisbane, Queensland, Australia: Griffith University.

Coyne, I., Seigne, E., & Randall, P. (2000). Predicting workplace victim status from personality. *European Journal of Work and Organizational Psychology, 9,* 335–349.

Coyne, I., Smith-Lee Chong, P., Seigne, E., & Randall, P. (2003). Self and peer nominations of bullying: An analysis of incident rates, individual differences, and perceptions of the work environment. *European Journal of Work and Organizational Psychology, 12,* 209–228.

Davidson, M. J., & Cooper, C. L. (1992). *Shattering the glass ceiling*. London: Paul Chapman.

Depue, R. A., & Monroe, S. M. (1986). Conceptualization and measurement of human disorder in life stress research: The problem of chronic disturbance. *Psychological Bulletin, 99,* 36–51.

Duffy, M. K., Ganster, D. C., & Pagon, M. (2002). Social undermining in the workplace. *Academy of Management Journal, 45,* 331–352.

Duffy, M. K., O'Leary-Kelly, A. M., & Ganster, D. C. (2003). Antisocial work behavior and individual and organizational health. In D. A. Hofmann & L. Tetrick (Eds.), *Health and safety in organizations: A multilevel perspective* (pp. 173–200). San Francisco: Jossey-Bass.

Einarsen, S. (1999). The nature and causes of bullying. *International Journal of Manpower, 20,* 16–27.

Einarsen, S. (2000). Harassment and bullying at work: A review of the Scandinavian approach. *Aggression and Violent Behavior, 4,* 371–401.

Einarsen, S., & Hoel, H. (2001, May 16–19). *The validity and development of the Revised Negative Acts Questionnaire.* Paper presented at the 10th European Congress of Work and Organizational Psychology, Prague.

Einarsen, S., Hoel, H., Zapf, D., & Cooper, C. L. (Eds.). (2003a). *Bullying and emotional abuse in the workplace. International perspectives in research and practice.* London: Taylor & Francis.

Einarsen, S., Hoel, H., Zapf, D., & Cooper, C. L. (2003b). The concept of bullying at work: The European tradition. In S. Einarsen, H. Hoel, D. Zapf, & C. L. Cooper (Eds.), *Bullying and emotional abuse in the workplace. International perspectives in research and practice* (pp. 3–30). London: Taylor & Francis.

Einarsen, S., & Mikkelsen, E. G. (2003). Individual effects of exposure to bullying at work. In S. Einarsen, H. Hoel, D. Zapf, & C. L. Cooper (Eds.), *Bullying and emotional abuse in the workplace. International perspectives in research and practice* (pp. 127–144). London: Taylor & Francis.

Einarsen, S., & Raknes, B. I. (1997). Harassment at work and the victimization of men. *Violence and Victims, 12,* 247–263.

Einarsen, S., Raknes, B. I., & Matthiesen, S. B. (1994). Bullying and harassment at work and their relationships to work environment quality. An exploratory study. *European Work and Organizational Psychologist, 4,* 381–401.

Einarsen, S., Raknes, B. I., Matthiesen, S. B., & Hellesøy, O. H. (1994). *Mobbing og harde personkonflikter. Helsefarlig samspill pa arbeidsplassen* [Bullying and severe interpersonal conflicts. Unhealthy interaction at work]. Soreidgrend, Norway: Sigma.

Einarsen, S., & Skogstad, A. (1996). Prevalence and risk groups of bullying and harassment at work. *European Journal of Work and Organizational Psychology, 5,* 185–202.

Fisher, R. J., & Keashly, L. (1990). Third party consultation as a method of intergroup and international conflict resolution. In R. J. Fisher (Ed.), *The social psychology of intergroup and international conflict resolution* (pp. 211–238). New York: Springer.

Frese, M. (1985). Stress at work and psychosomatic complaints: A causal interpretation. *Journal of Applied Psychology, 70,* 314–328.

Frese, M. (1989). Gütekriterien der Operationalisierung von sozialer Unterstützung am Arbeitsplatz [Psychometric criteria of measures of social support at work]. *Zeitschrift für Arbeitswissenschaft, 43,* 112–122.

Frese, M., & Zapf, D. (1987). Eine Skala zur Erfassung von Sozialen Stressoren am Arbeitsplatz [A scale for the assessment of social stressors at work]. *Zeitschrift für Arbeitswissenschaft, 41,* 134–141.

Gandz, J., & Murray, V. V. (1980). The experience of workplace politics. *Academy of Management Journal, 23,* 237–251.

Glasl, F. (1994). *Konfliktmanagement. Ein Handbuch für Führungskräfte und Berater* [Conflict management. A handbook for managers and consultants] (4th ed.). Bern, Switzerland: Haupt.

Groeblinghoff, D., & Becker, D. (1996). A case study on mobbing and the clinical treatment of mobbing victims. *European Journal of Work and Organizational Psychology, 5,* 277–294.

Gross, C. (2003, May 14–17). *Social conflicts and bullying at work—Results of a diary study with two waves.* Paper presented at the 11th European Congress of Work and Organizational Psychology, Lisbon, Portugal.

Hoel, H., & Cooper, C. L. (2000). *Destructive conflict and bullying at work.* Unpublished manuscript, University of Manchester, Institute of Science and Technology, Manchester, England.

Hoel, H., Cooper, C. L., & Faragher, B. (2001). The experience of bullying in Great Britain: The impact of organisational status. *European Journal of Work and Organizational Psychology, 10,* 443–465.

Hoel, H., Einarsen, S., & Cooper, C. L. (2003). Organisational effects of bullying. In S. Einarsen, H. Hoel, D. Zapf, & C. L. Cooper (Eds.), *Bullying and emotional abuse in the workplace. International perspectives in research and practice* (pp. 145–161). London: Taylor & Francis.

Hoel, H., Rayner, C., & Cooper, C. L. (1999). Workplace bullying. In C. L. Cooper & I. T. Robertson (Eds.), *International review of industrial and organizational psychology* (Vol. 14, pp. 195–230). Chichester, England: Wiley.

Hoel, H., Zapf, D., & Cooper, C. L. (2002). Workplace bullying and stress. In P. L. Perrewé & D. C. Ganster (Eds.), *Research in occupational stress and well being* (Vol. 2, pp. 293–333). Amsterdam, The Netherlands: JAI Press.

Hogh, A., & Dofradottir, A. (2001). Coping with bullying in the workplace. *European Journal of Work and Organizational Psychology, 10,* 485–495.

Huber, B. (1993). *Psychoterror am Arbeitsplatz—Mobbing* [Psychological terror at work—Mobbing]. Niedernhausen, Germany: Falken.

Kahn, R. L., & Byosiere, P. (1992). Stress in organizations. In M. D. Dunnette & L. M. Hough (Eds.), *Handbook of industrial and organizational psychology* (2nd ed., Vol. 3, pp. 571–650). Palo Alto, CA: Consulting Psychologists Press.

Karasek, R. A., & Theorell, T. (1990). *Health work. Stress, productivity, and the reconstruction of working life*. New York: Basic Books.

Kasl, S. V., & Cooper, C. L. (Eds.). (1987). *Stress and health: Issues in research methodology*. New York: Wiley.

Keashly, L. (1998). Emotional abuse in the workplace. *Journal of Emotional Abuse, 1*, 85–117.

Keashly, L., & Jagatic, K. (2003). By any other name: American perspectives on workplace bullying. In S. Einarsen, H. Hoel, D. Zapf, & C. L. Cooper (Eds.), *Bullying and emotional abuse in the workplace. International perspectives in research and practice* (pp. 31–61). London: Taylor & Francis.

Keashly, L., & Nowell, B. L. (2003). Conflict, conflict resolution and bullying. In S. Einarsen, H. Hoel, D. Zapf, & C. L. Cooper (Eds.), *Bullying and emotional abuse in the workplace. International perspectives in research and practice* (pp. 339–358). London: Taylor & Francis.

Knorz, C., & Zapf, D. (1996). Mobbing—Eine extreme Form sozialer Stressoren am Arbeitsplatz [Mobbing—An extreme form of social stressors at work]. *Zeitschrift für Arbeits und Organisationspsychologie, 40*, 12–21.

Lazarus, R. S., & Folkman, S. (1984). *Stress, appraisal and coping*. New York: Springer.

Leymann, H. (1986). *Vuxenmobbning—Psykiskt våld i arbetslivet* [Mobbing—Psychological violence in working life]. Lund, Sweden: Studentlitterature.

Leymann, H. (1990a). *Handbok för användning av LIPT-formuläret för kartläggning av risker för psykiskt vald* [Manual of the LIPT questionnaire for assessing the risk of psychological violence at work]. Stockholm: Violen.

Leymann, H. (1990b). Mobbing and psychological terror at workplaces. *Violence and Victims, 5*, 119–126.

Leymann, H. (1993). *Mobbing—Psychoterror am Arbeitsplatz und wie man sich dagegen wehren kann* [Mobbing—Psychoterror in the workplace and how one can defend oneself]. Reinbeck, Germany: Rowohlt.

Leymann, H. (1995). Einführung: Mobbing. Das Konzept und seine Resonanz in Deutschland [Introduction: Mobbing. The concept and its resonance in Germany]. In H. Leymann (Ed.), *Der neue Mobbingbericht. Erfahrungen und Initiativen, Auswege und Hilfsangebote* (pp. 13–26). Reinbeck bei Hamburg, Germany: Rowohlt.

Leymann, H. (1996). The content and development of mobbing at work. *European Journal of Work and Organizational Psychology, 5*, 165–184.

Leymann, H., & Gustafsson, A. (1996). Mobbing and the development of post-traumatic stress disorders. *European Journal of Work and Organizational Psychology, 5*, 251–276.

Leymann, H., & Gustavsson, B. (1984). *Psykiskt våld i arbetslivet. Två explorativa undersökningar* [Psychological violence at work places. Two explorative studies]. Stockholm: Arbetarskyddsstyrelsen.

Lindemeier, B. (1996, June). Mobbing. Krankheitsbild und Intervention des Betriebsarztes [Mobbing. Symptoms and intervention of the company physician]. *Die Berufsgenossenschaft,* 428–431.

Mackensen von Astfeld, S. (2000). *Das Sick-Building-Syndrom unter besonderer Berücksichtigung des Einflusses von Mobbing* [The sick building syndrome with special consideration of the effects of mobbing]. Hamburg, Germany: Dr. Kovac.

Matthiesen, S. B., & Einarsen, S. (2001). MMPI–2-configurations among victims of bullying at work. *European Journal of Work and Organizational Psychology, 10,* 467–484.

Matthiesen, S. B., Raknes, B. I., & Røkkum, O. (1989). Mobbing på arbeidsplassen [Mobbing at work]. *Tidskrift for Norsk Psykologforening, 26,* 761–774.

Meschkutat, B., Stackelbeck, M., & Langenhoff, G. (2002). *Der Mobbing-Report. Repräsentativstudie für die Bundesrepublik Deutschland. Schriftenreihe der Bundesanstalt für Arbeitsschutz und Arbeitsmedizin, Forschungsbericht Fb 951* [The mobbing report. Representative study for the Federal Republic of Germany]. Bremerhaven, Germany: Wirtschaftsverlag.

Mikkelsen, E. G., & Einarsen, S. (2002). Basic assumptions and symptoms of posttraumatic stress among victims of bullying at work. *European Journal of Work and Organizational Psychology, 11,* 7–111.

Mohr, G. (1986). *Die Erfassung psychischer Befindensbeeinträchtigungen bei Arbeitern* [The measurement of psychological dysfunctioning of workers]. Frankfurt am Main, Germany: Peter Lang.

Neuberger, O. (1995). *Mikropolitik. Der alltägliche Aufbau und Einsatz von Macht in Organisationen* [Micropolitics. The everyday construction and use of power in organisations]. Stuttgart, Germany: Enke.

Neuberger, O. (1999). *Mobbing. Übel mitspielen in Organisationen* [Mobbing. Playing bad games in organisations] (3rd ed.) München, Germany: Hampp.

Neuman, J. H., & Baron, R. A. (1997). Aggression in the workplace. In R. A. Giacalone & J. Greenberg (Eds.), *Antisocial behavior in organizations* (pp. 37–67). Thousand Oaks, CA: Sage.

Niedl, K. (1995). *Mobbing/Bullying am Arbeitsplatz. Eine empirische Analyse zum Phänomen sowie zu personalwirtschaftlich relevanten Effekten von systematischen Feindseligkeiten* [Mobbing/bullying at work. An empirical analysis of the phenomenon and of the effects of systematic harassment on human resource management]. München, Germany: Hampp.

Niedl, K. (1996). Mobbing and well-being: Economic and personnel development implications. *European Journal of Work and Organizational Psychology, 5,* 239–249.

Olweus, D. (1994). Annotation: Bullying at school—Basic facts and effects of a school based intervention program. *Journal of Child Psychology and Psychiatry, 35,* 1171–1190.

Piirainen, H., Elo, A.-L., Hirvonen, M., Kauppinen, K., Ketola, R., Laitinen, H., et al. (2000). *Työ ja terveys-haastattelututkimus* [Work and health—An interview study]. Helsinki, Finland: Työterveyslaitos.

Pryor, J. B., & Fitzgerald, L. F. (2003). Sexual harassment research in the United States. In S. Einarsen, H. Hoel, D. Zapf, & C. L. Cooper (Eds.), *Bullying and emotional abuse in the workplace. International perspectives in research and practice* (pp. 79–100). London: Taylor & Francis.

Rammsayer, T., & Schmiga, K. (2003). Mobbing und Persönlichkeit: Unterschiede in grundlegenden Persönlichkeitsdimensionen zwischen Mobbing-Betroffenen und Nicht-Betroffenen [Mobbing and personality: Differences in basic personality dimensions between individuals concerned and not concerned with mobbing]. *Wirtschaftspsychologie, 2.*

Randall, P. (1997). *Adult bullying: Perpetrators and victims.* London: Routledge.

Rayner, C. (1997). The incidence of workplace bullying. *Journal of Community and Applied Social Psychology, 7,* 199–208.

Rayner, C. (1999). From research to implementation: Finding leverage for prevention. *International Journal of Manpower, 20,* 28–38.

Roland, E., & Munthe, E. (Eds.). (1989). *Bullying. An international perspective.* London: D. Fulton.

Sacco, W. P., Dumont, C. P., & Dow, M. G. (1993). Attributional, perceptual, and affective responses to depressed and nondepressed marital partners. *Journal of Consulting and Clinical Psychology, 61,* 1076–1082.

Salin, D. (2001). Prevalence and forms of bullying among business professionals: A comparison of two different strategies for measuring bullying. *European Journal of Work and Organizational Psychology, 10,* 425–441.

Schuster, B. (1996). Rejection, exclusion, and harassment at work and in schools. *European Psychologist, 1,* 293–317.

Selye, H. (1971). The evolution of the stress concept—Stress and cardiovascular disease. In L. Levi (Ed.), *Society, stress and disease. Vol. 1: The psychosocial environment and psychosomatic diseases* (pp. 299–311). London: Oxford University Press.

Sheehan, M., Barker, M., & Rayner, C. (1999). Applying strategies for dealing with workplace bullying. *International Journal of Manpower, 20,* 50–56.

Spector, P. E., Zapf, D., Chen, P. Y., & Frese, M. (2000). Why negative affectivity should not be controlled in job stress research: Don't throw out the baby with the bath water. *Journal of Organizational Behavior, 21,* 79–95.

Stucke, T. (2002). Persönlichkeitskorrelate von Mobbing. Narzissmus und Selbstkonzeptklarheit als Persönlichkeitsmerkmale bei Mobbingtätern [Personality correlates of mobbing. Narcissism and self-concept clarity as personality correlates of mobbing perpetrators]. *Zeitschrift für Arbeits und Organisations-psychologie, 46*, 216–221.

Tepper, B. J. (2000). Consequences of abusive supervision. *Academy of Management Journal, 43*, 178–190.

Theorell, T., Leymann, H., Jodko, M., Konarski, K., & Norbeck, H. E. (1994). "Person under train" incidents from the subway driver's point of view: A prospective 1-year follow-up study. The design, and medical and psychiatric data. Special issue: Suicide on railways. *Social Science and Medicine, 38*, 471–475.

Thomas, K. W. (1992). Conflict and negotiation processes in organizations. In M. D. Dunnette & L. M. Hough (Eds.), *Handbook of industrial and organizational psychology* (Vol. 3, pp. 651–718). Palo Alto, CA: Consulting Psychologists Press.

Thylefors, I. (1987). *Syndabockar. Om utstötning och mobbning i arbetslivet* [Scapegoates. On expulsion and bullying in working life]. Stockholm: Natur och Kulture.

UNISON. (1997). *UNISON members experience of bullying at work.* London: Author.

Vartia, M. (1993). Psychological harassment (bullying, mobbing) at work. In K. Kauppinen-Toropainen (Ed.), *OECD Panel group on women, work, and health* (pp. 149–152). Helsinki, Finland: Ministry of Social Affairs and Health.

Vartia, M. (1996). The sources of bullying—Psychological work environment and organizational climate. *European Journal of Work and Organizational Psychology, 5*, 203–214.

Vartia, M., & Hyyti, J. (2002). Gender differences in workplace bullying among prison officers. *European Journal of Work and Organizational Psychology, 11*, 113–126.

Walter, H. (1993). *Mobbing: Kleinkrieg am Arbeitsplatz. Konflikte erkennen, offenlegen und lösen* [Mobbing: Micro war at work. Recognition, disclosure and solution of conflicts]. Frankfurt am Main, Germany: Campus.

Withey, M., & Cooper, W. (1989). Predicting exit, voice, loyalty, and neglect. *Administrative Science Quarterly, 34*, 521–539.

Zapf, D. (1993). Stress-oriented job analysis of computerized office work. *European Work and Organizational Psychologist, 3*, 85–100.

Zapf, D. (1999a, April 19–22). *Differences in mobbing (bullying) by supervisors and coworkers. Symposium on "Mobbing."* Paper presented at the 10th European Congress of Work and Organizational Psychology, Helsinki, Finland.

Zapf, D. (1999b). Mobbing in Organisationen. Ein Überblick zum Stand der Forschung [Mobbing in organisations. A state of the art review]. *Zeitschrift für Arbeits- und Organisationspsychologie, 43*, 1–25.

Zapf, D. (1999c). Organizational, work group related and personal causes of mobbing/bullying at work. *International Journal of Manpower, 20*, 70–85.

Zapf, D., & Einarsen, S. (Eds.). (2001). Bullying in the workplace. Recent trends in research and practice. *Special Issue of the European Journal of Work and Organizational Psychology*. Hove, England: Psychology Press.

Zapf, D., & Einarsen, S. (2003). Individual antecedents of bullying: Victims and perpetrators. In S. Einarsen, H. Hoel, D. Zapf, & C. L. Cooper (Eds.), *Bullying and emotional abuse in the workplace. International perspectives in research and practice* (pp. 165–184). London: Taylor & Francis.

Zapf, D., Einarsen, S., Hoel, H., & Vartia, M. (2003). Empirical findings on bullying in the workplace. In S. Einarsen, H. Hoel, D. Zapf, & C. L. Cooper (Eds.), *Bullying and emotional abuse in the workplace. International perspectives in research and practice* (pp. 103–126). London: Taylor & Francis.

Zapf, D., & Gross, C. (2001). Conflict escalation and coping with workplace bullying: A replication and extension. *European Journal of Work and Organizational Psychology, 10,* 497–522.

Zapf, D., & Holz, M. (2003, May 14–17). *On qualitative differences of workplace bullying at various levels of conflict escalation.* Paper presented at the 11th European Congress of Work and Organizational Psychology, Lisbon, Portugal.

Zapf, D., Knorz, C., & Kulla, M. (1996). On the relationship between mobbing factors, and job content, the social work environment and health outcomes. *European Journal of Work and Organizational Psychology, 5,* 215–237.

Zapf, D., Vogt, C., Seifert, C., Mertini, H., & Isic, A. (1999). Emotion work as a source of stress. The concept and development of an instrument. *European Journal of Work and Organizational Psychology, 8,* 371–400.

11

BULLYING AT WORK:
A PERSPECTIVE FROM BRITAIN
AND NORTH AMERICA

CHARLOTTE RAYNER AND LORALEIGH KEASHLY

The study of bullying at work emerged in the 1990s and is gaining momentum internationally. Bullying is persistent negative interpersonal behavior experienced by people at work. It can be applied to the boss who is too tough and the work mates who go beyond a joke—in other words, those who cause distress, anxiety, or feelings of intimidation in others at work. It can be counterproductive to the recipient causing increased stress that may lead to sickness absence or, in severe cases, total withdrawal from the workplace. It can be counterproductive for organizations because people simply leave (often quietly) as a method of resolution. Witnesses also leave. Replacement costs for these staff alone can represent a major drain on bottom-line profits. In addition we suspect that the breakdown of trust in a safe psychological environment means that, for example, employees fail to contribute their best, do not give extra ideas for improvement, do not provide feedback on failures, and may be less than truthful about performance. Organizations that can keep employees incur costs when investigating and resolving these situations. Without doubt bullying at work is costly and counterproductive to individuals and organizations.

This chapter provides an overview of research from the United Kingdom and North America on adult bullying at work. It is important to note that the bulk of research we review is from the United Kingdom and Europe. Persistent hostility at work such as bullying has only recently become the subject of systematic research attention in the United States (e.g., Duffy, Ganster, & Pagon, 2002; Keashly & Jagatic, 2003; Keashly & Neuman, 2002; Namie, 2000; Tepper, 2000). Much of the north European work has been completed by psychologists. We will begin with a discussion of the challenging area of definition, progress to the data regarding measurement and prevalence, then to our knowledge of causes. Bullying is perhaps best described as a process, however, and the nature of this process is outlined with the implications for organizations and opportunities for interventions are discussed at the end of the chapter.

The term *bullying* had its genesis in the school bullying literature that has received significant research attention over recent decades (Besag, 1989). This literature has provided some guidance for researchers of adult bullying (such as parameters to do with describing the phenomenon, which was originally called *mobbing,* a term that is still used by some authors). However, a school is a very different context than that of a workplace. School bullying has focused almost exclusively on children bullying other children, and as such does not reflect some of the hierarchical aspects that are encountered in the workplace—which would be the equivalent of teachers bullying children.

The development of European research into adult bullying at work began in the late 1980s. Scandinavian researchers, the first to turn their attention to the adult area of negative at-work behavior, initially carried over the term *mobbing.* British researchers have built on the field of mobbing (see chap. 10, this volume), but they and North American researchers have broadened the nomenclature of words associated with the phenomenon. In contemporary work most writers use the terms interchangeably. Where specific distinctions are made, the term *mobbing* has been used to describe situations in which colleagues group together to bully someone at the same hierarchical level (e.g., Davenport, Distler Schwartz, & Pursell Elliott, 1999). *Bullying* is the more encompassing term used to describe all situations of persistent hostile treatment in the workplace. Although the phenomenon under study is the same, the focus of the two research traditions is somewhat different. Psychologists have conducted much of the north European work, the focus of which is at the individual actor level and directed toward remedial action for severely damaged targets. In the United Kingdom and North America, more emphasis is placed on individual characteristics and organizational structural aspects that contribute to the existence of bullying in the organization. Thus, the difference in focus is on understanding in service of prevention of bullying versus understanding in service of remedial clinical action for the targets. Both of these areas of focus are critical to a better understanding of bullying, and as a result, there is active exchange of information between these sets of researchers. Thus, we encourage readers to also read the chapter on mobbing (chap. 10, this volume) to augment the information gained from our discussion of bullying.

DEFINITIONS OF BULLYING

Most researchers in this area have had concerns regarding definition and understand that the domain must be clearly identified (e.g., Keashly, 1998). Operational definitions of bullying in the United Kingdom contain some or all of the following elements:

1. the experience of negative behavior;
2. behaviors experienced persistently;
3. targets experiencing damage;
4. targets labeling themselves as bullied; and
5. targets with less power and difficulty defending themselves.

The Experience of Negative Behaviors

Bullying at work is about the experience of behaviors. Categorizing these behaviors has occurred in many different ways, because there is simply no definitive list (e.g., Leymann, 1990; Rayner & Hoel, 1997; Zapf, Knorz, & Kulla, 1996). The United Kingdom and north European researchers have concentrated on *what* is attacked rather than *how* it is attacked. This latter aspect has recently advanced as a result of U.S. contributions, and we now have a rounder picture of the phenomenon. Although physical aggression usually appears on item lists, it is infrequently reported. Instead there is a much higher prevalence of covert tactics, such as social isolation (being "sent to Coventry" or given the cold shoulder), undermining of professional status, tampering with tools or equipment that people need to do their jobs, feeling intimidated, micromanagement of one's work duties, and more personal attacks on credibility.

These findings are consistent with the North American literature on workplace aggression that finds that most aggressive behaviors at work are nonphysical, passive, and indirect (Keashly & Jagatic, 2003; Neuman & Baron, 1997). Although the typical aggression overt–covert dichotomy has support from the bullying literature, it is not sufficiently comprehensive. Both covert and overt behavior imply that something is done. In bullying at work, it is that which is *not* done that can be undermining, which can take away trust or create humiliation. An unsupportive boss who is not providing adequate information to allow a task to be done effectively is an example in which absence of action is the source of problems. In the United States, Neuman and Baron (1997) have argued for applying the three Buss (1961) dimensions of physical–verbal, active–passive, and direct–indirect to ensure that the full domain of aggressive work behaviors are identified. Keashly and Jagatic (2003) used the Buss framework to map items used in similar U.S. research. This makes interesting reading for those who wish to relate parallel studies within accessible U.S. literature to bullying at work. The broad construct of workplace bullying may serve to act as a meeting place for those interested in negative interpersonal treatment at work, especially for those who wish to extend their studies into persistent behavior within relationships.

Often these experiences are rather small instances when taken on their own. If one is looking to identify if someone has been bullied or not, it is rarely that a single (convenient) unwarranted public dressing down has occurred, but rather a collection of smaller covert behaviors (e.g., being ignored, not receiving needed information, rumors, glaring). The professional should be looking for a pattern of behaviors that, when taken together, show a set of negative events over time that add up to the targets feeling the way they do.

This collection of seemingly minor events presents challenges for the people who are wondering what these behaviors add up to and who are trying to "define" what is happening in their work environment. For the recipient, the apparently incidental appearance of single events may make them doubt that there is anything wrong and question themselves about why such small incidents are disturbing (Keashly, 2001). They may also be reluctant to tell others or complain as they may themselves judge the evidence to be flimsy (Adams, 1992). For the individuals to whom they complain, some training or skill may be necessary to sensitize them that small incidents can be taken as aggregate and that complaints should be taken seriously. For those investigating, the temptation may be to investigate each incident as a separate item, when actually it is the pattern that should be under investigation (Incomes Data Source [IDS], 1999; Ishmael, 1999; Keashly & Jagatic, 2003). Under current legislation in the United States, only extreme behaviors are actionable rather than an accumulation of seemingly minor incidents (Yamada, 2000). In the United Kingdom, legal action is usually taken under Health and Safety legislation, and thus the effect on the targets is the focus. This facilitates the presentation of aggregate events.

Persistency: A Core Concept

The late 1990s saw exploration of the *persistency* of hostile behaviors (e.g., Hoel, Rayner, & Cooper, 1999). British researchers have followed their north European counterparts in considering someone to have been bullied if they had experienced negative events at least weekly and over

6 months or more. The North American research literature on workplace aggression has only recently begun to explore the notion of persistent hostility, tending to focus on understanding isolated incidents or aggregated aggression (Keashly & Jagatic, 2003; Keashly & Neuman, 2002).

The notion of persistency is important conceptually to the field of hostile treatment in general and bullying in particular because it moves the focus away from negative acts to negative relationships (Keashly & Jagatic, 2003). Now it becomes important to know who the actors and targets are relative to one another and the dynamics of these interactions. This focus on persistent negative behavior within relationships distinguishes the study of bullying from many other areas of workplace research.

For example, workplace violence (which traditionally refers to physical assaults at work) is an area of concern in many countries (Denenberg & Braverman, 1999; Ishmael, 1999). Most often it occurs between strangers who have no history together, and often the person is attacked because of his or her role in the organization. Although Social Security office staff might be at risk from successive customers who are abusive when denied access to resources, this is not the persistent behavior that is part of the bullying *relationship*. It is possible that the staff member experiences certain customers as bullying, but this is a context that remains to be examined within this field.

The relationship context highlights the interpersonal nature of bullying at work. Thus when one considers broad-brush approaches such as workplace deviance (Bennett & Robinson, 2000) or organizational aggression (O'Leary-Kelly, Griffin, & Glew, 1996) then the overlap potential only exists for the interpersonal factors, not those in which the "target" is the organization, for example damage to equipment or sabotage that does not involve colleagues. Recent work on bullying that takes a phenomenological approach has demonstrated that employees also perceive a relationship with the organization (Liefooghe & MacKenzie Davey, 2003). In a study of two sections of a large bank in the United Kingdom, respondents raised the existence of organizational bullying consistently. That is, employees argued that certain work practices such as monitoring of calls and needing to justify leaving their workstation were experienced as bullying by the organization. These findings are highly challenging for current work in the area, which to date has perceived bullying as between *people* and can be linked to related fields such as perceived organizational justice (Colquitt, Conlon, Wesson, Porter, & Ng, 2001).

Damage

If a lawyer called someone bullied, the targets would need to have experienced damage of some kind—otherwise there would be no case to bring (Yamada, 2000). Most cases in the United Kingdom are linked to claims of injury under health and safety legislation, under which an employer has the duty to protect the physical and psychological safety of the employee, with bullying falling into the latter category. Lawyers also need to link the damage directly with those behaviors that have been experienced at work.

A human resource management professional will be worried about actual damage but probably also concerned about events "upstream" in the process to engage in preventative action before damage has occurred. They may hear that an employee has experienced negative behavior over a period of time that alone might be enough to warrant concern, even though damage may not (yet) have occurred.

Damage resulting from bullying at work is largely stress-related. A UNISON (the largest trade union in Britain and serving the public sector) study of members who are civilian staff with the English police service found 75% of those who reported being bullied also experienced health effects (UNISON, 2000). These effects included heightened anxiety, sleeplessness, and a dread of going to work, which would be typical of occupational stress reactions (Lazarus & Folkman, 1984). In another study of more than 5,000 British workers, it was found that negative effects were related to the experience of bullying behaviors, regardless of whether people labeled themselves as bullied or not (Hoel & Cooper, 2000).

Considerable work has been done in the Scandinavian countries and northern Europe on the health effects of those who have been severely damaged (e.g., Einarsen & Matthiesen, 1999; Leymann, 1996; Zapf et al., 1996). A few British studies have used qualitative data from severely affected targets to investigate their experience of bullying (e.g., Petri, 2002). These include reports of changes to personality that replicate findings in Scandinavia and back up work on the applicability of posttraumatic stress disorder (PTSD) or prolonged duress stress disorder (PDSD) to bullying. In these cases, changes to personality might be expected, thus highlighting the need for care when identifying cause and effect by means of personality data.

Labeling

Should people be included as bullied only if they label themselves as such? This aspect of definition has had considerable discussion (e.g., Hoel et al., 1999). Professionals in workplaces have been reluctant to include this as a strict criterion within their definitions because it is so dependent on the individuals' awareness and other mediating factors, such as whether this treatment is the norm within that specific work context. If one were to use this criterion, it may exclude staff that clearly have been bullied but for one reason or another do not label themselves as such (Adams, 1992).

The finding that damage was related to the experience of behaviors and not labeling per se reflects similar results in the field of sexual harassment (Munson, Miner, & Hulin, 2001). However the debate has moved into one that takes a more phenomenological view to understand perceptions of bullying (Liefooghe & Mackenzie Davey, 2003). In these studies there is an emphasis on understanding what bullying is from the perception of those in the workplace. These must be welcome developments, but they will challenge the wider academic community, because their early results are reconceiving definitions that previously saw bullying as between *people*, to a situation in which bullying could be between employee(s) and the *organization*, and the organization can be seen to be the bully.

Imbalance of Power

The final aspect of definition in this chapter suggests that there is an imbalance of power between the actors and targets with the targets being at a disadvantage. This imbalance in turn is related to the targets' ability to defend themselves (Keashly, 2001). To the extent the people involved have equal power (access to similar resources), their relationship would be better characterized as a conflict between equals than as an example of bullying (Einarsen, Hoel, Zapf, & Cooper, 2003). The power aspect of these relationships derived from early research in Germany and Scandinavia, where it is treated as an important conceptual aspect of definition (Leymann, 1990). It has received far less attention in the United Kingdom and North America. Perhaps there is less emphasis in the United Kingdom (and Australia) because typically 80% of bullies cited by targets are their managers, thus drawing on hierarchical power (McCarthy, Sheehan, & Kearns, 1995; Rayner, 1997). There is less dominance of reports that bosses are bullies in most other cultures studied (including the United States), where typically a 50% incidence would be recorded (Keashly & Jagatic, 2000; Neuman & Baron, 1997; see also chap. 10, this volume), with the remainder being mostly peer bullying. Another possibility is that defining power in terms of organizational position may be too limited and that other conceptualizations of power need to be considered when exploring this aspect of the bullying experience (e.g., Keashly & Jagatic, 2003).

But what of intent? What is notable in the defining features of bullying is the lack of actor intent. Although this is still a hotly debated topic in the North American literature on workplace aggression (e.g., Keashly & Jagatic, 2003; Neuman & Baron, 1997), United Kingdom and North European researchers have discarded actor intent as a critical defining element because it was anticipated that most bullies would deny intent, thus negating the existence of bullying (IDS, 1999).

Establishing Perspective

Any discussion of definition requires consideration of the perspective of the one doing the defining. Our discussion to date (like much of the research) has focused on definitions from targets. Recent work (e.g., Rayner, 2002) has highlighted how different professions emphasize different aspects of definition as it suits their purpose and shows a level of pragmatism. However, when someone asks what bullying is, he or she might receive a range of answers! Although all concerned would emphasize the importance of behaviors, unfortunately how each of the other parameters is used depends on who is being asked. Lawyers will stress damage (Yamada, 2000). Human resource professionals will stress labeling (Munson et al., 2001) but be concerned not to emphasize persistency because this may invite bullies to continue with their behavior until the required persistency is almost reached. Some academics are concerned about the imbalance of power (e.g., Einarsen et al., 2003).

In summary, workplace bullying is a field that examines interpersonal events in relationships at work. These events are about persistent negative interpersonal behaviors. Targets may label themselves as bullied, may also experience damage, and are likely to experience an imbalance of power between themselves and the bully. Some aspects of definition may hold for some professionals but not others.

MEASUREMENT

Measurement concerns the operationalizing of definitions. Aspects of definition will inevitably act as cornerstones to measurement. We should first consider who is the subject of measurement. It is rare to find studies that are done with students that seriously contribute to our understanding of bullying, although these do exist (e.g., Keashly, Harvey, & Hunter, 1997; Keashly, Trott, & MacLean, 1994; Rayner, 1997). Most studies have tried to use sampling methods with "normal" working populations. For most researchers this means that they have to find an employer or other organization (such as a trade union) through which to reach staff. Samples of workers provide the opportunity to assess the prevalence of bullying behaviors and factors that exacerbate or mitigate becoming a victim (e.g., Coyne, Seigné, & Randall, 2000; Rayner, 1998). Other studies have focused exclusively on people who self-identified as having been bullied, with an eye toward understanding who the bully is and the nature of the effects (Keashly, 2001; Namie, 2000).

Without doubt, persistency is fundamental for those academic researchers who are establishing incidence. Most studies (e.g., Archer, 1999; Duffy et al., 2002; Keashly & Neuman, 2002; Rayner, 1997; Tepper, 2000) present respondents with a list of negative behaviors and ask them to indicate (for a specified period of time, usually the past 6 to 12 months) how often they have experienced each behavior. Scales will typically be "never," "less than monthly," "monthly," "weekly," and "daily." How often and for how long must someone experience behaviors to be counted as bullied? The late 1990s saw exploration of this topic (e.g., Hoel et al., 1999), and British researchers have followed their north European counterparts in considering someone to have been bullied if they had experienced negative events at least *weekly* and over *six months* or more (Keashly & Jagatic, 2003; Rayner, 1997). There are still variations between studies (often imposed by factors beyond the researchers' control), and readers are encouraged to look carefully at the measures used for persistency when comparing studies. Thus someone who indicates any single behavior weekly for a six-month time period would be counted in incidence research. In addition, those who indicate four different behaviors monthly could be counted (Rayner, 1999b). Thus the incidence researchers may include aggregate patterns of reports.

The use of labeling is also important for those interested in establishing incidence. Respondents are asked whether or not they consider themselves to have been bullied, with reference to a definition provided by the sponsoring organization (e.g., UNISON, 1997, 2000). This is usually a yes–no item, although a recent study included "don't know," which had a small response rate (2%: Coyne, Smith-Lee Chang, Randall, & Seigné, 2002).

Opinion has varied within the academic Scandinavian literature (Einarsen & Skogstad, 1996; Leymann, 1990) as to whether only those labeling themselves should be counted. A British study compared the results of labeling to define whether people have been bullied (Rayner, 1999b). It was found that only half those who reported weekly negative interpersonal behavior for 6 months labeled themselves as bullied. Hoel and Cooper (2000) found that people experience negative health effects regardless of whether they labeled themselves as bullied or not. We still are unclear about why people do and do not label themselves in context. To some extent Hoel and Cooper's (2000) findings have placed this aspect in the background (see earlier section on labeling, this chap.). Currently most academic researchers would track labeling only as a matter of interest rather than one of definition. Indeed this reflects previous developments in the field of sexual harassment, where labeling is only one aspect in definition (Magley, Hulin, Fitzgerald, & DeNardo, 1999). Thus best practice is that all items on incidence surveys should be answered by everyone, regardless of whether they self-label. Researchers then identify who is bullied by the frequency and persistence of reported behaviors.

In some respects the current lack of emphasis on labeling presents an opportunity for researchers. Many employers are unhappy to allow studies that include the bullying label to be used in their organizations, perhaps for fear of heightening sensitivity around the issue of looking bad (Jagatic, 2001; Rayner, Hoel, & Cooper, 2002). Thus, some bullying studies are done by asking about behaviors and omitting the label. We should not forget though that only half those who experience negative behavior do label themselves as bullied. The processes by which people label their experiences are not well understood (Keashly, 2001) and thus continue to be an area of academic and practical interest for those who can gain open access to working populations.

Other aspects of measurement include whomever else the respondent perceives as experiencing the negative behaviors (e.g., others in the work group), information about the bully/bullies, and the effect on themselves (often revealed in open question format). For most studies there is no way of triangulating the data to corroborate the existence of behaviors in the work context (i.e., gathering observer and actor reports), and researchers tend to accept targets' reports at face value, which is clearly an issue for validity.

In summary, measurement for incidence implements some of the definitional aspects in a clear way. Normally respondents are asked about the persistency of experience of behaviors, the actors involved, and their reaction to their treatment in the time frame specified. In examining any research study, the operational definition used by researchers in measurement needs to be clearly understood, because it will define the nature and meaning of the findings.

NATURE AND PREVALENCE

So what do we know about the nature and prevalence of bullying? British studies have found that around 30% of people experience negative weekly behavior over 6 months, and half of these (i.e., 15%) *also* label themselves as bullied (Rayner et al., 2002). These rates are higher than those found in Germany and Scandinavia. Those who report negative behaviors at work and label themselves report more behaviors than those who do not label (Rayner, 1999b). As indicated earlier, the negative behaviors reported by all respondents tend to be covert and nonphysical. The number of people who report feeling bullied and do not report experiencing negative behaviors is negligible (Rayner, 1999b).

As noted earlier, the word *bullying* is not yet in common usage in U.S. studies in occupational settings. Thus it is often the case that labeling is not used in U.S. studies. Rather, the researcher judges whether or not someone has been persistently negatively treated through preset criteria such as exposure to a number of behaviors over a period of time. Using the at-least-weekly criterion of the United Kingdom and European research, Keashly and Neuman (2002) reported that 36% of employees of a U.S. federal agency responding to a survey on workplace stress and aggression would be categorized as bullied. The label of mistreatment has shown up in some U.S. studies. In a representative sample of Michigan workers, 27% of people reported mistreatment at the hands of someone with whom they worked in the previous year (Keashly & Jagatic, 2000). Price Spratlen (1995) took any frequent occurrence of negative behavior as indicative of mistreatment and reported an average incidence of 23% in a university setting. This rate varied for different occupational groups (e.g., 11% faculty, 25% classified staff, 38% professional staff). As with the British and European studies, most of the behavior reported is nonphysical and covert. Although early data suggest that bullying is a significant workplace issue in the United States, the lack of a common terminology makes it difficult to determine prevalence and hence to make comparisons to other countries (Keashly, 1998; Keashly & Jagatic, 2003).

Variations between sectors has been studied in the United Kingdom, although the differences seem to be at the higher end of incidence rather than any low rates being achieved in any particular sector (Hoel & Cooper, 2000). To date no sector has been devoid of reports of bullying. Reports from staff in prisons have recorded the greatest incidence of witnessed bullying at 64% in Britain (Hoel & Cooper, 2000), with high rates also prevalent in education (Lewis, 1999, 26%; Savva & Alexandrou, 1998, 30%). As with bullying in schools, Britain's closest counterpart for workplace bullying is Australia, where strong similarities are found in the nature and prevalence of bullying at work.

The most interesting findings in the descriptive data for targets are the nonsignificant differences on demographic characteristics. In the United Kingdom, men and women are equally likely to report being bullied, and age has not been found to be a significant factor in United Kingdom studies (Hoel et al., 1999, provide a review). In addition, Hoel and Cooper (2000) found that hierarchical status was not linked to victimization status. Similar nonsignificant findings are found in U.S. studies on persistent aggression (see Keashly & Jagatic, 2003, for review). Although reasons may differ for bullying, these particular groupings of individuals, the nonsignificant target differences along with low sector variability, provides ample evidence to back up early claims that bullying at work can happen to anyone, anytime (e.g., Adams, 1992).

In terms of the actors, the United Kingdom and Australia share the situation that targets see managers as the bully in approximately 80% of cases (McCarthy et al., 1995; Rayner, 1997), with coworkers being responsible for almost all other instances. In Scandinavian countries, coworker bullying is reportedly around 50%, and in the United States coworkers as sources of the negative behavior range from 40% to 50% (Keashly & Jagatic, 2000, 2003). Upward bullying is reported extremely rarely in all countries (around 1%). In the United Kingdom, men are reported more often as bullies, however after one factors in the fewer number of women in management, this gender difference disappears. The evidence is more mixed in the limited U.S. literature, with some reporting females more (e.g., Namie, 2000) and some finding no difference (e.g., Keashly, 1998). So although we may state that bullying is about the abuse of power, in the United Kingdom and Australia this appears to be power-derived from hierarchical position. In other parts of the world, such as the United States, the source of power may be more varied (see Keashly & Jagatic, 2003, for more discussion).

Although the frequency of reported behaviors from various actors may be somewhat similar, what differs is the appraisal of these behaviors. For example, Farrell (1999) found that nurses did experience negative behavior from doctors, but found it far less disturbing than when other nurses were the source of behavior. Also, in a health care setting, Keashly and Rogers (2001) found that nurses appraised similar behaviors differently from fellow nurses than when the behaviors came from patients. In the U.S. federal agency study mentioned earlier (Keashly & Neuman, 2002), behavior from supervisors was rated as more bothersome than behaviors from coworkers or customers. These findings highlight the bluntness of incidence measurement and may provide an indication about why some people do not label themselves as bullied when they are experiencing weekly negative behavior. These findings also highlight that it is the experience of behaviors that is critical, and research needs to be directed at what contributes to people's experience of feeling bullied (e.g., Keashly, 2001).

One might think that bullying at work is a one-on-one phenomenon. A British trade union study of public sector workers (UNISON, 1997) found that approximately one third of those who report being bullied also reported that their entire work group was treated likewise. This finding has ramifications if discrimination legislation were to be attempted. There are anecdotal reports in the United Kingdom of bosses accused of bullying calling as their witnesses all others who worked for them. If each member of the staff confirmed negative treatment, the idea of discrimination has been refuted. Similar arguments have been used in the few U.S. cases (Yamada, 2000).

Up to 20% of those reporting bullying in the United Kingdom indicate they have a one-on-one situation. These individuals almost exclusively populate calls to help lines and support groups (Field, 1996). Thus anyone sourcing respondents from help lines or activist groups should be aware that their population samples might be extremely biased. The remaining 80% of United Kingdom targets report one or more bullies to one or more targets. These different situations (the only one, one of several, one of all) must affect how the dynamic is perceived and played out, although as yet we have little data on these experiences (Lewis, 1999). Without doubt they raise problems for investigators, who are quite likely to have multiple players on both sides.

CAUSES

As in other areas of counterproductive work behavior (e.g., O'Leary-Kelly et al., 1996), causes and antecedents can be examined at several levels, such as the individual, interpersonal, work group, corporate, and societal levels (Lewis, 1999). This part of the chapter will examine these levels separately for both the bully and the target, and we would encourage the reader to embrace this complexity. Any studies that focus on a single level but claim all-pervading knowledge should instead be viewed in their context.

The Individual Level: The Target

This represents an area of great strength for Scandinavian and German research into workplace bullying. We recommend chapter 10 (this volume) for depth regarding personal and interpersonal factors and see this part of our chapter as an addendum to their more extensive work.

The vast majority of data regarding workplace bullying comes from targets. Our focus of the individual is on both the *targets* and their reports of the bullies. No longitudinal studies have been published to date, so determination of cause and effect has been limited. Therefore interpretation of findings must be carefully managed. After summarizing her findings of bullying in a British hospital, Quine (1999) posed some useful questions for consideration in all bullying research. Are these people more likely to report bullying? Are these people more likely to be bullied? Does bullying lead to these effects? The latter two questions provide us with a distinction between cause and effect that cannot be resolved easily through the use of cross-sectional studies. Finally, the ethical aspects of such data and interpretation must be handled carefully in case employers attempt to use psychometrics to prescreen and exclude staff that they (perhaps erroneously) perceive to be more likely to be targets of workplace bullying.

An unusual study used matched-pair methodology in an organization in which people who were being bullied were cross-matched in terms of age, gender, position, and home living situation (Coyne et al., 2000). This study found a profile of difference among targets that one would associate with targets of victimization (such as heightened anxiety and depression). Both United Kingdom (e.g., Quine, 1999) and U.S. studies (e.g., Keashly

& Neuman, 2002) found that targets of bullying reported higher stress levels, greater intention to leave, lower work satisfaction, and lack of support from colleagues. Rayner (1999a) found external locus of control was significantly associated with people who reported bullying behaviors compared to those who did not report behaviors. All of these findings demonstrate the dilemma of cause and effect well, in that it is quite possible targets had these characteristics before the bullying, or that they changed as a result of the bullying, or because they have these characteristics they are more likely to report. Longitudinal studies would provide the opportunity to shed light on the answers to these questions.

North European researchers have used Janoff Bulman's (1993) concepts to explain the negative effect on targets. The original work was used in victimization studies. The normal slow evolution of ideas about the world is different for victims of incidents, and their traumatic experience shatters basic assumptions that have been central to the individual's concept of self and the world. Janoff Bulman (1993) described these basic assumptions as the degree to which individuals perceive the world as benevolent, the meaningfulness of the world in relation to the distribution of outcomes, and the degree to which they perceive themselves as worthy. Although the notion of shattered assumptions has helped European researchers explain clinical studies (most of whom had left the workforce), it has had little application into the still-at-work group. A doctoral study (Rylance, 2002) in Australia provided initial support for the assumption of self-worth playing a part in the process of bullying at work but not meaningfulness or benevolence. Most of the sample were survivors of bullying episodes and still working in the same sector. This may explain the lack of linkage to *benevolence* and *meaningfulness*, because if these other two assumptions had been shattered, perhaps targets would not have been able to continue in their profession.

One aspect that has been raised is that of sensitization (Field, 1996). This can provoke two questions: Is someone more likely to be bullied after it has happened to them once, and do they react differently to the stimuli on a second encounter with bullying at work? These are clearly complex issues and have received little attention to date. Analysis of data collected from members of UNISON trade union has shown that people who are currently being bullied are not more likely to have been bullied before than people who have been bullied before and are not being bullied now (UNISON, 2000). These findings run counter to claims for vulnerability once bullied. However it is quite possible that employees do become more aware of bullying once it has happened to them and effectively avoid such situations in future employment. Such suggestions emphasize the need for longitudinal studies so that the dynamics can be positively established.

The Individual Level: The Actor

Few studies exist on bullies, although there are some interesting reviews of "tough" leaders (e.g., Baumeister, Smart, & Boden, 1996). In a British study (Rayner & Cooper, 2003), managers were labeled on the reports of their staff. No significant difference was found between bullies and nonbullies regarding their self-reported mental health, stress levels, or personality. However the sample was small ($N = 35$), so the findings should be interpreted as suggestive only. The study analyzed grouped reports from individual staff on managers and found confirmation of different patterns of bullying between work groups. That is, in some groups everyone reported bullying behavior, in other groups only some people reported negative behavior, and finally in some groups reports came from single individuals. These latter findings based on a larger sample ($N = 374$ individuals in 72 groups) give credence to the notion that managerial behavior at work does vary widely (Rayner, 1999a).

Studying bullies directly presents methodological problems regarding sampling or methods of identification. Asking people to volunteer and label themselves as bullies does not seem a valid approach (Rayner & Cooper, 2003). However, it is quite possible that people may be willing to report using negative tactics with others if anonymity is ensured (e.g., Greenberg & Barling, 1998; Neuman & Baron, 1998). Because of these challenges, studying bullies has been slow to develop and warrants more research attention in the future to truly understand the dynamics of the bullying process.

A popular idea is that workplace bullies were bullies at school (e.g., Field, 1996; Randall, 1996). Although a simplistically attractive proposition, the reality of data from school studies reveals a level of complexity that negates the validity of any easy link. First, no long-term study has tracked schoolchildren through school and into adult working life. Thus any data of the two situations are dependent on adult memories. Changes in perceptions over time would cast doubt on the validity of any labeling. In addition, British school data identify around 20% of pupils bullied at any point in time, and many children claim to be both a target *and* a bully (Besag, 1989). Such is the complexity that we cannot even infer a track of realities and roles through time. Thus it is not possible at this time to provide a starting point for testing the idea that bullies at school go on to bully in later life.

Another appealing and simple idea is that bullies themselves have psychological problems—for example, they are sociopaths (Field, 1996). This may indeed account for a small group of bullies, but the term *sociopath* is only applied to about 1% of the population, and given the incidence of bullying in workplaces, they do not add up to accounting for any large proportion of total bullies.

A sensible suggestion from Scandinavia is that there are two types of bullying: (a) predatory bullying in which the bully picks on and pursues target(s) (which may equate to sociopathy) and (b) dispute-related bullying that reflects an escalating conflict in which the process of interaction between both parties is more important (Einarsen et al., 2003). The authors used an adapted version of Glasl's (1994) model of conflict escalation in their analysis. In dispute-related bullying, the original problems that sparked the conflict become forgotten, as the dispute takes on a life of its own and behaviors of both parties become more destructive (Keashly & Nowell, 2003). The notion of the predatory bully has dominated the popular press with little empirical evidence to back it up. With the focus on individual and structural factors in the development and maintenance of bullying in the workplace in the United Kingdom and U.S. literatures, the notion of dispute-related bullying may receive a systematic test.

The consideration of bullying as a form of escalated conflict creates the opportunity for a connection between the bullying and workplace aggression literatures and the conflict literatures that have tended to operate in parallel (Keashly & Nowell, 2003). The conflict literature is rich with methodologies and findings on escalation and, fortunately, deescalation via third-party intervention that can provide some direction for research on and intervention into bullying. However, the conflict literature brings with it certain assumptions such as both parties being mutually responsible for the conflict and hence mutually capable of resolution. Some of these assumptions may not hold in the case of those who have been severely bullied (see Keashly & Nowell, 2003, for an in-depth discussion).

The evidence from targets on dealing effectively with bullying at work is sparse. One UNISON study (2000) asked nonbullied people if they had ever successfully stopped being bullied and to describe how they had dealt with that situation effectively. The respondents who had stopped bullying described a wide variety of tactics but most were confrontational, from highly aggressive (including the threat of physical violence) to rational appeal. Of real importance was the fact that *all* the interventions were very quick—that is, on the first or second appearance of the negative behavior (UNISON, 2000). Intervention had occurred before the behavior had become a norm within that relationship (Rayner et al., 2002).

For many people, however, by the time they have worked out what is happening, the behavior is already the norm and they are in the position of persistent and potentially long-lasting negative treatment. In conflict terms, the relationship is escalating to the point of destruction and violence. The conflict intervention literature provides some ideas about how such difficult and increasingly hostile situations can be halted and in some cases altered to be more productive (see Keashly & Nowell, 2003; Zapf & Gross, 2001, for a more in-depth discussion). Such intervention requires the involvement of interested and sometimes powerful third parties in a coordinated and sequenced effort. In the case of the workplace, such third parties include coworkers and supervisors (as witnesses) and all levels of management (e.g., human resources, the upper-level management) and unions in their role as power brokers in the overall labor–management relationships, as well as organizational outsiders (family, friends, consultants, police). We will discuss organizational actors that may be helpful (or not) in this process of intervention and management in the next section.

At the Organizational Level

Bullying occurs in a relationship, but it also occurs at work where a wider context needs to be taken into account. Accounts from targets are typically not only about an interpersonal struggle and failure but also the failure of organizational support systems (e.g., Ackroyd & Thompson, 1999; Adams, 1992; Bassman, 1992). These failures can lead to secondary bullying being felt by targets as they endeavor, with little perceived help, to defend themselves (Babiak, 1995; Keashly, 2001).

Much of the United Kingdom work has concentrated on the corporate and organizational structures that effectively support bullying. These can be demonstrated in a disturbing case that gained publicity in Britain in 2002 relating to Mr. Lee, who had committed suicide because of bullying at work (*London Times*, 2001). Mr. Lee had been working as a sorter in a postal unit and had been bullied both by colleagues and his boss. Mr. Lee tried to deal with the problem on his own. He then raised the problem with the trade union representative and was rejected, made complaints to managers and senior managers to no avail, and finally took his own life. His father, who wanted an apology from the employer, sought the publicity. This case illustrates the need for the involvement of others to be able to complement individual approaches to workplace bullying. When bullying occurs at work, it does so over a period of time. Often others in the workplace know what is going on and often structures and procedures that could be used to deal with the behavior seem to fail the targets (Adams, 1992). Considerable effort therefore has been applied to finding effective remedial actions so that situations such as Mr. Lee's suicide can be avoided (Bassman, 1992; Ishmael, 1999).

The overwhelming perception of third-party action (such as that taken by personnel, managers, and trade unions) by targets is generally scathing (e.g., Adams, 1992; Field, 1996; Lewis, 1999; Rayner, 1998) mostly in terms of its nonexistence. Data from the U.S. federal agency study found that even those who had been bullied did not bring their problem to the attention of a superior or union official or other formal grievance processes (Keashly & Neuman, 2002). The transition from personnel (that owns and incorporates issues of staff welfare) to Human Resource Management (HRM; providing support for managers to manage) has been seen as one reason in the United Kingdom (Lewis & Rayner, 2003), with a move away from welfare and internal support for staff.

The UNISON studies (1997, 2000) asked respondents what they thought caused bullying at work. Because there were no specific theories to be tested, participants were asked to respond to a set of statements that included inadequate management, poor training, oversensitive workers, and so forth. In short, the various players and their roles were highlighted. More than 90% of all respondents (some of whom were bullied or had witnessed it, some of whom had not) agreed with the two statements, "Bullies can get away with it" and "Workers are too scared to report it" (Rayner, 1998; UNISON, 1997, 2000). This implicates cultural organizational norms before that of any specific player.

It is unlikely that bullies can "get away with it" all the time or that workers are always "too scared to report it," but these perceptions of staff represent a phenomenon that has currency in its own right. Lewis's (1999) findings that workers get most of their information about bullying from each other reinforces the importance of being *seen* to deal with bullying. There is the danger that employers will be judged as active members in the process of escalation if they apparently fail to recognize, or do not have the processes to deal with, bullying at work (Keashly, 2001). Essentially, doing nothing about bullying at work is not a neutral act on the part of the employer (Rayner et al., 2002).

The anecdotal evidence from targets can be used to identify endemic support for bullying at work (Adams, 1992; Field, 1996). One of the first lines of defense might be to go to the bullies' boss and complain, but usually the perception is that nothing is done (Rayner, 1998), yet something may have been done that is neither shared with the target nor led to perceptable change. The lack of engagement by managers receiving a complaint was confirmed by a study in British hospitals that revealed that bosses did not do anything (see Rayner et al., 2002), claiming that they did not know what to do. This is a useful pointer for intervention through training.

Considerable work in the field of perceived justice can be applied to situations that are deemed to be bullying. If bullying is seen as a norm of working life, this suggests failures of interactional and procedural justice (Ferrell, Fraedrich, & Ferrell, 2002; Tepper, 2000). Most targets, if they complain successfully, are moved within the firm (Ishmael, 1999), which can cause great resentment and raise criticisms with respect to distributive justice, because they feel it is the bully who should be moved. The U.S. literature has paid more attention to this connection than the United Kingdom or European literatures, and the insights gained are informative for both understanding the bullying process and also the effects on targets.

For example, Neuman and Baron (1997, 1998) have proposed and demon-strated that perceptions of being treated unfairly are linked to people behaving aggressively. Tepper (2000) found that targets' perceptions of organizational justice mediated the impact of exposure to abusive supervision on various job attitudes and behaviors. Given our knowledge of the negative effect of perceived injustice on workplace attitudes in terms of demotivation and lowering of commitment (Colquitt et al., 2001), its connection to workplace bullying needs to be pursued further.

COSTS TO ORGANIZATIONS

There is a strong business case for dealing with bullying at work. Costs are associated with three areas: replacing staff members that leave as a result of being bullied, the opportunity costs from effort being displaced into staff coping with bullying incidents around them, and costs to do with investigations of ill treatment and potential court action.

In the United Kingdom, 25% of targets of bullying leave their job (UNISON, 1997), and 20% of witnesses also leave (Rayner, 1997). Taking a 15% average rate of bullying and the average cost of replacement, then the replacement bill becomes calculable (Rayner, 2000). In an organization of 1,000 staff, for example, this will mean that one can expect 150 to report being bullied. If 25% of the bullied leave, and the replacement cost is estimated at $20,000, the cost is $750,000. If one conservatively estimates that for every one of these events there are two witnesses and 20% of *them* leave, that bill alone is $1.2 million. These staff may leave quietly and quickly, finding alternative employment if they can. These exit costs will not be found on the balance sheet.

Those who stay in the organization may complain, may want to be moved, may be disruptive, actively resist the bully, may simply "work to rule" or other action that represents a token withdrawal or protest (Ackroyd & Thompson, 1999; Brodsky, 1976; Zellars, Tepper, & Duffy, 2002). We are not yet clear about the costs of dealing with these reactions. If an escalation of the situation occurs, then it is quite likely that the actors' time will also be taken away from productive employment. That is to say nothing of the variety of comment, gossip, and rumor that might engage other staff rather than their daily travail.

Internal investigations of bullying at work in the United Kingdom will cost around $150,000 each, mostly management time and again completely hidden from the balance sheet. If the situation were to get as far as legal action, then United Kingdom employers need around $250,000 to prepare, again mostly management time, and the lawyers' costs would be added on. British insurers are currently budgeting $400,000 per claim if the claim is lost to the complainant (these are just the damages; Earnshaw & Cooper, 2001). Those figures are for each individual case. A business case exists for doing something about bullying at work. Of course there is also the adverse publicity, avoidance of which can be a main driver for those in power.

ORGANIZATIONAL ACTION

There has been considerable work in developed countries over many years that have established some good practice as far as negative events such as bullying and harassment are concerned. These are well developed in the United States with the Federal Sentencing Guidelines for Organizations (FSGO; 1998). In general these guidelines refer to formal systems, and these need to include a policy against bullying (not just sexual or racial harassment) or, for example, suggesting dignity for all, communicating the policy, and raising awareness of it (perhaps through training). There also needs to be a formal complaints process and an appeals process. These actions need to be led at board level by an appropriate person. The system needs to be monitored, evaluated, and reviewed. Variations on the FSGO are in place in most countries.

Special note needs to be made that employers need to be careful to treat the accused bullies fairly in these situations, because they may also experience a major trauma on being accused. We will not spend more time in these well-established formal principles of good practice for dealing with negative behavior such as sexual or racial harassment and bullying.

Unfortunately many people do not want to use formal systems. In Britain, a confidential study estimated that only around 1 in 30 people who label themselves as being bullied would actually take formal action. This may help explain the exit rates of staff. In general a staff member is concerned that the system will not support him and her and that making a formal complaint will leave him or her worse off (Ishmael, 1999; Keashly, 1998). These individuals may be affected by the prevailing organizational culture in these judgments (Rayner et al., 2002).

It is arguable that formal systems are rather after-the-fact even though they give a good opportunity for the officers of the organization to demonstrate that they take negative treatment seriously, and this may in turn affect a culture of acceptability. To reduce bullying at work, informal systems need to be developed that allow negative behavior to be dealt with quickly and informally, before the situation escalates. The conflict literature is rich with research and best practices on developing entire organizational dispute systems that provide multiple mechanisms (formal and informal) and multiple entry points (e.g., Brett, Goldberg, & Ury, 1990; Costantino & Merchant, 1996; Slaikeu, 1999). Such information is highly relevant to any discussion of ways and means of managing bullying in the workplace (Keashly & Nowell, 2003).

Effective informal programs require training for regular managers to deal with ambiguous complaints from staff. This is not easy. In Britain we are currently seeing a spread of practice that can be termed as dignity at work initiatives. In these processes the organization establishes (ideally in consultation with staff) a statement of acceptable behavior. All staff members are then trained with two messages: that it is their right to expect decent treatment (as per the statement) and that they have a responsibility to treat others in an acceptable way.

These programs are interesting in that they provide equal expectations for and from everyone (including White men). As such this represents a departure from previous practice in the United Kingdom that had been driven by employers adhering to gender and race discrimination legislation. As a result United Kingdom employers' practices during the 1990s emphasized the need to ensure fairness for women and non-White employees. Dignity at work programs redress this balance, emphasizing fairness for all.

These initiatives are new, and it is too early for any evidence on their efficacy to be available. Without doubt some United Kingdom and U.S. organizations will have these policies in name only and move not one inch further. However, anecdotal evidence suggests that the overt fairness is appealing to staff, and staff are more willing to recognize their own responsibilities if they are also getting good treatment in return. For the organization, as costs fall, so the benefits may become apparent and the wisdom of such policies may be able to shine through.

CONCLUSION

This chapter has examined a problem that is endemic in most workplaces. Bullying has been systematically studied by British and, to a more limited extent, U.S. academics for less than a decade, and they have followed a good lead from the Scandinavian and German researchers (e.g., chap. 10, this volume). It is an area of counterproductive work behavior that can be extremely costly to organizations in terms of labor turnover, distracting staff from regular work, and in the costs associated with formal investigations and court cases. It can cost staff considerable anxiety and stress and ultimately affect their health. A wide range of negative behaviors can constitute bullying, many of which are individually minor when taken on their own, but when added together form a pattern of persistent negative treatment. The full dynamics of the process of bullying at work are far from understood, but the importance of organizational action has been stressed in this chapter. Standard formal organizational procedures for issues such as harassment and conflict provide guidance for the bullying at work field. However, we have suggested that these are often implemented after—or as—costs are occurring. For organizations to tackle this problem, informal practices hold the key. Resolving difficulties between staff at work quickly and with fairness is a potential vehicle for dealing with the problem and thus lowering costs to the organization and all involved.

REFERENCES

Ackroyd, S., & Thompson, P. (1999). *Organizational misbehavior*. London: Sage.

Adams, A. (1992). *Bullying at work—How to confront and overcome it*. London: Virago.

Archer, D. (1999). Exploring "bullying" culture in the para-military organization. *International Journal of Manpower*, 20(1/2), 94–105.

Babiak, P. (1995). When psychopaths go to work: A case study of an industrial psychopath. *Applied Psychology—An International Review*, 44(2), 171–188.

Bassman, E. (1992). *Abuse in the workplace*. New York: Quorum.

Baumeister, R. F., Smart, L., & Boden, J. M. (1996). Relation of threatened egotism to violence and aggression: The dark side of self esteem. *Psychological Review*, 103(1), 5–33.

Bennett, R. J., & Robinson, S. L., (2000). Development of a measure of workplace deviance *Journal of Applied Psychology*, 85(3), 349–360.

Besag, V. (1989). *Bullies and victims in schools*. Milton Keynes, England: Open University Press.

Brett, J. M., Goldberg, S. B., & Ury, W. L., (1990). Designing systems for resolving workplace disputes in organizations. *American Psychologist*, 45, 162–170.

Brodsky, C. M., (1976). *The harassed worker*. Lexington, MA: Heath.

Buss, A. H. (1961). *The psychology of aggression*. New York: Wiley.

Colquitt, J. A., Conlon, D. E., Wesson, M. J., Porter, C. O. L. H., & Ng, K. Y. (2001). Justice at the millennium: A meta-analytic review of 25 years of organizational justice research. *Journal of Applied Psychology*, 86(3), 425–445.

Costantino, C. A., & Merchant, C. S. (1996). *Designing conflict management systems*. San Francisco: Jossey-Bass.

Coyne, I., Seigne, E., & Randall, P. (2000). Predicting workplace victim status from personality *European Journal of Work and Organizational Psychology*, 9, 335–349.

Coyne, I., Smith-Lee Chong, P., Randall, P., & Seigné, E. (2002, September). *Subjective and objective measures of bullying and their impact on incident rates, individual differences, and perceptions of team effectiveness*. Paper presented to the International Conference on Bullying at Work, Birkbeck College, London.

Davenport, N. Z., Distler Schwartz, R., & Pursell Elliott, G. (1999). *Mobbing: Emotional abuse in the workplace*. Ames, IA: Civil Society.

Denenberg, R. V., & Braverman, M. (1999). *The violence-prone workplace*. Ithaca, NY: Cornell University Press.

Duffy, M. K., Ganster, D. C., & Pagon, M. (2002). Social undermining in the workplace. *Academy of Management Journal, 45*, 331–351.

Earnshaw, J., & Cooper, C. (2001). *Stress and employer liability* (2nd ed.). Harmondsworth, England: Penguin.

Einarsen, S., Hoel, H., Zapf, D., & Cooper, C. (2003). The concept of bullying at work. In S. Einarsen, H. Hoel, D. Zapf, & C. Cooper (Eds.), *Bullying and emotional abuse in the workplace: International research and practice perspectives* (pp. 3–30). London: Taylor & Francis.

Einarsen, S. E., & Matthiesen, S. B. (1999). Symptoms of post-traumatic stress among victims of bullying at work. *Abstracts for the Ninth European Congress on Work and Organizational Psychology*. Helsinki, Finland: Finnish Institute of Occupational Health.

Einarsen, S., & Skogstad, A. (1996). Bullying at work: Epidemiological findings in public and private organizations. *European Journal of Work and Organizational Psychology, 5*, 185–202.

Farrell, G. (1999). Aggression in clinical setting: Nurses' views. *Journal of Advanced Nursing, 29*(3), 532–541.

Ferrell, O. C., Fraedrich, J., & Ferrell, L. (2002). *Business ethics*. Boston: Houghton-Mifflin

Field, T. (1996). *Bullying in sight*. Didcat, England: Success Unlimited.

Federal Sentencing Guidelines for Organizations. (1998). Retrieved June 15, 2004, from http://www.ussc.gov/guidelin.htm

Glasl, F. (1994). *Konfliktmanagement. Gin Handbuch für Führungskräfte und Berater* [Conflict management: A handbook for managers and consultants] (4th ed.). Bern, Switzerland: Haupt.

Greenberg, L., & Barling, J. (1998). Predicting employee aggression against coworkers, subordinates and supervisors: The roles of person behaviors and perceived workplace factors. *Journal of Organizational Behavior, 20*, 897–913.

Hoel, H., & Cooper, C. L., (2000). *Destructive conflict and bullying at work*. Unpublished manuscript.

Hoel, H., Rayner, C., & Cooper, C. L. (1999). Workplace bullying. *International Review of Industrial and Organizational Psychology, 14*, 189–230.

Incomes Data Services. (1999). *Harassment policies*. London: Author.

Ishmael, A. (1999). *Harassment, bullying and violence at work*. London: Industrial Society.

Jagatic, K. (2001). *The influence of educational culture on experienced and witnessed hostility by faculty toward professionals in training*. Unpublished doctoral dissertation, Wayne State University, Detriot, MI.

Janoff-Bullman, R. (1993). *Shattered assumptions: Towards a new psychology of trauma*. New York: Free Press.

Keashly, L. (1998). Emotional abuse in the workplace: Conceptual and empirical issues. *Journal of Emotional Abuse, 1*, 85–117.

Keashly, L. (2001). Interpersonal and systemic aspects of emotional abuse at work: The target's perspective. *Violence and Victims, 16*, 233–268.

Keashly, L., Harvey, S., & Hunter, S. (1997). Emotional abuse and role state stressors: Relative impact on residence assistants' stress. *Work and Stress, 11*, 35–45.

Keashly, L., & Jagatic, K. (2000, August). *The nature, extent, and impact of emotional abuse in the workplace: Results of a statewide survey.* Paper presented at the Academy of Management Conference, Toronto, Canada.

Keashly, L., & Jagatic, K. (2003). By any other name: American perspectives on workplace bullying. In S. Einarsen, H. Hoel, D. Zapf., & C. Cooper (Eds.), *Bullying and emotional abuse in the workplace: International research and practice perspectives* (pp. 31–61). London: Taylor & Francis.

Keashly, L., & Neuman J. (2002, August). *Exploring persistent patterns of workplace aggression.* Paper presented at the annual meeting of the Academy of Management, Denver, CO.

Keashly, L., & Nowell, B. (2003). Workplace bullying and conflict resolution. In S. Einarsen, H. Hoel, D. Zapf, & C. Cooper (Eds.), *Bullying and emotional abuse in the workplace: International research and practice perspectives* (pp. 339–358). London: Taylor & Francis.

Keashly, L., & Rogers, K. A. (2001). *Aggressive behaviors at work: The role of context in appraisals of threat.* Unpublished manuscript, Wayne State University.

Keashly, L., Trott, V., & MacLean, L. M. (1994). Abusive behaviour in the workplace: A preliminary investigation. *Violence and Victims, 9*, 341–357.

Lazarus, R. S., & Folkman, S. (1984). *Stress, appraisal and coping.* New York: Springer.

Lewis, D. (1999). Workplace bullying—Interim findings of a study in further and higher education. *International Journal of Manpower, 20*(1/2), 106–118.

Lewis, D., & Rayner, C. (2003). Bullying and human resource management: A wolf in sheep's clothing? In S. Einarsen, H. Hoel, D. Zapt, & C. Cooper (Eds.), *Bullying and emotional abuse in the workplace: International research and practice perspectives* (pp. 370–383). London: Taylor & Francis.

Leymann, H. (1990). Mobbing and psychological terror at workplaces. *Violence and Victims, 5*, 119–125.

Leymann, H. (1996). The content and development of mobbing at work. *European Journal of Work and Organizational Psychology, 5*(2), 165–184.

Liefooghe, A. P. D., & MacKenzie Davey, K. (2003). Explaining bullying at work: Why should we listen to employee accounts? In S. Einarsen, H. Hoel, D. Zapf, & C. Cooper (Eds.), *Bullying and emotional abuse in the workplace: International research and practice perspectives* (pp. 219–230). London: Taylor & Francis.

London Times. (2001, January 15). *Post office says dead man bullied.*

Magley, V. J., Hulin, C. L., Fitzgerald, L. F., & DeNardo, M. (1999). Outcomes of self-labeling on sexual harassment. *Journal of Applied Psychology, 84*, 390–402.

McCarthy, P., Sheehan, M., & Kearns, D. (1995). *Managerial styles and their effects on employees health and well-being in organisations undergoing restructuring*. Brisbane, Australia: Report for Worksafe Australia, Griffith University.

Munson, L. J., Miner, A. G., & Hulin, C. (2001). Labeling sexual harassment in the military: An extension and replication. *Journal of Applied Psychology, 86*, 293–303.

Namie, G. (2000, January). *U.S. Hostile Workplace Survey 2000*. Paper presented at the New England Conference on Workplace Bullying, Boston, MA.

Neuman, J. H., & Baron, R. A. (1997). Aggression in the workplace. In R. A. Giacalone & J. Greenberg (Eds.), *Antisocial behavior in organizations* (pp. 37–67). Thousand Oaks, CA: Sage

Neuman, J., & Baron, R. A. (1998). Workplace violence and workplace aggression: Evidence concerning specific forms, potential causes, and preferred targets. *Journal of Management, 24*, 391–420.

O'Leary-Kelly, A. M., Griffin, R. W., & Glew, D. J. (1996). Organization-motivated aggression: A research framework. *Academy of Management Review, 21*, 225–253.

Petri, H., (2002). *A crime without punishment: Policy advocacy for European Union health and safety legislation as harassment at work*. Unpublished doctoral dissertation, Middlesex Univerisity, Middlesex, England.

Price Spratlen, L. (1995). Interpersonal conflict which includes mistreatment in a university workplace. *Violence and Victims, 10*, 285–297.

Quine, L. (1999). Workplace bullying in an NHS trust. *British Medical Journal, 318*, 228–232.

Randall, P., (1996). *Adult bullying: Perpetrators and victims*. London: Routledge.

Rayner, C. (1997). Incidence of workplace bullying. *Journal of Community and Applied Social Psychology, 7*, 199–208.

Rayner, C. (1998). Workplace bullying: Do something! *Journal of Occupational Health and Safety—Australia and New Zealand, 14*, 581–585.

Rayner, C. (1999a). *Bullying in the workplace*. Unpublished doctoral dissertation, University of Manchester Institute of Science and Technology, Manchester, England.

Rayner, C. (1999b). A comparison of two methods for identifying targets of workplace bullying. *Abstracts for the Ninth European Congress on Work and Organizational Psychology*. Helsinki, Finland: Finnish Institute of Occupational Health.

Rayner, C. (1999c). From research to implementation: Finding leverage for prevention. *International Journal of Manpower, 20*(1/2), 28–38.

Rayner, C. (2000, September 6–8). *Building a business case for tackling bullying in the workplace: Beyond a basic cost–benefit approach*. Paper presented at the Transcending Boundaries Conference, Brisbane, Australia.

Rayner, C. (2002, February). *What is this thing we call bullying? Revisiting our thinking after 10 years of study*. Paper presented at the Adelaide International Workplace Bullying Conference, Adelaide, Australia.

Rayner, C., & Cooper, C. (2003). The black hole in "bullying at work" research. *International Journal of Decision Making, 4*(1), 47–64.

Rayner, C., & Hoel, H. (1997). A summary review of literature relating to workplace bullying. *Journal of Community and Applied Social Psychology, 7,* 181–191.

Rayner, C., & Hoel, H., & Cooper, C. L. (2002). *Bullying at work: What we know, who is to blame and what can we do?* London: Taylor & Francis.

Rylance, J. (2002). *Affirmation processes: A study of the experience of responding to workplace abuse.* Unpublished doctoral dissertaion, Queensland University of Technology, Queensland, Australia.

Savva, C., & Alexandrou, A. (1998, July 1). *The impact of bullying in further and higher education.* Paper presented to the 1998 Research Update Conference, Staffordshire University, Staffordshire, England.

Slaikeu, K. A. (1999). Designing dispute resolution systems in the health care industry. *Negotiation Journal, 5,* 395–400.

Tepper, B. J. (2000). Consequences of abusive supervision. *Academy of Management Journal, 43*(2), 178–190.

UNISON. (1997). *UNISON members' experience of bullying at work.* London: Author.

UNISON. (2000). *Police staff bullying report.* London: Author.

Yamada, D. C. (2000). The phenomenon "workplace bullying" and the need for status blind hostile work environment protection. *Georgetown Law Journal, 88,* 475–536.

Zapf, D., & Gross, C. (2001). Conflict escalation and coping with workplace bullying: A replication and extension. *European Journal of Work and Organizational Psychology, 10,* 497–522.

Zapf, D., Knorz, C., & Kulla, M. (1996). On the relationship between mobbing factors, job content, social work environment, and health outcomes. *European Journal of Work and Organizational Psychology, 5*(2), 215–237.

Zellars, K. L., Tepper, B. J., & Duffy, M. K. (2002). Abusive supervision and subordinates' organizational citizenship behavior. *Journal of Applied Psychology, 87,* 1068–1076.

12

CONCLUDING THOUGHTS: WHERE DO WE GO FROM HERE?

PAUL E. SPECTOR AND SUZY FOX

In recent years, the area of counterproductive work behavior (CWB) and related negative acts by employees and other organizational stakeholders has become quite lively, although fragmented. This book attempts a much needed integration of this area, showing links among conceptually, although not necessarily operationally, distinct behavioral constructs. Taken as a whole, the literature in this area has provided insights into potential causes and consequences of CWB, providing models based on different theoretical bases, such as aggression, deviance, schoolyard bullying, and social exchange. The combined roles of environmental and personal factors have also been explored.

It was not the goal of this book to provide a single integrating theory that subsumes all others, and none has been provided. The various authors have offered a variety of theoretical positions that offer different insights and perspectives. Rather, the goal was to underscore connections as well as distinctions and to illustrate where the different research streams can inform one another—for example, by providing empirical support. Linkages among the various approaches have been highlighted throughout the book, as, for example, Figure 8.2, which provides a Venn diagram showing the overlap among these various forms of behavior. In this chapter we will take a look forward and suggest where the field should go from here and how we might proceed in a more integrative way.

DETERMINING THE NEXT STEPS

The past decade has seen considerable conceptual and empirical work in the CWB realm, but there is still much to be done. As is true of new areas of research, our early work has identified the nature and scope of the phenomenon of interest and has shown links to other variables. In this chapter we provide a number of suggestions for research that needs to be done. Much of our advice fits research on many if not most of the different theoretical concepts—in other words, they would fit aggression research as well as revenge research.

CLOSER TIE BETWEEN DEFINITIONS AND OPERATIONALIZATIONS

One of the striking things in this area, as we pointed out in chapter 7 (see Table 7.1) is that although the definitions may be quite distinct, operationalizations are less so. Thus, for example, researchers studying aggression as an act intended to harm and deviance as an act that violates norms might both include the same items in their scales of behavior, but the intent and norms are assumed rather than explicitly measured. An exception is the work on retaliation in which items specifically ask if the behavior was done in response to provocation. Whether this makes a difference in people's responses or not is an empirical question, but there is a closer tie in their work between definition and assessment.

Research that attempts a more explicit link between definition and operationalization has potential to provide additional insights into CWB. For example, deviance research could focus on norms in organizations at various levels (e.g., workgroup vs. organizationwide) and explore issues of norm development and communication, including flow from top to bottom and bottom to top of organizations. It can answer questions about how norms for various CWBs develop and what might be causes and consequences of norm violation. Work on revenge might help us understand when and under what conditions an employee is likely to respond or choose to ignore the provocation.

MORE STUDY OF MOTIVES FOR COUNTERPRODUCTIVE WORK BEHAVIOR

Considering that motives are important in definitions of CWB terms, it is interesting that more work has not been done on motives. Many of the behaviors studied in this area are not necessarily clear-cut in their intentions or results. For example, organizational withdrawal (e.g., coming to work late) could be done to withhold performance as a means of harming the organization intentionally or it could be a result of a sick child who had to be taken to the doctor. Many other behaviors could likewise have different motives and results. The work on incivility specifically acknowledges the idea that motives behind behaviors can be ambiguous, but the study of motives can help us understand even here the extent to which rudeness is truly unintended, in contrast to intent that is carefully and deliberately concealed.

Likewise with deviance, it would be instructive to study motives in relationship to norm violation. Do violations of norms for different behaviors reflect the same underlying motivations? Are motives underlying aggression the same as deviance, and do the same people who engage in aggression also engage in deviance? In cases of genuine value differences between individuals or groups, by definition norms of one party may be violated by the other party. Is this deviance, and if so, who defines counterproductivity?

DIMENSIONALITY OF COUNTERPRODUCTIVE WORK BEHAVIOR

There has been relatively little work done on the dimensionality of CWB. Most studies have either combined all CWBs into a single overall measure or they have used broad categories, the most popular being Robinson and Bennett's (1995) organization-versus-person dichotomy. Although broad categories have yielded interesting findings, we would benefit from taking a more fine-grained view as well. The broad categories can hide rather large distinctions among specific acts that might not all have the same causes and consequences. Thus a total CWB measure might relate to variables of interest with relatively few of the individual behaviors being related. Spector, Fox, and Penney (2003), for example, have shown that relatively few individual behaviors from their Counterproductive Work Behavior Checklist (CWB–C) of 45 behaviors related to criteria that correlated significantly to their overall CWB score. Thus one should be cautious in generalizing from total scores to the individual items.

CLOSER TIES WITH OTHER RELATED CONSTRUCTS

This book included chapters on a variety of constructs that seemed most related to our conception of CWB. However, there are additional constructs that have literatures that have not been integrated well with CWB. Two in particular stand out: Sexual harassment (SH) and withdrawal.

SH consists of acts that can produce a hostile work environment for an individual and therefore cause harm to well-being. From this perspective, SH overlaps conceptually with aggression (see review by Bowes-Sperry, Tata, & Luthar, 2003), abuse, bullying and mobbing, and to some extent with incivility. In fact Zapf and Einarsen (chap. 10, this volume) defined mobbing as *non*sexual harassment (italics ours). Of course, SH is limited to behaviors that include some sex-related features, but many of these behaviors fall under the more general categories. Furthermore, the causes and effects on the individual might be similar to the target-centered forms of CWB discussed in this book. Evidence that supports this is a meta-analysis by Lapierre, Spector, and Leck (2004), showing that SH correlates similarly to job satisfaction as other forms of verbal aggression, although the mean correlation of SH was somewhat lower. It would be instructive to integrate SH with these other forms of behavior, looking at behaviors that do and do not overlap.

There is a vast literature on employee withdrawal, particularly absence (which is often included in CWB measures) and turnover (which is included only indirectly, as intention to quit). There has been some work done on lateness as well, although generally defined purely in terms of getting to work after the scheduled time, rather than coming back from breaks or lunch late as is included in some CWB studies. The absence literature has shown that there are different kinds of absence—for example, absent when sick versus other reasons—and these can have different causes (Dalton & Mesch, 1991). This suggests that it might be important to investigate multiple reasons for a number of CWBs in addition to absence. For example, one item from the CWB–C (Spector et al., 2003) asks about not returning a phone call to someone you should. This could be because of having critical tasks that must be completed for the organization or it could represent a form of revenge against someone who performed a slight in the past.

Another place where the absence literature might integrate with CWB is the work on the absence culture (e.g., Nicholson & Johns, 1985). The idea that absence and perhaps other forms of withdrawal are in response to norms is relevant to work on deviance, because it suggests that absence can be affected by group norms and culture. However, the absence culture suggests that such acts can be nondeviant, with employees engaging in acts that are socially acceptable within their workgroups and organizations. Thus the same absence might be deviant in one setting and not in another, suggesting that there can be different underlying motives.

ADDITIONAL METHODOLOGIES BEYOND CROSS-SECTIONAL SELF-REPORTS

As is true of most new areas, CWB research has been dominated by cross-sectional, self-report surveys. This area is particularly difficult to study, given the sensitivity and in some cases illegality of the phenomenon. However, it is time to find new and perhaps creative ways to study CWB with additional methods. Steps in that direction have already been taken, but more research is needed. For example, Glomb (2002) interviewed employees about their CWB experiences and then content-analyzed their responses. Skarlicki and Folger (1997) asked coworkers to report on the retaliation of their target participants. Goh, Bruursema, Fox, and Spector (2003); Lee and Spector (2004); and Penney and Spector (2003) all assessed CWB from both employee and coworker reports.

One of the biggest problems with conducting CWB studies is the need for participant anonymity if more serious items are included, such as sabotage and theft. This is not an insurmountable problem, because questionnaires can be matched across sources and time with "secret" codes. For example, we have had good success asking the target participant to put his or her own identifying code on his or her own and a coworker questionnaire and then ask his or her coworker to complete his or her version and return it to us separately and anonymously. Return rates for coworkers have been quite good. A similar procedure could be used to acquire supervisor responses.

For longitudinal studies a different approach would be needed, because we could not rely on participant memory over time. This could be accomplished by asking a few factual questions that would allow matching questionnaires without identifying individuals. This might include asking the person the name of the first street they remember living on, the name of their first grade teacher, and their month of birth.

Experience sampling could also be useful, asking people to periodically record in diaries their experience as both an actor (record behaviors you have done) or target (record things done to you). Given the relative infrequency of many behaviors, asking at the end of the day to recall CWB during the day might be most reasonable. This approach could link CWB to both psychological (e.g., emotional experience) and physiological (e.g., ambulatory heart rate–blood pressure monitoring) factors. It could also help link CWB to other experiences at work that the individual would be asked to record.

Finally, a more qualitative approach could prove helpful, for example, asking people to describe in detail a CWB incident they experienced or performed using an approach like the Stress Incident Record (Keenan & Newton, 1985). Such incidents can be content-analyzed and placed into categories reflecting factors leading up to the incident (e.g., being assigned an unwanted task or being criticized by the supervisor), the nature of the incident (e.g., coming back from lunch an hour late or being rude to the supervisor), and effects (e.g., getting angry vs. being reprimanded). The categories can be related to one another—for example, is being assigned an unwanted task more likely than being criticized to be associated with getting angry? The categories can also be related to more quantitative data— for example, are those who report withdrawal-type behaviors more or less satisfied than those who report rudeness?

COUNTERPRODUCTIVE WORK BEHAVIOR CULTURE

There has been relatively little attention paid to the impact of organizational (as well as national) culture on CWB. One exception is Robinson and O'Leary-Kelly (1998), who showed that individual CWB is influenced by members of the work group. Boye and Jones (1997) discussed a number of organizational factors that can affect CWB, including the values communicated by organizations, honesty policies (e.g., antitheft), work-group norms, security, and company responses to CWB. Much of the support they noted concerned employee theft, but likely many factors that influence that behavior will influence others as well. Group-level studies could prove useful, relating frequency of behaviors to contextual factors. Studies focusing on entire supervisor–subordinate units could be useful for exploring the impact of supervisor variables on the CWB of subordinates as a group as opposed to individuals.

CONCLUSION

The recurring theme running through all the chapters of this book is that employees are both actors and targets of acts that harm organizations and people in organizations. The various chapters looked at different aspects of such acts, focusing in some cases on actors and others on targets. Chapter authors varied in their focus on interpersonal versus organizational acts and in organizational versus personal factors. They also varied in their underlying theoretical bases and positions—for example, Neuman and Baron's aggression (chap. 1) is based largely on the social–psychological aggression literature, whereas Bennett, Aquino, Reed, and Thau's deviance (chap. 5) was

TABLE 12.1
Characteristics of Different Counterproductive Work Behavior Concepts

Term	Person target	Organization target	Physical acts included	Intent to harm	Violates norms or standards	Pattern of behavior
Aggression	Yes	Indirectly	Yes	Yes	No	No
Bullying	Yes	No	Yes	Yes	No	Yes
Counter-productive work behavior	Yes	Yes	Yes	No	No	No
Deviance	Yes	Yes	Yes	Yes	Yes	No
Emotional abuse	Yes	No	No	Yes	Yes	Yes
Incivility	Yes	No	No	Ambiguous	Yes	No
Mobbing	Yes	No	Yes	No	No	Yes
Retaliation	Indirectly	Yes	Yes	Yes	No	No
Revenge	Yes	No	Yes	Yes	No	No
Violence	Yes	No	Yes	No	No	No

based on the work of Hollinger (1986) in criminology. Such diverse backgrounds and theories have enriched the study of these behaviors, even though at times it has resulted in researchers overlooking where others' work might inform and support their own.

Taken as a whole, the chapters of this book describe organizational (e.g., injustice and stressors) and personal (e.g., negative affectivity and hostile attribution bias) factors as well as their interactions that contribute to CWB. Many of the same variables can be found in chapters throughout the book as work based on different conceptual underpinnings has converged on conclusions about the role of these variables. Table 12.1 contrasts the key characteristics of the 10 different terms that form the basis of our various chapters, including whether they include acts directed toward people or organizations, whether they include physical acts, whether they assume an intent to harm, whether they include reference to norms or standards of behavior, and whether or not they require a pattern of behavior over time.

The distinct terms and conceptualizations of the individual chapters are by no means mutually exclusive. Many of the specific behaviors we study could be included in several or most of the terms and concepts represented in this book. For example, if one employee insults another, it might be considered aggression, revenge (if the employee was previously insulted), retaliation (if the employee insults the supervisor in response to unfair treatment), deviance (if it violates norms), CWB, incivility, and abuse, bullying, or mobbing if it is part of a pattern of harassment. If that employee punches another, it might be considered aggression, violence, revenge (if in response to a previous attack), retaliation (if in response to injustice), deviance, CWB, and possibly bullying or mobbing. It would not be incivility or abuse because they exclude physical acts.

Whatever our various authors call the phenomenon, we undoubtedly agree that it is important to research these harmful acts at work. A better understanding of the causes and consequences of aggression, violence, revenge, retaliation, deviance, CWB, incivility, abuse, mobbing, and bullying will help inform organizations about the best way to manage such behaviors that harm them and their employees.

REFERENCES

Bowes-Sperry, L., Tata, J., & Luthar, H. K. (2003). Comparing sexual harassment to other forms of workplace aggression. In A. Sagie, S. Stashevsky, & M. Koslowsky (Eds.), *Misbehaviour and dysfunctional attitudes in organizations* (pp. 33–56). Hampshire, England: Palgrave Macmillan.

Boye, M. W., & Jones, J. W. (1997). Organizational culture and employee counter-productivity. In R. A. Giacalone & J. Greenberg (Eds.), *Antisocial behavior in organizations* (pp. 172–184). Thousand Oaks, CA: Sage.

Dalton, D. R., & Mesch, D. J. (1991). On the extent and reduction of avoidable absenteeism: An assessment of absence policy provisions. *Journal of Applied Psychology, 10,* 810–817.

Glomb, T. M. (2002). Workplace anger and aggression: Informing conceptual models with data from specific encounters. *Journal of Occupational Health Psychology, 7,* 20–36.

Goh, A. P. S., Bruursema, K., Fox, S., & Spector, P. E. (2003, April 11–13). *Comparisons of self and coworker reports of counterproductive work behavior.* Paper presented at the meeting of the Society for Industrial and Organizational Psychology, Orlando, FL.

Hollinger, R. C. (1986). Acts against the workplace: Social bonding and employee deviance. *Deviant Behavior, 7,* 53–75.

Keenan, A., & Newton, T. J. (1985). Stressful events, stressors and psychological strains in young professional engineers. *Journal of Occupational Behavior, 6,* 151–156.

Lapierre, L. M., Spector, P. E., & Leck, J. D. (2004). *Sexual versus non-sexual workplace aggression and overall job satisfaction: A meta-analysis.* Unpublished manuscript, University of Ottawa, Canada.

Lee, V. B., & Spector, P. E. (2004, April 2–4). *Sources of conflict at work and targets of counterproductive behaviors.* Paper presented at the meeting of the Society for Industrial and Organizational Psychology, Chicago, IL.

Nicholson, N., & Johns, G. (1985). The absence culture and the psychological contract—Who's in control of absence? *Academy of Management Review, 10,* 397–407.

Penney, L. M., & Spector, P. E. (2003, April 11–13). *Workplace incivility and counterproductive workplace behavior.* Paper presented at the meeting of the Society for Industrial and Organizational Psychology, Orlando, FL.

Robinson, S. L., & Bennett, R. J. (1995). A typology of deviant workplace behaviors: A multidimensional scaling study. *Academy of Management Journal, 38,* 555–572.

Robinson, S. L., & O'Leary-Kelly, A. M. (1998). Monkey see, monkey do: The influence of work groups on the antisocial behavior of employees. *Academy of Management Journal, 41,* 658–672.

Skarlicki, D. P., & Folger, R. (1997). Retaliation in the workplace: The roles of distributive, procedural, and interactional justice. *Journal of Applied Psychology, 82,* 434–443.

Spector, P. E., Fox, S., & Penney, L. M. (2003). *To sum or not to sum: Development of the Counterproductive Work Behavior Checklist (CWB–C).* Unpublished manuscript, University of South Florida, Tampa.

AUTHOR INDEX

Numbers in italics refer to listings in reference sections.

Damasio, A. R., 93, *102*
Damon, W., 113, *122*
Darden, M., 177, *199*
Darwin, C., 94, *103*
Davenport, J., 46, *59*
Davenport, N., 22, 36, 272, *293*
Davidson, M. J., 248, *264*
Davis, H., 43, 44, *59*
Davison, H. K., 128, 143, *145*
Deal, T. E., 109, *122*
Deffenbacher, L. J., 112, *122*
Delaney, C., 216, *232*
del Barrio, C., *263*
DeNardo, M., 279, *295*
Denenberg, R. V., 275, *293*
DeNeve, K. M., 30, *35*, 156, *170*
Dengerink, H. A., 156, *172*
De Nicholas, M. E., 116, *121*
Depue, R. A., 253, *264*
Deshpande, R., 118, *122*
Deuser, W. E., 30, *35*, 156, *170*
DeVore, C. J., 163, *173*
Dickson, R., 49, *61*
Dietz, J., 188, 189, *197*
Dill, K. E., 30, *35*
Distler Schwartz, R., 272, *293*
Dodge, K. A., 128, 131, 133, *146*
Dofradottir, A., 257, *265*
Dollard, J., 156, *171*
Donnerstein, E., 24, *36*
Donovan, J. J., 141, 143, *147*
Doob, L. W., 156, *171*
Douglas, S., 42, 50, *59*, 112, *121*, 159,
    164, *171*, *172*, 180, 188, *197*,
    198, 212, 214, *230*
Dow, M. G., 253, *268*
Downey, G., 94, *102*
Drasgow, F., 223, *231*
Drum, M. L., *234*
Duck, S. W., 178, *200*
Duffy, M. K., 14, 24, *36*, 162, *171*,
    180, 188, *197*, *198*, 203, 205,
    207, 208, 210, 213, 215, 223,
    224, 227, *230*, 233, *235*, 236,
    261, *264*, 272, 278, 289, *293*,
    296
Dumaine, B., 21, *36*
Dumont, C. P., 253, *268*
Duncan, L. E., 128, *150*
Dupré, K. E., 43, 50, 51, *59*, *60*
Dwight, S. A., 129, *146*

Dwyer, D. J., 228, *235*
Dyck, R. J., 99, *103*

Eagly, A. H., 187, *197*
Earnshaw, J., 290, *293*
Eavis, P., 110, *122*
Eckenrode, J., 224, *230*
Ehrensaft, M. K., 51, *60*
Ehrlich, H. J., 177, *197*
Einarsen, S. E., 8, 22, *36*, 205, *231*, 237,
    238, 239, 240, 242, 243, 244,
    245, 246, 247, 248, 249, 250,
    251, 253, 254, 255, 256, 258,
    259, 260, 262, *264*, 265, *267*,
    270, 276, 277, 278, 279, 286,
    293, 300
Elias, N., 178, 195, *197*
Elias, R., 212, *231*
Elliott, G. P., 22, *36*
Elo, A-L., *268*
Emler, N. P., 75, *79*
Epstein, S., 115, *122*, 129, *146*, 186, *197*
Erdelyi, M. H., 129, *146*
Erikson, E. H., 113, 114, *122*
Esser, H., 120, *122*

Falbe, D. M., 219, *235*
Faragher, B., 249, *265*
Farrell, G., 282, *293*
Fass, P. M., 45, *62*
Fazio, R. H., 120, *122*
Felson, R. B., 128, *146*, 180, 185, 186,
    189, *199*
Fendrich, M., *234*
Ferrell, L., 288, *293*
Ferrell, O. C., 113, *122*, 288, *293*
Field, T., 282, 284, 285, 287, 288, *293*
Finch, J. F., 116, *121*
Finchum, F. D., 133, *145*
Finnegan, W., 134, *146*
Fischbein, R., 14, 23, *38*
Fisher, R. J., 259, *265*
Fiske, A. P., 93, 99, *103*
Fiske, S. T., 129, *146*
Fitzgerald, L. F., 204, 206, 209, 213, 218,
    223, 228, *231*, *234*, 241, *268*,
    279, *295*
Flaherty, J. A., 204, 205, 221, 223, *234*
Flanagan, J. C., 84, *103*

Fletcher, J. K., 187, *197*
Flin, R. H., *149*
Flinn, M. V., 109, *122*
Folger, R., 6, 14, *39*, 42, 51, 52, *60*, 65, 66, 70, 71, 73, 75, 79, 80, 83, 84, 85, 87, 88, 90, 95, 97, 100, *102, 103, 104, 105*, 112, *124*, 127, *149*, 153, 154, 156, 157, 161, 165, 168, 169, *171, 173*, 185, 186, 188, *197*, 199, 225, 228, *231*, 235, 301, *305*
Folkman, S., 159, *172*, 220, 233, 254, 266, 276, *294*
Ford, D., 113, *123*
Forehand, M., 118, 120, *122*
Fox, S., 7, 14, 25, 27, 31, *37*, 39, 68, 75, 76, 79, 112, *122*, 156, 157, 160, 161, 162, 163, 164, 165, 166, *171, 172, 174*, 179, 180, 188, 189, *197*, 228, *231*, 299, 301, *304, 305*
Fraedrich, J., 288, *293*
Frank, R. H., 93, *103*
Freels, S., 223, *234*
Freeman, L. V., *196*
French, J. R. P., 255, *263*
Frese, M., 158, 159, *171, 174*, 253, 254, 255, *265, 268*

Gabor, T., 45, *60*
Galperin, B. L., 112, *121*
Gandz, J., 251, *265*
Ganster, D. C., 14, 36, 162, *171*, 188, *197*, 205, 230, 261, 264, 272, *293*
Gardner, W., 114, *121*
Garrett, C., 44, *60*
Gay, P., 128, 133, 134, *146*
Geddes, D., 13, 18, *36, 37*, 43, 59, 188, *196*
Gee, J., 90, *105*
Geen, R. G., 15, 21, 30, *37*, 127, *146*
Geva, N., 15, *37*
Gewirth, A., 95, *103*
Giacalone, R. A., 188, 190, *197*
Glasl, F., 258, 259, *265*, 286, *293*
Glew, D. J., 14, *39*, 42, 62, 65, 80, 128, 148, 153, *173*, 179, 198, 212, 233, 275, *295*

Glisson, C. A., *147*
Glomb, T. M., 31, *37*, 161, *171*, 205, 207, 208, 209, 219, 223, 226, *231*, 301, *304*
Goh, A. P. S., 159, 160, 161, 162, 163, 166, 168, 169, *171, 174*, 301, *304*
Goldberg, S. B., 290, *292*
Gollwitzer, P. M., 120, *122*
Gonthier, G., 177, 178, *197*
Goranson, R., 24, *39*
Gottfredson, M. R., 141, *146*
Gottlieb, N., 202, *233*
Gough, H. G., 26, *37*
Graham, J. P., 51, *60*
Graydon, J., 177, *197*
Green, P. D., 128, 139, 143, *145, 146*
Greenberg, J., 32, 36, *37*, 112, *122*, 130, 148, 188, 190, *197*
Greenberg, L., 50, 51, 52, 57, *60*, 161, *172*, 214, 216, 217, *231*, 285, *293*
Greenberger, D. B., 163, *170*
Greenwald, A. G., 129, 130, 135, 141, 143, 144, *147*
Greenwell, J., 156, *172*
Gresham, L. C., 113, *122*
Griffin, R. W., 14, *39*, 42, 62, 65, 80, 128, 148, 153, *173*, 179, 180, 198, 203, 212, 233, 275, *295*
Grisso, T., 130, *147*
Groeblinghoff, D., 239, *265*
Gross, C., 249, 255, 256, 257, 258, 259, 260, 262, *265*, 270, 286, *296*
Grover, S., 205, *229*
Grubbs, L. M., 47, *62*
Gundlach, M. J., 159, *172*, 188, *198*
Gustafsson, A., 237, 247, 254, 256, 266, 267
Guterman, N. B., 47, *60*

Haidt, J., 95, *103, 104*
Hales, S., 116, *122*
Hall, S., 44, *60*
Hammock, G. S., 128, *147*
Hanson, L. R., 73, *79*
Harakka, T., 187, *198*
Hare, C., 214, *235*
Harris, M. B., 29, *37*
Harrison, C. A., 45, 56, *60*
Hart, D., 113, 114, *122, 123*

London, M., 187, 200
Long, L. W., 180, 197
Lonsway, K. L., 196
Loomis, D., 43, 61
Loughlin, C., 162, 172
Luckenbill, D. F., 185, 198
Luckmann, T., 111, 121
Lundell, J. A., 42, 55, 62
Luthar, H. K., 215, 230, 300, 304
Lyman, S. M., 116, 124
Lyndon, K., 46, 61

MacEwen, K. E., 218, 230, 233
Mackensen von Astfeld, S., 247, 267
MacKenzie Davey, K., 275, 277, 294
MacKinnon, C., 180, 198
MacLean, L. M., 188, 197, 203, 232, 278, 294
Magley, V. J., 177, 178, 184, 188, 196, 210, 225, 230, 279, 295
Mannix, J., 47, 61
Mantell, M. R., 14, 38
Marais-Steinman, S., 22, 38
Marcus-Newhall, A., 27, 38
Marshall, S. W., 43, 61
Martin, C., 83, 103
Martin, J., 177, 178, 198, 221, 235
Martinko, M. J., 42, 50, 51, 59, 62, 159, 164, 171, 172, 180, 188, 189, 197, 198, 212, 214, 230
Matthews, C., 73, 80
Matthiesen, S. B., 4, 10, 237, 239, 242, 251, 253, 264, 267, 276, 293
May, D. D., 47, 62
Mazerolle, M. D., 129, 131, 134, 147
McCarthy, P., 277, 281, 295
McClelland, D. C., 127, 129, 141, 147
McClure, S., 46, 62
McGue, M., 51, 61, 165, 172, 214, 232
McGuire, T. W., 192, 198
McIntyre, M. D., 128, 135, 141, 143, 145, 147, 148
McLean Parks, J. M., 52, 60, 65, 73, 80, 108, 125
Meadows, R. J., 42, 62
Menzel, H., 111, 123
Merchant, C. S., 290, 292
Merchant, J. A., 42, 55, 62
Merrill, G. L., 55, 61
Mertin, P., 53, 62

Mertini, H., 255, 270
Mesch, D. J., 300, 304
Meschkutat, B., 247, 252, 255, 257, 258, 262, 267
Metcalfe, J., 94, 104
Metts, S., 180, 197
Meyer, J. P., 109, 121
Mikkelsen, E. G., 240, 253, 254, 255, 256, 264, 267
Mikula, G., 72, 80
Miles, D., 14, 37, 68, 79, 160, 161, 162, 164, 171, 172, 179, 197, 228, 231
Miller, J. B., 119, 123
Miller, J. L., 129, 148
Miller, N., 27, 38
Miller, N. E., 156, 171
Miller, R. S., 178, 198
Miller, S. M., 130, 148
Miller-Burke, J., 45, 57, 62
Millon, T., 128, 129, 133, 134, 148
Miner, A. G., 31, 37, 219, 231, 277, 295
Mischel, W., 94, 102, 104, 133, 141, 148, 150
Misner, T. S., 48, 61
Moag, J. S., 184, 196
Moberg, P. J., 14, 23, 38
Mohr, G., 255, 267
Mohr, P. B., 53, 62
Monahan, J., 128, 130, 148
Monroe, S. M., 253, 264
Moore, R. W., 129, 148
Morgan, C. D., 143, 148
Morrell, J. S., 53, 62
Morrill, C., 6, 10, 71, 74, 80
Morris, J., 178, 198
Morrison, B., 50, 63
Mount, M. K., 141, 145
Mowrer, O. H., 156, 171
Munn, M., 53, 54, 62
Munson, L. J., 277, 278, 295
Munthe, E., 238, 268
Murphy, C. M., 202, 233
Murphy, K. R., 25, 38
Murray, H. A., 128, 143, 148
Murray, V. V., 251, 265

Namie, G., 214, 215, 219, 233, 272, 278, 282, 295
Namie, R., 214, 233
Nault, A., 162, 172

Reed, A. II., 6, 113, 114, 118, *122, 121, 124, 125,* 302
Reheiser, E. C., 165, *174*
Remington, R., 177, *199*
Rest, J. R., 108, 113, *124*
Richardson, D. R., 16, 19, 30, 36, 128, 133, *145, 147*
Richman, J. A., 204, 205, 207, 208, 210, 212, 221, 222, 223, 224, 227, 228, *234*
Riger, S., 54, 63
Ritter, B., 14, 23, 38
Robins, R. W., 115, *124*
Robinson, S. L., 6, *10,* 14, 25, 26, *39,* 65, 66, 68, 80, 107, 108, 109, 110, 112, *121, 124,* 154, 156, 157, 160, 161, *170, 173,* 179, 180, 186, 188, 190, *196, 197, 199,* 207, 208, 213, 230, *234,* 275, 292, 299, 302, *305*
Robinson, T., 83, *103*
Rogers, A. G., 47, 59
Rogers, K. A., 48, *63,* 207, 208, 215, 216, 218, 219, 221, 222, 224, 225, 226, *232, 232, 234,* 282, 294
Røkkum, O., 4, *10,* 237, *267*
Roland, E., 238, *268*
Rosenberg, E., 95, *104*
Rosenfield, D. D., 83, *103*
Rospenda, K. M., 204, 205, 219, 221, 223, 226, 227, 228, *234*
Ross, L., 88, *104,* 130, *148*
Rosse, J. G., 129, *148*
Rothleder, D., 187, *199*
Rothstein, M., 141, *149*
Rotter, J. B., 166, *173*
Rowland, K. M., 187, *200*
Rubin, J. Z., 219, *234*
Rubin, L. J., 53, 62
Rule, B. G., 99, *103*
Runyan, C. W., 42, 43, *61, 63*
Ryan, K. D., 223, *234*
Rylance, J., 284, *296*

Sacco, W. P., 253, *268*
Sackett, P. R., 152, 163, *173*
Saito, M., 186, *198*
Salancik, G., 112, *124*
Salgado, J. F., 163, 165, *173*
Salin, D., 249, *268*

Salmivalli, C., *37*
Santos, A., 52, *63*
Savva, C., 281, *296*
Scanlon, T. M., 96, *104*
Schaal, B., 120, *122*
Schaffer, K., 42, *63*
Schat, A. C. H., 48, 49, 55, 56, *63,* 221, *234*
Schaubroeck, J., 159, *173*
Schaufeli, W. B., 259, *263*
Schein, E. H., 109, 110, *124*
Scher, S. J., 129, *145*
Schlosser, E., 44, *63*
Schmiga, K., 253, *268*
Schmitt, N., 129, *148*
Schneider, D. J., 130, *148*
Schneider, K. T., 206, 208, 218, *235*
Schoop, R. F., *148*
Schroth, H. A., 74, *80*
Schuessler, K., 209, *235*
Schulz, M., 188, *197*
Schuster, B., 253, *268*
Schwab, D. P., 206, *235*
Schwartz, R. D., 22, *36*
Schwarz, N., *149*
Scott, M. B., 116, *124*
Sears, R. R., 156, *171*
Seifert, C., 255, *270*
Seigne, E., 253, *263,* 278, 279, *292*
Selye, H., 240, *268*
Shah, P. P., 74, *80*
Shapiro, D., 133, *145,* 186, *199*
Shaw, J. D., 162, *171,* 223, *235*
Sheehan, D. V., 204, *235*
Sheehan, K. H., 204, *235*
Sheehan, M., 243, *268,* 277, *295*
Shepardson, D., 44, *60*
Shoda, Y., 113, *121*
Shullman, S. L., 204, 206, 218, 228, *231*
Siegel, J., 192, *198*
Simpson, D., 4, 9
Sims, R. R., 110, *124*
Sinclair, R. R., 221, 227, *235*
Skarlicki, D. P., 6, 14, *39,* 42, 51, 52, *60,* 65, 66, 70, 71, 73, 75, 79, 80, 83, 84, 85, 97, 100, *103, 104,* 112, *124,* 127, *149,* 153, 154, 156, 157, 161, 165, 168, 169, *173,* 185, 186, *197, 199,* 228, *235,* 301, *305*

SUBJECT INDEX

Bullying at work, *continued*
  causes of, 283–289
  damage from, 275–276
  defined, 272, 273
  dispute-related, 286
  financial costs of, 271, 289–290
  intent and, 277
  labeling, 276–277, 279–280
  measurement of, 278–280
  vs. mobbing, 238, 243–245, 272
  nature and prevalence of, 280–283
  organizational, 275, 287–289
  perpetrators of, 285–287
  persistency and, 274–275
  perspective of perpetrator, 244
  and power imbalance, 277
  predatory, 286
  vs. revenge, 66
  and school bullies, 285
  studies of, 14
  targets of, 283–284
  training for the management of, 291
  UK and North American origin of
    research, 9, 272
  victim and perpetrator perspectives
    for bullying and mobbing
    (figure), 244

Census of Fatal Occupational Injuries, 55
Characteristics of counterproductive work-
    place behavior concepts (table),
    303
Civility. *See also* Incivility; Workplace in-
    civility
  defined, 178
Cognitive processes
  and dispositional aggressiveness,
    129–130, 143–144
  and revenge, 74–75
  and self-regulation of moral identity,
    115–116
Conditional reasoning, 131–135
  defined, 131–132
  measurement system for, 135–138,
    143
Conditional Reasoning Test for Aggres-
    sion (CRT–A)
  described, 135–136
  developmental work on, 138–141,
    143

example items of (exhibit), 137
number of problems on, 139
reading level of, 138–139
scoring of, 140–141
uncorrected validities for (table), 142
visual–verbal version, 139, 140
Conflict, studies on interpersonal, 160–
    161
Consequences of mobbing from stress per-
    spective (figure), 255
Control
  and counterproductive work behav-
    ior, 4, 162–163, 166
  locus of, 3, 166, 167
Coping
  and emotional abuse, in the work-
    place, 222–224
  and mobbing, 256–258
  and victims of robberies, 56
Counterproductive work behavior
    (CWB), 7, 25, 151–170, 297–
    304. *See also* Bullying at work;
    Employee deviance; Emotional
    abuse, in the workplace;
    Mobbing at work; Personality,
    and counterproductive work be-
    havior; Revenge, in the work-
    place; Stressor–emotion model,
    of counterproductive work behav-
    ior; Targets, of counterproductive
    work behavior; Workplace aggres-
    sion; Workplace incivility
  accountability for, 4
  and aggression, 27
  areas for future research, 9, 298–302
  and autonomy at work, 163, 165
  characteristics of counterproductive
    behavior concepts (table), 303
  constructs of, 153–156
  and control, 162–163, 166
  defined, 151–152
  and emotions and job satisfaction,
    161
  and employee withdrawal, 300–301
  examples of similar items from scales
    that assess aggression, deviance,
    and retaliation (table), 157
  forms of, along with workplace inci-
    vility (figure), 191
  job stressors and, 160–161
  as label for field of study, 3, 5, 68

methodological issues in the study of, 167–169

motives for, 299

vs. organizational retaliatory behavior, 85–86, 101

overlapping set of behaviors, 4

personality and, 3–4, 163–166

self-reports and, 301

and sexual harassment, 300

stressor–emotion model of, 7, 156–160

tie between operationalizations and definitions, 298–299

vs. workplace aggression, 153

Counterproductive Work Behavior Checklist (CWB–C), 299

Culture

counterproductive workplace behavior, 302

deviant organizational, 7, 25–27, 112

and incivility, 192

organizational, 109–111, 118–119

Deonance. *See also* Emotions; Organizational retaliatory behavior

and anger, 92–95, 96–99

defined, 88–89

and guilt, 99

and retaliation, 83

Depression, 214, 217, 223

"Desk rage," 3

Deviance, 66, 68–69, 101. *See also* Employee deviance

and counterproductive work behavior, 154

directed toward organizations vs. people, 154

examples of similar items from scales (table), 157

organizational, 25–27, 112, 115–118

vs. revenge, 66

types of, 26

Dictator decision game studies, 90–92, 96

Domestic abuse

and absence, from work, 54

and posttraumatic stress disorder study, 53

and workplace violence, 53–54, 57–58

Effects of emotionally abusive behaviors on targets (table), 227

Emotional abuse, in the workplace, 8, 69, 201–229. *See also* Counterproductive work behavior; Targets, of counterproductive work behavior

actor characteristics, 214–216

and counterproductive work behavior, 155

defined, 202, 203–205

defining features of, 204–205

effects of emotionally abusive behaviors on targets (table), 227

examples of behaviors (table), 207–208

framework for approach to, 210–211

and gender, 215, 217

measurement of, 206–210

organizational response to, 225–226

persistence of, 218–219

process framework (figure), 203

similar terms for, 204

situational forces, 212–214

and stressors, 210–216, 219–220

target-oriented factors, 216–218

target perspective of, 8, 210, 220–228

Workplace Aggression Research Questionnaire, 209

Emotions. *See also* Anger; Deonance; Emotional abuse, in the workplace; Frustration

and counterproductive work behavior, 161–162

moral, 83, 87, 88, 94–95, 98

negative, 164–165

Employee deviance, 6–7, 25–26, 107–120, 190, 302–303. *See also* Counterproductive work behavior

and behavioral norms, 108–109

bidirectional feedback, 118–119

defined, 101, 107, 111

and moral identity, 6–7, 112–115

and organizational culture, 6, 109–111, 112–113

relationship of moral identity to deviant organizational norms (figure), 117

and self-regulation of moral identity, 115–118

Organizations. *See also* Culture; Organizational retaliatory behavior
and bullying, 290–291
culture in, 109–111
delinquency in, 26–27
deviance in, 25–27, 112, 115–118
and emotional abuse, 225–226
financial costs of counterproductive work behavior, 193–195, 271, 289–290
and justice, 84–86, 96–101
misbehavior in, 27–28
and mobbing, 252–253, 259
norms, 298
relationship of moral identity to deviant organizational norms (figure), 117
response to robbery, 56
response to targets, 225–226
and workplace violence, 56–57

Persistency
and bullying, 274–275
and emotional abuse, 205, 218–219
Personality, and counterproductive work behavior, 3–4, 158, 163–166
and affective traits, 165
and conscientiousness, 3
and narcissism, 3, 165–166
and negative affectivity, 164, 214
and trait anger, 3, 164, 165, 214
and trait anxiety, 3, 165
Personality Research Form (PRF), 144
Petty tyranny, 23, 189, 251
studies of, 14
Police officers
effect of aggression on, 52
Positive and Negative Affect Scale, 164
Posttraumatic stress disorder (PTSD), 8
and bullying, 276
and domestic abuse, 53
and mobbing, 239, 256, 262
Power
and bullying, 277
and mobbing, 241–242, 261
and revenge in the workplace, 67–68
and workplace incivility, 186

Process framework, for emotional abuse (figure), 203
Protocall, Inc., 53
Psychological terror, 14, 22–23
Public Agenda poll, 177

Questionnaires, 84, 167, 168, 301

RAGE system, 93
Reasoning, conditional. *See* Conditional reasoning
Reconciliation. *See also* Organizational retaliatory behavior
and organizational retaliatory behavior, 99–101, 102
Referent cognitions theory, 83, 87, 90
Relationship of moral identity to deviant organizational norms (figure), 117
Retaliation, 6, 24–25, 65. *See also* Counterproductive work behavior; Organizational retaliatory behavior; Revenge, in the workplace
vs. counterproductive work behavior, 153
and dictator decision game studies, 90–92, 96
examples of similar items from scales (table), 157
and organizational retaliatory behavior, 89–92, 102
and retribution bias, 133
Retaliation behaviors, list of (exhibit), 85
Revenge, 24–25. *See also* Revenge, in the workplace
vs. bullying, 66
and counterproductive work behavior, 153–154
defined, 66
vs. deviance, 66
Revenge, in the workplace, 6, 24–25, 65–77. *See also* Counterproductive work behavior; Retaliation; Revenge
conceptual and ideological issues of, 66–70
defined, 66–67
and emotions, 71–72, 73
employee-centered approach to, 76–77

forms of, 75
and label for field of study, 67–69
manager-centered approach to, 75–76, 77
and moral imperative, 73–74
vs. organizational retaliatory behavior, 66
as provoked behavior, 70–71
research on, 70–75
and sense of violation, 72–73
and severity of provocation, 69–70
and social cognitive dynamics, 74–75
unified conceptual approach to, 77
Robberies. *See also* Workplace violence
organizational responses to, 56
and psychological symptoms of victims, 45
and violence, 44–45
Rudeness. *See* Incivility
Rules
violations of, 71

Sabotage
and stressors, 160
Self-determination, 216, 217
Sexual harassment. *See* Harassment, sexual
Shame, 99, 101
deontic, 100
Social learning theory, 109
Social support
and mobbing, 255–256
for targets of emotional abuse, 224–225
Social undermining, 24, 224
and emotional abuse, 205
and mobbing, 261
studies of, 14
Status
and power derogation, 71
Strain, on targets of emotional abuse, 211, 226–228
Stress, job. *See also* Stressor–emotion model, of counterproductive work behavior; Stressors
and bullying, 276
and counterproductive work behavior, 4, 160–161

and workplace aggression, 7, 156–161
Stress Incident Record, 302
Stressor–emotion model, of counterproductive work behavior, 7, 156, 158–170. *See also* Counterproductive work behavior
causality of, 158
and environment, 159
and frustration–aggression link, 156
illustration of (figure), 158
interpersonal conflict studies, 160–161
Stressors. *See also* Stressor–emotion model, of counterproductive work behavior
and anger 159, 160
and anxiety, 159
and emotional abuse, 210–216, 219–220
and frustration, 160
and mobbing, 238–239, 254, 256–258
Substance abuse. *See* Abuse, alcohol
Supervision, abusive. *See* Abusive supervision

Targets, of counterproductive work behavior. *See also* Counterproductive work behavior
appraisal process of, 221–222
and bullying, 283–284
and coping, 222–224
derogation of target bias, 133
effects of emotionally abusive behaviors on (table), 227
and emotional abuse, 8, 210, 216–228
and mobbing, 240, 244
organizational response to, 225–226
social support for, 224–225
strain on, 226–228
victim and perpetrator perspectives for bullying and mobbing (figure), 244
and workplace aggression, 17–18
and workplace incivility, 180, 184–185, 192, 194
Technology
and workplace incivility, 183, 192–193

and informal climate, 188
moderators of, 186–188
organizational pressures and, 183,
 195
and other forms of counterproductive work behavior (figure), 191
social contextual shifts and, 181–
 183, 195
studies of, 14, 179–185
targets and, 180, 184–185, 192, 194
technology and, 183, 192–193
vs. workplace aggression, 28–29
Workplace victimization, 205
Workplace violence, 3, 5–6, 41–58, 65,
 189, 218. *See also* Counterproductive work behavior; Homicides;
 Robberies; Violence

areas for future research, 54–56
client–customer–patient-initiated
 (type II violence), 5, 46–49, 57
decline in U.S., 43
domestic abuse and, 53–54
insider-initiated (type III violence),
 5–6, 49–52, 57
organizational responses to, 56–57
partner-initiated (type IV violence),
 6, 53–54, 57–58
and psychological aggression, 52
statistics on homicides, 55
strange-initiated (type I violence), 5,
 43–46, 56
studies of, 14, 43
types of, 42–43

ABOUT THE EDITORS

Suzy Fox, PhD, is assistant professor at the Institute of Human Resources and Industrial Relations, Graduate School of Business, Loyola University, Chicago, where she teaches organizational behavior, global human resource management, and ethics. Her two research areas focus on barriers to employee well-being and cross-cultural studies of successful women. Her work has appeared in numerous journals and book projects. She is associate editor of *Human Relations.*

Paul E. Spector, PhD, is a professor of industrial/organizational psychology and the industrial/organizational doctoral program director at the University of South Florida, Tampa. His work has appeared in many journals, and he has written books on both methodology (research design and SAS programming) and content, including a textbook (*Industrial and Organizational Psychology: Research and Practice*, 3rd ed., 2003). He is an associate editor for the *Journal of Occupational Health Psychology* and the point/counterpoint editor for the *Journal of Organizational Behavior*. He is also on the editorial boards of the *Journal of Occupational and Organizational Psychology, Organizational Research Methods,* and *Personnel Psychology*. In 1991, the Institute for Scientific Information listed him as one of the 50 highest impact contemporary researchers in psychology.